EXPLORATIONS IN ENTERPRISE

EXPLORATIONS IN ENTERPRISE

EDITED BY

Hugh G. J. Aitken

HARVARD UNIVERSITY PRESS

Cambridge, Massachusetts

1965

Distributed in Great Britain by Oxford University Press, London

All royalties earned by this book are to be given to the
Council on Research in Economic History

Library of Congress Catalog Card Number 65–12782
Printed in the United States of America

TO

A. H. C.

Counselor of Scholars

PREFACE

IN ASSEMBLING THIS COLLECTION of articles I encountered many difficulties of selection and organization, and I am painfully conscious of the fact that no one is likely to agree fully with the choices I have made. Most of the articles are drawn from *Explorations in Entrepreneurial History,* the journal of the Research Center in Entrepreneurial History at Harvard University. I have not hesitated, however, to include material written by persons associated with the Center but published in other journals, and I have also thought it desirable to reproduce three articles from *Change and the Entrepreneur,* a modest and little-known volume published by the Center in 1949. On the other hand, I am well aware that the articles selected for reprinting here fall far short of representing adequately the full range of the Center's work. I regret very much, for example, my inability to include James S. Duesenberry's well-known contribution, "Some Aspects of the Theory of Economic Development" (*Explorations,* vol. III, no. 2); and my failure to find a selection from the pen of Dr. Fritz Redlich which would fit the space limitations and organization of the book is a fault for which his many friends and admirers will not soon forgive me. But the constraints of space were rigorous, and no editor can please everybody. The selection represents my personal judgment of what is most likely to be of continuing interest and importance; the collection could have been twice as long without any serious lowering of standards.

As regards organization, after experimenting with more complex systems I decided that the simplest was probably also the best. The articles have therefore been arranged in four groups, the first presenting examples of the better-known "approaches" to the study of entrepreneurship, the second a number of articles on social and cultural factors in entrepreneurial behavior, the third a set of portraits of individual entrepreneurs, and the last a series of attempts to define and describe entrepreneurial types. Each group, as well as the book as a whole, I have introduced by a brief editorial essay which, I hope, will not detract unduly from the virtues of the articles themselves. I have been warned by friendly critics that the nonprofessional reader may well find the articles in the first group hard going; if so, he has editorial dispensation to move on quickly to the more colorful descriptive material that follows.

The articles are reprinted as they were originally published, with only the most minor editorial corrections. I am most grateful to the authors and original publishers of each article for granting me permission to reprint in this collection. And I must express my thanks to the many friends and colleagues who encouraged me to proceed with the venture.

H. G. J. A.

Riverside, California
4 August 1964

CONTENTS

PART V

PART I

INTRODUCTION

Entrepreneurial Research: The History of an Intellectual Innovation

HUGH G. J. AITKEN

THIS BOOK CONTAINS a collection of articles designed to illustrate some aspects of research in entrepreneurial history. However defined, entrepreneurship always involves, explicitly or implicitly, the idea of innovation, and it is as an intellectual innovation that I propose to discuss the origins and development of entrepreneurial history. This approach will, I trust, excuse a more informal and personal tone than normally characterizes an editor's introduction.

Proposals for organized research in entrepreneurial history first came to my attention in 1947–1948, when I was a graduate student at the University of Toronto. The idea of entrepreneurial history as an area of research was then a novelty; to some extent it still is. Like anyone else with a smattering of classical economics, I knew what the word "entrepreneur" meant, or at least some of the things it could mean. But the idea of carving out a field of historical research that should have this concept at its center seemed new and strange. Equally strange at first was the fact that the men under whom I was working at Toronto—notably W. T. Easterbrook and the late Harold Innis—seemed to take the idea seriously.

This should not have surprised me. Like many an apprentice economist, I had acquired a rather jaundiced view of economic history, principally because it had been presented to me as a collection of facts already known. It was only at Toronto that I had come into contact with men who had a different view of the matter, who thought of it as an area for exploration in which even the most competent had only a vague idea of "the lie of the land." The seriousness with which men like Innis and Easterbrook responded to the idea of entrepreneurial history was part and parcel of their approach to history in general.

Another reason why they took it seriously was the fact that they knew the men in the United States who had conceived this new approach. In particular, they knew Arthur Harrison Cole of Harvard University. The guild of economic historians, as I later learned, is not in the habit of recognizing any individual as the acknowledged leader or dean of the profession. Edwin F. Gay, Cole's former mentor, had once played that role, but since Gay's death in 1946 a kind of collective leadership had emerged which—in so far as it was formalized at all—resided in the Committee on Research in Economic History, a body of which more later. Cole was at this time chairman of the Committee; partly for this reason, but more because of the great personal respect and affection in which he was held by his colleagues, any project to which he lent his support commanded attention.

My first personal acquaintance with Cole was made in the spring of 1948, when I learned that he intended to establish a research center in entrepreneurial history at Harvard University, that he had secured financial support from the Rockefeller Foundation, and that he was looking around for one or two younger men interested in doing research on the subject. Associated with Cole at this time were the late Joseph A. Schumpeter of Harvard University and two other scholars—Leland H. Jenks of Wellesley College and Thomas C. Cochran of New York University—who proposed to take leave the following year to study at the new center. These four became the senior members of the Research Center in Entrepreneurial History when it was formally established in the fall of 1948. With them was associated Dr. Fritz Redlich, already well known for his work on American and European entrepreneurship. Five junior members were also appointed, all graduate students at Harvard: R. Richard Wohl, Fr. Adrien Taymans, Wingfield N. Chamberlain, Harold C. Passer, and I.

It was only after taking up my appointment at the Research Center that I began to learn something of the history of Cole's project.[1] One thing became clear very early: the Research Center was *at* Harvard University, but in a sense it did not belong to Harvard at all. It belonged to the economic history profession. It was at Harvard because it had to be somewhere, but its precise location was a matter of convenience only. In practical terms, neither Cole nor any of the other senior members thought of it as being a creation of the Harvard faculty, or as existing exclusively or primarily for the benefit of people who happened to be at Harvard. This had certain advantages: the funds at our disposal could be used to promote research wherever it was carried out, and discussion and planning groups could be assembled from a wide variety of institutions. But it had disadvantages too, some of which were later to prove serious: the Center and its personnel were never integrated into the teaching functions of the University (although a few of those working at the Center held appointments in the teaching departments); and just as the Center regarded itself as being at Harvard but not of it, so the administrative officers of the University understandably tended to think of the Center as an institution whose survival was no important concern of theirs or of the University. The fact that Harvard provided no financial support other than office space also meant a certain diversion of energy from research to fund-raising.

Few of these problems were unique to the Research Center in Entrepreneurial History. What was unique, I think, was the unspoken assumption that the Center existed for the benefit of the entire profession of economic history, that more than our own private futures depended upon what we accomplished, and that success had to be defined in terms of reinvigorating economic history as a whole. Entrepreneurial history, in short, was never thought of as the private preserve of a splinter group, but rather as a "leading sector" in the development of a discipline. Those who pioneered in entrepreneurial history were prepared to contemplate with equanimity the possibility that in time their ideas and methods would come to seem hackneyed and out of fashion. No great foresight, indeed, was required to consider such an outcome entirely probable.

The explanation for this state of affairs lay in the character of Arthur Cole and in the way in which, almost imperceptibly, his colleagues absorbed his ideas of what the Center was for. This had been spelled out prospectively as early as 1944, when the Committee on Research in Economic History had published its program for research in the postwar period. Originally presented as a report to the Social Science Research Council (then the Committee's parent body), this document was subsequently published in full in the *Journal of Economic History* (May 1944).[2] In it, Cole surveyed the state of research in economic history at that time ("largely at a standstill") and described four fields of inquiry which the Committee recommended for support in the postwar years. Two of these were termed "major fields": the role of government in economic change and the role of entrepreneurship. Two were "minor fields": the development of the corporation and the history of American banking.

The report reflects, of course, not only Cole's thinking but also that of his colleagues on the Committee.[3] In the section on entrepreneurship, however, ideas that in retrospect can be identified as clearly his are prominent, and the concrete proposals foreshadow the organization of the Center as he later established it. In addition to proposing the holding of a conference on current problems in economic history and the establishment of a system of postdoctoral fellowships, the Committee stated that it was "pondering the desirability of sponsoring temporary institutes . . . devoted to the study of the fields of its research program." One such center was suggested for the "role of government" area, another for entrepreneurial history.

The Research Center in Entrepreneurial History at Harvard was, to my knowledge, the only such institution formally established, but it is worth noting that the other "major area" selected by the Committee was by no means neglected. In fact, the substantial monographs that have since appeared under the Committee's sponsorship on the role of government—particularly state government—in American economic development outnumber the published books on entrepreneurial history.[4] These works, however—which form in a sense the ideological complement to the studies of entrepreneurship—were produced either by scholars working independently or by informal groups such as that which grew up under the leadership of Carter Goodrich at Columbia. Some such strategy might well have been followed for entrepreneurial history. My impression is, however, that the fact that the Center had a corporate identity clear enough to evoke loyalty and a sense of membership was one of its major strengths.

The ideas on entrepreneurship that Cole presented in the 1944 Report were an extension and elaboration of suggestions he had made some two years earlier when, as participant in a symposium on "profits and the entrepreneur" at the annual meeting of the Economic History Association, he had undertaken to survey "Entrepreneurship as an Area of Research."[5] This early paper displayed the uneasiness about problems of definition that was later to harass the Research Center, but its primary purpose was to assess the potential of alternative research strategies: business biographies, company histories, histories of business methods, and so on. Cole noted that everyone he had consulted agreed on the importance of studying entrepreneurship but disagreed about almost everything else:

> What is meant by the terms "entrepreneur" and "entrepreneurship"? If there were once such elements as the "entrepreneur" and "entrepreneurship" in the American economic system, what happened to them as a result of the rise of the corporation, of large-scale enterprise, or of high income taxation? What functions have, in the past, been essential to entrepreneurship and what changes, if any, have come in these functions over time?

Cole himself tended to favor a functional approach—"the idea of a managing, innovating, and inspiring entrepreneurship of which the *locus* changes over time but which even to the present has been an essential element in the operation of private enterprise"—and suggested a cross-sectional analysis—"entrepreneurship as of a given point in time"—the virtues of which he was to advocate more strongly in later years. But clearly at that time the game was wide open; anyone's ideas were as good as anyone else's, and no one really knew the best way to proceed.

This uncertainty regarding meanings and purposes was partly dissipated by Cole's presidential address to the Economic History Association in 1946. Reprinted in this volume, the paper can be taken as representing the best considered thinking on the subject in the period immediately before the founding of the Center. In it Cole states his conviction that "To study the 'entrepreneur' is to study the central figure in modern economic history, and, to my way of thinking, the central figure in economics;" he attempts a pragmatic definition—"entrepreneurship boils down in basic functions to innovation upon a solid operational base achieved through the medium of business decisions;" he suggests a set of stages of entrepreneurial development—empirical, rational, and cognitive entrepreneurship; and, with remarkable foresight, he points out one probable line of development in entrepreneurial research—the construction of "a historical sociology of entrepreneurship." Firmly locating his subject in the mainstream of the history of economic thought, tying it explicitly to the ideas of his mentor, Edwin F. Gay, Cole describes the possibilities of the new field in language that approaches eloquence. The sense of personal dedication and commitment is unmistakable.

No less unmistakable in Cole's address was his conception of entrepreneurial research as an inclusive, integrating branch of scholarship. He drew no hard boundary lines. Almost anything that might conceivably concern a historian or social scientist was possibly relevant. Directly or indirectly, if you were interested in research in the social sciences and had some sense of history, what you were working on probably had something to do with entrepreneurship. It could be "tied in." This conception of entrepreneurship as an integrating focus for historical research pervaded all the later work of the Research Center. Its implications were obvious. It meant that the Center was unusually hospitable to interdisciplinary work and that people from a wide variety of specialties could find in it a reasonably comfortable intellectual home. But it also meant difficulty in the construction of rigorous theory and, as a result, problems in maintaining liaison with those social scientists, and particularly the economists, who regarded rigorous theory as the hallmark of respectability. It is no accident that, at Harvard, the Center was more widely known and respected in the Departments of History and of Social Relations than it was in the Department of Economics.

Although Abbott Payson Usher was deeply interested in the Center's work, and both Alexander Gerschenkron and John E. Sawyer later served as senior members, its principal link with the Department of Economics was, in the early days, Joseph A. Schumpeter. In view of the fact that Schumpeter had presented to the world of scholarship, long before the Center was established, a fully elaborated theory of entrepreneurship and that his status among economists was very high, a legitimate question can be raised as to why he did not influence the direction of the Center's theorizing more decisively. One answer to this question is that Schumpeter was preoccupied at this time with the preparation of his monumental *History of Economic Analysis* and with numerous other concerns related to his teaching and research. He gave the Center his blessing and took an avuncular interest in its progress. He presented to the Economic History Association in 1947 a brilliant article on "The Creative Response in Economic History" which placed his earlier theorizing on entrepreneurship in novel perspective. And, in the early months of the Center's existence, he read at an evening meeting a paper on "Economic Theory and Entrepreneurial History" (reprinted in this volume). He was present at most of our early discussions, and was always available for advice; but, in my judgment at least, the work of the Research Center absorbed only a small fraction of his attention, and the full weight of his tremendous intellect was never brought to bear on its problems. This is said not as criticism, but merely in order that the later evolution of the Center's theorizing—which was in important respects non-Schumpeterian in emphasis—can be properly understood.

But there is more to it than this. Schumpeter, alone among all those associated with the Center in its early days, knew where he stood theoretically and pragmatically. His thinking on the nature and problems of entrepreneurship had been done many years before. In his *Theory of Economic Development* (first published in English in 1934) and his two massive volumes on *Business Cycles* (1939), he had presented his ideas with great intellectual sophistication and in considerable detail. There existed, in fact, a "Schumpeterian system" which, though perhaps vulnerable to criticism on points of detail, stood open to inspection, monumental and monolithic, a completed theoretical construct. If one accepted this system, what more was there to do? The work of exegesis and commentary, perhaps, to clear up obscurities and make plain what the master really meant. Minor correction of details, which might make the system a little tidier but would leave it, in the large, unchanged. And the pedestrian work of historical illustration. What excitement was there here?

I speak now with some confidence regarding the attitudes of the junior members of the Research Center, of whom I was one, and I would ask the reader to bear in mind that we were a group of rather aggressively egotistic young men, anxious to make our own marks in the world of scholarship. We were very much in awe of Schumpeter. He was one of the great men of the profession, a scholar who by his authority of intellect, by his tremendous accumulation of knowledge, and by his very manner could, almost without knowing it, make a young man who questioned his views look and feel very foolish. Our reaction to the presence of this intellect in our midst was one of respectful but wary neutrality. We would prefer, if you please, not to become known as Schumpeterians. We would rather start afresh, with new assumptions and a new point of view, and create our own theories.

In retrospect, there is little here in which one can feel pride. But something can be said by way of extenuation. It may be that, in rejecting the Schumpeterian approach, we were wiser than we knew, for the Schumpeterian system is an integral whole, to be accepted or rejected entire. It would not, I think, have been in the best interests of the Research Center if we had said, in effect, "Very well, here is our theory already prepared; our task is to apply it and refine it." And particularly is this true if we remember that the primary *raison d'être* of the Research Center was to revitalize the study of economic history. Better, from this point of view, to spend time re-examining assumptions and searching for new approaches, than to take over an already elaborated model. There was, too, much in the Schumpeterian system that we found hard to digest. Our positivistic stomachs rebelled at the taint of mysticism in Schumpeter's concept of creativity; and our ideological palates, conditioned during the late 1930's, found the heroic and aristocratic elements in his thinking distasteful. None of this was reasonable, of course; but it is perhaps understandable.

It is also true, however, that what appeared on the surface to be rejection was on a more subtle level unconscious assimilation. None of those who worked at the Center—indeed, none who ever worked in the field of entrepreneurial history—could escape completely from the influence of Schumpeter's ideas. He set his permanent mark on the subject. The concept of innovation, for example, though analyzed and criticized until at times there seemed nothing left of it, has shown remarkable vitality and continues to serve as the central element in any definition of entrepreneurship and the principal link with theories of economic development—which is precisely what Schumpeter intended. The same is true of his refusal to describe entrepreneurs as a social class, his emphasis on the particular personality requirements of successful entrepreneurship, and his insistence on the need for "protective strata" in society if private entrepreneurship is to function. An overt rejection of the Schumpeterian model on the part of the younger members of the Center there may have been; but no one who reads the material reprinted in this volume can question Schumpeter's enduring influence.

If any attempt has been made to impose the Schumpeterian schema upon us younger men, some kind of minor palace revolution might well have resulted. But nothing like this ever happened. Cole, as we have already seen, concerned himself with questions different from any that Schumpeter's model was designed to handle—questions about the evolution of business practices, the pace of business life in different periods, and the interdependence of parts in the business system. While we "junior members" took our bearings from the academic departments around Harvard Yard, Cole was at least equally concerned with relations with the Business School on the other side of the Charles River, and particularly with the group of business historians there who had received their training from N. S. B. Gras. What was the relation between entrepreneurial history and business history? Was there any significant difference, and if so, what? To questions such as these Cole attached an importance which some of the rest of us—at a time when entrepreneurial history had no literature of its own—failed to understand. As we then saw it, business history was nontheoretical and even antitheoretical, and that was all that needed to be said.

The man to whom the younger members increasingly looked for intellectual leadership as the first year of the Center's existence wore on was Leland Jenks. Trained originally as a historian, Jenks was known to us when we first came to Harvard primarily for his early work on the migration of British capital. Some of us also knew his book on Cuba, and a more recent article in the *Journal of Economic History* on railroads in American economic development had attracted considerable attention.[6] But, besides his training as a historian, Jenks had acquired in the course of his career at Wellesley College the skills and outlook of the sociologist and was in fact chairman of the department of sociology at Wellesley at the time. Of this side of his professional character we at first knew little. Yet it was through this distinctive combination of historical and sociological training that Jenks was to make a decided impact on the work of the Center.

Had we known it, we might have been intrigued by the fact that, whereas most of us had prepared for the year by rereading

Schumpeter and Cole's articles, Jenks had spent the previous summer working his way through the major economic journals, in a determined attempt to acquire a "feel" for the way contemporary economic theory was moving. As a result of this self-imposed purgatory, he had convinced himself that, if there was to be any "theory of entrepreneurship," it could not be an economic theory in the conventional sense. Being already familiar with current theorizing in sociology and social psychology—the only senior person at the Center who was—he turned naturally to the task of translating what we knew or suspected about entrepreneurship into the language of culture-and-personality. He accepted Cole's axiom that entrepreneurship was an organizational phenomenon: as Cole defined it, "purposeful activity . . . undertaken to initiate, maintain, or aggrandize a profit-oriented business unit." He pointed out that the only hard evidence available was of "what men do in situations which they perceive as affording business opportunities." And he proposed that entrepreneurship be thought of as a social role—a role played *in* the business unit but also *in* society—the precise functions associated with the role being defined not *a priori* by the theorist but in the process of social interaction itself.

Here was a type of theorizing strange to most of us, and particularly to those accustomed to the simpler "other-things-being-equal" propositions of classical economics. It did not sit comfortably at first. Implied by Jenks's approach was a concern with values, with perceptions, with social sanctions and social definitions, with motives and with how people *saw* situations rather than with situations-as-they-really-were—with all sorts of seemingly "soft" and "subjective" variables, in short, that induced in the conventional economist a reflex shudder of rejection. To be accurate, of course, Jenks's search for a "field" theory of entrepreneurship was more modern and methodologically sophisticated than most theorizing that a graduate student in economics would encounter, but few of us realized this at the time. Nor was appreciation of what he was up to facilitated by the involuted language and specialized terminology that seem to be inseparable from this sort of speculation. For a considerable time Jenks was; as far as the rest of the Research Center was concerned, far out in left field. Mutual understanding depended on the rest of us catching up with him.

Catching up with Jenks was made easier by the presence at the Center of a sympathetic historian and a highly intelligent enthusiast. Thomas C. Cochran was the historian. Then on leave from New York University, he was starting work on the study of nineteenth-century American railroad entrepreneurs that was to culminate in 1953 in his classic *Railroad Leaders, 1845–1890,* perhaps the most solid piece of historical scholarship to emerge from the Center's research.[7] Concerned as he was with the way his "general entrepreneurs" saw the world in which they were operating—the things they took for granted as right and proper as well as the things they regarded as uncertain—the concept of the entrepreneur as playing a social role and responding to positive and negative sanctions appealed to him immediately. Fortunately for him, the material with which he was working—the business correspondence of a relatively homogeneous group of businessmen facing a common set of problems and opportunities—lent itself admirably to this approach. What impressed us most, however, was not the success with which Cochran applied Jenks's concepts, for at the time this was uncertain, but the calm, methodical, matter-of-fact way in which he went about the job, as if the assimilation of these rather complex notions were, for a competent historian, the most natural thing in the world. Cochran, in short, took much of the heat out of the controversies and misunderstandings that were then developing, demonstrating by his work—the only way that could carry conviction—that there was nothing in the new concepts and hypotheses that need divert an honest craftsman from doing an honest job.

R. Richard Wohl, whom I have described above as a highly intelligent enthusiast, was that certainly, but much more besides. A graduate student at the time, pursuing the unconventional doctoral degree in social science, he was intensely concerned to systematize the study of entrepreneurial behavior and to bring to bear upon it the ideas and methods of sociology and anthropology. Intellectually, he and Jenks thought along the same lines, although they were poles apart in personality, and it was to no small extent because of Wohl's strenuous advocacy and intense enthusiasm that others, originally hostile or indifferent, became convinced that the sociological approach to the study of entrepreneurship had at least to be taken seriously. As a catalyst of ideas, Wohl was a most valuable asset to the Center. A brilliant talker and formidable disputant, he compelled one to clarify one's own ideas, if only to avoid being swamped by his.

If I have conveyed any sense of how the Center was organized and how it functioned, it should not be necessary to state explicitly that none of the analytical approaches suggested by its members ever won universal assent. What emerged was a mosaic of approaches and points of view. To the individual participant, the continuing problem was to decide where one stood in relation to the various alternatives available: in relation to the Schumpeterian system, for example, or to Jenks's social role approach, or to business history, or to the emerging theories of economic development. The more cautious among us were unashamedly eclectic. Others chose to adopt one approach, work with that, and see how far it would take them. The prevailing sentiment was thoroughly permissive. Nevertheless, with the benefit of hindsight, it is apparent that the concern with sociological method which Jenks introduced, which Cochran absorbed, and for which Wohl served as the advocate, gave to the Center's work a characteristic flavor. This tendency was reinforced by the studies undertaken by other scholars who became affiliated with the Center after its initial establishment. William Miller's work on the social origins of the American business elite was not directly influenced by Jenks's theories, but was certainly compatible with them.[8] The studies of French business and businessmen undertaken by David Landes and John E. Sawyer showed a sensitivity to cultural and social factors that a social theorist could not but applaud.[9] Sigmund Diamond's research on the public reputations of American businessmen had similar characteristics.[10] And Wohl's rapidly emerging concern with the cultural elements in economic development, which he was to carry further at the University of Chicago until his untimely death in 1957, stemmed from the same intellectual roots as Jenks's analysis of entrepreneurial roles.[11] This convergence of research interests was not accidental, and to the outside observer it must have seemed as if the Center had committed itself to a particular mode of analysis.

If there was any such commitment, it was never total, and it was accompanied by a growing tension between those who adopted what may be called a broad sociological approach and those who felt uncomfortable about the gap that was appearing between the work of the Center and the established discipline of economics. On occasion this tension came to the surface in unmistakable form, as for instance in a vigorous controversy in print between Alexander Gerschenkron of the Harvard Department of Economics on the one hand, and Sawyer, Landes, and Cochran on the other. More frequently, however, it remained covert. Some of those attached to the Center—Noel G. Butlin of the Australian National University is, I think, a good example—learned what Jenks and Wohl were talking about, grasped the essentials of the approach, and decided that, though it might have merits, it was not for them. Others reacted by castigating the economic theorists, the suggestion being that it was about time that economists learned what modern social science was all about. And still others ignored the issue completely, concentrating on their own research projects with the comforting reflection that methodological disputes were usually a waste of time anyway.

This last reaction was the most unfortunate of all, for important issues were involved. These issues appeared at several different levels. First, there was a conflict of methods: to proceed by isolating and abstracting, as did economics, or by adopting a more open-ended approach which was unlikely to produce a coherent, logical system of theory but which left room for the inclusion of whatever variables seemed relevant to the problem at hand. The economic approach, except in the Schumpeterian system, tended to eliminate the entrepreneur completely, converting him into a mere formal relationship between inputs and outputs, and seemed to require, moreover, a distinction between economic and noneconomic factors which many found difficult to make. The alternative approach, however, at least in the eyes of its critics, seemed impressionistic and unsystematic: when one tried to formalize it, one ended up with some version of the Parsonian system which, whatever its other virtues, was clumsy to work with in historical research. Secondly, there was a conflict of personalities, which can best be described as a temperamental difference between those who were primarily historians and those who were primarily theorists: the first concerned with depicting the past, the second with the construction of systems of thought. Intellectually, perhaps, this gap can be bridged; temperamentally it could not. And thirdly, there was a conflict of objectives, of different views regarding what the Research Center was for and what kind of work it should try to do. Was it to attempt the construction of a systematic theory of entrepreneurship, or was its proper role that of facilitating the carrying-out of interesting pieces of historical research? If the latter, substantial tolerance of different points of view could be afforded. If the former, agreement on definitions, assumptions, and research procedures was necessary.

Conflicts of this kind are probably intrinsic to any attempt to treat history as a social science. History is concerned with irreversible, discontinuous change over time, and conventional modes of theorizing in economics are not readily adapted to such a subject matter. Historians, too, are uneasy in any theoretical garb that hampers their freedom of movement. They like their theories custom-tailored, fitting so easily that they can forget they are wearing them. It is not without significance that theorists of economic development—likewise concerned with irreversible, discontinuous change—have encountered problems similar to those experienced by the Research Center in Entrepreneurial History.

I would not leave the impression that the emerging conflict I have described was altogether unfortunate. On the contrary, it had its uses. The Center needed something of this kind to prevent its members from growing complacent and intellectually lazy. It was, in addition, excellent raw material for the journal which was established at the Center halfway through the first year of its existence. Wohl was the moving spirit behind this enterprise, and the effectiveness of his driving enthusiasm was never better displayed than in the way he pushed through the idea of publishing a journal despite much initial skepticism. What Wohl wanted was a medium by which the ideas then floating around the Center could be pinned down and subjected to responsible criticism. He was little concerned at this time with reaching an audience outside the Center itself. More effective internal communication was what he was after. From this point of view what was wanted was an informal, economically produced journal, of very limited readership, containing material that was tentative and preliminary, not yet ready for formal publication. It would appear at frequent intervals—once a month, if possible—and it would circulate primarily within the Center.

The initial reaction to this proposal was that a journal of any kind was premature; that not enough good material was being generated around the Center to fill its pages; and that its production would require too great a diversion of time and energy from our other responsibilities. And if Wohl had suggested that the journal be launched as an official publication of the Center, these objections might well have defeated him. Instead of this, however, he proposed that the journal should be edited and produced by the younger men around the Center and that it should be regarded, not as a formal publication, but rather as a series of "occasional papers," to be read, discussed, and then perhaps discarded. Expressed in these terms, the innovation appeared at once more modest and more acceptable. It would be a journal, but not really a journal. It would be produced at the Research Center, but it would not really be a publication of the Research Center. Its editors and contributors would, at least to begin with, be members of the Center, but it would be a responsibility of the junior members only.

Friends have sometimes commented on the apparent ease with which the Center's journal was born and contrasted it with the painful and prolonged birthpangs of other learned journals. One element in the explanation is that the costs of producing the journal were carried almost wholly by the Center itself. These costs were relatively small—less than $500 for the first year—but assurance that they would be covered freed us from the necessity of building up a list of paying subscribers. No efforts were ever made, throughout the ten years of the journal's existence, to persuade people to subscribe. The original conception of the journal as being primarily for internal circulation was never entirely lost.

On the other hand, the quick acceptance of the journal and the rapid expansion of its "outside" readership were the result of considerations that had nothing to do with costs. Wohl's proposal had struck a responsive chord, particularly among the younger people working in entrepreneurial history. Consider our situation at the time: we were committed to research in an area that was not yet academically recognized, that had no clear identity or boundaries, and that could be described only by an awkward French adjective on whose definition no one seemed able to agree. An uncomfortable state of affairs, one must admit, for graduate students worried about their dissertations and their acceptability on the academic job market. What could we do to improve matters? We could talk, of course, and this we did, at great length. But we talked mostly to ourselves, and at the evening meetings of the Center—which took place every few weeks and were then the only formal meetings of the whole group—our talk was overshadowed and inhibited by the presence of senior scholars whose authority we hesitated to challenge. The journal, explicitly assigned to the junior members as their responsibility, gave us a chance to talk with a louder voice and to a wider audience. It gave us a sense of identity and direction and lent to our ideas an authority partly spurious but wholly delightful. Small wonder, then, that Wohl received from his young colleagues all the cooperation he could have wished. The title selected—*Explorations in Entrepreneurial History*—accurately reflected the spirit of the venture.

Most of the material reproduced in this book has been drawn from the pages of *Explorations,* and in this there is a certain paradox. The original concept of the journal was that it would be a medium in which ideas could be "tried out," as it were. It was not our intention to publish articles in final polished form, far less articles that a decade or more later would merit assembly between hard covers. In the first year or two of publication this idea was maintained rather consistently. Part of the reason for this, I am sure, was the fact that our pages were mimeographed, not printed. They had a tentative, preliminary look about them and lacked the solid authority of the printed page. Mimeographing was at first an economy measure, but the question may well be raised whether it would not have been wise to have retained this form of reproduction even after more generous financial backing became available. Instead, we graduated first to photo-offset printing, with a notable gain in elegance, and finally to the full dignity of double-column linotype on fine paper. And, paralleling this rise to respectability, the articles we published grew more scholarly and more authoritative. But *Explorations* lost something in the process. Print is the enemy of spontaneity, and what had at first been an informal magazine of ideas became eventually a learned journal.

Before the Research Center, its supporting grants finally exhausted, officially went out of existence in 1958, it had produced a not unimpressive series of monographs and, through its influence on the scholars who at one time or another had been associated with it, had left a definite imprint on the writing and teaching of economic history. Yet it was through *Explorations* that the Center had exercised its widest influence, in other countries as well as within the United States, and it is in the pages of *Explorations* that the character of its work is most accurately reflected. This is in itself, I believe, sufficient justification for reprinting in book form a selection from the articles that appeared in the journal, for many of the volumes are now no longer available except on microfilm.

Beyond this, however, and quite apart from the intrinsic value and interest of the articles themselves, there are lessons to be learned from the history of the Center and its attempt to open up for exploration a new area of scholarly research. Organized research units such as the Center are becoming increasingly common in American universities, in the social sciences and humanities as well as in the natural sciences, and the analysis of how they may best be organized and operated, where they are appropriate instruments and where they are not, has received very little attention. The experience of the Research Center in Entrepreneurial History has some relevance in this respect. On one score the record is clean: the type of leadership that Cole and his senior colleagues provided was close to ideal. Their intellectual tolerance, their patience with the brash aggressiveness of their younger coworkers, the free rein they gave to innovations and experiments—these were necessary if the task for which the Center had been created was to be carried out. The problems the Center encountered, and in particular its failure to bring order into the particular area of the intellectual universe that it claimed as its own, were caused not by its internal organization but by the intrinsic difficulties of the subject matter. At the present stage of knowledge in the social sciences, any attempt to integrate theory and history, whether in the analysis of entrepreneurship or in any other way, would have found itself entangled in similar thickets.

PART II

POINTS OF VIEW

Points of View

IN THIS PART there are presented two surveys of entrepreneurship as an area of research by Cole and Schumpeter, a critical article by Easterbrook designed to delimit the field, and two essays by Jenks and Cochran exemplifying the analysis of entrepreneurship as a social role. Cole's "Approach to the Study of Entrepreneurship" has been briefly discussed in the Introduction. This was the article that set the stage for the early discussions of the Research Center. Indeed, if memory serves, the first two formal meetings of the Center were called to discuss the "errors and inadequacies" of Cole's "Approach." The article is, however, difficult to criticize, largely because of its irenic tone and the modesty of its hypotheses. Certain of its basic assumptions are worth noting. Cole takes for granted that entrepreneurship can exist only in societies with considerable decentralization of economic power. At the center of the stage is the "restless, innovating businessman" operating through and on behalf of a business unit that is assumed to have considerable freedom of maneuver. This implies that entrepreneurship is not distributed evenly or randomly through history, but is found only in situations in which social controls over economic behavior are relatively relaxed and the "cake of custom" can be broken by the innovating activity of individuals. This point of view leads Cole to impute an essentially conservative role to government and to define entrepreneurship not in terms of innovation—for surely governments can innovate—but in terms of profit-oriented decision-making. Such a definition is at one and the same time highly restrictive and extremely loose. It is restrictive in the sense that entrepreneurship so defined is, in the broad sweep of history, a relatively unusual phenomenon. And it is loose in the sense that it encompasses practically everything that goes on in a capitalistic business enterprise.

Cole's point of view is natural for a scholar whose primary interest is in nineteenth and twentieth century American economic history and who has always had as one of his purposes the systematic analysis of the American business system. Unwilling to define entrepreneurship in terms of a particular type of *act* (as, for instance, innovation), he deprives his theory of the hard cutting edge of the Schumpeterian theory. But on the other hand, by leaving his definition relatively "open," he leaves the field unobstructed for subsequent research.

Schumpeter's discussion of economic theory and entrepreneurial history, originally presented as a formal paper at an early meeting of the Center, should be read in conjunction with his paper on "The Creative Response in Economic History."[1] The argument in both papers starts from the simple assertion that economic processes are not automatic; there is a "designing, directing, leading, co-ordinating function" to be performed in every economic system. The way in which this function is performed determines the rate and direction of economic development. If, confronted with a change in its data, an economy or a sector of an economy reacts by doing something within the realm of existing practice (or, as Schumpeter characteristically put it, "in the way that traditional theory describes"), it is making an adaptive response. If, however, the reaction is outside the range of existing practice, we may speak of creative response. The study of creative response in economic history is, for Schumpeter, the study of entrepreneurship, for the defining characteristic of entrepreneurship is simply innovation, or "the doing of new things or the doing of things that are already being done in a new way."

Schumpeter's approach and Cole's are compatible with one another, but there are significant differences of emphasis. Cole, for example, tends to view the act of innovation as one end of a spectrum, at the other end of which is the purely routine, and makes no such sharp dichotomy between creative and adaptive responses as does Schumpeter. And while Schumpeter would undoubtedly have recognized the importance for entrepreneurship of good administration, he leaves the reader with the impression of a *toto caelo* difference between the creativity involved in innovation and the mere efficiency required to run a business successfully. Schumpeter's entrepreneur seems on occasion to be depicted as a particular type of individual, and not just as the personified carrier of a particular economic function. Cole, on the other hand, is quite explicit in regarding efficient organization as the essential foundation for effective entrepreneurship, and indeed as part of the phenomenon itself. It is for this reason, I think, that Schumpeter's theory is pedagogically more effective than Cole's: analytic distinctions which Cole, with his intense appreciation of the complexity and continuity of history, leaves blurred at the edges, remain in Schumpeter's argument sharp as a razor.

So at least it appears. But anyone who defines entrepreneurship functionally as essential to economic development in general can hardly restrict it to capitalistic or "free enterprise" economies. Cole explicitly defines entrepreneurship in terms that restrict its denotation to market economies. Schumpeter writes of entrepreneurship in terms that suggest that it is a purely capitalistic phenomenon, but in terms of his own theory it cannot be so. If innovation or the creative response is a *sine qua non* for economic development, and if entrepreneurship is defined in terms of innovation, one has no alternative but to conceive of noncapitalistic entrepreneurs. Schumpeter in fact does so. In the article reprinted below he describes the U.S. Department of Agriculture as an entrepreneur; and in a cryptic footnote to his earlier article on the creative response, he claims that, although "the function itself" is not absent from other forms of society, capitalist entrepreneurship is "a sufficiently distinct phenomenon" to be singled out. These suggestions were never fully integrated into Schumpeter's theory, which is distinctively a theory of capitalist development, but one may speculate what difference they might have made, if elaborated, to the conclusions of *Capitalism, Socialism, and Democracy,* for example. This is, in any event, one case in which Cole's definition is more restrictive than Schumpeter's.

These matters of definition are important because they determined what kinds of research would be done under the general rubric of entrepreneurial history. Both Cole and Schumpeter, if pressed, would have had to agree that the general economic function known as entrepreneurship must be present in all developing economies, whether organized on the decentralized model of classical capitalism or along some more centralized lines; both, however, make it clear that they do not intend to study the phenomenon in its general aspects, but only that specific variety described as capitalistic or profit-oriented entrepreneurship. Cole narrows his field of view by a restrictive definition, Schumpeter by saying that other species of entrepreneurship are not his present concern and that he proposes to talk about the capitalist variety.

Easterbrook's article on "The Climate of Enterprise" is reprinted here, despite the fact that it has not yet provided the foundation for much empirical research, because it grapples directly with the problem of nonprofit-oriented entrepreneurship. The profit-oriented, capitalistic, market-economy entrepreneur, Easterbrook argues, is historically unusual: "an extremely elusive entity, at times difficult to find, or not to be found at all, and frequently so subservient to other entities and ideas that he does not warrant the search." If we choose to define this elusive entity as the entrepreneur—and not merely as one particular subspecies of entrepreneurship, tied to a specific set of institutional and ideological conditions—then we must face up to the fact that we are proposing to study an uncommon type of change-producing agent and that much of our theorizing will be simply irrelevant to what happened in history. The entrepreneur so defined, Easterbrook suggests, is best regarded as an ideal type—"an idealized economic category operating freely in an idealized institutional environment"—and, interpreted in this way, may serve as a useful point of reference. But if we do this, we must bear in mind that the more common and more typical type of change-producing agent is nonentrepreneurial or, as Easterbrook calls it, bureaucratic.

It is an open question whether, in selecting the term "bureaucratic," Easterbrook did not burden himself with as many definitional headaches as afflicted the analysts of entrepreneurship. But in arguing that entrepreneurship as conventionally defined can function only within a rather specific and unusual institutional and ideological environment—one providing, in his terms, certain basic "securities"—he was raising fundamental questions as to the future direction of research. Only two types of definition of entrepreneurship are possible: one which emphasizes the general economic function performed, no matter what the social framework, and one which links the phenomenon to a particular set of economic, political, and social parameters. The latter alternative usually results in a Colean definition in terms of profit-oriented decision-making in a market economy. By such a definition entrepreneurship becomes historically specific and historically unusual and Easterbrook's objection—Why spend time studying the atypical when we know so little about the typical?—is difficult to meet. A broader functional definition, on the other hand, unspecific with respect to the institutional and ideological environment, is so abstract that its utility becomes questionable. Why not just say that you want to study the history of economic development and leave it at that?

Jenks's article, "Approaches to Entrepreneurial Personality," is a revised version of a talk given at an early meeting of the Research Center and presents ideas and hypotheses which were subsequently spelled out with greater rigor in his "The Role Structure of Entrepreneurial Personality," published in *Change and the Entrepreneur* in 1949.[2] The problem Jenks tackles is not one of definition, but of method. No matter what the specific definition, entrepreneurship refers to a pattern of probable behavior. Can we say anything sensible and empirically testable about the personality of people whose behavior follows this pattern? Not, Jenks argues, by assuming the existence of a particular set of personality traits. The differences in behavior between, say, professional criminals and other people are discontinuous, but empirical research has failed to demonstrate any analogous discontinuity in personality traits. Personality, then, cannot be thought of as something innate and fixed, determining uniquely what people will or will not do. Rather, it is something that grows and changes as the individual interacts with his environment, his personality and the situations in which he finds himself being part of a single "field." Specifically, Jenks suggests, personality should be thought of as an organization of the resources of the individual *with respect to* the situations in which he tries to act. As far as entrepreneurial research is concerned, this means that it is not necessary to know everything about an individual in order to understand why and how he acts as an entrepreneur. All that is necessary is to understand those aspects of his personality that are relevant to the requirements of the entrepreneurial role. "No given role exhausts personality; it represents merely one kind of organization of personality for limited purposes, an organization largely in terms of the requirements of the social situations."

The attempt to understand why and how people act as entrepreneurs leads Jenks directly to the analysis of entrepreneurial roles. This analysis is merely sketched in the article reprinted here. It is systematically presented in the later article on "The Role Structure of Entrepreneurial Personality" referred to above. Jenks there bases his analysis upon the organizational requirements of the business unit, regarded as a system of exchanges, a system of productive performances, and as an organization. The essential point made is that the requirements of the entrepreneurial role are not random or haphazard. They are determined within limits by the very nature of the business firm on the one hand, and by the commonly shared expectations of what constitutes proper and improper behavior in particular roles on the other. The business firm is seen as an organized system of interdependent and interacting roles, and behavior in these roles is regulated by positive and negative sanctions.

The problem of entrepreneurial personality serves Jenks as the entering wedge for an analysis of entrepreneurship completely different in character from any that might stem from Cole's or Schumpeter's approaches. The vocabulary and point of view are different; the lines of research suggested are also different. Two lines of inquiry in particular are indicated. First, one might investigate the requirements of entrepreneurial roles in a particular historical setting, perhaps in a particular industry, building up from analysis of what people actually said and did in particular situations to an understanding of what it meant to be an entrepreneur at that time and place. Alternatively, one might begin with an analysis of the dominant themes of a particular culture, investigate how they were expressed in the sanctions governing business roles, and relate these sanctions to what is in fact known about how businessmen behaved in that culture. In other words, we may proceed from a lower level of abstraction to a higher, or from a higher to a lower. Each of these modes of inquiry is excellently exemplified in the work of Thomas C. Cochran, the first in his *Railroad Leaders,* the second in his study of the Puerto Rican businessman,[3] and in his article on cultural factors in economic growth reprinted below in part III. The article reprinted in this part was originally published in *Change and the Entrepreneur* and represents an early attempt to "work down" to business roles from an analysis of the dominant themes of American culture. Difficult enough in itself, this task is made even more challenging by Cochran's interest in deviance from established roles as a source of social change. Identification of deviance from a role clearly requires prior identification of the role itself, and the attempt to impute social change to deviant behavior may lead to confusion if—as may have been the case with entrepreneurial roles in nineteenth century America—departure from established patterns of business behavior is itself expected and positively sanctioned. In such a case what appears to be deviance in role behavior will, on closer analysis, prove to be not deviance but conformity. Attempts to infer the characteristics of entrepreneurial roles from an analysis of cultural themes are particularly susceptible to traps of this kind. The detailed dissection of the actual content of entrepreneurial roles, such as Cochran carried out in his *Railroad Leaders,* is less vulnerable to error, but the evidence required is not always easily assembled.

These five articles illustrate the variety of approaches and points of view that characterized the early discussions of the Research Center. Despite the obvious differences with respect to definitions, assumptions, and methods of analysis, there was general agreement that the area selected for research was a fruitful one; indeed, the very heterogeneity of "approaches" testified to the rich harvest that was anticipated. Failure to agree upon a single point of view caused some distress at the time, but this was probably misplaced. In the early stages of research, virtue lay in variety—in preserving the ability to look at the evidence from different directions, in different lights, and with different perspectives. No single theory or set of concepts could yield all the understanding that was desired. A theory that threw one aspect of the problem into sharp relief by that very fact threw other aspects into the shadows. The soundest strategy was probably the one that was in fact adopted: to walk all round the subject and see how it showed itself differently to different observers. The five articles that follow describe what five people saw.

An Approach to the Study of Entrepreneurship: A Tribute to Edwin F. Gay

ARTHUR H. COLE

THE FIRST FORMAL MEETING of the Economic History Association after his death should not close without appropriate tribute to our initial president and the first real American economic historian, Edwin F. Gay. More than most members of the Association, I feel his loss, since in one capacity or another I had the good fortune to be associated with him for almost thirty-five years. And I am the more appropriate agent to render our common tribute, since, more than others, I am indebted to him. I realize that, without his instruction, encouragement, and stimulation, I should not be standing here as a successor to him in office.

I shall not attempt to compete with all the eulogists who, speaking for a score of institutions, have endeavored to phrase their debt to Professor Gay. Rather, I shall try to pay my homage by taking my evening's text from one of his interpretative essays, and by attempting to carry a bit further the thought that he impounded therein. Mr. George O. May has described Mr. Gay as "the scholar in action," and I doubt if Mr. Gay could be more pleased than by realizing that documents (or institutions) which felt his living hand were still of real service after he had gone.

Twenty years ago Mr. Gay gave the Phi Beta Kappa Commencement address at Harvard. He entitled it "The Rhythm of History," and not infrequently in his later years he referred to the theme that he embodied in it:

This article was originally given as the Presidential Address to the Economic History Association in 1946. It was published in *The Journal of Economic History*, Supplement VI, The Tasks of Economic History, 1946, pp. 1–15 and is reprinted here by permission of the author and the Association.

The amount of permissible free competition . . . varies with the social need. In differing degree it must always be active—this is what the socialists fail adequately to recognize—but it must always be subject more or less to group control, for the interest of the group predominates, and each member of the group consciously or unconsciously acknowledges this. The self-centered, active individual is a disruptive force, and there are periods in the rhythm of history when the cake of custom must be broken, when that disruptive, innovating energy is socially advantageous and must be given freer opportunity. But the social or group motive is even then latently powerful, while for normally longer periods of the rhythm the motive of social stability and order enjoys the more marked social approval. It then becomes active in building and defending social institutions and in seeking security for its members.[1]

Perhaps Mr. Gay liked to recall this thesis long after its first formulation because he could observe its increasing confirmation as the years and decades passed. Surely with him we can note the ever rising aspirations toward economic security and the continuing development of group organizations. Possibly we are also justified in thinking that this tide has begun to turn, the rhythm reached another turning point—with the rebuff to totalitarianism, with the moderation of English socialist beliefs, and with the prevailing contentment of American labor unionists to get along without Communist aid. Of course, the future direct and indirect influence of Russia constitutes the largest present question mark.

As historians, however, we may be allowed to take a longer view. Whether we stand at a turning point or must watch the trend toward socialization proceed yet further, surely we can look back upon and examine critically the extended period when "disruptive, innovating energy" was breaking through the "cake" of pre-existing customary forms, and "social need" appears to have condoned, even supported, a high degree of "permissible free competition" on the part of "self-centered, active" individuals. Surprisingly enough, this aspect of economic life has attracted less scholarly attention than it has deserved.

Reasons can be found for this relative neglect. Possibly the conjuncture of a rising interest in economic history with an evolving socializing economy may be a factor. The novel elements in recent history have been the new regulatory bodies or the new social groupings. The restless, innovating businessman could be taken for granted, a wholly familiar figure, even as, a hundred years ago, McCulloch thought that free trade was a self-evident truth.

A factor yet more potent may well have been the course of economic thought. Here the villain of the piece is David Ricardo. Building upon Adam Smith, but in important ways altering the scientific method, he influenced processes of thinking in that area, which, transmitted through Mill and Caines and Marshall, have not wholly lost their potency to the present day. Economists since Ricardo have been largely preoccupied with "long-run" conditions, "static" analysis, and the like, and thereby have tended to distract attention from short-run, but repetitive, forces that are productive of change.

But my quarrel with the eminent stockbroker is more specific. In the construction of his economic principles, Ricardo failed to pursue the suggestion supplied by Cantillon and Jean-Baptiste Say that the entrepreneur be distinguished clearly from the other agents of production. This failure is somewhat difficult to understand, since Say had formalized the term "entrepreneur" and given it definition some fifteen years before Ricardo's *Principles* appeared, and he had repeated the notion several times in the interim, at least one version of which was available to Ricardo in English translation. Not merely is the term itself absent in Ricardo's writings, but no concept of business leaders as agents of change (other than as shadowy bearers of technological improvements) is embraced in his treatment of economic principles. In neglecting to follow Say, Ricardo seems to me to have rendered a great disservice to economics, and secondarily to economic history.[2]

Say had presented a characterization of extraordinary insight and imagination. The entrepreneur is the economic agent who

> unites all means of production—the labor of the one, the capital or the land of the others—and who finds in the value of the products which result from their employment the reconstitution of the entire capital that he utilizes, and the value of the wages, the interest, and the rent which he pays, as well as the profits belonging to himself.[3]

This person, this entrepreneur, must have special personal qualities:

> . . . judgment, perseverance, and a knowledge of the world as well as of business. He is called upon to estimate, with tolerable accuracy, the importance of the specific product, the probable amount of the demand, and the means of its production: at one time, he must employ a great

number of hands; at another, buy or order the raw material, collect laborers, find consumers, and give at all times a rigid attention to order and economy; in a word, he must possess the art of superintendence and administration . . . In the course of such complex operations, there are an abundance of obstacles to be surmounted, of anxieties to be repressed, of misfortunes to be repaired, and of expedients to be devised.[4]

This appraisal seems to me exceptionally full, as I have already suggested. Indeed, after a perusal of more modern authors—Walker and Knight, Schumpeter, Chamberlin, and divers others—I am inclined to paraphrase Say in an effort to blueprint the individual or institution that exhibits and has for centuries exhibited the "disruptive, innovating energy," of which Mr. Gay wrote. Say's analysis does fail to emphasize the spirit of adventure and the element of innovation, without which, it seems to me, a complete formulation of the entrepreneurial function is impossible.

I

Entrepreneurship may be defined in simplest terms as the utilization by one productive factor of the other productive factors for the creation of economic goods. But such a definition means little until we have answered a barrage of questions: Why? How? Through what institutions and instrumentalities? With what concessions to the prevailing political and social environment? Elaborated as a result of such a catechism, entrepreneurship may be described as follows: the integrated sequence of actions, taken by individuals or by groups operating for individual business units, in a world characterized by a large measure of uncertainty, such actions being modified in greater or less degree by contemporary economic and social forces. This sequence of actions is intended to increase the residual element in business income for those business units, namely, profits, or to achieve some other business gain, for example, power, efficiency or the survival and growth of these units (or the avoidance of loss). Thereby an advantage or satisfaction is hoped for (directly or indirectly, immediately or shortly) by those planning and executing these actions either for themselves or for the institutions with which they are affiliated and have identified themselves. At this point, it becomes essential to fragmentize the problem.

Obviously, we are concerned primarily with individual business units, with their creation, their preservation, and their demise, in whatever portion of economic and business life they may chance to be concerned, and in whatever form—proprietorship, partnership, or corporation—they chance to be organized. Also we are interested in the one person or in the several or many persons who alone, counseled by external advisers, or as a joint undertaking carry the destiny of each enterprise in his individual or in their co-operating hands. In the case of group entrepreneurship, such as we find in many large corporations, our concern is primarily with the so-called "top executives" or "top management"; but the diffusion of authority seems often so great that sovereignty may be no less difficult to locate than in the British form of government. I am inclined to think the lower edge of entrepreneurial power in group executive situations to be more like an uneven fringe than a neat clear line.[5]

In the promotional and survival purposes which entrepreneurship serves relative to individual business units, three processes alone seem important: innovation, management, and adjustment to external conditions, with the last including the imitation by some enterprises of the innovations initiated by other business units that are directly or indirectly competing, and the utilization by enterprises in one industry of innovational services provided by ancillary concerns.[6] Innovation and adjustment, in turn, are the resultants of business decisions—business decisions motivated, as just suggested, by a purpose of increasing some differential business advantage or some satisfaction, or avoiding some differential or positive business disadvantage or unpleasantness.[7]

Under such a concept, risk bearing and profit receiving obviously become mere negative or passive elements. The real purpose of business strategy is to minimize risks and uncertainties and, if possible, to pass them off upon other business units; while the distribution of profits within business enterprises is a function of law, custom, and internal pressures, and, except in simple business organizations, has no close relation to the active derivation of profits.[8]

Since adjustment to forces external to given business units—economic, business, or social forces—may be regarded as a sort of necessary evil (inasmuch as no single enterprise can enjoy a monopoly of business talent and since business cannot generate its own environment), entrepreneurship boils down in basic functions to innovation upon a solid operational base achieved through the medium of business decisions. Innovation without a solid base tends to be ineffective—as witness the thousands of concerns that yearly die before their first birthdays; while management without innovation gives a poor prognosis, being the "dry rot" of enterprises on the way toward ossification and extinction.

In turn, these activities—and the decisions behind them—relative to innovation, management, and the adjustment to external forces may be conceived as directed along a half-dozen channels, which together, in fact, comprehend all the important phases of purpose in the individual business unit, whether it be large or small, or concerned with commercial, industrial, banking, or other business activities. Of course, the proportionate importance of the several phases will differ with size and with the nature of the business unit, as well as with some other factors. The half-dozen spheres of action are:

1. The determination of the business objectives of the enterprise, and the change of those objectives as conditions require or make advantageous;
2. The development and maintenance of an organization, including efficient relations with subordinates and all employees;
3. The securing of adequate financial resources, the retention of them, and the nurture of good relations with existing and potential investors;
4. The acquisition of efficient technological equipment, and the revision of it as new machinery appears;
5. The development of a market for products, and the devising of new products to meet or anticipate consumer demands; and
6. The maintenance of good relations with public authorities and with society at large.

In any of these phases of enterpreneurial activity there is constant need for decisions, and in any of them there is opportunity for innovation, management, and the adjustment to external conditions, including alterations of public opinion. It is through these avenues of operation that entrepreneurial power functions.

Thus, in brief, we have at the base of our pyramid a half-dozen lines or avenues of activity—from organizing the enterprise to getting along with the general public—in following which entrepreneurship really does things. Then we have three objectives or purposes which occasion activities along these several lines: innovation, management, and the imposed adjustments. The actions for these three purposes along any of the six lines are the resultants of executive decisions; these decisions are the acts of a real person, or a real, but variantly composed, group of persons at or near the top of individual business units; and these decisions are made in response to divers psychological imperatives and are conditioned by various and changing environmental forces.

II

The economic significance of such business phenomena is patent, although infrequently adumbrated. Economic advance, at least insofar as it springs from business and not from governmental or other forces, is largely a consequence of innovations by individual enterprises copied by competing business units. These innovations may be of any sort, from the organization of a business unit itself—the launching of an enterprise novel in product, place, or form—to a new method of packaging a manufactured item. They may be innovations of technological equipment and productive processes, or they may be purely innovations of management.[9] Also, one may properly conceive of innovations pushing out, first in one sector of operations and then in another, first by one enterprise and then by another, like the advancing front of a long battle line. Advantageous innovations, made effective by efficient management, are copied by other enterprises; the differential advantages of the innovating institutions are repeatedly lost; marginal expenses are reduced; and the phenomenon of economic progress—greater productivity at lower human cost—is attained. Such surely is an adequate social reason for studying entrepreneurship.

The central position of entrepreneurship in other economic relations is suggested by consideration of the fact that entrepreneurial decisions (including those of banking "entrepreneurs") constitute the chief element in business cycles. Albert Hart and George Shackle have paid special attention to this situation in their analyses of "anticipations"; Sumner Slichter and others have studied businessmen's reactions in their examination of "turning points" in business cycles; while, of course, to Joseph Schumpeter, innovations and other entrepreneurial phenomena are pivotal. Again, one may say that entrepreneurial policy has been half (or more) of the problem of industrial relations; and it forms an equivalent proportion of public relations. In short, entrepreneurship cannot, it seems, be regarded as other than a potent change-producing force in a free or relatively free economy.[10] To study the "entrepreneur" is to study the central figure in modern economic history, and, to my way of thinking, the central figure in economics.[11]

Such strong statements may well demand support, and I offer a few brief explanations. Entrepreneurship seems to me central in economics for a number of important reasons, some of which are of significance for economic historians. I agree with my friend G. Heberton Evans that the development of sound theory in dynamic terms and the forging of links between aggregative economics and the economics of the individual firm are urgent present-day problems in economic theory, and that here the study of entrepreneurship should be productive. Again, the hypothesis—almost invariably taken as self-evident—that the aim of all businessmen is and always has been the maximization of profits has been a primary element in economic theory over many decades, but actually no one has collected evidence to establish the truth of this contention. Undoubtedly other forces have had influence, while also without doubt the strength of the lure of profits has varied among time periods. For instance, there is good reason to believe that few entrepreneurs have really made decisions on the grounds of "the public be damned"—while probably there are still fewer who have operated on the policy of "my church, my family, my friends, my social and business relations be damned." Joan Robinson, with a liberty appropriate to her sex, speaks of the "horrors of inflation" being "sucked up with the milk of the mothers of bank presidents";[12] and surely—with more seriousness—other, less specific attitudes are derived by entrepreneurs from their family and social or business milieus. Again, one may quote Sir Sidney Chapman who, at the end of a long experience, has ventured recently to assert that "in nine cases out of ten" the assumption of crass money seeking would not be true: chiefly the entrepreneur strives for efficiency and assumes an enhanced pecuniary gain only as a related consequence.[13] And do we not know that men have frequently measured their success by the growth of the enterprises with which they have identified themselves, that others have kept active at business after they had more wealth than they could themselves utilize, that still others—in mutual savings banks or similar institutions—have long operated with a feeling for social service? Actually we know precious little about the motivations of entrepreneurs or the changes in motivations over time. Success in entrepreneurship may itself actually prevent the maximization of profits, as was suggested by my predecessor in office, Harold A. Innis, in his presidential address: "Large-scale effective mechanization of distribution necessitated a single price and the search for devices to prevent outbreaks of competitive warfare. The price system weakens the profit motive by its emphasis on management."[14]

On the other hand, it may be contended that a study of entrepreneurship in its historical setting provides an opportunity to synthesize the work going forward in economics and in business administration, in economic history, business history, and social history, in the history of entrepreneurial thought and the history of social thought. It is not without significance that economists like Taussig or Schumpeter or Gordon, psychologists like Thorndike and Katona, political scientists like Dimock, historians of social thought, business historians, and divers others have paid some, if inadequate, attention to entrepreneurship and its characteristics.

III

For those economic historians concerned with the development of a logical framework of our subject, I would suggest the potentiality of devising "stages" of economic evolution—or, as I prefer to think of it, plotting the longitudinal segments of change—which would have greater pertinence to basic conditions in a world of private economy, even for business history (and would have greater logic), than the "commercial capitalism," "industrial capitalism," "financial capitalism," etc., which now have broad acceptance among us.[15] I have no intention of belittling such categories. However, one may fairly ask whether these conceptual tools are sounder than "commercial initiative," "industrial initiative," "financial initiative," and the like—even "commercial," "industrial," and "financial" law.

I should propose the analysis of business and economic evolution in terms of the "disruptive, innovating energy" which over recent centuries has been a continuingly important factor in evoking change; and, until some more imaginative and more profound student devises a superior formulation, I suggest the categories of empirical entrepreneurship, rational entrepreneurship, and cognitive entrepreneurship. Somewhat less elegant terms might be rule-of-thumb, informed, and sophisticated entrepreneurship. However, I have yet to find any set of appellations that conveys the full concepts at each level.

I do not believe that the character of the decision-making organ —whether singular, plural, or institutionalized—is a crucial element, although rational entrepreneurship would be likely to be less individualized than the itinerant peddler or the primitive textile proprietor, while a cognitive entrepreneurship would usually coincide with the multiple leadership of which Robert Gordon has written.[16] Again, I do not find that the business form—whether proprietorship, corporation, international cartel, or what not—is a determining force. Nor does it seem to be vital for differentiating change in this social institution whether entrepreneurship be concerned with commercial or industrial pursuits or be temporarily (and partially) linked to a set of financial advisers.

What seems most important for economic evolution is a composite of elements which together condition efficiency of entrepreneurial activity. First there must be a favoring environment: the prevalence of an adventurous spirit either in men or in organizations; the existence of potent incentives, whatever their nature; an opportunity to reap rewards adequate to continued initiative; and, if entrepreneurship is to have sustained development, provision for succession and the training of successors to those who launch new enterprises. Then within that general climate of beneficence, the significant factor appears to be the growth in skill of making wise decisions relative to innovation, management, and the adjustment to external forces. Here the most noteworthy changes over time seem to pertain, first, to knowledge of what really is going on within and outside the individual business unit (where entrepreneurship draws on accountancy, statistics, systematic business information, and the like); secondly, to the rise of advisers—away from the local lawyer or general storekeeper to well-chosen boards of directors, and to permanent administrative staffs; and, thirdly, to the development of ancillary business agencies and institutions, by aid of which some of the uncertainties of the individual business unit are passed to other shoulders, and some of the rule-of-thumb expedients eliminated, or through which increased knowledge or superior advisers come to its service.[17]

To be sure, the criteria just suggested are two dimensional, if not three. The business leader of modern decades not only must know more facts about more subjects than his eighteenth-century counterpart, synthesize more appraisals of experts and advisers, and be cognizant of more services from more service institutions, but he must relate his decisions to a longer time space of past and future. Also he tends to approach or handle his greater body of data for his longer range decisions in a different manner—with an attitude more akin to that of the so-called "learned professions," with more awareness of the data that he does not possess, and with higher appreciation (at least in large situations) of the repercussions of his actions upon the various parts of his own business unit, upon his direct and indirect competitors, upon the customers whom he desires to influence, or upon the public or the governmental officials with whom he seeks to maintain amicable relations. Ideas along these lines are implicit—some explicit—in much of the recent literature on monopolistic competition; while other aspects of the development are suggested by Mr. Barnard's stimulating study of the executive in operation.[18]

While those segments of entrepreneurship—empirical, rational, and cognitive—all persist today; while, like the use of snuff, empirical businesses are quantitatively more important than they were two hundred years ago; and while empirical procedures can still be found in business units of the most advanced quality, yet I do not believe the statement likely to be challenged that empirical or rule-of-thumb entrepreneurship prevailed universally in this country (and with few exceptions elsewhere) until the nineteenth century; that informed entrepreneurship, waxing steadily in its rationalizations, grew to prominence a hundred years ago and especially after about 1860; while, evolving particularly since 1890 or thereabouts, a cognitive entrepreneurship has come to characterize the leading, and some medium-sized business units of the present day. In short, I offer you the concepts of empirical, rational, and cognitive entrepreneurship as a growth sequence, and offer them in the hope that they may be improved and refined as research progresses.

Such a series of evolutionary phases, though obviously defined by business criteria, does have an economic basis and possesses an economic significance of no small moment. Even as, in other connections, man's progress is measured by his increasing knowledge of and control over nature, so the terms tendered here express (or are intended to express) a varying, increasing degree of effectiveness in the utilization of economic factors by that fourth factor in production: entrepreneurship. Thus we come back finally to our starting point, the simple definition of entrepreneurship as the employment of other productive factors by the fourth.

IV

For those who find little satisfaction in system framing, the study of entrepreneurship offers a rich opportunity from the fact, suggested in my earlier definition of this economic function, that in entrepreneurship "an individual or group operating for an individual business unit" takes an "integrated sequence of actions." The entrepreneur, whether individual or multiple, does not "decide" in the abstract, "adjust" in the abstract, innovate, or maintain an organization in the abstract. Always such actions are taken relative to concrete living institutions, and therefore they can best be examined in concrete historical settings. Again, not only are decisions arrived at, and indeed conditioned by an environment of social, political, and economic factors (including contemporary thought), but one decision in some measure conditions all subsequent decisions. Moreover, one phase of entrepreneurship as a whole conditions subsequent phases. Accordingly there seems to be a rich opportunity for business history—as Thomas Cochran has emphasized in other connections[19]—to provide the necessary data for broad generalizations respecting business behavior. In this regard, N. S. B. Gras has had a proper intuition, and we can welcome the spread of interest in the field which the latter has done so much to establish. Out of the work that N. S. B. Gras's group, and now a host of research workers, are providing may yet be evolved a new emphasis in economics and business administration and a new outlook in economic history.

Sometimes, though with limited objectives, it will be possible to indulge in studies cross-sectional in time. For example, we could learn a good deal about the Colonial merchant entrepreneur by an intensive examination of those men who were active in the later pre-Revolutionary days: Hancock, Laurens, Morris, and the rest.

To the data of Robert East,[20] I can add a few facts as yet unassimilated. In this early environment, men could and did set themselves up in independent business or entered partnerships in the first years of manhood: Hancock at twenty, Laurens at twenty-three, Christopher Gadsden (of Charleston) at twenty-two, and Robert Morris at twenty—a considerable contrast to the ages at which men in recent years have reached the top executive positions in large modern enterprises. Again, I know that Thomas and John Hancock made (or had made) annually an average of 950 credit entries in their ledgers in the period 1755–1770—or about three transactions per working day[21]—while the number of daily transactions at country stores seems to have been not much greater. On the other hand, a typical department store in Boston is confronted annually with the job of handling 1,700,000 transactions, or better than 5,000 per day. And the daily transactions of a large grocery "chain" must approach or exceed 100,000 per diem. What do such contrasts mean as far as entrepreneurial history is concerned?

Similarly we could study the plantation owners of the 1850's, the railroad executives of the 1870's, or the investment bankers of the 1890's. We would, of course, want to know much more than their entering ages or volume of transactions: their origins, their burdens of uncertainties (with the collateral facts regarding their accountancy, controls, etc., or regarding ancillary institutions), the sources of their business information, the availability of counselors, or their attitudes toward business and economic problems of their times. The investigator would here be dealing more with the externals of entrepreneurship than with motivations or personal characteristics or specific business decisions, into which business biographies and company histories can hope to penetrate; but he would be blazing trails through what is now largely *terra incognita* and often he would be doing all that is possible to do with situations so far removed in time. Perhaps we would wind up with a historical sociology of entrepreneurship—comparable possibly with existing studies of the church or the immigrant or the public school.

Again, there is opportunity for longitudinal studies of particular entrepreneurial functions or relations: the use of the corporate form, trends in personnel policies, employment of accountancy, and the like.

In a few instances, the investigator can survey even broader areas, areas toward which perhaps all narrower studies should trend, and areas that bring once more to mind Mr. Gay's thesis. One such inquiry is reported in E. Lipson's effort to apply economic history to the solution of current problems: his *Planned Economy or Free Enterprise.*[22] Here in words that Mr. Gay might have used, "the entrepreneur" is viewed as "the powerful dissolvent of a communal regime which had been organized on the basis of craft gilds and village courts."[23] And he suggests the manner whereby this result was achieved when he notes how "the richer members" of the guilds could begin the breakdown of these units by gathering "into their hands a monopoly" of the business; or how the "large traders [in regulated companies] . . . managed to squeeze out the 'young beginners' and men of 'lower estates.' "[24] Surely these "pushing" individuals (as Mr. Gay used to characterize the corresponding figures of a later period) were entrepreneurial in type—innovating businessmen squirming like unborn chicks to break out of the shell of communal life.

Here in England from the later Middle Ages onward, or in the entrepreneurs of "hard cutting edge" in the Industrial Revolution (again to employ a favorite phrase of Mr. Gay), in the "robber baron" period of our post-Civil War days (of which Chester Destler has told us), or in the growth in social responsibility which various observers think to detect in the American business leaders of the past few decades—here can one work closely indeed in the theorem that Mr. Gay propounded.

In short, there are opportunities for factual investigations as diverse as the differences among us of temperament and intellectual values—from the intensive examination of a company's or an individual businessman's career to a wide-ranging effort at co-ordinating known facts into fruitful hypotheses.

V

The area of entrepreneurial history stands open to the present generation of research workers, almost as unworked as the "significance of the frontier" when Frederick Turner first voiced his hypotheses. Some tools of analysis—some ploughs and harrows, if you will—have been fashioned, although we do not know but what they will "foul" as did the cast-iron ploughs in prairie land. A few specimens of the soil have been treated scientifically. A few uncertain maps have been sketched. But the main rich territory awaits the intellectual explorers and exploiters who will locate and develop the more valuable sections—explorers and exploiters who, it is to be hoped, will maintain contacts with the older parts of the country—in this case, the parts of the historical world that Mr. Gay described. Thus in the end the new may be achieved by reaching out from the old: we can honor our distinguished first president by examining systematically a hazy segment of his "rhythm" of history" and offering our new facts and theories as tributes to his memory.

Economic Theory and Entrepreneurial History

JOSEPH A. SCHUMPETER

IN THE AREAS of economic theory and entrepreneurial history, I propose to deal with three topics. First, I shall present a brief survey of the history, within economic literature, of the notions that economists have formed at various times on the subject of entrepreneurship and economic progress (I). Secondly, I shall deal with some aspects of enterprise as it actually evolved through the ages (II). And, thirdly, I shall briefly comment on the possibilities of what might be termed "general economic history" as viewed from the standpoint of the phenomenon of economic enterprise (III). The first topic will also provide the conceptual apparatus to be used in the treatment of the other two.

I

In the field to be discussed, as in others, early economic analysis started from the notions evolved by common experience of everyday life, proceeding to greater precision and refinement of these notions as time went on. From the first, the businessman was a familiar figure that did not seem to call for elaborate explanation at all. The particular forms of business enterprise that every particular environment produced—the artisan, the trader, the moneylender, and so on—took a long time in merging into the general concept of businessman. But by the end of the 17th century this

This article is reprinted, by permission of the Harvard University Committee for the Schumpeter Fund, from Harvard University Research Center in Entrepreneurial History, *Change and the Entrepreneur* (Cambridge, Mass.: Harvard University Press, 1949).

modest generalization was pretty much accomplished. It is, however, worth noting that at least from the beginning of the 15th century on, the scholastic doctors in their economics had a very definite idea of the businessman and his functions, and that in particular they distinguished clearly between the specific *industria* of the merchant and the *labor* of the workman. The same applies to the laic successors of the scholastic doctors, "the philosophers of natural law," and still more to all those pamphleteers of the "mercantilist" age that laid the foundations of classic economics. Cantillon's work, which is usually, though not quite correctly, described as the first systematic treatise on economics, then introduced the term "entrepreneur." It is worth our while to note that Cantillon defined this entrepreneur as the agent who buys means of production at certain prices in order to combine them into a product that he is going to sell at prices that are uncertain at the moment at which he commits himself to his costs. I think that this embryonic analysis was not infelicitous. Besides recognizing business activity as a function *sui generis,* it emphasizes the elements of direction and speculation that certainly do enter somehow into entrepreneurial activity. Like most of Cantillon's ideas, including the idea of the *tableau économique,* this one was accepted by the physiocrats as a matter of course. Since directly and through the physiocrats Cantillon's teaching continued to be known in France, it seems fair to say that J. B. Say only continued the French tradition by developing this analysis further. In this he was greatly helped by the fact that, knowing from experience what business practice really is, he had a lively vision of the phenomenon which most of the other classic economists lacked. With him, then, the entrepreneur is the agent that combines the others into a productive organism. It could be shown both that this definition might be expanded into a satisfactory theory of entrepreneurship by analyzing what this combining of factors really consists in, and that Say himself did not do much with it beyond stressing its importance. Let us note in passing, however, that he put the entrepreneur into the center of both the productive and the distributive theory which, though it is disfigured by many slips, first adumbrated the analytic structure that became fully articulate in the hands of Walras, Marshall, Wicksell, Clark, and the Austrians. Still more clearly the nature and importance of entrepreneurship were perceived by Jeremy Bentham. It is a curious fact (curious, that is, considering the tremendous influence that Bentham exerted in other respects) that his views on this subject—which were not fully given to the public until the posthumous publication of his collected works—remained almost unnoticed by professional economists.

In spite of the great influence of the physiocrats and of Cantillon upon Adam Smith, English thought took a quite different line. To be sure, Adam Smith repeatedly talked about the employer—the master, the merchant, and the undertaker—but the leading or directing activity as a distinctive function played a surprisingly small role in his analytic scheme of the economic process. His reader is bound to get an impression to the effect that this process runs on by itself. Natural law preconceptions led Adam Smith to emphasize the role of labor to the exclusion of the productive function of designing the plan according to which this labor is being applied. This shows characteristically in his turn of phrase that asserts that "capitalists" hire "industrious people," advancing them means of subsistence, raw materials, and tools, and letting them do the rest. What the businessman does in the system of Adam Smith is, therefore, to provide real capital and nothing else: the identification of the capitalist's and the entrepreneur's function was thus accomplished. Let us note: first, that this picture of the industrial process is entirely unrealistic; but that, considering the prevalence at Adam Smith's time of the putting-out system, and also for other historical reasons, this identification was then less absurd than it became fifty years later; and that Smith's authority explains why it survived so well into times that presented different patterns. Since capital, according to Adam Smith, is the result of saving, and since providing capital is the only essential function of the businessman, the latter's profit was essentially interest to be explained on the lines of either an exploitation or an abstinence theory. Adam Smith elaborated neither, but no doubt suggested both.

With Ricardo and Marx the processes of production and commerce are still more automatic. The designing, directing, leading, co-ordinating function has practically no place at all in their analytic schemata. To avoid misunderstandings, let me emphasize that there is no doubt but that, if pressed, both Ricardo and Marx (and this goes for a majority of the writers of the classic period) would certainly have recognized the importance of entrepreneurship or business management or however they would have called it, for the success or failure of the individual concern. But it is possible to recognize this and to hold, nevertheless, that for the social process as a whole individual differences in this respect are of no great moment. John Stuart Mill who, at an early age, had experienced the influence of Say, abandoned Ricardianism in this as he did in other points. He emphasized the function of direction in the productive process and went out of his way to say that very often it required "no ordinary skill." His perception of the importance of entrepreneurial activity shows among other things in the fact that he regretted that there is no good English word for the French "entrepreneur." But this was all. When we observe that he analyzed the entrepreneur's profits into wages of management, interest on owned capital, and premium of risk, we wonder why he should not have been content with the perfectly good English term "business management," which was in fact to satisfy Marshall. For, after all, his entrepreneur does a type of nonmanual work that does not essentially differ from other types, and therefore reaps a return that is analogous to wages. There should be no need for a distinctive term.

Just as the understanding of the phenomenon of rent of land was facilitated by the English land system that showed up the distinction between the owner of land and the agricultural producer with unmistakable clearness, so the distinction between the entrepreneur and the capitalist was facilitated in the second half of the nineteenth century by the fact that changing methods of business finance produced a rapidly increasing number of instances in which capitalists were no entrepreneurs and entrepreneurs were no capitalists. Though the owner-manager remained for a time still the ruling type, it became increasingly clear that a link between owning and operating the physical shell of industry is not a necessary one. Economists accordingly began to emphasize distinctions between the two functions and to devote more attention to the specifically entrepreneurial one. Fundamental change in the analytic setup was very slow, however. Among other things, this shows in the survival of the risk theory of entrepreneurial profit. If providing the capital is not the essential or defining function of the entrepreneur, then risk bearing should not be described as an essential or defining function either, for it is obviously the capitalist who bears the risk and who loses his money in case of failure. If the entrepreneur borrows at a fixed rate of interest and undertakes to guarantee the capitalist against loss whatever the results of the enterprise, he can do so only if he owns other assets with which to satisfy the creditor capitalist when things go wrong. But, in this case, he is able to satisfy his creditor because he is a capitalist himself and the risk he bears he bears in this capacity and not in his capacity of entrepreneur. To this point I shall return below. The economists, therefore, who went on to emphasize the entrepreneurial function more and more, such as Francis A. Walker in the U.S., Marshall in England, Mangoldt and others in Germany, added very little to its analysis.

Two lines of thought that issued in distinctive theories of entrepreneurial profits as distinguished from interest should not go unmentioned. Mangoldt, following up a generalization of the rent concept that may be traced to Samuel Bailey, defined the particular element of total receipts that goes to the entrepreneur as a rent of ability. The underlying idea is very plausible. All current disturbances of the economic process, the whole task of adaptation to ever changing situations, impinges primarily upon the heads of business concerns. Obviously this is a very personal task of which some people acquit themselves very much better than others. There is a common-sense impression to the effect that there is such a thing as a distinct business ability, which includes aptitude for efficient administration, for prompt decision, and all that sort of thing; and it is very generally recognized in spite of some votes to the contrary (in this country, mainly from economists of Veblenite persuasion) that successful survival of difficult situations and success in taking advantage of favorable situations is not merely a matter of luck. The concept of a rent of ability expresses the element involved quite well. Again the cognate idea that business decisions in a world that is full of uninsurable risks ("uncertainty") will in general produce results that diverge more or less widely from the expected ones and thus lead sometimes to surplus gains and sometimes to losses, is one that common experience presses upon us very strongly. This idea may be but need not be added to the element of business ability and is of course, still more obviously, not quite the same as the element of risk: but we need not stress these relations. So far as I know, Böhm-Bawerk was the first to make use of this notion for the purpose of explaining entrepreneurial profits as distinct from interest. But this line of thought culminates in the work of Professor Knight.

It does not seem far-fetched, however, to analyze the entrepreneurial function in a different direction which moreover leads to a result that comprises also some of the elements of other theories. I shall try to convey this analysis by starting from two different standpoints. The first standpoint to start from is given by Say's definition of the entrepreneurial function. If production in the economic, as distinguished from the technological, sense consists essentially in transforming or combining factors into products, or as I have put it above, in providing the design of production, then we certainly have in this combining or planning or directing activity a distinct function before us. But this function would be an exceedingly simple matter and essentially a matter of administration if the combinations that have been carried into effect in the past had to be simply repeated or even if they had to be repeated subject to those adaptations which common business experience suggests in the face of conditions that change under the influence of external factors. Administrative or managerial activity of this kind, however necessary, need not be distinguished from other kinds of nonmanual labor; but if we confine Say's definition to cases in which combinations that are *not* inherited from the past have to be set up anew, then the situation is obviously different and we do have a distinctive function before us. Naturally, to some extent, even current decisions contain elements that have not been contained in inherited routine. There is, therefore, no sharp dividing line between entrepreneurial activity in this restricted sense and ordinary administration or management, any more than there is a sharp dividing line between the *homo neanderthalis* and the types which we recognize as full-fledged human beings. This does not, however, prevent the distinction from being possible and useful. And the distinctive element is readily recognized so soon as we make clear to ourselves what it means to act outside of the pale of routine. The distinction between adaptive and creative response to given conditions may or may not be felicitous, but it conveys an essential point; it conveys an essential difference.

The other standpoint from which to get a realistic understanding of the entrepreneurial function comes into view when we try to analyze the nature and sources of the gains that attend successful entrepreneurship. This can be done in many ways, for instance, by analyzing the sources of a sufficient number of industrial fortunes. We find immediately that industrial activity in established lines and by established methods hardly ever yields returns that are much greater than is necessary to secure the supply of the factors required. Furthermore, we find that the earning capacity of almost any industrial concern peters out after a time that varies from a few months to a few decades. And, finally, we find that the great surplus gains are in general made in new industries or in industries that adopt a new method, and especially by the firms who are the first in the field. These propositions await scientific investigations in order to be fully established, but are strongly suggested by universally known facts.

If then we have, on the one hand, a distinctive function and, on the other hand, a distinct return on the exercise of this function, we can start with the task of conceptualization. First, we need a word. I have myself suggested that the word "entrepreneur" be harnessed into service, but it is quite clear, of course, that since this "entrepreneurial function" is not a neologism other meanings are bound to creep in. I should, therefore, have no objection to some such expression as "business leader" or simply "innovator" or the like. The essential thing is the recognition of the distinct agent we envisage and not the word.[1] Secondly, in applying our conception to reality we find, as we do in other such cases, that real life never presents the function in and by itself. Even the English landlord is not merely the owner of a natural agent but does various other things besides. In the case of the entrepreneur it is even difficult to imagine a case where a man does nothing but set up new combinations and where he does this all his life. In particular an industrialist who creates an entirely new setup will, in a typical case, then settle down to a merely administrating activity to which he confines himself more and more as he gets older. On the other hand, the entrepreneurial element may be present to a very small extent even in very humble cases and in these the entrepreneurial function may be all but drowned in other activities. It will be seen, however, that while this makes it difficult to deal with entrepreneurship irrespective of the other types of activity of the same individual and while Professor Cole is therefore quite right in emphasizing the necessity of considering business activity as a whole, the distinctive element and its *modus operandi* should not and need not be lost from sight.

Thirdly, since entrepreneurship, as defined, essentially consists in doing things that are not generally done in the ordinary course of business routine, it is essentially a phenomenon that comes under the wider aspect of leadership. But this relation between entrepreneurship and general leadership is a very complex one and lends itself to a number of misunderstandings. This is due to the fact that the concept of leadership itself is complex. Leadership may consist, as it does in the arts, merely in doing a new thing, for instance, in creating a new form of pictorial self-expression, but in other cases it is the influencing of people by methods other than example that is more important. Take, for instance, the phenomenon that we call the ability of being obeyed. Here it is not so much example as a direct action upon other people that matters. The nature and function of entrepreneurial leadership, its causes and effects, therefore constitute a very important subject of investigation for our group.

Fourthly, the distinctive return to entrepreneurship presents difficulties of its own. It is certainly a return to a personal activity. In this sense we might be tempted to call it a form of wages as has in fact been done in the past by many economists. Furthermore, it is clear that if all people reacted in the same way and at the same time to the presence of new possibilities no entrepreneurial gain would ensue: if everybody had been in a position to develop the Watt condenser, prices of products to be produced with the new steam engine would have adjusted themselves instantaneously and no surplus over costs would have arisen for the firm of Boulton and Watt. Therefore, entrepreneurial gain may also be called a monopoly gain, since it is due to the fact that competitors only follow at a distance.[2] But if we called it either wages or monopoly gains we should be obscuring very important characteristics that do not apply to other wages or to other monopoly gains. Moreover, the entrepreneurial gain does not typically consist, and in any case does not necessarily consist, in a current surplus *per se*. If a man, for instance, sets up a new industrial organization such as United States Steel, the value of the assets that enter into this organization increases. This increase no doubt embodies, at least ideally, a discounted value of the expected surplus returns. But it is this increase in asset values itself rather than the returns that constitute the entrepreneurial gain, and it is in this way that industrial fortunes are typically created—another subject to be investigated.

Finally, as has been often pointed out, the entrepreneurial function need not be embodied in a physical person and in particular in a single physical person. Every social environment has its own ways of filling the entrepreneurial function. For instance, the practice of farmers in this country has been revolutionized again and again by the introduction of methods worked out in the Department of Agriculture and by the Department of Agriculture's success in teaching these methods. In this case then it was the Department of Agriculture that acted as an entrepreneur. It is another most important point in our research program to find out how important this kind of activity has been in the past or is in the present. Again the entrepreneurial function may be and often is filled co-operatively. With the development of the largest-scale corporations this has evidently become of major importance: aptitudes that no single individual combines can thus be built into a corporate personality; on the other hand, the constituent physical personalities must inevitably to some extent, and very often to a serious extent, interfere with each other. In many cases, therefore, it is difficult or even impossible to name an individual that acts as "the entrepreneur" in a concern. The leading people in particular, those who carry the titles of president or chairman of the board, may be mere co-ordinators or even figureheads; and again a very interesting field of research opens up into which I do not wish to go, however, since this problem is in no danger of being forgotten.[3]

We have now briefly to advert to the relation that exists between economic change (usually called economic progress if we approve of it) and the entrepreneurial activity. At present there is, as has been stated above, a whole range of differences of opinion on this subject that extends from a complete or almost complete denial of any importance to be attached to the quality of leading personnel to the equally reckless assertion that the creative individual is nothing less than everything. It need hardly be pointed out that most of these opinions carry the stamp of ideological preconception. It is no doubt part of our work to put provable results into the place of such ideologies. The fundamental question is one of fact, but the necessity of a theoretical schema to start with is nevertheless obvious. I submit that the material under observation may be classed into two masses: on the one hand, there are the given data of the physical and social (including political) environment and, on the other hand, there are the observable reactions to these environmental conditions. But it is better perhaps to include those facts that may be independently observed concerning the quality of leading personnel among the conditions in order to display the interrelation between this and the other factors and to emphasize from the first that on principle there are never any causal chains in the historical process but only mutual interaction of distinguishable factors.

We can then attempt to construct an analytic model of the mechanism of economic change or else, for different countries and periods, different such schemata or models. Let us, in order to visualize this method, consider for a moment the situation that existed in England around 1850. A unique set of historical conditions had produced a uniquely able political sector, the bulk of the members of which hailed from a distinct social class. This sector, while very efficient in certain respects, was entirely unfit and unwilling to undertake anything that we now call economic public management or economic planning. Neglecting for the rest the agrarian sector, we find industry, trade, and finance substantially left to themselves; and if we add a number of other unique historical circumstances we are pretty much able to draw the picture of economic change that is in fact drawn in the ordinary text-book of economic history. In this process of change it is possible to identify a number of factors and events that are entirely impersonal and in some cases random. But looking more closely we see not only that these factors do not determine outcomes uniquely but also that they do not tell us how the actual changes such as the tremendous increase in exports actually came about. In order to make headway with this problem we must investigate how the thousands of individuals actually worked whose combined action produced these results. And for this purpose it is useful as a first step to assume all the environmental factors to be constant and to ask the question what changes we might expect under this assumption. We immediately see that simple increase of population and of physical capital does not constitute the answer. It is not simply the increase of the existing factors of production but the incessantly different use made of these factors that matters. In fact much of the increase in factors and particularly of physical capital was the result rather than the cause of what we may now identify as entrepreneurial activity. What we observe is rather a behavior pattern, possibly supplemented by a schema of motivation; a typical way of giving effect to the possibilities inherent in a given legal and social system both of which change in the process; the effects of entrepreneurial activity upon the industrial structure that exists at any moment; the consequent process of destruction and reconstruction that went on all the time. All these things may be conceptualized in a more or less complicated schema, every item of which has to be nourished with facts and corrected and amplified under their influence. And this is all.

I shall add, however, that in investigations of this kind the notion of an economic process that merely reproduces itself and shows neither decay nor progress has been found to be of considerable use. It is called the stationary state, and plays two distinct roles in economic theory. On the one hand, economists, ever since Adam Smith and perhaps earlier times, have envisaged the possibility that the energetic advance they were witnessing would some day subside into what we now call a stagnating or mature economy. John Stuart Mill differed from Ricardo not in his expectation that a stationary state would one day emerge but in the optimistic view he took of its features—a world without what he considered an unpleasant bustle, a world much more cultured and at ease than the one he observed. Now, as everybody knows, this "stagnationist thesis" has emerged once more, but it has emerged with two differences. First, the stationary state is by some authors not looked upon as something that looms in the far future but as something on which we are actually about to enter. Let us note in passing that the experiences of the crises 1929–1932 may have a lot to do with the emergence of this frame of mind. Secondly, a problem has arisen which did not worry the classics at all. Smith or Ricardo did not anticipate any particular difficulties that would arise from the very process of settling down into stationality: rates of change would converge towards zero in a slow and orderly way. But our modern stagnationists anticipate difficulties in this process of settling down. Keynes in particular anticipated that habits of saving to which equally strong or still stronger propensities to invest corresponded would run on in spite of the fact that there would be no longer any investment opportunties left. With everything indicating now that a new period of unheard-of "progress" is at hand it might be thought that we need not greatly worry about this. But I do not think that we can entirely overlook the problem and history's contribution to it.

II

Whether we define the entrepreneur as an "innovator" or in any other way, there remains the task to see how the chosen definition works out in practice as applied to historical materials. In fact it might be argued that the historical investigation holds logical priority and that our definitions of entrepreneur, entrepreneurial function, enterprise, and so on can only grow out of it *a posteriori*. Personally, I believe that there is an incessant give and take between historical and theoretical analysis and that, though for the investigation of individual questions it may be necessary to sail for a time on one tack only, yet on principle the two should never lose sight of each other. In consequence we might formulate our task as an attempt to write a comprehensive history of entrepreneurship.

So far as the institutional framework is concerned we are, comparatively speaking, well off. The social, legal, technological, and other conditions in which entrepreneurship has run its historical course, from the primitive tribe to the modern large-scale corporation, have been on the whole satisfactorily worked out already. But until relatively recent times it is this framework only that is really known: the actual activity of the entrepreneur, what he really was and did at various stages of historical development, is largely construction. It is true that this construction is in many cases quite safe. For instance, when we know the trade routes in the Near East during the first ten centuries A.D., the commodities that were transported, the political history of the territories through which they were transported, it is not very difficult to imagine the kind of tasks and difficulties that the trader met on these routes and the kind of chap he must have been in order to overcome them. When we know the history of the later trading companies such as the Trading Company of Ravensburg, we again have little difficulty in complementing this by a picture of the kind of man that a member of this company must have been. And to a certain extent we might hope to answer the question directly how environment, public authority, corporate action, and individual initiative must have co-operated and what relative weight we are to attach to each. However, these are favorable cases. In others, much digging may have to be done before we arrive at reliable results. Let us then note that the forms of organization of trade and later on of manufacturing are an acquired asset all along. The same applies largely to the fields and methods of what provisionally we should call entrepreneurial activity. That is to say we know or readily understand that at some times under certain conditions entrepreneurial activity must have consisted largely in trading and transporting, in manufacturing and organizing and financing at others. Finally, the history of entrepreneurial types and of the nature of entrepreneurial performance, the action of these types on the social organization and the reaction of the social bodies on the entrepreneurial impulse should not be too difficult to analyze. Having thus adumbrated my ideas about what that history of entrepreneurship should do, I want now briefly to touch upon a number of problems and stumbling blocks that will inevitably be met with on this road.

The first of all these stumbling blocks is that most of us do not approach the material with a perfectly unbiased mind. In other words, every age and every social organization approaches these problems from an *a priori* of its own, that is to say, from a conviction (all the more dangerous if subconscious) that individual initiative in the matter of economic development counts for almost everything or else for almost nothing, and it is easy to see how such a conviction supplies the basic colors of the picture. For some of us the problem of economic development is all but solved so soon as natural and social conditions and political measures are stated—the rest follows automatically, and if entrepreneurs have anything to do with what actually happens they are a sort of beast of prey withholding the fruits of technological advance from the community and sabotaging progress in their own interest. It is needless to point out that this attitude is very prevalent in this country and that any attempt to take another view is for many a modern economist stigmatized as apologetics. Nevertheless, it should be clear from even a superficial survey of facts that this view is as wrong as is the exactly opposite one and that careful discussion of ever more numerous situations is the only method of arriving at a more tenable one.

Secondly, in connection with this we frequently meet with an attitude that is indeed a necessary prerequisite for the "theory" just alluded to. This attitude may be expressed by saying that the entrepreneur or money-maker simply does nothing but take advantage of technological progress, which therefore appears, implicitly or explicitly, as something that goes along entirely independently of entrepreneurial activity. Now how far is this true? It is perhaps not difficult to understand that technological progress, so obvious in some societies and so nearly absent in others, is a phenomenon that needs to be explained. For instance, it is necessary to find out whether the rational or rationalist attitude to life has or has not been formed by the type of mind that pervades bourgeois society. In this case technological progress would be related to entrepreneurial action in a way that may not always be obvious but would be very important all the same. I have always emphasized that the entrepreneur is the man who gets new things done and not necessarily the man who invents. As a matter of history, the entrepreneur is almost as often an inventor as he is a capitalist but it seems to me that analysis shows that neither of these capacities is essential to him. I can adduce plenty of examples by which to illustrate what seems to me to be the true relation, but only extensive research can present really reliable results.

Thirdly, let us consider a very old problem that has played more of a role in economic literature than it does now under the title of "original accumulation." Some command over physical and personal factors is no doubt necessary in order to start any enterprise: but how is such command acquired in the first place? The old classical answer, that resources came from savings, was understandably unpopular with socialists and is equally unpopular with modern radicals. And it is quite true that, however great the role of self-financing may be in the course of the development of an enterprise, the original nucleus of means has been but rarely acquired by the entrepreneur's own saving activity—which in fact is one of the reasons, and a significant one, for distinguishing the entrepreneur as sharply as I think he should be distinguished from the capitalist. One important source of the means for early enterprise is no doubt to be found in the fact that such means were available in the hands of extra-bourgeois strata and in particular in the hands of temporal and spiritual lords. As everybody knows, this source has been particularly stressed by Sombart and drew so much critical fire that Sombart himself practically surrendered it. But the last word has certainly not been spoken on this affair and if we command co-operation from medieval historians we might well ask them to go into the matter. Another explanation is in the fact that for many types of enterprise the minimum of means to start with was very small: a shack which a man could put up with his own hands, very simple tools, and very few assistants were sometimes all that was required. Means of that order of magnitude many people would possess for a variety of reasons. A third source was tapping the savings of other people and "created credit." The roles of these two last-mentioned sources, though in a general way obvious, also deserve further research. "Credit creation" introduces banks and quasi-banking activities. Here we meet with the difficulty that orthodox banking theory, emphasizing as it does current financing of current trade transactions as the main function of banks, did its best to obliterate all that banks had to do with bringing into existence new industries. French and German experience offers a rich field for the study of this phenomenon, and the common saying that in the United States enterprise developed so well because its banking system was so bad also indicates an important truth: after all, we should not simply shut our eyes or sanctimoniously disapprove when we find that in certain cases even railroad building was financed by the issue of bank notes. Fourthly, it stands to reason that a bank which finances the overhead of a new enterprise must at the very least supervise very closely the behavior of the enterprise founded. That is to say, the necessity of supervising customers which exists to some extent even for the most ordinary routine business acquired in the case envisaged a novel importance. In consequence, two phenomena are observable which are so essential for capitalist life that they are well worth our attention. On the one hand, banks have, though to a very different extent in different countries, established themselves as a social organ of entrepreneurial activity. What this supervision actually consisted in, what the means were by which it was actually carried out, and the success with which it was exerted, has been frequently discussed but quite inadequately, even if we neglect the fact that many social critics have seen nothing in this institution (and it is an institution of later capitalism) but abuse. On the other hand, entrepreneurs and industrialists generally have fought against the restrictions imposed upon their freedom of action by bankers' interference, and important features of modern industrial policy are precisely explainable by the wish of industrialists to free themselves from it. For instance, this has been an important feature of industrial policy in this country during the first World War and in the 1920's. But an entrepreneur can also gain freedom from interference by bankers by turning into a banker himself. John Law and the brothers Pereire are outstanding examples. They illustrate also something else, namely, the fact that the economic and social meaning of this kind of activity has been almost invariably misunderstood.

However, if we could poll business leaders, we should, I am convinced, establish that according to their opinion it is self-financing from earnings which constitutes the soundest method of providing the means for raising an enterprise to its full size. This method, too, is highly unpopular with modern economists and its investigation is a matter of urgent necessity—as is, by the way, the opposite phenomenon, namely, the phenomenon that expenditure on current replacement of equipment is very often financed on credit. The actual results of the method of self-financing, for instance, the question whether or not it involves malallocation of resources, are so much blurred by preconceptions that a reopening of the case promises to add considerably to our knowledge of how modern business works.

III

In the enterprise economy the entrepreneur will inevitably exert some influence on things in general; hence the study of his interests, positions, and so on necessarily constitutes one of the possible approaches to an understanding of economic history or even of history in general. A recent paper by Professor Cochran may be referred to for the general philosophy of this approach as against the approach embodied in what he calls the "presidential synthesis."[4]

It has been emphasized above that when we speak of the entrepreneur we do not mean so much a physical person as we do a function, but even if we look at individuals who at least at some juncture in their lives fill the entrepreneurial function it should be added that these individuals do not form a social class. They hail from all the corners of the social universe. For instance, if we list all the entrepreneurs mentioned in Mantoux's work on the Industrial Revolution we find among them the Duke of Bridgewater and we may, starting from him, go through practically the whole extent of the social ladder until we reach men who rose to entrepreneurship from the ranks of manual labor. This seems to me a very important fact. How important precisely it is can again be only said after extensive research. However, all the men who actually do fulfill entrepreneurial functions have certain interests in common and, very much more important than this, they acquire capitalist positions in case of success. The modern corporation has not entirely done away with inheritance of this capitalist position and so we may say that entrepreneurs do in the end land in the capitalist class, at first as a rule in its most active sector until they wind up in its less active and finally in its decaying sector. I believe that this statement can be supported successfully but I do confess to a wish to see it established.

Now the man whose mind is entirely absorbed by a struggle for entrepreneurial success has as a rule very little energy left for serious activity in any other direction—some philanthropy and some more or less well-advised collector's interests usually fill the bill. From where then stems the influence or the power which most economists and historians attribute to him? I shall state frankly that I consider power to be one of the most misused words in the social sciences, though the competition is indeed great. So firmly entrenched in our popular psychology is the idea that entrepreneurs or else the capitalist class into which they merge are the prime movers of modern politics that it is very difficult to make headway against it and to point out how very little foundation there is to this opinion. Let me take an example that is far enough removed from us to be looked at with something like detachment: Ehrenberg's book on the Fuggers.[5] There, the rise and decline of that industrial, commercial, and financial family is in my opinion described in a perfectly responsible way. Among other things, the report itself clearly shows that in the time of Charles V the two Fuggers who came into contact with the imperial policy and especially its financial needs exerted no influence on this imperial policy other than is implied in their getting various concessions, especially mining concessions, in the Emperor's Latin territories. For the rest, however, they were ruthlessly exploited, so much so in fact that their wealth declined in consequence, and there is no sign whatever that they influenced the Emperor's policy in such matters as his attitude toward the Protestants, toward France, toward the Turks, and so on. Although all this is quite clear from Ehrenberg's own report, he is, nevertheless, so imbued with the idea that in a capitalist age the capitalists rule as to emphasize repeatedly what he considers to be the proud position of power of that family. Now this instance could be multiplied as everyone knows and at the end of a long list of instances, if I could present it, I should mention a conversation I had with an otherwise quite intelligent lawyer who defended the legislation that was to subject the insurance companies to federal control on the ground that "we cannot allow the insurance companies to run the country."

It seems to me that at the outset it is necessary to distinguish two entirely different things. Naturally, as has been pointed out above, the mere emergence of a quantitatively significant number of entrepreneurs presupposes, and its existence contributes to, a certain type of civilization and a certain state of the public mind. Entrepreneurs will be few and without great importance in situations where this activity is despised and frowned upon, and entrepreneurial success in turn will tend to change such a situation. If I had space to develop this point, I should end up by saying that to some extent entrepreneurial activity impresses the stamp of its mentality upon the social organism. In any cultural history, therefore, the entrepreneurial factor will have to come in as one of the explaining elements, but this is not the same as saying that the wishes and interests of entrepreneurs or even of the capitalist class into which they merge is a political factor that counts by direct influence or else at the polls. It is quite true that in individual cases, for reasons of self-defense primarily, individual entrepreneurs need to acquire and do acquire political positions of their own. But the importance of these positions seems to be limited, and the way to show this is to analyze the means at their disposal in order to exert influence, such as contributions to politicians' war chests, or ownership of newspapers, and so on. I think it can be shown that the influence that can be acquired in these and other ways is much smaller than it is usually supposed to be. In fact, little more is necessary in order to convince one's self of this than to look at the modern situation in practically all countries. Methodological questions of great interest arise in the course of an attempt to investigate these matters. To begin with, we should have to have a much more realistic theory of politics than any that has been developed so far, but this is not enough. In order to see what entrepreneurs or the capitalist class as a whole can and cannot do, it is necessary to establish facts which are extremely difficult to get at and the appraisal of which requires a kind of experience of life which, even in those cases in which it is present in a research worker, is confined to individual environments, inferences from which may easily mislead.

The attitude of the state to entrepreneurial activity is a most fascinating study and raises questions of interpretation such as these: what was the nature of that amphibial condition of society that culminated in the state of Louis XIV? The court and the bureaucracy which ruled that state were no doubt alive to the fact that in order to spend as they did they needed adequate objects of taxation and that the most promising of these objects was a powerful community of traders and manufacturers. Thus a large group of measures find a ready explanation in the wishes to further the wealth and taxable capacity of the bourgeoisie. But what precisely does this mean and how would all parties concerned fare as a result? Colbert has had among historians his fervent admirers. To my immense amusement, I have also found that Sir John Clapham described him as a big, stupid, brutal fellow, who never had an idea in his life. Whatever else such judgments prove or do not prove they certainly establish one thing: that the nature and amount of influence exerted by public administration in the period in question really is no more than a big question mark; and if we leave the time of Louis XIV and transfer ourselves into our own I feel that the question mark is still bigger.

IV

Students interested in the history of economic thought and in the writings upon economic development will draw two important, though variant conclusions from their inquiries as far as entrepreneurship and entrepreneurial history are concerned. First, I believe that they would be justified in the view that theories of past economists relative specifically to entrepreneurship will not form a very firm support for future investigations of facts. New hypotheses and the marshalling of factual data, old and new, must proceed together.

Secondly, I would commend to economic historians—and, for that matter, to economic theorists, if they will interest themselves in the problem—that they examine the already available secondary literature for data upon entrepreneurial characteristics and phenomena. A miscellany of such writings—from general economic histories to biographies of businessmen, and from local histories to studies of technological change—all hold information, which sifted and arranged with definite hypotheses in mind will carry us a goodly distance toward our goal. New facts will doubtless be needed in the end, but already we have a multitude that have as yet not been digested.

In the handling of old and new facts, the historian will gain from keeping in touch with theorists. Neither group should ever be distant from one another—but here the promise from collaboration is particularly great for both parties. As I have said before, the study of economic change is an area of research where "economic historians and economic theorists can make an interesting and socially valuable journey together, if they will."[6]

The Climate of Enterprise

W. T. EASTERBROOK

I

THE SUBJECT OF THIS PAPER may be best indicated by reference to a wire sent to me some months ago from Cambridge, Massachusetts. The communication was very brief and to the point. It read, simply, "Schumpeter impatient." Narrowly interpreted, this could be taken to mean that a title to this paper was long overdue. Interpreted more broadly, it suggests something much more disturbing; namely, the impatience of theorists with historians, an impatience which is frequently, sometimes forcibly, expressed by those in theory and statistics and which is not without justification. Apart from a few striking and well-known exceptions, historians have not bothered to consider how historical study and method may be of assistance to those working in closely related fields of endeavor. In this respect, the failure of historians has not only its drawbacks for others but its perils for history as well. These "others" are now taking history seriously and while good things may emerge, there is apparent an increasing tendency to use history in a way that most historians cannot accept. And in part, this paper[1] is an attempt to suggest what the historian might do about this novel and dangerous situation.

By way of introduction, I should like to point to the striking contrast apparent between the preoccupations of economists in the 1930's and their preoccupations of the present. In the 1930's interest was mainly in short-period change, and significant advances were made in business cycle analysis, imperfect competition, and

This article is reprinted, by permission of the author and the American Economic Association, from *The American Economic Review,* 39:322–335 (May 1949).

what might be called "depression economics." There was present the general assumption that with the discovery and use of more adequate antidepression techniques economies could be coaxed into high gear when the necessity arose, and that, fundamentally, the analysis of the short run was the logical province of enquiry. Now, in the late 1940's, there is a noticeable shift to interest in structural change, and much is being said about problems of time and development and, particularly, of growth. These new preoccupations seem to me to reflect greater awareness of deep-rooted changes in institutions and ideas—changes which are altering or modifying the whole setting of economic life and which are of the greatest consequence to theory and the relations between theory and history. They have, for example, greatly complicated the theorist's search for constants so fundamental to the initial choice of parameters for dynamic models and his problem of distinguishing between endogenous and exogenous factors. Empirical study is necessary for the determination of conditions that may be regarded as constant, and it is at this stage that the historian may be of some assistance, although for the most part he seems to have been unaware of the problem. Without pursuing this further at this point, it is clear that the theorist's increasing interest in "reality" and "time" demands a greater self-consciousness on the part of the historian as to the methods and objectives of historical writing.

In this connection, A. H. Cole's unpublished paper on the "Essence of Economic History" is most suggestive. It is pointed out that there are four principal approaches to the study of economic history. The purpose of the first, the "cultural," is to leave the reader better informed about the past and its main interest is in the telling of a good story. Most writings in economic history have been of this sort, but the trend is away from this to other and more promising approaches. Of these, the "analytical" approach is probably the most popular among economists in general and would reduce history to a testing ground for theoretical models and statistical tools. Its exponents tend to overlook (or to make light of) differences between historical and analytical method and between the theoretical model and the reality it seeks to explain. It also raises the very difficult problem of "not going too far back" when one step backward may be too far. The remaining approaches consist of the study of "problems," certain problems being viewed as focal points for the assembly and study of historical materials, and, finally, variants of the "sociological" approach, including the structural (which rests on the attempt to use Talcott Parson's brand of sociology in the study of history) and another, the examination of economic change in the light of all the factors that go to make up or explain such change.

These last two, the "problems" and "sociological" approaches, appear to have the most general appeal to present-day historians and many would be inclined to agree with Kenneth Boulding that "it may well be that the slovenly borderland between economics and sociology will be the most fruitful building ground during the years to come . . . ,"[2] although other "slovenly borderlands" between economics and the disciplines of social psychology, anthropology, and politics promise to be equally fruitful building grounds. At any rate few historians will accept the "analytic" approach so popular these days with theorists and others, not as a matter of vested interest, but rather as a result of the conviction that theory and history are fundamentally unlike in purpose and method, and that to confuse these disciplines is to weaken prospects for fruitful work in both. When in the nineteenth century, partly as a result of the influence of the historical school, theorists pulled in their horns and turned increasingly to abstraction, the change was all to the good. And in spite of the misguided institutionalist attacks of this century, it remains important to emphasize the separateness of these disciplines, methodologically speaking. T. S. Ashton is helpful here. He writes:[3]

> The theorist has taught us that economic phenomena are bound together in ways that the uninstructed would not suspect. He has created an apparatus which explains any given economic situation in terms of profit expectations, the propensity to consume and so on. But beyond that he cannot go. It rests with the historian to trace the causes, or as he would prefer to say, the antecedents and predisposing circumstances of these expectations and propensities: to say how it came about that at one time men were inclined to spend freely, and at another to hoard their resources, how it was that men were enterprising and optimistic in this year, cautious and penurious in that.

I shall assume here that at least some of the questions of history should be asked by historians, and, again, that historians must consider the problems that history poses for other disciplines and consider phrasing their questions in a way useful to these. The historian's neglect (possibly fear) of theory and quantitative method has greatly vitiated his work, but greater awareness of the possibilities (and limitations) of these does not imply an opposite extreme: that history is simply a happy hunting ground for the theorist and statistician.

In the remainder of this paper, I want to consider, in the light of the above, instances of what the historian might do about history—one very briefly, another at greater length. The first, the work of the Research Center in Entrepreneurial History, appears as one line of attack which has already demonstrated its worth. Many readers will be familiar with its method and the questions it asks of history. As I see it, the approach involves broadening or extending the range of entrepreneurial functions and activities as commonly described in economic literature, and then placing the entrepreneur as the central figure in economic change. An entity once identified as a creature of theory now becomes a creature of history. The emphasis is on the functions of the entrepreneur rather than the environment in which he innovates, makes his decisions, and provides the dynamics of change to the accompaniment of uncertainty. There is no question of the great possibilities of this approach for the purpose for which, I think, it was originally designed: the study of business organization, motivation, and techniques in nineteenth and twentieth century United States.

For reasons which I have indicated elsewhere, this approach seems to me to be less useful for long-period study or for comparative history. The "entrepreneur" as visualized becomes a concept much too broad and general for such purposes. He turns out to be an extremely elusive entity, at times difficult to find, or not to be found at all, and frequently so subservient to other entities and ideas that he does not warrant the search. Primary orientation in economic life is commonly noneconomic. Causation is extremely complex, and, as a result, very serious difficulties arise from divorcing the entrepreneur from the institutional setting and "psychological atmosphere" with which he has been most commonly identified. Concentration on entrepreneurial functions or "tasks" tends to a neglect of change initiated by nonentrepreneurial forms and such change is very common in economic history. The act of innovation, per se, is very often less significant historically than the structural and motivational aspects of those situations in which the innovational act takes place. This one-sided emphasis on the act reflects, I suspect, the bias of those concentrating on the economic aspects of change, and particularly the short-run aspects (short-run from the historian's point of view). The hypnotic effect of the term "innovation" like that of "dissaving" is itself becoming an interesting historical fact.

There is no disagreement here with the definition of entrepreneurial functions. Criticism rests, as indicated, on the generality of the concept of "entrepreneur," a result of the failure to identify him with any specific set of conditions, institutional and "ideological." For comparative study of long-period change, I have found the entrepreneur most useful if visualized as an "ideal type" in the Weber sense, and hence to be regarded as an objectively possible entity even though one we would not expect to find in all its purity in real life (and quite different in this sense from the imaginative construct of economic man). This *Idealtypus* may be taken as one responding to a free competitive market, making his decisions, innovating and managing in response to competitive market forces: in short, an idealized economic category operating freely in an idealized institutional environment.[4] As thus conceived, this ideal is to be regarded as a useful point of reference in studies of historical change.

The antithesis of "free enterprise" in the sense of intensive or "watertight" regulation and control, may be referred to as "authoritarian" or "bureaucratic." The distinction between these polar extremes of freedom and control rests on, first, the locus and use of power in each instance. Free enterprise is to be identified with complete dispersion of economic power via the competitive market (this is not to neglect the place of coercion in making such a situation possible), as contrasted with concentration of economic power in the production and distribution of goods and services. This alternative control type may be ecclesiastical, military, administrative (service state), or corporate, or a mixture of two or more of these. Historically, the authoritarian (or bureaucratic) form is more interesting than enterprise but is not the subject of this paper.

A second point of distinction, scarcely less significant, appears in the attitude of the entrepreneur and his opposite number to "time." With the ideal entrepreneur, emphasis is on the short-run "maximization of returns" as contrasted with the emphasis on continuity and permanence of the authoritarian entity; this last has been referred to as "the principle of organizational preservation." Oswald Knauth[5] has written of the primary importance of stability and continuity and concern for the future in what would be referred to here as "corporate bureaucracy." The idea of eternity is, of course, most commonly associated with the most perfect bureaucracy of all, the Church. The entrepreneur, then, maximizes his net income as his primary motivation; the ideal authoritarian form maximizes period of existence as its most compelling purpose. Maximization of income with the limitations set by the market is the criterion in the one instance; in the other, dominance of the market provides the means of ensuring continuity of income as more significant than highest returns.

This approach and these distinctions lead to the phrasing of certain historical questions; for example: (1) What are the elements which appear to be basic to freedom of enterprise, historically considered? (2) What environmental conditions appear to have been most commonly associated with the presence of these elements (and conversely, with the absence of some or all of them)? (3) Concerning alternative forms of organization, what significant differences appear when these elements and conditions are considered? Are certain institutions and attitudes unique in this sense that their presence (or absence) may be regarded as decisive? (4) Is there a pattern of change to be discerned here? With reference to theory, may periods of time be discerned in which slowly moving variables have no upsetting effect on fast-moving ones?—or, in other words, can study of long-period change throw any light on the theorist's search for constants? And finally, what are the possibilities of ascertaining by statistical investigation the quantitative aspects of change in periods of relative freedom as compared with those of control and restrictionism? Comparative study of alternative forms of economic and political organization seems to me to offer exceptional opportunities for collaborative work in closely associated disciplines.

II. *The Security Environment of Enterprise*

The traditional and probably still the typical view of the entrepreneur in enterprise literature is that of an independent (even autonomous), rugged, and dynamic innovational type making his way largely by his own efforts. Closer attention to the conditions of enterprise leads to a somewhat different conclusion: that actually he has thriven only in a highly selective environment. This may be provisionally described as an environment in which various security elements have been combined. Study of conditions favorable to the enterprise system suggests that the presence of these essential security elements has been as much a matter of historical accident as anything else. And if some feature of the enterprise system appears to be worth preserving, closer examination of environments favorable to (and destructive of) enterprise should not be without interest or value. There is no suggestion here that the entrepreneur does not, at times, modify or even shape institutions and attitudes to his own ends. And more than one writer has commented on the fact that self-destructive urges are not an uncommon feature of his activities (as entrepreneur). In short, he is not to be taken as a passive figure submitting meekly to circumstances. His influence as an active agent, however, varies greatly from period to period and area to area, and the nonentrepreneurial factors present in an enterprise system and the interaction between entrepreneurial and nonentrepreneurial activities merit more attention than they have so far received.

References to security are extremely common in the literature of the social sciences.[6] In this paper it is necessary to narrow the problem down to a consideration of the securities essential to the existence of free entrepreneurial action. I shall treat these in a summary fashion, and then outline even more summarily the conditions which appear to have been most commonly associated with these securities. It is scarcely necessary to point out that the interrelations of these securities and conditioning factors are very close and that they are dealt with separately only for analytical purposes.

The first and most obvious manifestation of security I shall label "entrepreneurial security," this referring to the freedom of the businessman to take "the ordinary and legitimate risks of doing business," or what the late Henry C. Simons described as "risks of investing in the wrong places—risks of demand changes, of technical obsolescence in plant facilities, and of guessing badly only because too many others guessed the same way."[7] In the main, this is the manifestation of security which liberal economists have been most concerned about, and their proposals relate to defense of competition against coercive elements in business, labor, and government, and to "sound" taxation, monetary, and commercial policies. Professor Lionel Robbins (the "new" Robbins), for example, looks "to adequate action to maintain reasonably stable the volume of aggregate demand with which the system of market and enterprise has to function," and the establishment and maintenance of "a deliberately created competitive order." Where prospective returns to enterprise are not such as to compensate for risks associated with threats to entrepreneurial security, then entrepreneurship languishes and the "corporate" form[8] of business organization appears to be the logical (only) form of organization—a point sometimes overlooked in studies of medieval guilds, trading leagues, regulated companies, and joint-stock organizations.

Whether this variant of security is examined from a historical or contemporary point of view, the tendency to examine it as a separate and distinct problem in itself seriously weakens prospects for either realistic analysis or sound reform measures. Commonly, threats to entrepreneurial security originate in the destruction of other and equally fundamental securities. This is not to overlook the fact that entrepreneurs themselves are active agents in preserving or destroying entrepreneurial security; certainly exhortations to entrepreneurs to behave themselves and to act as statesmen imply that this belief is held in high circles. But examination of the whole set of conditions to which businessmen have responded in the past, and are responding now, will produce more fruitful results than the most eloquent appeals to their finer instincts.

A second and closely related manifestation of security is that of social or "want" security which may be defined as security against want for that part of the population which matters politically (either in terms of the use of force or the vote), want being an elastic term the meaning of which has changed greatly from one period to another. Professor Helleiner has written of this problem in the medieval world, and recent interest in social security has seen a spate of writings on social legislation in later centuries to the present. It has always been a major problem facing Church or state, and appeals to noneconomic symbols have not been the least valuable of solutions. It presents an acute problem today in some areas because the so-called "masses" now count in national policies as they have never counted before, and slogans of social security or full employment cannot be suppressed or ignored, as sporadic, ill-organized revolts once were.

And once again, indeterminateness as to what is a "fair" share strengthens the case for a strong central authority to define "fairness" and guarantee "social justice." There are very dangerous implications for entrepreneurial freedom in policies which define social security as the great and overriding objective of reform rather than entrepreneurial security as the logical starting point. The issue here is sometimes stated, erroneously, I think, as one involving a choice between stability and progress. There are many forms of stability and many types of progress. From the standpoint of the entrepreneur, however, unless he can sell the idea that the straightest, perhaps only, road to social security is via entrepreneurial security, the immediate future offers very unhappy prospects indeed—which takes me to a third manifestation of security, that of ethical security, or Weber's "psychological atmosphere."

This variant of security, the ethical, rests on the presence of social sanctions sufficiently strong to ensure general acceptance of entrepreneurial activities as "good." A healthful "enterprise" environment is out of the question without a popular faith in enterprise. And it is highly important in this connection that people in general feel that they have a stake in, and form an integral part of, the system. This is in itself an act of faith—a faith which must rest on such sanction elements as religious feeling, nationalism, legalism, tradition, custom, and even education (I shall touch very briefly on some of these sanction elements at a later point) and the close identification of entrepreneurial health with the welfare of society. In this sense, "free enterprise" has become a fighting slogan, although it has been pointed out very recently that in the United States this slogan has been used much more effectively by the corporation than by the individual.[9]

And finally, the fourth manifestation, that of political security, which is closely bound up with the above. Political security has two aspects, the first being that of defense against external enemies as more important than opulence. Threats of hostile action (genuine or "manufactured") if of long duration will, in the end, destroy enterprise. Protection against the foreigner has been a common problem of economic organization over history, and methods of solving this problem have been highly significant to the character of organization. Frederic C. Lane's study of Andrea Barbarigo, for example, notes the tendency to collusive action (in economic affairs) among those merchants banding together for defense, and

John U. Nef's studies of war and economic progress in the two centuries following 1540 have thrown new light on factors which help to explain contrasts between the course and character of continental and English economic development.

Long preoccupation with military frontiers and the resulting strength of the military caste (Mannhein has interesting things to say about the military mind and Hanson Baldwin has suggested certain implications for our time) runs directly counter to preoccupation with the "ordinary business of getting a living." Recent developments in the technology of waging war give little promise of restoration of this variant of political security in the near future. Over history, the origins of threats to this security have been many and complex—religious and ideological differences, dynastic aspirations, the presence of unsolved economic problems.

The second aspect of political security is that of internal stability or order (Adam Smith's "order and good government, and along with them, the liberty and security of individuals"). Threats to this variant of security have taken different forms at different times—the disappearance of accepted status, the breakdown of traditional restraints upon the behavior of the individual, the tyranny of absolutist ruler or majority. Tensions are most likely to originate in the economic sphere, but it is dangerous to assume that, historically, this is the general case. But whatever the source, risks of this sort are beyond the ordinary risks of doing business, and in this sense are destructive of enterprise, involving as they do the tendency to action infringing on essential freedoms, since the problem is fundamentally one of a ruling group maintaining its power and position by all the means at its disposal.

It is clear, as stated, that the security elements, taken as a whole, are closely interrelated. Serious threats of any duration to any one (or its destruction) upset the security balance and lead to organizational change, and no one-factor explanations will do. The liberal answer, I suppose, would emphasize that strong entrepreneurship offers the greatest hope of internal stability, of economic and military power, and of adequate employment opportunities. I have identified this entrepreneurship with dispersion of economic power and suggested that it is helpful to analyze threats to enterprise as threats to the basic security elements, and that the nature and direction of these threats is different in different situations if long-period change is considered. If, alternatively, our concern is with administrative bureaucracy (socialist or "service state") or with some variant of the corporate form of economic organization (for example, a working combination of business, labor, and agricultural groups), then the security problem appears in a different form. The security elements of these power structures may be similarly examined, and the absence of entrepreneurial security reflects a simpler, if no less vulnerable, structure. The stability of bureaucratic structures has been discussed by Max Handman and has been the subject of long and intensive study by H. A. Innis.

III. *The Conditions of Security of Enterprise*

So far I have outlined a historical model to be used as a point of reference in comparative studies of different areas and periods.[10] A more adequate treatment than I can present here would be to consider the underlying conditions which have been most commonly associated with the presence of the basic securities. Of these, the most significant has been the institutional setting (in terms of structure and ideas), although this is closely bound up with the nature of the physical environment and the rate of technological change. I confine myself here to a few scattered comments on how these conditions might be examined in one particular context; namely, their bearing on the presence (or absence) of free enterprise with its central attribute of dispersion of economic power.

Geographic influences, for example, are highly significant in the historical long run in establishing limits to the range of economic activities and in determining types of organization. To mention only three, we may note the geographic factors bearing on the problem of national defense (isolation—geographic barriers to easy invasion), the long-run significance of maritime as contrasted with continental backgrounds, and the abundance or paucity of strategically located resources. These and others may be related to the securities mentioned and hence to their tendency to strengthen or weaken entrepreneurial action. Changes in techniques, whether considered in terms of accounting and finance, production, exchange, transportation or communications, may be considered with reference to their relation to increasing concentration (or dispersion) of economic power; e.g., their effect on the extension of the market in relation to the size of the units operating within it. Again, technical advance in the means of destruction or in terms of media of communication and their influence in shaping mass sentiment and opinion (the most pervasive technique of all)—these are very closely related to the security environment referred to.

Of the institutional factors, the state as the center of coercive power in its political aspects is the most significant to enterprise and its environment. "State" in this connection may refer to the political authority of the small medieval town, or the Council of Augsburg, the Senate of Venice, the mercantile oligarchy of Antwerp, the absolutist state of Colbert's France, or the government of mercantilist and liberal England. From the standpoint of the entrepreneur, state action has three principal aspects: protective, promotional, and corrective. The first, protective, relates to the maintenance of entrepreneurship within the area of control; the second, promotional, refers to the expansion of the area of enterprise by, say, military or diplomatic action or public works; the third, corrective, involves action against tendencies destructive of competition. (It should perhaps be added that these are not sharply demarcated and that state action may be repressive as well as "constructive.") There is a tendency to overemphasize the importance of the state as a positive agent. In the main, its actions and policies are necessarily adaptive to conditions, whether of military necessity or mass unemployment; but Professor A. P. Usher pointed this out long ago. It is impossible to separate state from law, the most "specialized and highly finished engine of control employed by the state," and the legal system as a stabilizing force, a sanction element, protector of property rights and so on, is to be regarded as one of the elements most crucial to the power and freedom of the entrepreneur.

Again, the organizational aspects of religion have been of the greatest consequence to enterprise—whether, for example, the "church" appears as a militant and disruptive force or as a center of social stability and social welfare, and its immense importance as an economic organization in the past has not been overlooked by historians. Finally, social organization—the importance of a strong and distinct community life, and the status of the entrepreneur in the social structure—has been from the beginning one of the great formative influences in the history of enterprise. Closely related to such institutional factors is the climate of ideas or *Zeitgeist*. The bearing of religious feeling and attitudes on economic life has been the subject of an extensive and controversial literature. Equally important is national feeling, and it is of the utmost consequence to the entrepreneur whether the prevailing sentiment is that of the statism of the absolutist, mercantilist or neomercantilist varieties, or the liberal nationalism which is commonly identified with the nineteenth century. Finally, social attitudes, and the almost overwhelming importance of social respectability—these have been among the most decisive of sanction elements.

This bird's-eye view of the principal conditioning factors is used here to suggest one way of getting at the essential conditions which seem to promote (or for that matter, destroy) prospects for free entrepreneurial action. By considering the basic securities and their conditions in selected periods and areas, some light may be thrown, I think, on the determinants of freedom of economic activity in history, and conversely, on the absence of such freedom in periods of authoritarian control.

IV. *Concluding Observations*

In discussing the climate of enterprise I have been talking about freedom and power in only one context. There is no assumption that other freedoms of other entities (than the entrepreneur) resting on other power relationships may not exist and be talked about; i.e., enterprise, whether spontaneous or consciously planned and supported, may be seen as but one sort of answer to the broader problem of human freedom, although the one most familiar to us (and to many the most acceptable). It is legitimate, I think, to speak of concentration or dispersion of economic power when distinguishing certain categories of action and organization, but wrong to see in dispersion of economic power the only means of maximizing individual freedom of action and thought. Liberalism is best seen as "a method of social adjustment." If, upon examination of the environmental conditions of enterprise, it becomes apparent that increasingly stormy weather lies ahead, the problem becomes that of seeking to establish the possibilities of freedom where concentration of economic power must be taken as an accepted fact and where competition, however fierce, is significantly unlike that of the competition of the free market and more akin to the competition of power aggregations in terms of perpetuation of organization and extension of control.

The almost universal desire for peace and quiet appears to be a reflection of a sadly upset security balance. Corporate action of some kind, whether on the part of business, labor, agriculture, or even the lowly consumer, must be viewed, in part at least, as a defense against insecurity conditions which entail risks beyond the abilities of the entities concerned to bear without reorganization to meet the conditions of a dangerous world. Until well into this century, there was the general assumption that apart from threats to entrepreneurial security there were present no decisive changes in the environment of economic life; yet threats to entrepreneurial security present but one aspect of far-reaching changes of the greatest import to the expectations and propensities referred to by Professor T. S. Ashton. Investment and savings patterns reflect fears much more deep-rooted than those associated with temporary or short-lived periods of depression followed by recovery and a new start. Now politics rather than economics is looked to for solutions, ideological differences loom as portentous threats to external security, and national feelings appear in a form even more dangerous than that of the sixteenth and seventeenth centuries.

If a pattern of change is to be discerned over the historical long run, it is one mainly notable for the duration and stability of authoritarian structures. In many areas (e.g., Spain and Russia) the entrepreneur has at no time made any significant headway (this is not to overlook the Russia of the thirteenth and fourteenth and early twentieth centuries, and Spain's feeble effort in the eighteenth). In other areas where the entrepreneur has for a time stepped into the limelight, very powerful authoritarian supports have, in large part, provided the essential securities, and in such areas the wave of enterprise has been preceded and followed by one (or a mixture of) the nonentrepreneurial forms referred to earlier. These waves have originated in marginal areas where centralized controls have been weak; and, where of any magnitude, they have profoundly altered the older rigid structures of control. Over history, the margins have been those of continents, and trade and finance have been the most typical (although, of course, not the only) spheres of entrepreneurial action. Apart from developments in the Mediterranean (first) and the North Sea area (later), the most striking and momentous event in entrepreneurial history is the transplanting of enterprise in North America, this continent taking what it could use, modifying or rejecting the rest. (It would take me too far afield at this point to raise the problem of preserving enterprise, whose origin is maritime, in a continental background or environment with its tendencies to giantism and centralism so inimical to enterprise.)

For economists, the most comfortable environment for analytical study is either the area and period in which there is sufficient approximation to freedom of economic action that it may be labeled "entrepreneurial," and where natural laws or tendencies and cyclical patterns of change may be discerned or at least sought with some grounds for optimism; or the area and period in which authoritarian control is associated with a fair degree of peace and quiet, where the essential securities (apart from the entrepreneurial) are present. In the latter, constants and uniformities may be sought, and although economic analysis lacks the precision and scientific air it attains in the entrepreneurial society, since greater breadth and inclusiveness is necessary, prospects for realistic analysis are considerably brighter than in periods like the present, when solid ground for analysis is difficult to find and short-run predictions turn out to be extremely risky.

The problem of the historian is to stand sufficiently far back to see the terrain as a whole—the long ground swells of authoritarianism, the shorter, sharper, more jagged peaks of comparative freedom (of the sort discussed in this paper). And in the attempt to see historically the relative heights, extent, and direction of these historical movements, the "ideal entrepreneur" and his environment seem to me to be a useful point of reference.

Approaches to Entrepreneurial Personality

LELAND H. JENKS

HISTORY AND ECONOMICS, not to say their neglected love-child, economic history, have of late years managed to omit personality as problematic. That is to say, their practitioners have tended to take it for granted, and have not regarded it as an essential part of the phenomena under investigation and to be understood. In the present, when they do take personality into account, they frequently make casual assertions about it that seem naïve, old-fashioned, or wrong-headed to other social scientists. I have the definite impression that this condition has been getting worse rather than better in recent years.

The consequences have been especially serious for scientific consideration of the entrepreneur—the businessman responsible for decision-making in an economy decentralized in terms of a multitude of business units. What social scientists have been saying about the businessman ranges from the tendency of some economic theorists to treat him as though he were a rational automaton maximizing profits, to the disposition of some American historians to be aware only of a few businessmen, whom they regard as robber barons. Sociologists have pretty generally ignored economic agents except in the context of status systems. Scarcely any "industrial sociologist" explicitly recognizes the top executive in an organization as an object for careful inquiry, and those who do so characteristically overcompensate for the limitations of economic theory by minimizing the orientation of business units with respect to profits. The recent nostalgic spate of business histories and biog-

This article is reprinted, by permission of the author, from *Explorations in Entrepreneurial History,* 2:91–99 (January 1950).

raphies of business leaders has yielded astonishingly little for the advancement of social science.

This lag is not to be imputed wholly to the pressure of public relations departments, business secrecy, the libel laws, or to the necessity in any scientific pursuit to take something as a matter of course. The specific functions which differentiate entrepreneurs from other economic agents constitute a serious problem for scientific method. For they are seen, at least in part, as functional to change in social and economic structure—specific, irreversible, historical change. It is precisely this sort of phenomenon that has resisted interpretation in terms of systematic theory in the several social sciences.

If this methodological problem is solvable at all, it seems certain that an empirically testable approach to entrepreneurs as actors must be involved. What would such an approach be like? How may entrepreneurial personality be most profitably approached in the context of historical change?

An answer would differ in detail according to our conception of the task. Are we trying to account for the performance of particular individuals? Or are we trying to account for the performance of similar functions by a considerable number of individuals? The former is the more romantic, glamorous sort of inquiry, of course. But I doubt whether much of social science significance can be accomplished without some prior answer to the latter question. How are we then to approach the study of what is common in the probable behavior of entrepreneurs or a plurality of them as distinct from that of other people?

Let us first examine the prevalent assumption that personality is not part of the phenomenon of business behavior. This has meant substantially that the personality, in our case of the entrepreneur, was taken as "given."[1] We recognize some consequences of this in those economic theories which have economic processes going on without perceptible intervention of human agency.

It is true that assumptions about man must be made, explicitly or implicitly, even by economic theorists. But they have been assumptions which tend to preclude historical investigation. Two general ones of a seemingly contradictory nature are common: (i) Men are all alike, or vary from each other in constant ratios (as in a normal distribution curve), or change at a constant rate;

(ii) Each man is unique. It is quite common for both such assumptions to be made, for different purposes, in different parts of the same economic theory. So we can say on the one hand that there is always a fairly constant reservoir of entrepreneurial propensities, ready to pour forth when obstacles are removed. Or we can say that over time men become increasingly rational or calculating. Or we can say that the appearance of entrepreneurs is a matter of chance. None of these propositions (all of which have figured in the literature of economic theory) has the slightest probability of being demonstrated historically. The list of assumptions can be extended from these starting-points in detail, implicitly or explicitly, without abandoning the conception of the personality function as given, or putting us in any position to find out whether the assumptions are right or wrong.

Of course, plenty of social scientists have also faced up to the fact that human behavior, as they encounter it, does not seem to swing between the poles of universality and indeterminate uniqueness. History, at least for remote periods, can scarcely be written in those terms. One encounters specifiable differences in the behavior of the London merchant of 1400 and of 1900. Mexican businessmen seem alike to Kansans in that they behave differently from Kansas businessmen. How can sense be made of such phenomena? The first resort in our culture both by numerous social scientists and by laymen has been to make more assumptions about the "given" personalities. Behavior differences between collections of individuals are to be accounted for in terms of differences in the "traits" or "capacities" of the individual composing the collections. We can try to enumerate the personality traits common to entrepreneurs and then try to relate this to what they do. As an historical task this sort of thing is of course very difficult, if not impossible, for lack of statistically manageable data. But where this sort of inquiry is not impossible, for instance where adequate samples are safely under control for the study of criminal personality, it has proven sterile. It has not been possible to get an inventory of personality traits for burglars, let us say, which is convincingly different from that for nonburglars, from the same general stock and background. One always comes up with sets of distribution curves which, no matter how they are manipulated, show a high degree of overlapping. But the differences as to criminal behavior are discontinuous. It is this discontinuity that is to be accounted for.

Lack of evidence has not been a serious obstacle to theorizing. It is easy to assume some one factor or other which can also be taken as "given," and from which the missing facts can be deduced. So the phenomenon of Mexican business behavior can be imputed to the peculiar heredity of Mexicans. It is a mere matter of convenience, or more usually a matter of stereotyping, whether typical traits which are supposed to have been inherited are specified or not. The literature not many years back is full of accounts of American economic success which attribute it implicitly to entrepreneurs of old Yankee stock. This line of theorizing is particularly tempting when it is accompanied by conceptions of the "right" kind of entrepreneurs as distinct from a "wrong" kind. With such a combination, an imposing edifice of historical speculation can be projected out of the hopes and fears of the social scientist, which is virtually impregnable to criticism in terms of any number of objective facts.

It is not my task to argue about racism or any other single-factor theory of history. All such theories manage effectively to take personality as given, as no problem, as either fixed or random with respect to the problem under investigation. None of them can be adequately tested empirically. All of them tend to detach business activities from the actors who carry them on. Most of them manage to treat activities as dependent variables with respect to remote general factors which make of personality, or personality traits, something fixed and constant and hence negligible, unless perhaps as a universal element of "cussedness" in the working out of equations. None of them makes room for the possibility that personality is a locus for dynamic organization and reorganization for the multiple determinants of social events.

Criticism of approaches to entrepreneurial personality as something given, either in the innate qualities of all men who are not thwarted, or the genetic character of some of them or in some determinate principle of increasing rationality, or in the heaven-sent genius of unique individuals, is not directed at the detailed assertions that may have been made in terms of such assumptions. Phenomena can be correctly apprehended even in terms of unsound theory. Current social psychologies build on the inadequacies of older approaches. What is criticized is the whole way of looking at personality qualities as separable from the social situations, past and present, in which actions are performed. This view is being definitely rejected from current trends in the social sciences specially concerned with personality. To the contrary, it is asserted that no personality, unique or otherwise, can be understood apart from the context of social situations, past and present, in which it has functioned. Nor are social situations to be adequately understood except in terms of the way persons actually or typically involved define and deal with them. These are basic assumptions of what writers of quite different disciplines and methods are coming to call the "field theory" of personality.

In this type of theory, initiated by Lewin but now available in several distinct variants, individuals are not viewed as simply the resultants of external social conditions. On the other hand, what is referred to as their "personality" is explicitly not to be looked for exclusively inside their skins. There are two other points of contrast between "field" theory and the more familiar conceptions. In the older view there was a tendency, even in psychology, to see personality as an aggregate of traits and mechanisms having no determinate connection with each other, except at the organic level. In field theory, personality at every level of analysis is seen as some degree of *organization* of all the resources of the individual with respect to the situations in which he tries to act. This view, on which a wide variety of experimental, statistical, projective, observational, and other techniques have been converging, involves in some constructions which have been placed upon it a return to pre-Lockean and teleological considerations. We hear again of processes and mechanisms in the brain which are "regnant" with respect to others which tend to be held in their place. Even biochemists are busily extending their interpretations to account for human processes as complex as those we are now able to build into our electronic machines, which choose, remember, and solve new problems. But if there is return, it is with a further marked difference.

The "given" personality tended to be viewed as static. If there was change, it was of a standard sort like maturation. "Capacities," "abilities," "traits" were simply there or not there. In the new conception things are not so simple. Murphy tells us not what personality is, or how it is *formed,* but how it *grows.* Personality is dynamic; it undergoes irreversible changes, not merely of an autonomous character, arising from continuous interplay with environment, especially the social environment. Persons are viewed from the cradle as making efforts, realizing goals, taking account of things, singling out cues to respond to, forming active likes and dislikes, and undergoing incessant change in the process. Feuerbach could say "Man is what he eats." Without undertaking to explain man, we can now say almost that his personality is the way he will probably interact with others.

Now this theory of personality as dynamic and organized with reference to the situations individuals encounter, has the merit of accounting for the plausibility of a good many of the assumptions which older psychologies encouraged. Kluckhohn and Murray declare that men are alike, in some respects; that they are all unique, in some respects; and that some men are, so to speak, more alike than others, also in some respects. None of these matters is attributable to a single principle, hereditary, constitutional or cultural. All of these aspects of personality are also in part to be attributed to the fact that all individuals interact with other people and acquire their "human nature," group-typical and idiosyncratic features in the process.

It is a fact that at any given time and place some men are more likely to make a go of a particular venture than others; they are more likely to come through with a hit with the bases loaded. In that sense, differences in ability (and the assumption that they can be recognized) are the basis of all personnel, promotion, and credit policies. Field theory traces some of them to physiological differences (called "constitutional" factors,[2] our knowledge of human heredity as a clue to human behavior being virtually zero). But these operate interdependently with things like diet, emotional disturbances, and the social meanings which people impute to the way a man looks, to his size, his complexion, his bodily gestures. Even constitutional factors are to be viewed with respect to the situations the individual has met and has to meet. The whole point of the Boudreau shift was that Ted Williams' constitutional make-up was not the only component in his batting prowess. He verified this experimentally by shifting the field.

Personality traits and capacities then enter into the purview of field theory only for the specific ranges of social situations in which they are expected to become manifest. One important corollary for the empirical study of entrepreneurial history may be drawn. It is not necessary to ascertain everything that may have been true about all individuals in the past in order to be able to make significant statements about pluralities of them, or about the way they were related to the activities that they carried on. This point will now be developed in somewhat broader perspective.

Field theory is, of course, not the only view of personality which has been influential in the social sciences, in which personality can be reckoned in as part of the problem of entrepreneurship. There are echoes in Sombart of what may be called the idealistic tradition, which was once dominant in Germany. In this tradition (which goes back to Plato), history is viewed as a sequence of unique periods or ages. Each has its unique patterning for business practices, economic processes, and so on. Each also exhibits distinct personality types. On principle Sombart, unlike some philosophers of history, would insist that the existence of such types should be established empirically. On the other hand, the coincidence of such types with certain business practices, forms, techniques, and various nonbusiness institutions, is not to be understood in terms of the way actual men interact. Historical likenesses and convergences all across the board are to be understood as manifestations of a common factor—a unique historical spirit—the spirit of an age—the spirit of capitalism, to be specific. The personality of entrepreneurs on the one hand and economic processes and institutions on the other, along with the state and the other phenomena of modern society, are understood as manifestations or expressions or emanations of a spirit in this sense. It is a complete misunderstanding of the whole position to suppose that Sombart is merely asserting that modern men have a unique psychological drive to make money.

In my view this attempt to account for everything in terms of a single historical spirit is not to be dismissed as metaphysical nonsense, especially if "spirit" is not viewed as a primary efficient cause. If I understand him Sombart did not do so. "Spirit" is rather for him a formal cause in the Aristotelian sense. If we view it simply as a symbol of integrative tendencies in the manifold patterns of culture; if we see it simply as a term for what Sumner called "the strain to consistency in the mores," we find anthropologists and others busily looking for notions that will perform similar functions in current conceptions of culture and personality. These notions as applied to culture are variously spoken of as "configurations" or "themes" or, following Sumner, as "ethos." As applied to individuals, such terms as "basic personality structure" and "social character" are employed.

But they are explicitly recognized to be high-degree abstractions; it is assumed that several can be found for any society at any time; and there is no assumption that the personal and social behavior of any society is completely organized or integrated, in terms of them or any other particular entity.

We may use universalism and materialism and achievement as hypothetical themes of American culture in an analytical sense to discern congruences between the behavior of businessmen, let us say, and our practices of child-care, our family structure, political leadership, foreign policy, our personality traits, and some biases in social science, such as those with which I began. There is growing up quite a literature on American character structure, most of it highly readable, all of it to be viewed as highly tentative and exploratory, with more agreement on some general ideas than upon distinctness in the use of terms. All of it, including the more fanciful psychoanalytic versions, finds a typical American character structure with a considerable range of variation and tension, maintained and transmitted and undergoing change by mechanisms involving the interactions of individuals in carrying out a considerable variety of activities. Personalities and the socially standardized activities are interdependent.

Thus we have themes and character structure as two conceptions linking the culture and personality patterns which tend to be prevalent in a given society. For practical purposes, they enable us to predict some degree of persistence. We see them as limiting the range of what can happen for a given society. The highly imperfect techniques and conceptions already developed enabled a group in Washington to predict accurately what the Japanese would do if surrender was brought about in the way it was; they managed to make their advice prevail. For historical inquiry, themes and character structure support the hope that firm anchorage points may be ascertained in the flux of past events. Realization of this hope depends upon the development of more publicly testable techniques of inquiry and more precise specifications, conceptual and empirical, of the mechanisms by which themes and character structure enter into the behavior of pluralities of individuals. For instance, it is still to be demonstrated that complex economic functions derive from such mechanisms as toilet-training, which some writers seem to think account for everything.

Fascinating as these notions are, I think that for the study of the entrepreneur another conception developing in the context of field theory, and similarly linking together individual and society, will be more directly useful. This is the notion of "role."

Just as "character structure" refers to the organization of personality traits and action patterns prevalent among all the members of a total society, "role" refers to an organization of personality with respect to differentiated functions or positions in a social group. It is a much lower-degree abstraction than themes or character structure or spirits. Specifically, reference is made to such matters as age and sex roles, kinship roles, occupational roles, and positions of all sorts in formal organizations. Role stands in one sense for the patterned expectations in a society or group which an individual tends to fulfil; in another, for a socially differentiated personality type. On the one hand, John Jones, besides being an adult male, husband, father, and member of the country club set, is a banker; on the other, being a banker is assumed to have positive social functions the exercise of which is a matter of social definition, expectation, and sanction. It seems quite easy to speak of the role behavior expected of various types of businessmen. It is from such materials that it seems possible to construct conceptions of entrepreneurial roles for given periods and areas.

Some practical implications of this sociological notion of role for our purposes may be mentioned.

1. It designates certain aspects of personality as relevant to, not apart from, the study of entrepreneurial activities. By specifying socially shared expectations, it provides a basis for selecting what is relevant about the personalities of entrepreneurs from the mass of things that by some technique or other, or in some other frames of reference, might be found true about the individuals who perform entrepreneurial functions. No given role exhausts personality; it represents merely one kind of organization of personality for limited purposes, an organization largely in terms of the requirements of the social structure. We are not required to know everything about every individual before making fruitful general assertions.

2. Role theory enables us readily to think of the individuals who are entrepreneurs as performing numerous roles, some of them concurrently, some in sequence or alternation. We may find it conven-

ient to view some of these other roles as virtually fused with entrepreneurship in various times and places. Fusion of entrepreneurship and ownership, for instance, is one way of referring to a well-known phenomenon. For certain historical purposes, it may be desirable to separate them systematically; but we shall miss something important if we fail to take account of the ways in which ownership interpenetrates and fuses with other functions in the performance of many entrepreneurs.

3. In role theory, any role is considered as related reciprocally to other roles. The role of entrepreneur is to be thought of in relation to other roles performed in the business unit or in the wider society, whether performed by the same individual or by others. Any role involves some sort of place in a social structure, consisting of other roles and their relationships. Biographies of businessmen that tell us nothing about their relations to other people, as competitors, customers, colleagues, and so on, are not of much help.

4. The notion of role directs us to take account of the degree and ways in which entrepreneurial behavior, both in form and content, may be socially sanctioned. By social sanction is meant, for practical purposes, simply any social mechanism of rewards and/or punishments, the carrot and the stick, whether deliberately enforced by definite agents or a matter of the diffuse reactions of one's fellows; whether consisting in the approved operations of a market, or in prevalent conceptions of good form, fair play, good sense, "a business-like way of doing things," efficiency; or in pressures to conform to the average, to get on the band-wagon; or in claims of the customers, shareholders, employees and other persons with whom one has necessary relations in carrying on a role; or in the model personalities, real and mythical, in which societies embody their ideals of success.

5. The notion of role provides a conceptual scheme in which two separably observable sets of phenomena can be viewed as systematically interlinked: on the one hand, the patterned sanctions and expectations and, more broadly, the social requirements for any one in typical entrepreneurial positions; on the other, the patterned behavior which individuals in those positions are motivated to carry out. It is true that in modern society the roles which individuals are motivated to fulfil are not likely to be completely a matter of social sanction. In so far as there are such sanctions for entrepre-

neurial behavior, it is safe to assume that a considerable range of deviation in personal behavior is permitted. But it is permitted within the framework of the business unit, which imposes a fairly complicated set of structural requirements for any action that we are likely to call entrepreneurial. Hence my pragmatic suggestion is that we view the sanctioned elements in roles as among their more general and more persistent features. It seems methodologically necessary to establish what they are before one can make meaningful statements about such deviations as creative innovations or about "spontaneous" and idiosyncratic performances.

6. Finally, I suggest that by viewing individual situations in terms of a plurality of roles and a plurality of sanctions, we are able to give systematic context to the problems of variation in role performance by entrepreneurs, their successes, their innovations.

It must not be supposed that even in their penal aspects, role sanctions are necessarily or merely frustrating to individuals. Role performance may be precisely the more effective the more completely sanctions are internalized by the individuals, the more completely external rewards and punishments are transformed into internal urges. This is one meaning for the Greek myth of the vulture that gnawed at the vitals of the innovating hero, Prometheus. Moreover, what we know about character structure in general enables us to suppose that some forms of it may be more congenial than others to the acquisition of entrepreneurial roles. It is in such terms that I would attack the problem of the South American businessman.

On the other hand, people are not indefinitely malleable; they differ for constitutional and other reasons in the degree to which a given role is congruent to their personal resources. There is probably some role tension in most individuals in complex societies, particularly between the different roles that they have to assume at the same time or in sequence, or between their more general predispositions and the social role requirements, or between different sources of sanction for the same role. Such sociologists as Parsons are finding in this tension between roles—and between roles, their sanctions, and constitutional factors—a sociological explanation for a good deal of the anxiety and other pathological symptoms in American society. That is to say, much personality conflict is referable to conflict between the sanctioned contents of different roles, or between the sanctions for behavior in the same role. When large numbers of individuals are inconsistent in their conduct, this is viewed as interdependent with the inconsistencies of society. I gather that Barnard regards such a situation of tension as typical for any top executive. Instead of being called upon to apply a rationally consistent preference scale to known data, it is the crux of his responsibility to reconcile inherently conflicting claims of owners, employees, customers, colleagues, and agents of other formal organizations.

In the light of such considerations, it appears that a rigid or narrow definition of the role of an entrepreneur will not work either for him, for society, or for students of the phenomenon. For entrepreneurial roles to be flexible, it seems probable that a lot of other roles in modern society must be also. Societies with rigid definitions of the claims of kinship, for instance, which definitely sanction for concrete individuals the bulk of their conduct, present almost insuperable obstacles to the effective working out of entrepreneurial roles.

For possible inquiry I suggest that tension between incompatible claims may provide one clue to numerous problems that have been encountered in this area, such as the early development of entrepreneurship, the adaptability of individuals to enterpreneurial roles, the innovating tendencies of entrepreneurs. Along these lines we may be able to approach our creative entrepreneur in an adequate theoretical and empirical setting. We can account for his vulture. By the same theory we account for his ulcers. Can we get rid of one without the other? Can we minimize personal strains without destruction of the flexibility which is inherent in the extent to which the entrepreneur must decide how he plays his role?

Some comments of a programmatic nature to pull this together. Whether we attack problems on an extensive or intensive scale, we do not start with atomistic personality inventories or with matters of unique motivation. In taking account of personality as part of our problem, we look first for structured relations with other people and the actual or typical rewards and penalties of all kinds that impinge on entrepreneurial behavior. Once we abandon the notion that all doors are to be unlocked with a single key, that all American society or all entrepreneurs in that society at a given time are to be accounted for by some comprehensive social definition, it is possible to see sanctions on every hand and to take them into account without asserting their range of application or asserting that all operative sanctions have been discovered. It is a definite step to be able to say that such-and-such specific sanctions operated in the experience of definite businessmen. It would be a further step to do this by period, or region, or industry, or type of market, or some other situational variable. Study might well be directed toward some particular type of sanction such as bankruptcy and its range of application. Perhaps we can quickly decide which elements of sanctions, or institutional elements, as Parsons calls them, are relatively constant, and focus attention on those that are more variable in combination with such constants.

Role and Sanction in American Entrepreneurial History

THOMAS C. COCHRAN

I

THE THEORY OF ROLES provides a nondeterministic explanation of historical change. Necessarily, change is seen against an assumed background of stability. In modern industrial societies this is probably an illusion, but every culture has many stable elements, and for a given analysis it is often convenient to regard the patterns that are changing slowly as relatively stable. On this basis, when an individual's behavior in fulfilling a role, such as father or business executive, accords closely with the conceptions of the role held by people in general, he can be regarded as fulfilling a normal or stable social role. In other words, his individual interpretation of the role falls within the scope of the existing social role, and he initiates no significant or cumulative change. In a static society all the personal deviations in such role performance would be minor and without lasting social effect. Presumably no two medicine-men have ever performed rituals in precisely the same way, but their little variations establish no new patterns.

Historical or social change is initiated when personal idiosyncrasies or the perception of new opportunities lead an individual to deviant behavior that alters the physical environment or is successful enough to lead to persistent imitation.[1] In either case a new social conception has to be formed regarding man's expected be-

This article is reprinted, by permission of the author, from Harvard University Research Center in Entrepreneurial History, *Change and the Entrepreneur* (Cambridge, Mass.: Harvard University Press, 1949).

havior in the situation, and this conception shapes the new social role. J. Pierpont Morgan, for instance, by successfully assuming responsibility for the management of companies financed by his bank, led other bankers to do likewise, and gradually altered the social role of the investment banker.[2] The prestige of the deviant individual will be a factor in the readiness and speed with which others imitate new actions. The Standard Oil group of entrepreneurs in the nineteenth century set many standards of behavior, both good and bad, for lesser businessmen, whereas the novel actions of a small manufacturer might find no imitators and be without lasting social effect.

Social change spreads as deviance in individual roles, and new social roles react on reciprocal roles, such as new behavior by a father altering the roles of the children, or that of an executive altering those of his subordinates; or it spreads by new roles creating new conditions to which other people must adjust. When, for example, some chief executives in the twentieth century began to decide that their role should be more that of cultivated gentlemen than of hard-driving bosses, the reciprocal roles of vice-presidents necessarily had to change. But the alteration of social roles by new conditions, created by some initial deviant behavior, appears to be the most usual cause of change. Our personal roles are reshaped largely in this way. Sometimes the new situation created by an innovation that alters roles forces conformity to the new pattern as the price of survival. The motor car, for example, soon destroyed the role of carriage builder, and those entrepreneurs who wished to continue to act in the larger role of suppliers of pleasure vehicles had to conform to the role of automobile manufacturers. But often the new situation, while making some part of a role nonfunctional, does not require a complete adjustment. In such cases, the persistence of the ceremonial or socially sanctioned elements of a role after they have lost their functional utility creates a situation vulnerable to sudden or sweeping change. Henry Ford's individual and social role as the purveyor of a cheap, simple black automobile was persisted in for some years after the market demand had shifted toward more elaborate cars, with the result that Ford lost his leading position and had ultimately to make drastic changes at large expense. On the broad social scene the rapid triumph of a reform movement that has long been resisted may illustrate the same phenomenon.

Just as altered roles are the impelling forces of social change, sanctions or ceremonial patterns (traditional habits) are the anchors of social stability. Most men will not persist in a policy that meets social disapproval and resulting penalties, and they will be led to assume roles that carry social praise and added prestige. Psychological characteristics of the average individual, which we cannot explore here, make in practice for inertia in social beliefs and attitudes. The social sanction against canned goods, developed in the experimental days of the nineteenth century, operated nonfunctionally against canned beer a hundred years later. Thus sanctions tend to protect the exponents of established practice. In the banking community, for example, the traditional sanctions regarding proper behavior worked strongly against a deviant like Giannini.

The pattern of sanctions in any culture may be seen as the expression of certain implicit cultural themes, or basic attitudes, in interaction with social environment.[3] A theme such as the disposition to perceive and value the importance of the individual manifests itself in a great variety of universal and special sanctions ranging from legally protected civil rights to styles in architecture. The logic of deductive analysis would dictate that we start with these universal culture themes and then show how they inspire specific roles and sanctions, but the actual building from empirical evidence has proceeded mainly in the opposite direction. By starting with some of the definite actions and attitudes that can be learned from contemporary documents, and inducting the more general beliefs from such evidence, we start, at least, from a factual basis.

This concept of change as the result of the interplay of roles and sanctions admittedly is in the form of a group of tentative hypotheses which require testing. The general historian working in the American field might readily turn it to use in studies of the Protestant ministry or national politics, since either such segment of our social life presents some rather definitely structured roles and rigid sanctions. But our task here is to attempt an application of the concept to the more amorphous and difficult area of business entrepreneurship.

II

American entrepreneurship offers unusual difficulties from the standpoint of role. To begin with, in the essentially agrarian society of 1790 where a national industry and a national money market were only beginning to develop, most roles were somewhat novel and, aside from trade, there were relatively few social specifications for business roles. A multiplicity of individual roles, and a minimal content for general social roles persisted, particularly in businesses that did not deal directly with the public, through the nineteenth century.

Some types of behavior such as that of the nineteenth-century banker or the general-store proprietor, however, acquired sufficient characteristic structure to create a contemporary social role. On the basis of Lewis Atherton's studies, it may be said that the social role of the back-country storekeeper was conceived as embracing broad social functions such as dissemination of news and advice on manners and customs, while on the purely business side it permitted a latitude for sharp practices on prices and products that could not be part of the present-day social role of successful chain-store managers. Similarly, from the writings of Bray Hammond, Fritz Redlich, H. E. Miller, and others we see the emergence of quite definite ideas as to what constituted proper and improper conduct for bankers. By the late nineteenth century these had become set in a quite elaborate social role. The banker, for example, was expected to do business in a stately or, at least, dignified establishment, to be grave and cautious in manner, to give objective and "sound" financial advice, to lend money only under certain conditions, and to have a high moral character that would inspire confidence in his trusteeship. Such structuring went down to many of the rather minute details of conducting business. A leading New York banker of 1900 would not accept deposits from an out-of-town bank unless he knew the character and appearance of its president.

Since performance of the purely economic aspects of the social roles in the two preceding examples involves the general public in important ways, these roles involve numerous social forms and functions. In contrast, the role of the manufacturer of an unbranded commodity sold through wholesalers scarcely touches the public. The noneconomic aspects of this manufacturer's social role will be guided or perceived only by those more or less directly connected with his operations. It may be assumed that the uniform social aspects of such a role will be relatively fewer and simpler than in cases where the role is shaped by wide and diverse interrelations.

Assembling data for structuring the social roles of the many and changing varieties of American businessmen will require a great deal of research. Meanwhile, social scientists, with whom the concept is still quite new, will further refine the theoretical elements in role.[4] The fact that Americans have acted time and again upon the assumption that they knew the role a man would play in a given situation, and that on an implicit level we constantly employ such calculations in everyday life, offers hope that the task of setting up entrepreneurial roles sufficiently explicit to reveal deviation and change is by no means impossible.

III

Social role is a concept twice removed from historical data. That is, material bearing on role has first to be abstracted from accounts of real action or ideas, and then on a theoretical basis this selected material has to be structured or interpreted in a social role. Social sanction, on the other hand, is a label for certain types of opinion or attitudes that can be read directly from historical evidence. It is a general concept that stresses the stabilizing function of adages, admonitions, social ceremonies, traditional practices, and other such devices for protecting society from unpredictable behavior.

One may question at this point the particular historical value of the concept of sanctions beyond the more familiar ones of culture or habit patterns. The answer is that whereas the general concept includes too many diverse elements, a sanction is one specific type of culture pattern that performs a definite social function and can hence be used as an analytical tool. A social habit, for instance, is also a culture pattern, but it does not necessarily imply the pressure for conformity that is characteristic of a sanction. Cleaning automobiles on Sunday is an American habit or culture pattern, but failure to conform to it involves neither social penalties nor rewards. A history written in terms of cleaning automobiles on Sunday, like much antiquarian social history, will not directly reveal any social dynamics. In contrast, take the original John D. Rockefeller's use of his time on Sunday in conformity with the sanctions for religious conduct. His behavior in this religious role was soon rewarded by the office of treasurer of the church, and also aided early in establishing his business standing. Here we could study the initial dynamics that led to the great oil company.

Since social beliefs are shaped by various age, sex, and interest groups, particular sanctions may be contradictory. Americans, for example, have generally believed in the virtue of material progress and accorded high prestige to the inventor. That is, they have established sanctions that reward innovation or deviant behavior in the realm of technology. Yet the same people who support this sanction have, on occasion, ridiculed inventors, and turned their backs on innovators. Opposed to the sanction for material progress is the primitive and deep distrust of the unknown, manifest in such a sanction as praise for doing things "the good old-fashioned way." The historian can only suggest that sanctions of the type that would lead to role changes have been more numerous and stronger in some areas of American culture, and sanctions that would hinder such changes have been weaker, than in the culture of the Latin American nations discussed by Professor Bradley.

Because of the ease of identifying sanctions, it is possible without additional research to go much further with an analysis of their part in the history of American culture than in the case of other elements of role. The rest of this section will be devoted to some examples of the nature and alteration of the sanctions bearing upon entrepreneurial conduct during the history of the United States.

Professor Jenks's analysis of sanctions shows them to be of varying types and dimensions. The following are some distinctions that will be of use in relating them to the interpretation of history. Sanctions incorporated in official codes of any character may be called *formal;* those sustained by popular feeling and expression, *informal.* The incidence of formal sanctions on the individual is likely to be *external:* he obeys the pure food laws for fear of arrest or he dresses in evening clothes and attends a tedious formal dinner in order to improve his business contacts, but in neither case is the formal action a part of his own internal code for conduct. Informal sanctions, on the other hand, are more likely to be incorporated in *internal* checks and urges. In a highly homogeneous society, parents can indoctrinate children with almost all the sanctions necessary for socially approved conduct. It is a mark of the heterogeneity of urban industrial society that so many attitudes have to be formalized. Sanctions that admonish against a type of behavior are *negative,* those promising social approval for doing certain things are *positive.*

Sanctions may also be seen as varying from *universal* (within a particular culture) to *special,* from *compulsory* to *permissive,* from *undefined* to *explicit,* and from socially *important* to socially *unimportant.* For example: the sanction against lying has been universal in American culture, but never compulsory; that dictating great speed in filling orders has been almost compulsory in mail-order houses but special to that and certain other business groups; that admonishing care of one's family has been universal and effective, but general in character, while certain religious precepts have been less effective but more explicit; and laws prohibiting card-playing on Sunday have been less socially important than those formerly prohibiting the running of trains. It is also clear that differing sanctions have been limiting or compulsory for particular groups. Cleanliness is a legal sanction for restaurant proprietors, in most large communities, but not for the operators of blast furnaces.

IV

While bearing in mind that analytical dissections of culture are wholly artificial, let us divide the sanctions that appear to have operated on the American entrepreneur over the last century into those that encouraged changes in role, those that were neutral or ambiguous toward change; and those that tended to prevent change. The diverse character of entrepreneurs makes it difficult to rate the general effectiveness of many sanctions. To move in "society" and belong to the right clubs, for example, was a sanction with business implications for the stockbroker, while it lacked the same force for a patent medicine manufacturer. I will merely note some of those sanctions that appear on the basis of research in the history of American business to have approached universality, to constitute part of the common heritage of American entrepreneurs. Since most of these sanctions were informal, their incidence was internal as well as external. Prior to the twentieth century, formalized codes, while providing certain security from robbery or violence, bore but lightly on the daily activities of American businessmen.

Among the sanctions likely to encourage deviant behavior that would lead to changes in role was the attitude that a businessman should be technologically progressive. While new machinery was to some extent forced on the businessman by the necessity of holding his position in the market, beyond such necessities the entrepreneur found that most Americans liked to patronize the firms that had new offices and new equipment. The rather steady pressure of this external sanction led to an internal one that gave the entrepreneur a feeling of virtuous pride in having new things.

Somewhat similar to the sanction for progress was that for efficiency. This was expressed specifically in maxims about the value of time and the evil of waste. In business, efficiency was generally associated with keeping down costs, and working continuously. The operation of the sanction was, however, quite uneven and can only be understood in relation to other cultural patterns. While the American entrepreneur appears in some measure to have made a virtue of long hours and hard work, he does not appear to have been as alert to the possibilities of better cooperative and bureaucratic arrangements as were his cousins in England and Germany.[5] That is, his role called for an alertness to new physical devices, but not to new social arrangements. Englishmen visiting America in the mid-nineteenth-century thought that New York business procedures were crude and labored compared with those of London. While having the newest machines, regardless of their precise effect on costs, satisfied a sanction, this did not apply to efficient use of national resources. Cheap raw material discouraged care in its utilization, and short-run gain often obscured long-run efficiency. But sanctions are almost always qualified in operation, both by the physical needs of the situation and the roles of the people involved.

The sanction to acquire personal wealth, the easiest path for most Americans to prestige and high social status, generally acted as a cause of change. Some sociologists have gone so far as to assume that Americans are unusually motivated and emotionally disturbed by the feeling of need to acquire higher prestige and status. To achieve these aims, young men have deliberately sought deviant behavior that will gain them favorable recognition or material advantage. Certainly among owner-manager entrepreneurs, such as John D. Rockefeller, R. H. Macy, or Marshall Field, the pursuit of personal wealth and the willingness to innovate and to assume the risks of new business behavior were closely allied.[6]

As the large corporation superseded the owner-managed firm as the dynamic force in American industry, roughly around 1900, the operation of the sanction to acquire prestige from wealth altered. On the one hand, the opportunity to acquire wealth or fame by starting a small owner-managed business became less, and, on the other, a new scale of prestige appeared in the form of place and rank in the larger corporations. A man might in fact acquire wealth by becoming a top officer of a big company, but his ascent had to be governed by sanctions other than those surrounding the direct pursuit of monetary gain. He had to adjust to a new series that was more politico-administrative and less market-oriented or economic. And even after he reached the top, he was hemmed in by new sanctions governing proper administrative conduct in large institutions. The boss of the small enterprise could be a dictator subject to few sanctions in his conduct toward employees. The leader of a great managerial hierarchy needed, in spite of the success of the occasional dictatorial leader like Sewall Avery, to understand and respect the sanctions of his colleagues. He needed not only the obedience, but also the respect and loyalty of the members of the organization. For giant companies selling in monopolistic competition to a large portion of the nation's consumers, the approval of the general public also became important. From these roles and sanctions there grew a literature on the sociology of industry, personnel management, morale problems, and public relations.

A number of the sanctions that have channelized entrepreneurship throughout American history have been ambiguous in their relation to change, sometimes operating to force and at other times to inhibit new behavior. The sanctions surrounding the central entrepreneurial function of making a profit have been of this order. Furthermore, their relative effectiveness has undergone considerable change in the last hundred years. To begin with, there was the positive sanction that individual profit-making resulted in general economic welfare and was, therefore, one of the most important social functions. This attitude was undoubtedly a major cause of the vigor of American entrepreneurship. It is scarcely an exaggeration to say that in the real, as distinct from the ideal, culture of America from 1830 to 1930, at least, profit-making was the most respected activity. The result was a nation of potential entrepreneurs, in strong contrast to the small supply of entrepreneurs in cultures that have regarded profit-making as ignoble, or lacking in prestige. From this standpoint this sanction undoubtedly stimulated change. But it could also work the opposite way. Large stockholders, content with existing profits, might insist on "letting well enough alone," and prevent the introduction of new procedures. Bankers in control of industry have, rightly or wrongly, become notorious for this short-sighted or "conservative" emphasis on immediate profit.

With profit-making the accepted sanction for economic activity, businessmen regardless of their own motives rationalized their activities in terms of profit. If they failed to make a profit, they suffered inner penalties in loss of self-esteem as well as in loss of standing with their colleagues. Unpleasant or antisocial actions were explained inwardly and outwardly as necessary to preserve profits, or minimize losses. Subscribing, on occasion, to the theory of the self-regulating market, entrepreneurs viewed profits as an index of business (and social) efficiency, and a proof of laudable acumen. This type of thinking obscured the changed relationship of the executive of the big corporation toward the pursuit of personal wealth. Even though he might in reality be seeking prestige, or wealth not connected with the profits of his firm, he talked the sanctioned language of company profits, and pledged his loyalty to the traditional "interests of the stockholders."

The sanction to look after the interests of the stockholders, therefore, has altered in effectiveness over the last century. It was practically compulsory in the nineteenth-century small company, or in any company where the board of directors was composed of the important stockholders. As the large company grew, however, its stock became more widely held, and its board composed of men whose personal shareholdings were relatively unimportant both to them and the company. In this situation, businessmen from Nathan Appleton in 1841 to Oswald Knauth in 1948 have seen the weakening or virtual disappearance of the sanctioning force of stockholder interest.

Stemming from the eighteenth-century days of small industry and independent traders, competition was sanctioned as the mechanism that insured business efficiency. But as heavily capitalized big business developed in the nineteenth century, the "ideal" sanction had to be applied in somewhat contradictory ways. A function of competition was to eliminate the unfit, but in an industry of large overhead costs too much competition might ruin the fit as well. Therefore, competition should, by implicit or explicit agreements, be kept within bounds, and preferably removed from the area of pricing—the only one dealt with in the then current economic theories of competition.[7] This meant that until well into the twentieth century most business behavior went on in areas not sanctioned by any economic theories or philosophies. Yet on a deeper level the ordinary businessman believed that "natural" economic laws such as supply and demand would ultimately assert themselves: that if a pool set prices too high it would invite new competition, or if a railroad was too grasping producers would shun its territory; and in the fluid economy of the earlier part of our period, at least, reality tended in the long run to support their belief.

Another sanction ambiguous in its effects was that praising courage or perseverance. Since the business community approved such action either in assuming well calculated risks or in standing by a position, this sanction could operate strongly for or against change. Thomas A. Edison who had the perseverance to invest years of labor and thousands of dollars of capital in producing a commercially practicable electric light, also had the courage to support his financial backers in a reactionary scientific stand to perpetuate the use of direct current. This also illustrates that the sanction for courageous action was generally modified in operation in the business world by the sanctions of profit and efficiency. A man would not be blamed for abandoning a course that involved certain loss, regardless of the fact that in better times he had said he would pursue it under any circumstances, while on the other hand he would be praised and feel virtuous for sticking through many vicissitudes to an enterprise that ultimately made money. Businessmen, and presumably most other Americans, liked to be thought of as having "guts." They also admired forceful, aggressive personalities more than hesitant or compromising types.

Some sanctions, such as that for honesty, bear little theoretical relation to change, although in a specific situation almost any factor may be favorable or unfavorable to new action. Some of the large "trusts," for example, were put together by buying out competing firms through dummies, a means for building large-scale industry that was contrary to the honesty sanction, while the later belief that a big corporation could not afford to violate this sanction helped to make it easy for the larger companies to raise capital for new ventures.

As the old adage "honesty is the best policy" indicates, the immediate basis of the general sanction against dishonesty was business efficiency rather than abstract morality. Operating from such a functional base, the impact of the sanction varied greatly. In the nineteenth century, for example, there was general social recognition of, if not acquiescence in, the fact that the honesty sanction could not be expected to inhibit the statements of western town-site entrepreneurs. Their conduct was rationalized under the looser sanction that it was desirable to settle the country. But, at the same period, the honesty sanction would rather strictly limit the statements of the president of a leading Boston bank, and, to that extent, restrict his role. Activities such as trading on the New York stock exchange involved strict sanctions on honesty in some parts of the process and none in others: between members of the exchange a nod or raised finger signifying a decision was as binding as a legal contract, while there were no sanctions against price manipulation by false sales or deliberate misinformation.

An indication of the necessity of honesty sanctions in the development of some new business roles was illustrated in the gold diggings of California where the miners themselves erected an elaborate code whose provisions had all the coercive force of law. In general, a reputation for honesty, within the meaning of the formal and informal codes of the particular industry, was a business asset valuable to one seeking support for deviant behavior, and a reputation for trickery was a heavy liability.[8] Exceptions to this statement arose most often in areas such as the stock and commodity markets where transactions were entirely impersonal. These men typified by Drew, Fisk, and Gould could gain wealth and power to innovate without regard to their reputation in the business community.

Another group of sanctions must be regarded as conservative pressures generally working against change. Sociologists and anthropologists, for example, have recognized an American "cult of the average man." They claim that Americans are embarrassed by unusual characteristics or abilities, that they want to be just like their neighbors. Ambiguities in the cult or its sanction have, of course, been recognized. The average man wanted a house about like those of his neighbors, only a little nicer; the able entrepreneur wanted to be "one of the boys" even with the workmen, but wanted a margin of respect for his abilities and position. To this extent these sanctions permitted some leeway for deviant behavior, but their total effect has undoubtedly been toward conformity and against innovation.

In some respects the exaltation of the average man was combined with another retarding or stabilizing sanction, the entrepreneur's distrust of book learning and his faith in experience. Experience was common to all, whereas the use of higher education set one apart. If a railroad president said his decision was based on thirty years' experience in railroading, everyone in the organization would respect it as being well founded, whereas if he said it was based on a treatise on railroad management, it would immediately be suspect. This exalting of experience inevitably worked against new ideas. It made a virtue of "soundness," of the well-tried. To some extent this type of negative sanction was necessary in large-scale mass-production industrialism, where false steps were ruinously expensive. But it has made it difficult for many entrepreneurs to espouse and maintain a progressive attitude.

Whether the trend toward expert advice and the hiring of men with college degrees in the industries that employ a majority of working Americans will gradually undermine the "cult of the average man" remains to be seen. The resulting emphasis on higher education indicates that perhaps the sanction of averageness or normality will be respected, but change will be made easier by raising the average level to include a certain familiarity with books and theories.

A number of conservative sanctions not directly related to business impinged on the role of the entrepreneur. The universal sanction to look after and protect the family manifested itself in nepotism or family dynasties, sometimes resulting in progress in the enterprise but more often the reverse. Since the repeal of the laws for imprisonment for debt, few American entrepreneurs have gone to jail. If enforcement of the law by the courts was likely, the sanction against being a jailbird operated to restrain entrepreneurs from new actions or ideas that would violate the criminal code. The civil law, however, has been a sanction of varying effectiveness in checking deviant behavior. The 19th-century big business entrepreneurs, for example, ranged in attitude from Commodore Vanderbilt who is reputed to have said: "What do I care about the law, I've got the power," to Henry B. Ledyard who wrote, "We must in all matters obey the law."[9]

Let us point up this discussion of the interplay of roles and sanctions in business change by an explicit illustration taken from Marquis James's *Biography of a Business,* the history of the Insurance Company of North America.[10] In 1895 Benjamin Rush, an ambitious man of twenty-five, anxious to create an outstanding individual role in business, became assistant to President Charles Platt. At this time the marine department of the company was steadily losing money, and Rush saw a chance to make a reputation by determining the cause. Since his method of procedure was based essentially on new ideas of cost accounting, that is on theory, it violated the sanction that experience was the best teacher and that, therefore, a twenty-five-year-old youth couldn't guide his elders. And, since the elders expected no useful results from such an analysis, the sanctions for efficiency and for protecting the interests of the stockholders would prevent his using working time for the research. Being an astute observer, Rush foresaw the operation of the sanctions and accordingly he kept his deviant behavior a secret by doing it after hours. From time to time he gave President Platt little bits of his new information. And although the president made no use of the new data, he finally allowed Rush to prepare a statement for the board of directors based on his two years of research. Rush organized this document so convincingly that he was made second vice-president in charge of the marine division, and empowered to put his ideas into operation.

But this marked only the beginning of his struggle to alter the social role of the marine insurer. His fundamental deviation consisted in setting up some 198 new classifications of risk, based on long-run individual profit-and-loss figures for each category. With these calculations he completely overhauled premium rates and re-insurance practices. The immediate result was loss of much business on which the new rates were out of line with those of competitors. Clients, agents, officers, and board members all complained to the president. To turn away business through prohibitive rates violated a powerful sanction, and to take apparently great risks on the basis of new theoretical calculations, not in accord with existing practice, violated still another. Had President Platt not stood by Rush's innovations during the years when loss of new business and claims resulting from unsound old policies ran deficits up higher than ever, the innovation would have been crushed by the sanctions. But when the old marine policies had expired and the sales organization had readjusted itself to the desirable types of risk, the plan proved a great success. Other companies then adopted similar classifications and the social role of marine insurance was correspondingly altered. The modified role included an element of scientific determination in place of the old and fallacious rule-of-thumb judgment, while the sanction against theoretical research had lost a small portion of its social force.

V

In playing an individual role that violated a sanction the entrepreneur was likely to incur the disapproval of a wider group than his business associates. Most of the important sanctions bearing on business were specific manifestations of general social sanctions. Those such as the "cult of the average," or the value of honesty, courage, protection of the family, and avoidance of criminal penalties operated in much the same way in the rest of American society as in the business world. Business emphasis on profit-making was only the special manifestation of a general belief that risk and personal endeavor for practical ends should be rewarded. Efficiency had as its more generalized form the assurance that material progress was desirable and attainable by well directed effort. Belief in the value of competition as a mechanism for eliminating the unfit in the business world was, after the mid-century, an expression of the widespread faith in competitive struggle that found its philosophical rationalization in Social Darwinism. Except for special groups like ministers and teachers who made professional use of knowledge, Americans in general also sanctioned experience as against higher education in the same fashion as businessmen. Learning as a useful tool for mathematical calculation, geographical understanding, or the reading of necessary instructions was sanctioned, but learning as a means to abstract thinking that might produce new ideas was in relatively low esteem.

These correlations between business and social beliefs seem to have been unusually close in American culture. Neglecting the complexities of the older European heritage, the mores or sanctions peculiar to the culture of the United States appear to have had three major sources in the domestic environment: the Calvinistic or Puritan teachings; "frontier" agricultural life (using the term to include all the back country); and the operations of business. And, ironically, all three produced much the same codes and maxims. From the mid-nineteenth century on, however, business became the most dynamic and prestigious of these environments and American culture became increasingly a business culture. But in so becoming, it should be emphasized, society had to discard very few of the sanctions of Calvinism or the frontier.

VI

With these considerations in mind, we see that sanctions are resistant to alteration or modification because they are surface manifestations of deeper implicit attitudes and beliefs that are not immediately affected by any temporary behavior that operates against the sanction. Furthermore, these implicit beliefs, or basic cultural themes, appear to form an interrelated complex in which the whole tends to resist alteration in any of its component parts. As far as cultural data on such an abstract level can be analyzed, and there is surprising agreement among social scientists in both conversation and writing as to the nature of these elements, there seems to have been relatively little change in American cultural themes over the last hundred and fifty years.

The following themes are often phrased in different ways and sometimes subdivided into many more headings, but they or their counterparts would probably appear in any summary of the traits or underlying assumptions that are peculiarly American: First, *the importance of the individual and his right to self-determination with happiness as a goal.* This seems responsible for historical patterns such as democracy, freedom of enterprise, emphasis on "getting ahead," and American conceptions of social justice. (Its far-reaching implications—it is perhaps the fundamental difference between the culture of the eastern and western worlds—call attention to the fact that each element in a complex of homogeneous culture themes can be derived as a corollary of any other element. All the discussion up to this point could be derived from the sanctioning force of this one belief, but might also flow from those that follow.) Second, *the ability of men to control their society and ultimately to control the forces of nature.* This proposition, nearly equivalent to the belief that man can find salvation on earth as well as in heaven, marks another basic theme of post-Reformation western culture that gained unusual strength in the American complex. It emphasizes the underlying unity between entrepreneurship and all forms of human planning—that they are all manifestations of a society dedicated to self-improvement, as distinct from fatalistic or religious orientations. Since understanding has been assumed as the means to control, this theme has emphasized the value of education or free access to knowledge. Third, *the order or structure of nature is equalitarian rather than hierarchical.* Not only are all men created equal, but all creatures and things are on an equal plane in the eyes of God. This assumption underlies the ambiguous attitude toward leadership which has led Americans to attack and belittle the leaders, while in power, who later become famous as symbols of American achievement. It has also found expression in the cult of the average, and in the belief that opportunities should be, and in America are, open equally to all men. The questioning of this latter belief among urban workers in the twentieth century has produced deep cultural uncertainties. Fourth, *the importance of the usable.* This heading represents an effort to state the core of the American's respect for increased production, material resources, and useful information; and his relative distinterest in the abstract, the supernatural, and the impractical. It derives, no doubt, to a large degree from the national experience of continual physical progress. Fifth, *the importance of the physically spectacular.* This, no doubt, also stems partly from the national experience with a new continent. Big waterfalls, big buildings, or other examples of bigness, are generally valued more than the small, the delicate, or the complex.

One major theme of the earlier period, *the assumption that change is desirable because it normally represents progress,* seems to be losing its generative force in the mid-twentieth century. Accumulating social difficulties have weakened the assurance typical of the older America, and led to the strengthening of a thematic fear of change.

This alteration illustrates the assumption that different themes of the implicit culture are emphasized by differing social situations, and that even the same theme may help to generate new or contradictory sanctions in a changed environment. A sanction is merely an attitude that has been generated by the desires or necessities of people at some time and place. When carried over to a new situation involving new roles the sanction may be nonfunctional, although it remains a direct expression of a still dominant cultural theme. The force and meaning of themes and sanctions must be interpreted, then, in relation to their origins and apparent functions in specific roles.

VII

In addition to providing an explanation of the mechanisms of social change, the theory of roles and sanctions leads to some interesting corollaries. It shows that economic change is not autonomous, and it explains why the operation of the same economic quantities may show little similarity of effect in two diverse cultures. From this it follows that adequate statistics and other physical facts are somewhat less than half the battle in understanding historic evolution. Unless the dominant cultural themes, and the resulting types of sanctions and social roles are understood, any assumed chain of causation is merely descriptive of a sequence rather than explanatory of real causal interaction.

This description of reality as seen by the social scientist has upsetting implications for the historian. No modern complex culture has, as yet, been systematically analyzed for cultural themes, sanctions, and roles. By joining the sociologists and anthropologists in pointing to these lacks, entrepreneurial historians are, in fact, demanding a new history—one for which some of the materials are available but unused, and some are still undiscovered. An historian trained in such an approach, for example, could find data at once for a satisfactory history of American cultural themes and universal sanctions, while other materials, such as those for a typology of social roles, are so vast and scattered that usable generalizations will require years of new research.

Cultural analysis calls attention to the possibility of new "tools" for detecting the rate and direction of social change. The changing effectiveness of a sanction under approximately the same physical circumstances indicates basic social movement more reliably than many statistical series. The declining effectiveness of the two sanctions, that management worked directly and solely for the stockholders, and that profits were their primary aim,[11] for example, indicates more about the nature of the evolution in the organization of American economic life than do statistics on the size of the largest corporations. Or, on the deeper cultural theme level, the weakening of the implicit belief in the reality of equality of opportunity over the last fifty years has had profound political and economic effects.

Finally, and perhaps more important than supplying tools for detecting change, is the emphasis that role-sanction-theme analysis places on continuities. This balanced view is particularly important for entrepreneurial history where the emphasis has been so concentrated on innovation. If the analysis in this essay has validity, the reader cannot but be struck by the number of cultural themes and universal sanctions that have scarcely altered over a century of American history. And analyses of other cultures would presumably yield the same result. A favorite aphorism applied to these basic cultural themes or patterns by anthropologist Clyde Kluckhohn is "Plus ça change, plus c'est la même chose." Even a cross-sectional analysis on this level of Russian culture before the first World War and today would no doubt indicate far more continuities than changes.

An economic or administrative innovation may produce a new constellation of roles and physical situations that somewhat reshape sanctions and other cultural patterns, as did factory industry a century ago, or government welfare spending from 1933 onward. But the "nuclear" or major cultural themes and their related sanctions are powerful and tough, and they at once start reshaping the physical situation in their image. When the result is a defeat of the new role or physical change, as in the success of community legal sanctions against the steam and gasoline automobile from 1803 to about 1885, it is easy to overlook the whole struggle.

In general, major changes in sanctions require the span of a generation or more. They have to wait for men, conditioned to some degree by the new situations, to develop new conceptions of their proper social roles. It is not due to economic causes alone that there has appeared to be a ten- to twenty-year lag between successful invention and commercial adaptation, or between the agitation of a reform and its achievement. In this sense some sanctions may be seen at any given time as limits to entrepreneurial action, but in thinking in this way it is necessary to remember that a sanction is not like a fence or geographical boundary; it is a pressure that must be judged in relation to counterpressures arising from other aspects of the given role.

By defining the innovating acts that produce change as aspects of behavior deviating from a social role, in place of generalizing them as actions by men of genius or unusual originality, our theory places the emphasis on observable social phenomena, that is, on deviance from an anticipated norm of social behavior, rather than on unexplored qualities of character structure. The role concept, then, puts the emphasis on historically ascertainable elements in a situation. By defining the chief social forces that interact with deviant behavior as sanctions, rather than by such vague terms as habits, traditions, interests, and inertias, the theory again uses a definite type of social data that is both historically distinct and available. The theory will gain predictive value, presumably the aim of all social science analysis, as the nature and probabilities of deviant behavior in various roles are studied and classified, and the relations of sanctions to roles and themes are better comprehended. But meanwhile the structuring of historical movement in these terms will undoubtedly call attention to new aspects of each situation and add immediately to the depth of historical understanding.

PART III

ENTREPRENEURSHIP IN THE COMMUNITY

Entrepreneurship in the Community

THE TITLE CHOSEN for this section betrays the difficulty of classifying systematically the types of work done under the general heading of entrepreneurial history. To the extent that studies of entrepreneurial behavior show any sensitivity at all to the milieu in which the entrepreneur acts, to that extent they are studies of entrepreneurship in the community. The four articles that follow have been selected not because they are unique in their concern with cultural factors, but rather because they attempt to confront the problems involved in this approach explicitly and directly.

Thomas Cochran's essay on "Cultural Factors in Economic Growth" was his presidential address to the Economic History Association in 1959. It represents a historian's attempt to make use of concepts derived from anthropology, and thus differs from the type of analysis Cochran had earlier used in his study of railroad executives. The central concept is no longer social role, but cultural attitudes. Cochran justifies this change of method on two grounds: first, because social structure is a static concept and "does not properly include social process"; and second, because of the complexities involved in analyzing business roles. To these one might add the greater flexibility of presentation and wider scope for intuitive judgment that a cultural approach permits.

Cochran's purpose is to sketch the characteristics of the Latin American entrepreneurial style and to explain, by reference to other aspects of Latin American culture, why and how business behavior in Latin America differs significantly from business behavior in the United States. He proposes the hypothesis that certain identifiable characteristics of Latin American culture have been unfavorable to economic development; one of the "middle terms" in this relationship—presumably not the only one—is the way in which the culture defines acceptable and correct ways of behavior for the businessman. These cultural definitions are to be thought of not primarily as external constraints upon business behavior, though they can appear in this guise, but rather as internalized values and presuppositions. Thus the Latin American entrepreneur, as Cochran describes him, enjoys talk, theory, and speculation. He lacks the compulsion to act characteristic of his North American counterpart. He seeks prestige and status principally in fields other than business. He is deeply concerned with personal integrity and dignity, finds it difficult to take criticism objectively, and gives his loyalty only to particular individuals, not to the group or the institution.

Why does the Latin American entrepreneur act and feel in this way? For an explanation Cochran turns to a description of the Latin American family, arguing plausibly that it is in the child-rearing process that cultural values and attitudes are passed on from one generation to the next. Child-rearing in Latin America, he suggests, is more "family centered" than in the United States. The family is the universe in which one competes and it is in family relationships that a man learns what he is and what he should strive to be. Conversely, the family sets restraints and imposes responsibilities on its members in their life and work "outside" the family.

The idea that important relationships exist between the family system and entrepreneurship occurs in other essays in this volume; there seems on this point to be some convergence of insights. Cochran's general hypothesis—that values later evinced in entrepreneurial behavior are learned in childhood within the family—is plausible. But to point out specific relationships between particular aspects of business behavior and particular aspects of the family system is difficult for a number of reasons. The evidence is flimsy: As Cochran points out, the middle and upper middle class families in Latin America which are the source of most entrepreneurs have received less attention than peasant families. We are dealing with averages at both ends of the comparison—typical Latin American entrepreneurship and typical Latin American family systems—and the unspecified variance around these averages leaves the reader uneasy. Above all, no set of general theoretical relationships enabling us to relate family structures to modes of entrepreneurial behavior is yet available. In the circumstances, to assert that there are important linkages and to suggest a few examples is probably all that can be hoped for.

Cochran moves onto firmer ground in his discussion of the implications of these cultural characteristics for economic development, placing his emphasis primarily on the managerial problems to which they lead and in particular on the difficulty of securing effective delegation of authority. Expressed in the most general terms, his hypothesis is that values and attitudes historically rooted in an economic context of slow growth, limited markets, and gradual or nonexistent technological change are likely to prove incompatible with the requirements of more rapid economic expansion. Such incompatibility may show itself in various ways: in internal political and social tension; in the breakdown of old ways of living and thinking; and in more or less overt resistance to the forces and groups making for change. New groups of entrepreneurs emerge, often with personality characteristics markedly affected by contact with the more highly commercialized culture of the United States. Yet in many cases the transition is incomplete, traditional ways being preserved in the home and outside office hours.

Clearly Cochran is discussing situations in which the forces impelling economic development do not emerge from the traditional culture but are in some way imposed on it. In this context the traditional culture can hardly appear otherwise than as an impediment to change and the analysis tends to hinge on the modifications necessary if change is to proceed. Cyril Belshaw, in the article that follows, carries the analysis further. Granted that, in relatively backward economies, the basic personality type of the culture is probably resistant to change, it is still true that the number of people who vary more or less from this basic type may be considerable, and such individuals may exert an appreciable influence in support of change. Entrepreneurs, he argues, must be leaders. This means, on the one hand, that they must be in some sense deviants from the traditional culture. But it also means that they must, if their leadership is to be effective, retain membership in the traditional culture and share to some extent its values. For otherwise the leaders will have no followers. Thus whereas Cochran's attention is focused mainly, though not exclusively, on the task of delineating the modal personality type of a traditional culture, Belshaw is more interested in those who deviate from the mode, finding in them the source of potential entrepreneurship. Consideration of the characteristics of the traditional culture is still highly relevant, but such characteristics now play a different part in the analysis. They are regarded, not primarily as impediments to change, but as influencing the organization and techniques that successful entrepreneurship in such a culture must have. One implication of this is Belshaw's recurrent insistence that technologies and forms of organization appropriate for entrepreneurship in "marginal" cultures must be discovered; they cannot be merely transferred from more commercialized societies. The traditional culture, as he views it, is a resource, but a resource that requires particular techniques for its exploitation.

Belshaw's attempt to "focus attention on significant variables rather than probably insignificant uniformities" leads him to inquire into the role of the entrepreneur as community leader. Leadership roles, he points out, are competitive; ceremonial activities provide an alternative outlet for the energies that might be diverted into entrepreneurship. The emergence of entrepreneurial leadership depends partly on the potential fields for leadership in general, partly on the attractiveness of competing alternatives. The defining characteristic of the entrepreneur is his orientation toward expansion and growth, and such individuals in a traditional culture must be almost by definition deviants from the cultural norms. Deviants are always present; no society is ever completely static. The analytic problem is to identify the factors that attract such deviants into entrepreneurial roles and the conditions necessary for them to perform such roles successfully.

The entrepreneur in traditional societies, as Belshaw interprets him, cannot completely identify himself with the norms of the culture; his personality cannot fit the matrix perfectly. On the other hand, he must be sufficiently in tune with traditional values and institutions to be able to use them for his own purposes. For example, the traditional kinship system with its familiar structure of authority and mutual obligations can serve as an important organizational resource; the same may be true of traditional communal and tribal organization. All such social subsystems provide potential fields for entrepreneurial leadership. It must be borne in mind, however, that the objectives of entrepreneurship in such societies, the forms of entrepreneurial organization that prove effective, and the criteria of successful entrepreneurship, are all culturally determined and may be very different from those that outside observers assume to be normal. In extreme cases objectives and organization may be so different from western norms as, on superficial inspection, to escape identification as entrepreneurial.

Belshaw's article and that by John Pelzel which follows it differ considerably in scope and refer to different parts of the world. Yet it requires no strained interpretation to show that they have much in common. Pelzel, analyzing a group of small-scale metalworking establishments in one of Tokyo's industrial suburbs, finds that kinship ties play an important role in the establishment, operation, and expansion of the firms concerned. This perhaps could be expected. More important than the family itself, however, is the network of patron-client relationships which, Pelzel shows, covers almost every type of transaction in which the firms are involved. Entrepreneurship, in the case study presented here, is but one aspect of a traditional and formal set of relationships whose implications extend far beyond the market place.

Analysts of Mexican culture have called attention to the institution of *compadrazgo,* a process by which family ties can be extended and multiplied by the deliberate selection of godparents. The economic and political uses of this institution have also been noted, and in particular the way in which it lends itself to the creation of systems of personal allegiance and patronage that are frequently very extensive in their membership and powerful in their ability to mobilize resources. Pelzel's stress on the essential role of patron-client relationships in Japanese culture suggests that such "artificial" kinship systems, if we may call them that, may well be a not unusual framework for entrepreneurship in traditional cultures. And perhaps not in traditional cultures only. Historians of business enterprise in North America and Europe have long been familiar with the close intertwining of family and firm, particularly in earlier periods when capital markets were imperfectly organized and businesses relatively small in size. The notable success of such groups as the Quakers and the Jews in certain lines of business suggests that the type of relationship typical of the family could be and was extended to include persons not linked by kinship. Belshaw's conception of entrepreneurship as a form of community leadership is clearly relevant to situations of this kind.

David Landes' article on French business and the French businessman was originally published in 1951 and reflects in its presentation some of the anxieties felt about French economic growth at that time. For its method and content, however, it retains a permanent importance. Its central thesis is succinctly stated: "Given the same machines and the same funds as an American, the French businessman will not use them in the same way or for the same ends." Such a statement is, of course, fully consistent with the point of view reflected in the earlier articles in this section: What Landes says of the French businessman, Cochran could say of the Puerto Rican, Pelzel of the Japanese, and Belshaw of the Melanesian. What each writer is saying is that entrepreneurship is culturally determined. The entrepreneur acts in and is part of a cultural context which influences his goals and his choice of methods. Landes' particular contribution in this essay is to spell out in lively detail the ways in which this context modulates business behavior in France: how it affects the size of the firm, the relationship between firm and family, the restraints on competition, the nature of the market, and the rate of innovation.

Noteworthy in Landes' presentation is his argument that the normative standards and patterns of behavior characteristic of the small family firm do not affect such firms alone but are carried over into the business practices of large corporations run by professional salaried managers. The beliefs and attitudes of which he writes, in other words, are not to be thought of as vestigial remnants of an earlier day, limited in their present influence to the small-scale sector of the economy. They are to be regarded, rather, as shaping the cultural definition of business roles in general. Their potency is reinforced by the distribution of income, by the slow growth of population and purchasing power, by the diversity of products insisted on by the French consumer, and by the fact that until recently there has been no overriding and generally recognized need for change. They are, as Landes puts it, the logical continuation of centuries of entrepreneurial tradition.

It is small wonder, therefore, that Landes, writing in 1950, found the prospects for economic development in France far from good. The characteristic behavior patterns of the French entrepreneur could not, as he saw it, be modified quickly or easily, for what was involved was "a whole way of life, the values and standards of a people." Yet it is undeniable that, in the years since Landes wrote, the rate of economic development in France has proved remarkably healthy. This raises important questions, both with reference to

Landes' particular analysis of France and with reference to the cultural approach to entrepreneurial analysis in general. Some of these questions Landes himself has explored in a recent article in which he analyzes the array of forces underlying France's recent spurt of rapid growth and defends his earlier emphasis on the entrepreneurial factor and on the family firm.[1] On this particular problem, the debate continues. But more fundamental issues are at stake. Is it perhaps the case that a cultural approach to the analysis of entrepreneurship, emphasizing as it apparently must the element of continuity and persistence in value systems, leaves with the analyst and with the reader an impression that the resistances to change are more potent than the forces making for change? Is there a tendency to bias in the methodology itself? If there is, it requires special effort and attention on the part of the analyst to avoid distortion. Each of the authors represented in this section is careful to point out that he is describing what is generally true, that the norms identified are merely norms and do not imply that deviance is nonexistent, that the seeds of change are there and must not be overlooked. Belshaw and Pelzel, who are trained anthropologists, are perhaps the most cautious in this respect, but even in their analyses the reader, unless he too is alive to the possibility of unintentional bias, is likely to depart with an ill-defined hunch that resistances to change are formidable indeed.

This may be one reason why economists, with a few exceptions, tend to be somewhat impatient with the findings of cultural analysts. And perhaps it is only to be expected that, reacting against the depressing array of "cultural obstacles to economic development," they sometimes overcompensate by developing a professional bias of their own. This bias takes the form of rating very highly the ability of the economic process, once development is fairly begun, to compel modifications in cultural values in such a direction that development can continue. From this point of view, the problem for policy is how to get development started; once the process is under way, the culture will adapt to its imperatives.

The two points of view have been stated here in starkly simplified form for the sake of contrast and to make the point that the differences between them can in principle be resolved by empirical research. Few will deny that the process of economic development, particularly when accompanied by large-scale industrialization and urbanization, does set its stamp on a culture and does induce a wide variety of conforming changes in values and attitudes. Equally, however, it can hardly be questioned that some cultural traditions have greater resistance to modification than others, and that the rate at which the matrix of cultural values can be modified exercises an important influence on the rate at which productivity grows. The problems at issue, therefore, relate to the malleability of cultural traditions in the face of pressures, of varying degree, for change. This is a matter of more-or-less, not of black-and-white alternatives.

Cultural Factors in Economic Growth

THOMAS C. COCHRAN

In 1940, when our Association was founded, this paper might have borne the same title as Caroline Ware's book: *The Cultural Approach to History*. In the meantime, however, world events have brought economists and historians together around the problem of economic growth. So, while pursuing the same interests illustrated in my contribution to Caroline Ware's book, I have chosen the more fashionable title of "Cultural Factors in Economic Growth."[1]

I

Economic theorists bringing their analytical methods to bear on problems of growth have quickly discovered what had been gradually becoming apparent to economic historians: that growth or change is a cultural process in which it is difficult to segregate the economic factors. As Professor Buchanan and Ellis have said: "the really fundamental problems of economic growth are non-economic," or as Irving Siegel recently put it: "man's ends are overwhelmingly cultural."[2] The obvious corollary of such conclusions is that economic history and growth theory have to be broadly inclusive social studies.

As early as the 1920's a small group of economic historians were extending their interest to the social institution of business. But these pioneer business historians came to devote themselves so exclusively to the problem of administration in the firm that social

This article was originally given as the Presidential Address to the Economic History Association in 1959. It was published in *The Journal of Economic History*, 20:515–530 (December 1960) and is reprinted here by permission of the author and the Economic History Association.

patterns affecting economic growth were not emphasized. The beginning of the general application of anthropological and sociological materials and concepts to what was conventionally regarded as the field of economic history came during World War II. Inspired by Arthur H. Cole the Committee on Research in Economic History sponsored conferences that ultimately led to the Research Center in Entrepreneurial History at Harvard. From this and several other groups came new concentration on man and his culture. By the late 1950's an economist, Albert Hirschman, could write: "The fundamental problem of development consists in generating and energizing human action in a certain direction."[3]

Obviously the new interests pose the same elusive problems in the integration of economic, social, and psychological knowledge that the historian has always had to face—problems that cannot be laid out in a brief paper, even were you willing to listen or I competent to try. With T. S. Ashton I feel "it would be unwise to begin with a disquisition of economic theory—for the fruit of that tree often turns out to be an apple of discord."[4] Since the same aphorism applies to the other social sciences I shall walk cautiously through the theoretical orchard to avoid shaking any of the trees. While in the famous controversy between Gustave Schmoller and Carl Menger the historian has to be on the side of Schmoller, it is not necessary to revive the arguments. Rather, I shall discuss some findings on the effect of cultural differences on business or entrepreneurial behavior, and suggest possible relations to economic change.

Among historians the necessity of comparative studies has long been a cliché—a need that everyone talked about and no one met. During the last fifteen years, however, economic growth has been one of several interests that have made comparative study a reality. When trying to understand the relations of the wide array of variables present in most real situations, comparison with what has taken place in analogous situations in other times and nations offers special insights. Most of the following discussion is grounded on comparisons and contrasts between United States and Latin American experience. The three Latin countries studied represent different modifications of Spanish culture overseas. Puerto Rico, a Spanish military bastion until 1898, has strong elements of traditional Spanish culture. Argentina represents a blending of an original Spanish background with the cultures of waves of immigrants from other European nations, particularly Italy. Less cosmopolitan than Argentina, Mexico has modified Spanish traditions with indigenous Indian customs. Yet all three share a number of cultural characteristics that differ from those of the United States.[5]

II

A North American turning to the study of Latin American entrepreneurial behavior is at once impressed by the fact that responses to apparently similar situations are not the same. In the economic language of Arthur Spiethoff their respective entrepreneurs are acting in systems having different *styles*, or spirits. "The aim of a style model," says Spiethoff, "is to mirror economic life as a specific set of economic institutions, economic life in its concreteness."[6] Present-day students of economic growth, however, pushing their inquiries beyond what Spiethoff regarded as "economic institutions," have found it necessary to assign many important factors to an area generally referred to as "social structure." The problem becomes one of finding specific social components which differentiate economic styles. Social structure, however, is a static concept that does not properly include social process and the sociological concepts involved in analyzing business roles are quite complex. For studying entrepreneurial behavior, therefore, it is easier to use the anthropological language of culture and personality.

In this vocabulary the Latin American and the United States styles can be said to be the result of certain persistent basic cultural attitudes related to different economic behavior. If one were to pursue the concept of general cultural attitudes in detail it would appear that they are a combination of generally held beliefs acting on the modal personality types of the culture. For purposes of the present survey it is not necessary to hypothesize the details of such interconnection. The term "cultural characteristics" will be used to indicate either the attitudes or behavior arising from the culture-personality complex.

I propose the general hypothesis that certain characteristics of Latin American culture have been relatively unfavorable to economic development. If this is true, it follows that diverse rates of development in the two culture areas are not adequately explained by differences in the physical situation. There is a generally uniform difference in human response that will upset calculations based on short- or long-run theories developed under the suppositions of any one culture.

By contrast to his counterpart in the United States the Latin entrepreneur enjoys talk, theory, and speculation, and lacks the compulsion to act. John Gillin finds Latin American culture "characterized by logic and dialectics, rather than empiricism and pragmatics; the word is valued more highly than the thing; the manipulation of symbols (as in argument) is more cultivated than the manipulation of natural forces and objects (as in mechanics)."[7] John Fayerweather, on the basis of studies in Mexico, calls one form of this addiction to speculation *projectismo.* "It consists essentially," he says, "of constructing plans without much critical analysis and then assuming the plans to be an accomplished fact."[8] Another facet of the tendency to postpone action is acceptance of the leadership of the occasional man who is both *sympatico,* or in tune with his followers, and prepared to act vigorously. While dictators appear less likely in United States culture, it is also less likely that entrepreneurs will receive the Latin degree of support from their chief subordinates.

The Latin American strives more for status not based on business success. This may be a disappearing vestige of agrarian aristocracy, but in Latin America it remains strong. Artistic achievement, professional status, landownership, and government or military office still outrank anything short of outstanding business success. In Mexico "the best men go into the professions and those who do not, no matter how good their reasons, are always aware that they are considered professionally inferior."[9] Hence Latin entrepreneurs divert their resources to achieving prominence in more prestigious fields. The leading businessman of Puerto Rico, for example, is also a member of the Commonwealth legislature and the leader of the conservative party. One of the most important Argentinian entrepreneurs, a man unusually engrossed in his business, took the time to study for and achieve an engineering degree at the University, subsequently held an associate professorship and developed a large *estancia,* all during the most active years of his business career.

A further aspect of seeking prestige in other terms than money is illustrated by the same Argentinian. Between 1928 and 1930 he organized companies in Brazil, Chile, and Uruguay to manufacture some of the products of the parent firm. All of these ventures lost money, and on the average continued to do so for many years. The losses in 1931 and 1932 put a severe strain upon the whole system, yet all three ventures were kept going. There are strong indications that he suffered these losses for reasons other than anticipation of large returns in the future. Among these reasons was probably the prestige that accrued from being an international businessman and the head of a family with international interests in a culture where industrialists were not highly respected.

Child-rearing, education, and family life are the chief processes by which culture and personality are perpetuated with a high degree of stability. According to present ideas of personality development the general characteristics favorable or unfavorable to entrepreneurship and economic growth are largely acquired at this early stage. For example, David C. McClelland argues that "countries where stories told to children have a high 'achievement content' show a higher rate of economic progress."[10] Similarly, the traits of cooperation that have produced the "organization man" were probably acquired more from family conditioning and schooling than from an adult environment of large corporate enterprise.

Latin American child-rearing is more family centered, particularly in country areas, than appears to be the case in the United States.[11] "In Mexico," writes Professor Fayerweather, "there is a much smaller universe with which one can compete . . . You don't give a darn about the neighbors. That's another world, but you care intensely whether you have as good a refrigerator as your brother-in-law."[12] Along with the restraints imposed on competitive goals by the tendency to look no further than the family, Professor McClelland thinks that the "solidary" family itself is associated with low achievement motivation.[13] The Latin family conditioning also appears to produce individuals who place more emphasis on the *forms* of politeness and obedience than on the facts of behavior.[14] This characteristic may appear in later life in the Latin liking for discussion rather than action. In making use of such hypotheses it must be remembered that the middle and upper-middle class Latin American family, the source of most entrepreneurs, has not been adequately studied.[15]

In periods before the use of corporations and holding companies family relationships in all countries have been the cement of the business structure. The operation of the family as an informal social and economic organization of relatives living in the same area was general in the eighteenth century in the older parts of the English colonies and persisted in the later centuries in the east coast agricultural regions. Since people move as a household, not as an extended family group, rapid migration in all newer parts of the United States minimized the influence of the family system.

In Latin America the family system has had a greater strength, a longer persistence, and a more clearly defined structure of authority than existed even in North American regions of out-migration such as the old South. The Latin family recognizes a head (*jefe*), who is not necessarily the oldest living relative, and he is expected to look out for the family interests. The head, when not the eldest, gets his authority by a sort of implicit democratic process, a recognition of his success and leadership by the members of the family. The head, in turn, particularly in a rich and powerful family, takes his responsibility very seriously. Obligations to the family may readily take preference over the obligations or ethics of business.[16] Rich men wishing to lead carefree, footloose lives may deliberately avoid becoming the head of the family. The superimposing of the family structure on business is a complex process with many ramifications.

III

The most intricate and in many ways the most important differences between United States and Latin American culture are in the area conventionally covered by the term individualism. For purposes of a clear analysis it would be well to eliminate this term and talk only of more special cultural traits. But "individualism" has such a firm place in both colloquial and official language that it seems necessary to use it as a category and then define some of its divergent meanings.

If the Latin family system is a way of limiting individual competition with the outside world, Latin individualism can be seen as an inner penetration of the same devices. A man prides himself on possessing a unique inner quality that is divorced from external matters. Only by long intimacy can this inner uniqueness be appreciated and any premature opening of the "soul" to a friend is degrading. Yet all human contacts are approaches to this ideal understanding, and at an early stage the Latin feels or does not feel a mutual sympathy and reacts accordingly. *Sympatico* may be evident quickly to sensitive Latins and the ultimate success or failure of a negotiation may be established within the first few minutes. Professor Gillin notes the lack of the type of impersonal confidence that men in the United States place in the salesman of large respected corporations. In Latin America "you have to know him as an individual and to understand his 'soul' really to have confidence in him."[17] The attitude gives rise to the characteristic of *personalismo,* loyalty to one with whom an understanding has been achieved.

In contrast so-called individualism in the United States is characterized by striving for status and success in the eyes of a peer group —to be as good or better than the next man. In other words, it is an individualism supported by external criteria. "It is not, on the whole," wrote Clyde Kluckhohn, the American's "privilege to develop individual uniqueness, to cultivate individuality."[18]

Another way of expressing the difference in attitudes is to say that the Latin American has an ego-focused image of a situation, while the North American has a cooperative or group-focused approach. Overemphasis by social scientists on the creative side of entrepreneurship has obscured the importance of these cooperative qualities. Albert Hirschman, on the basis of his wide Latin American experience, argues that the "ego-focused image of change" is a deterrent to economic development because success is not conceived as the result of systematic work and creative effort by a term or group, "combined perhaps with 'a little bit of luck,' but as due either to sheer luck or outwitting others through careful scheming . . . The ego-oriented approach," continues Hirschman, hinders the ability "to bring and hold together an able staff, to delegate authority, to inspire loyalty, to handle successfully relations with labor and the public and a host of managerial talents."[19] William Schurz, a lifelong observer of Latin customs, wrote that the Latin American "is not a good organization man, and his conferences and committees would be the despair of an American chairman."[20]

In contrast to the value placed on objectivity and impersonality among United States businessmen, the Latin American tends to regard seeking inner satisfaction, giving in to his "feelings," as the proper course, one which is taken for granted by people of his culture and needs no apology. This means, in turn, that he may refuse to do business with someone he dislikes, that he follows prearranged plans only so far as they suit his feelings, and that he may initiate unsound projects chiefly because they appeal to his emotions. Furthermore, since these characteristics are well understood the Latin American anticipates them in his fellow businessmen. What might be regarded as a breach of faith in the United States is understood to be a justifiable change in feeling.

Egocentric personality is also associated with greater emphasis on personal dignity. *Dignidad,* as the attitude is often called, can be seen as another facet of the devices to protect the ego from competition. The Latin Americans may scheme just as imaginatively for advantage, but they are disinclined to take overt acts which might expose them to humiliation in case of failure. Former Governor Rexford G. Tugwell said that the Puerto Rican "possesses a pride which is almost an obsession and which leads frequently to the substitution of fancy for fact . . . to the avoidance of outside competition, to the protection of mediocrity and so to a general lowering of levels of competence."[21]

Like other people, Latin Americans have always had to take criticism. "Offenses to *dignidad* have been commonplace . . ." But "they cannot take criticism *and* respond to it as part of a democratic context . . . one side of a democratic process of exchanging views . . ." For example, "in one apparently well-established relationship, critical pressure on an operating problem unnerved a Mexican executive to the point of making several unwise decisions."[22]

The Latin American relation between the chief and his subordinates reproduces the family pattern of paternalism with its emphasis on formal rather than real obedience. The normal framework for decision is superordinate-subordinate rather than one of equalitarian interchange of ideas or cooperation. The inferior will not risk the humiliation he might feel if he openly contradicted his superior and was then overridden, but orders *may in fact* be neglected. When the subordinate does act he feels safer from assaults upon his dignity when carrying out specific orders.[23]

Consequently delegation of authority is one of the critical points in registering the difference between Latin American and United

States attitudes. Often one must look below the surface of organization charts or routine controls to detect the operation of this cultural difference. In giving orders in the factory the Latin in lower- or middle-management acts with fully as much authority as his counterpart in the United States, but he is to a greater extent passing on orders from one he looks to as a superior rather than using, and *risking,* his personal judgment in meeting the situation. Extremes of the United States type of delegation are indicated by the policy in some large companies of leaving the problem of improving poor operating results up to the local manager, or by the statement of the president of a large company that he never made decisions because by the time matters reached his office the decisions had all been made. In many large Latin American companies what the United States manager would call delegation of authority from the chief to the subordinate has never taken place.

For example, in the 1930's one of the largest Argentine manufacturing firms had no officer conferences and no elaborate charts or manuals for managerial procedure. The chief walked through the main plant about twice a week conferring with all levels of subordinates down to the foreman and issuing direct orders. His manner was humble and he showed proper respect for the inner uniqueness of the men who talked with him, but he gave the orders on the basis of his personal judgment.

In 1941, however, the Argentinian entrepreneur decided that his plants, employing nearly four thousand people, might profit from more systematic management. A very large United States firm, one of the principal licensors, was asked to send an expert to Argentina to introduce North American efficiency. The United States company sent a recently retired executive who spent nearly a year in Buenos Aires installing a complete system for management and shop procedures. But, when put in operation, the system ran into difficulties. To begin with, it was hard to select the new departmental and divisional heads because under the system of one-man control few of the available men had really exercised their own authority, and hence their executive abilities were unknown. Men were finally fitted into the chart, however, and the plan put in operation. After eight months the expert from the United States reported that "organization functions are being ignored . . . engineers are doing shop work, shop officials are doing engineering work, building construction undertaken without informing Maintenance Department, salesmen giving instructions direct to the shop." "During the war," concluded the chief engineer of the company, "they did not do much about the new system. After the war they started again."[24] But even in 1960, with many plants and over ten thousand employees, the company is still highly centralized with ultimate decision largely in the hands of the successor of the original leader. Many United States ideas have been absorbed, but reshaped to fit the customs of Argentine culture.

That these differences are an effect of the personality-culture complex rather than just current fashions in management is further indicated by the fact that able American managers were urging delegation in the nineteenth century. Charles E. Perkins of the Chicago, Burlington & Quincy Railroad, for example, argued in 1882 for a system of semiautonomous divisions under general managers who could run them more effectively than if "one management were put over the whole."[25]

Contrasts in the environment in which business takes place in the two areas, a reflection of the cultures, accentuates the underlying differences. Valuable information on business or government policy in Latin America is gained in more indirect ways, such as prolonged luncheon conversations. While to be hurried in the United States is a sign of importance, to appear to be a cultured gentleman with leisure is more prestigious in Latin America. Consequently, Latins may linger over lunch and delay important conferences within their company, or enter into some long time-consuming and apparently nonbusiness discussion, ultimately to get useful business information.[26]

The person wishing to argue against the differentiating effect of cultural elements on economic growth could match the examples used with ones from the United States. North American entrepreneurs have taken uneconomic actions because of personal antagonisms, embarked on poorly planned ventures, and perpetuated inefficient family control. Failure to develop the careful rationalization and cooperation of modern American management may only indicate a greater nearness to the days of agrarian-mercantile attitudes. The number of cases that have been accumulated in published research on Latin American business is too small to carry quantitative weight. The argument for cultural differentiation has to rest on accumulated observation and historical judgment as to norms. The scholars who have been most deeply immersed in these materials would, I believe, be in substantial agreement that the examples cited illustrate widely shared traits of Latin culture, and I think that in a similar stage of industrialism these were not normal traits of United States culture.

In speculating upon the effect of these cultural differentials on economic growth it is soon apparent that the impact varies with the type of activity, the size of business units, and the level of economic development. Evon Z. Vogt writes: "The widest proposition that I think can be defended with our present evidence is that the importance of value orientation in shaping the direction of change is proportional to the amount of economic and technological control a society has achieved."[27]

The highest level of such control is presumably found in United States big business run by professional management. Looking at this sector of the economy Paul F. Lazarsfeld notes that culture strongly influences the selection of matters for executive decision. He sees three factors influencing such personal decisions: "informal groups, the relations of statuses, and visibility."[28] As advanced management becomes ever more politically and socially oriented and less concerned with technological problems the question arises, according to Professor Lazarsfeld, "whether sociological concepts like social visibility may not one day themselves become determinants of managerial activities."[29]

Obviously historians do not now have to confront these problems, but such thinking emphasizes the probability that the cultural characteristics favorable to growth at one level may differ significantly from those favorable at even a slightly higher level of complexity in business and social organization.

In Puerto Rico, for example, the traditional Spanish type of culture did not appear to impede the building of strong importing houses, moderate sized sugar centrals, and successful small embroidery, ready-made clothing and furniture factories. Of these last three, only hand embroidery was sold on the mainland. Viewing the island market as a limited one that had to be divided among competitors, even sugar having a quota after 1934, entrepreneurs seldom took the risk of trying to expand.[30] Thus a small and fairly static business community could cultivate personal relations, eschew group activity, and look for prestige outside the business world without running counter to the economic situation.

With the stimulation of manufacturing by the insular government from 1945 on, selling more products outside the Puerto Rican market became a possibility, and at the same time new technology and new marketing methods menaced the stability of the old internal arrangements. It was at this point that the lack of cooperative or group orientation began to appear as a hindrance to growth. Many sugar centrals had become uneconomically small, yet in spite of wide recognition of this fact there were no mergers, as distinct from outright sales, of these family-owned mills.[31] Even more striking was the last-ditch stand of small food wholesalers against the supermarkets and bigger distributors with better mainland connections. In Ponce in 1955, for example, there were 20 small wholesalers where two or three could have handled the business. But these entrepreneurs would not reconcile themselves to giving up their proprietorships by merging their interests with those of other families.

Granted that Puerto Rico was to become a mature industrial area, these delays to the logical course of economic development illustrate not only the poor adjustment of Latin type individualism to the cooperative demands of mass production and distribution, but also the hindrances that a strong family system can impose on changes in the ownership of enterprise.

VI

The dominant role of communication in economic development has been well recognized. Much of the writing of Harold A. Innis dealt with this theme. Arthur H. Cole made changes in communication the basis for his stages of entrepreneurship.[32] Recently Richard L. Meier has said that change in the magnitude of economic factors, or growth, depends on "the flow of information and changes in the state of informedness."[33] These, in turn, are closely related to other cultural characteristics. If people are industrially oriented they will absorb more and more technological learning, and progress accordingly, whereas if there is a lack of interest in such knowledge the rate of transfer may be too slow to affect economic change. Professor Gillin points out that in contrast to the normal pattern in the United States, Latin Americans have not been particularly receptive to ideas regarding technology.[34]

As has been emphasized, their attitudes regarding delegation of authority, free discussion in committees, and objective experimentation with change also run counter to modern United States managerial concepts. Among seventy entrepreneurs in Puerto Rico only those who had prolonged schooling in the United States seemed able to make the full transition to the attitudes current in advanced management.[35] Some of the northern-educated Puerto Ricans made only part of the transition. They talked the language of United States consultants but still reacted emotionally in the traditional patterns. Sometimes they displayed the fashionable United States type of personality at the office and the traditional Spanish type at home.

In Mexico "delegation may involve fundamental personality changes if it is to be effective."[36] Of the group of executives interviewed by Professor Fayerweather only two, "both of them young men who had rather exceptional educational experience, including extended stays in the United States, spoke intelligently about changes in their own attitudes. The rest were essentially lacking in what I shall call a learning attitude."[37] He calls the partial transition described above "the formal behavior level of learning" as distinct from "alterations in basic attitudes."[38]

There are, of course, a number of elements not directly connected with particular types of personality that also affect the rate of transfer of information and attitudes. Three such factors are: the size of firms; the stage of technology; and the type of products available.

While the small entrepreneur has to be personally motivated to learn, the large firm can appoint a specialist to study new information. In 1950, for example, small businessmen in Puerto Rico had a tremendous amount of useful literature beamed at them by government and private agencies, but they paid little attention to it, taking their ideas from conversations with equally poorly informed fellow businessmen or necessarily biased traveling salesmen.[39] As might be expected, the lack of cooperative tendencies in Puerto Rican culture kept trade associations weak and their contributions to technical information slight. On the other hand, relatively big business firms kept in touch with the latest developments in the United States through frequent visits by both specialists and chief executives. In the big company studied in Argentina 34 trips by a wide range of executives were made to the United States during the single year 1958.

As a country reaches higher levels of technology with an almost inevitable increase in the size of firms the intake of outside information becomes greater, but its content is more complicated and more difficult to put into practice. This proposition becomes obvious when comparing widely separated periods of industrial development. At an early stage in industrialism the most advanced machines were not complex. In 1811 Francis Cabot Lowell surreptitiously observed English and Scotch power looms, and with the help of a good mechanic constructed satisfactory copies in the United States. In the 1930's college-educated Italian engineers in the large plant in Argentina were unable efficiently to produce sealed compressors for refrigeration even though they had United States blueprints to work from.

The transfer of knowledge regarding managerial practice appears, in part, to obey this same rule of increasing flow and increasing difficulty. In the 1830's ideas of efficient bank management could be acquired by talking to cashiers in London or other large banking centers. By the 1950's the largest Puerto Rican bank found it worthwhile to pay a firm of consultants from Chicago a very large fee for redesigning the system of management.

The acquisition of good working habits or "industrial discipline" in the lower ranks has been speeded by products that create new wants or goals. The Latin countries discussed here, and a large part of the world area classed as underdeveloped, lie in the tropical or subtropical zones. Warm climate and long growing seasons reduce the need among the working class for costly housing and special preparation for winter. Habits of accumulation appear to be less developed; leisure may seem preferable to the discipline of steady employment. In the twentieth century, however, new forms of consumer durables, at prices that workers can meet if given long-term instalment credit, have changed tropical attitudes. Everywhere radios, televisions, refrigerators, washing machines, motor scooters, and automobiles have had great mass appeal. Like the Calvinistic force of doing God's work, desire for these objects converts idlers in the sun to machine tenders and office workers. The goals of the culture having been partially reshaped from preference for leisure to preference for consumer durables, the effect becomes cumulative.[40] Employees become more reliable and real wages rise; this, in turn, provides for larger consumption and makes the durables into more universal and mandatory marks of social prestige.[41] During the politico-economic confusions of the Péron regime this process was going on in Argentina, and was obvious during the same period in Puerto Rico.

V

This paper must be as unsatisfying and inconclusive as the present state of the analysis of culture and personality or of theories in social psychology. My aim has been to indicate by argument and example that the cultural elements that have to be included in any comprehensive approach to either economic growth or economic history can be analyzed.

From the material discussed, the following propositions may be offered regarding differences important for economic growth between United States and Latin American culture and personality. Comparatively the Latin American complex: 1) sacrifices rigorous, economically directed effort, or profit maximization, to family interests; 2) places social and personal emotional interests ahead of business obligations; 3) impedes mergers and other changes in ownership desirable for higher levels of technological efficiency and better adjustment to markets; 4) fosters nepotism to a degree harmful to continuously able top management; 5) hinders the building up of a supply of competent and cooperative middle managers; 6) makes managers and workers less amenable to constructive criticism; 7) creates barriers of disinterest in the flow of technological communication; and 8) lessens the urge for expansion and risk-taking. These Latin qualities are not necessarily detriments to the good life, perhaps just the opposite, but they are hindrances to material progress under the Anglo-American concepts of a market-oriented capitalist economy.

As one inadequately versed in current economic and psychological hypotheses it would be presumptuous for me to say just how these elements should be utilized by theorists. Certain limitations, at least, seem apparent to the outsider. In spite of the work of Professor McClelland and others, measurement of these cultural differentials still seems rather remote. Yet, as qualities or tendencies they appear reliably identifiable. At present they suggest that the anticipated responses on which North Americans base economic or political activities may not be the same in Latin American or other countries. As against our inevitable desire to apply universal historical analogies and formulate general economic laws, to behave as though roles were played everywhere as in the United States, cultural differentials are warnings that each area will make its own amendments.

Lastly, the growing recognition of the inescapable importance of these basic cultural considerations may be ushering in a new period of the generalist in contrast to more than a generation of increased specialization. If so, the economic historian can hope that his methods of descriptive integration and tentative generalization may regain the prestige they enjoyed in the social science of the late nineteenth and early twentieth centuries. He may still lack answers or often fail to hit on the right question, but he has to work with all the variables, and the results of their interaction, as historical record.

The Cultural Milieu of the Entrepreneur

CYRIL S. BELSHAW

THERE ARE SEVERAL WAYS in which anthropologists may legitimately interest themselves in the study of entrepreneurs. First, they may assess the function of enterprise in the economies of primitive or peasant peoples. This would include the examination of the way in which leadership embodies enterprise and is reflected in organization.

Secondly, they may study entrepreneurs as persons involved in the processes of cultural change.

Thirdly, anthropologists may deal with the complex problems of modern business administration as an aspect of the working of small groups more or less integrated with cultural elements external to the firm. To suggest this problem, however, is to look somewhat into the future, for the entry of anthropological analysis into such fields is recent and not yet clearly defined.

It is with the second problem, that of the entrepreneur in relation to cultural change, that this article primarily concerns itself. I wish to show, as far as my data will allow, certain principles which relate the form of society and the characteristics of culture to the facility with which entrepreneurs emerge; to demonstrate some ways in which the forms of business leadership are related to social and cultural factors; and to indicate difficulties in obtaining criteria by which to judge the success or failure of business leadership in alien cultures. I intend my remarks to apply only to "underdeveloped" countries, and I base them mainly on field experience in various parts of Melanesia, together with more general published references.

This article is reprinted, by permission of the author, from *Explorations in Entrepreneurial History,* 7:146–163 (February 1955).

There are several foci with respect to this problem. As entrepreneurs are in some sense leaders, it is relevant to relate their behavior to general theories about leadership. In their capacity as leaders, entrepreneurs represent and influence directions of social change. Their values and methods are a reflection of the synthesis between old and new that is the developing culture. Hence theories of social and cultural change can help to explain the emergence and methods of entrepreneurs; and the study of case histories against the background of social institutions can influence the confirmation and modification of the theories. Then again, anthropologists are often critical of the ethnocentric assumptions that lie behind many theories of economic development, but their generalizations are often imprecise or too historical to make the appropriate impact upon economists. The study of entrepreneurs as persons involved in cultural change may do something to bring anthropologists and economists together.

To begin with, it is advisable to explore a little more the implications of the term "entrepreneur." The meaning of the word has been discussed at considerable length in the pages of this journal, and is destined for still further argument. I enter the controversy only because the anthropologist has a particular point of view in the matter.

When L. M. Fraser[1] published his valuable analysis of economic terminology in 1937, he was able to distinguish several meanings of the words "enterprise" and "entrepreneur." In summary, the connotations included (a) the management of a business unit, (b) profit taking, more especially in industry, (c) business innovation, (d) uncertainty bearing. If my interpretation is correct, the treatment of entrepreneurs as reflected recently in this journal is to emphasize the role of innovation at the expense of the other factors. Indeed, one could regard (a), (b), and (d) as being merely aspects of normal management, whereas (c) gives a peculiarly dynamic character to management. There is a further distinction. In theoretical models, it is the *function* of enterprise that is important, and innovation can be abstracted from the other functions of management. But in historiography, the data are the behavior of persons fulfilling social roles. That is, the ethnographer and social historian must usually, though not always, see the innovator in a relationship with the other tasks of management as well. Indeed, he is probably not an entrepreneur unless he does undertake ordinary management tasks. I will suggest later in this essay that, from the point of view of the anthropologist in studies of culture change, even innovation is not a necessary criterion, but expansive management is.

Like the economic historian, the anthropologist studies the behavior of historical persons, though by the method of contemporary observation and discussion rather than by the method of analyzing records. His subjects are actually living out their social role as managers and leaders. Since he usually deals with small communities, at best on the verge of a dynamic economy, the number of innovations that the anthropologist can relate to management is usually very small. Of equal interest to him is the way in which they are taken up or rejected by others in the community, and the way in which the ordinary role of management is a part of contemporary cultural synthesis. That is, the anthropologist's data, and the theories he builds upon them, are concerned with a broad problem and not with its minute break-down—with all four aspects of enterprise as Fraser set them out, and not merely with innovation. In other words, an entrepreneur is someone who takes the initiative in administering resources.

While this definition is suitable for the discussion of entrepreneurs in traditional economic systems, it is still too broad for the problems of entrepreneurs in expanding economies and changing cultures which this essay is to consider. In the first place, we are here interested in enterprise related to marketing products for cash. Note, I do not use the phrase "enterprise in the market economy." The distinction is important. Melanesian entrepreneurs, for instance, do not as yet hire labor to any extent as a commodity marketable for cash; the use of resources does not involve the payment of either rent or interest in a cash form. They produce goods or obtain them by exchange (in semitraditional ways) for ultimate sale to European firms or government agencies who give a cash value to the product. The entrepreneur may even reduce his handling of cash by using store accounts: although the firm keeps the accounts with money entries, the Melanesian entrepreneur often simply hands over his product and receives goods in return without taking into consideration the monetary implications of the transaction. Yet the procedures are accompanied by an "economic growth" and hence have relevance for the theory of economic development.

Further, not all those who administer resources in relation to cash marketing need to be considered as entrepreneurs, though perhaps strictly speaking they are. I have in mind two types of Melanesian enterprise which an anthropologist would wish to set apart in this analysis. First, there is the Melanesian who depends for cash upon the sale of his labor, either under indenture or freely. On one reading, of course, he is an entrepreneur—he must make important decisions as to how long to be away from his village, whether the return is worth social sacrifices he must make, and whether he could obtain greater satisfactions from some kind of peasant farming. His role as a cash earner may be very much akin to that of the local Melanesian businessman; he may, for instance, lean upon the resources of his kinsfolk in much the same way, and may distribute his income in the same manner as the businessman. Some laborers even take the initiative in gathering a team together to work continuously as a labor group on some plantation.

There are several distinctions between Melanesian laboring and business management: perhaps I may single out two. First, the decisions of the laborer are only of two kinds: (a) the decision to go to work and to leave work, and (b) decisions made during the course of the work, principally on behalf of the employer, and particularly if some managerial responsibility is allocated. The village businessman must make decisions continuously, and usually on his own behalf, or, if not, on behalf of a corporate organization which is part of the Melanesian community. The second distinction is that the wage laborer uses resources which his employer controls and provides for him. The businessman depends almost entirely on village resources.

Another type of enterprise that should be excluded consists of those with a static rather than a dynamic character. There are perhaps thousands of Pacific island families, particularly along the coastline of New Guinea and the more easterly islands, and still more in Polynesia and Micronesia, who customarily produce for sale to the cash market. They cut coconuts and dry the flesh for copra; they produce vegetables for European or plantation consumption; they fish for trochus or pearl shell; occasionally they grow coffee, cocoa, bananas or citrus fruit. Such families have done these things for decades. There may have been an increase in their numbers since the turn of the century, but the kind of things they do and the scale of their operations (save for bananas and citrus) have hardly varied, if we exclude certain limited responses to fluctuations in prices. My point is that such families are not concerned primarily with the expansion or growth of their business, and it is concern with *expansion and growth*[2] that makes the entrepreneur significant, both from the point of view of cultural change and of economic development. That is, we should exclude such families from our purview and make concern with growth a criterion of the entrepreneur in situations of change, anthropologically considered.

Now the economist may say that this is what he has in mind by innovation. The contention, if made, would seem to me to be dubious, and the concept is certainly distinguishable from innovation. Innovation implies the introduction of a new kind of behavior; cultural change implies acceptance of or reaction to the innovation; growth implies increased intensity of action, through expansion and intensification within an organization, through expansion of the boundaries of the organization, or through repetition of the organization's procedures which other organizations copy with suitable variations. Many of the *individuals* whom the anthropologist would wish to study as entrepreneurs are thus not innovators in a cultural sense although *society* must have accepted innovation at some stage for there to be growth. The idea of growth and expansion may be new to them as individuals who use it as an orientation for their action, but it has already been introduced into the community and in some sense accepted by at least sections of the community. Orientation towards expansion, whether successful or not, is therefore a criterion for an entrepreneur in this meaning, whereas innovation may or may not be characteristic.

Expansion may or may not involve accumulation of capital. It usually does, and capital accumulation may indeed mark off a truly dynamic society from one which is culturally static. Conceptually however we must recognize that expansion may simply involve increased consumption derived from more intensive effort, from greater use of existing resources which have hitherto been used below potential, and from increased velocity of circulation of working capital.

II

In the Pacific Islands, as in other parts of the underdeveloped world, the entrepreneur is involved in the processes of cultural change in differing degrees, which we can represent in terms of his relationship with his home group—that is, the group in which he grew up and which he feels was responsible for the formation of his early values. The home group is usually the one to which his kinsfolk belong. There are four possible major variations in this relationship, with a number of significant subvariants.

1. The entrepreneur has completely broken away, by migration, rupture of communications, and full amendment of values and preferences, from the home group. If we use concepts rigorously, then the "achievement" of individualism, where the individual was brought up in a primitive or peasant society, would involve such an extreme change. Many observers have pointed to individualists who have completely "broken away from" their home group, and who no longer share its values. No doubt there are many instances. In Melanesia I have had occasion to observe quite a number of such cases, labeled in this manner by officials, European residents, and even anthropologists. But closer checking has shown that the rupture has never been complete. There has always been a carry-over in the form of retention of an attitude toward personal relations which makes "impersonal" market relations only a facet of the total; or there has been retention of some channel of communication with the home group. Thus to label such a person individualist often conceals questions which should be investigated, and the observer tends to put the entrepreneur into this category instead of into the following one, where he rightly belongs.

2. The entrepreneur makes a break with the home group, but this is incomplete. (a) He breaks social links with the group through migration and rupture of communications, but he retains elements in his values and preference patterns which derive from his earlier upbringing in the home group. (b) His values and preferences, because of some factor such as differential education or experiences gained through travel, are more sophisticated than those of other members of his home group. He works to achieve a different standard of living. But yet he retains communications with his home group. Thus, if he is a migrant, members of his home group may occasionally visit him, or he may send them wealth. Cases (a) and (b) are of course not mutually exclusive.

Thus there are instances in which the man of enterprise becomes impatient with the social bonds he associates with his group membership; he decides that his community will never make the move to free itself from lethargy or the tie of old ways, that his income is dispersed too widely among his kinsfolk, or that the labor that the community supplies for his use (according to traditionally accepted procedures) will not submit to his discipline. He may then turn his back on his own society. But the claims of kin die hard, and even those who remove to cities, who become "urbanized," are still likely to maintain some exchanges of wealth with their old connections. Standards and levels of living are still likely to retain important traditional elements—preferred foods, the rhythm of work, ceremonial demands, qualities given to human relationships. This is true even of highly acculturated Indian peoples in North America.

When the entrepreneur differs from the home group only in his assessment of the value of certain kinds of material things, and retains the interest in traditional relationships and the village community, the rise in demand is often in terms of those things which other members of the community also value, but not so much. The leader may, for instance, be stimulated because he dislikes regular periods of undernourishment and sees a way to avoid it; he may wish to clothe *all* of his family instead of only a few. On the other hand, of course, he often attempts to obtain articles that his neighbors must do without, such as a radio set, a bicycle, or a motor car. Though many instances of this occur, the situation is relatively infrequent. Individual conspicuous consumption is often disliked in primitive communities, unless there is a real opportunity for others to achieve similar standards, or there are ceremonially authorized channels of achievement. Overconspicuous consumption leads to jealousy, with specific consequences such as social ostracism, community schism, sorcery and political or religious rivalry.

3. The entrepreneur continues to identify himself with the home group in every way: the home group is interested in development according to our criteria of growth.

(a) The entrepreneur bases his organization upon traditional modes, though of course he and the community amend these insofar as they perceive change to be necessary to their objectives. The entrepreneur obtains his factors of production in the framework of established patterns of ownership, and through the convergence of interest of his kinsfolk, who supply materials, labor, and funds in accordance with traditional relationships. The factors are combined and the product marketed under the entrepreneur's direction. Occasionally there are specific rewards, such as the payment of a wage rate; but, in Oceania at any rate, the rewards are not usually completely specific, but are regulated more with reference to the increased returns which kinsfolk render as an aspect of their reciprocal obligations. I shall refer to this point later in the essay, as it is essential to our understanding of the entrepreneur's organization. Through these means the entrepreneur contributes to the increased level of living of the group associated with him, and hence satisfies some of their wants as well as his own.

(b) The community may be organized specifically in a joint venture, such as a cooperative, or a local authority with responsibility for and interest in commercial development. In such a case the entrepreneur is the leader or the responsible head of the organization and not an individual operating on private account. The distinction may be merely formal and legal, because it is sometimes difficult to determine whether operations under heading (a), which the European often regards as a kind of emasculated private enterprise, are not in fact cooperative in spirit.

(c) The entrepreneur acts as head of a small unit comprising his own biological family, or at most an extended family consisting of the biological families of himself and his siblings. The unit is repeated within the group, each unit striving for expanded operations, thus giving a dynamic character to the group.

4. The man who leads in the administration of resources continues to identify himself with his home group as in 3. But the group has simple and static cash needs; thus there is no incentive for expansion, and the leader simply sees to it that current levels of consumption are more or less maintained. Since by definition we are not interested in such people as entrepreneurs unless they are aiming at expansion, this case falls outside our present scope, important though the anthropologist considers it in the general analysis of peasant societies.

III

A number of factors are likely to stimulate the emergence of entrepreneurs of the types I have listed. We may consider them under the rough working heads of (a) commercial conditions and institutions, (b) technical conditions, (c) potential fields of leadership in general, and (d) the cultural environment of potential leaders. No doubt other headings and arrangements could be arrived at readily, but these seem to be the most suitable for the points I wish to make.

In this paper it is unnecessary to attempt a thoroughgoing economic analysis of commercial conditions and their influence on the emergence of entrepreneurs. It is, however, relevant to point out that many if not most of the underdeveloped regions of the world are marginal in a number of senses. They are marginal in the economists' sense in that a given increment of effort or capital is likely in such areas to result in very small yields in comparison with the application of similar increments in other areas. Where this rule does not apply, the effective units of capital and management have generally been most readily available when foreign entrepreneurs have controlled them, and the type of enterprise which can most readily produce for the given markets has been outside the technical knowledge of the indigenous groups. Anthropologists have been using the word "marginal" in a sense which takes in something of this last point. Underdeveloped areas are marginal in that they are off the beaten track. They are far from highly developed markets geographically, because of the arrangement of world communications, and in organization, because they do not possess market contacts. Their peoples are similarly isolated in spirit; their thought does not embrace the philosophical, political, and commercial speculations of the capitalist world.

We should not overdraw such a picture. In all such communities there is some enterprise.[3] There is much indigenous production, both in agriculture and in limited handicrafts, and there is a great deal of trade, though not necessarily through impersonal markets. There is also speculation and a willingness to learn about the thoughts and behavior of peoples who are not quite so marginal. But all in all one should not be surprised that the emergence of entrepreneurs is relatively slow when commercial conditions have this character. Where indigenous peoples feel that it is in their capacity to produce for a market that is within their reach, without domination or double-dealing by outsiders, and with every step of the process reasonably well delineated, it is seldom that they do not take up the opportunity.

Of course, such emergence may only be temporary. The Maori of parts of New Zealand once held a virtual monopoly of the supply of fresh food and wheat to the growing colonial townships, and operated their own mills and fleets of vessels in the trade. After some years the enterprises dwindled and disappeared, and the descendants of those enterprising people have had in recent years to start once again from scratch. One reasonable hypothesis would be that as Europeans immigrated in increasing numbers they began to compete with the Maori, gradually forcing them out of the trade, and that the Maori found that the new conditions of competition injected an insecurity into the situation which they were not prepared to combat. Such is not a complete explanation or a necessary response to changing commercial conditions, but there are similar instances from other parts of the world.

All theories of economic development, by definition, must provide an analysis of the commercial conditions necessary for the emergence of an increasing number of entrepreneurs (at various levels of responsibility). It would be beyond my competence and take me beyond my field to try to summarize them. But abstract and mechanical models of economic development, though valuable and necessary steps in the construction of adequate theories, often fail because the apparently universal assumptions do not apply to particular societies or to particular stages in their development. Many anthropologists would also argue that they must fail simply because they are mechanical and oversimplified, but this is not a point of view I wish to stress. Duesenberry's article on the theory of economic development, published in this journal in December 1950, illustrates the limitations of some apparently universal assumptions.[4]

Duesenberry makes the point that in backward countries elementary labor saving devices, requiring very little capital, are not used, because there is so much labor available relatively to land that there is no need to conserve labor. This may be a valid description of conditions in a country such as India, at least as a first approximation. But ultimately it is not very helpful because it does not take into account other variables which might be present. On the one hand, under such conditions of overfull employment of one factor of production, *any* increase in the application of any other factors is likely to have highly disturbing consequences.[5] Duesenberry's own remedy of combining minimum capital and maximum labor on public works, and siphoning off increasing purchasing power by means of taxation, will be disturbing, because *any* economic growth must result in increased pressure on the land, and this, on the assumptions of the model, cannot be borne.

On the other hand, this land/labor ratio does not apply in large numbers of backward countries where technical conservatism seems to operate. In New Guinea, for example, there are vast areas of land which the Papuans have at their disposal to use more intensively. It is only recently that technical innovations have occurred, leading to the emergence of entrepreneurs as I have defined them; and the acceptance of such innovations is by no means widespread even yet. My conclusion from this is obvious. There are other factors influencing technical conservatism apart from the land/labor ratio; hence the attempt to introduce a dynamic element into a static society by means of a mechanistic injection of a "multiplier" factor, selected on the above assumption, will not necessarily provide the answer.

To put the matter more concretely, few anthropologists would agree that the creation of significant public works by combining minimum capital with maximum labor, siphoning off purchasing power through taxation (because the private sector cannot provide goods to purchase) would of itself create a dynamic society out of a static one. They would rather suggest that the question was bound up with (a) securing an expanding demand for goods and services, culturally determined and (b) ensuring a supply of technical innovations which the entrepreneurs of the private sector recognized as being more efficient in terms of achieving their own, culturally determined, objectives. Similarly, although it may be true that there is no unemployed land, it does not follow that the land could not be turned to more productive uses, were the people persuaded of the feasibility of this.

That control over appropriate techniques is a factor essential to the successful emergence of the entrepreneur is sufficiently obvious. Indeed, it is so obvious that it is in considerable danger of becoming overemphasized in official programs, at the expense of economic and sociological factors. The overemphasis comes from two sources. Westerners, however aware they may be of the importance of economic and sociological conditions, either find the techniques of control beyond their means (as, for instance, when the achievement of satisfactory economic conditions is an international question, or when sociological conditions impinge upon religious ideas), or else lack the training and ability to deduce definite propositions from the mass of economic and sociological data available to them. Westerners turn much more readily to technological analysis, even applying technological routines to situations which are not always suitable.

And on the other hand the representatives of underdeveloped countries often fall into a similar error. As Toynbee has pointed out, it is easier to understand and accept a technological process, while rejecting or being suspicious of alien economic or cultural institutions. I do not agree with Toynbee that this is a universal phenomenon—there are innumerable cases of peasantries which have accepted institutions or ideas, but have resisted technological change. But I think it is true to say that governing classes in underdeveloped countries often fall into the Toynbee pattern. This is particularly so when, as in Indonesia, a vigorous nationalism, associated with a strong religious movement, asserts its cultural identity as against the values and institutions of the technologically oriented West. Here again, the demand is for techniques, not wider culture. At this point, the position is probably justified, for if the people command the techniques they may be able to devise their own institutions to fit their culture. But sometimes it implies a refusal to analyze their own institutions, and a rejection of thinking out the implications of changing them.

The increasing awareness of the importance of technique and of technological training still needs continual reappraisal. United Nations and other agencies still seem to be "discovering" that it is often inappropriate to talk of advanced techniques, even in medicine, when the people concerned do not have the educational background or capital resources to enable them to obtain, maintain, and use the suggested equipment. The most valuable technical expert is usually the man with a sound theoretical training, and sufficient practical ability to be able to leave all his gadgets behind him and start working out the remedies in the villages with his brain, his bare hands, the enthusiasm of the people, and the resources on the spot or near at hand. Such techniques are likely to be taught and transmitted easily from villager to villager, they may obviate delays and indebtedness, and, as Duesenberry had indicated, may provide an initial impetus which enables future capital savings, and sets the community on a dynamic path. The point here is that an entrepreneur needs technical knowledge, but this, at an early stage, is more valuable if it is inventive rather than merely the application of taught alien methods.

By contrast, indigenous entrepreneurs often run into difficulties because they lack some type of technique which the educational system does not provide. In many colonial countries the educational emphasis has been upon classical, clerical, theological, legal, medical and handicraft work; re-emphasis upon commercial trades has been relatively recent, and there are still many resistances to the teaching of skilled crafts.[6] Although such crafts may be more important to artisans than to entrepreneurs, without them the numerous small workshops which form a backbone to any well developed middle class cannot exist. However backward technical training has been, commercial training has been even less developed. For instance, in Oceania there are several colonies where stenography and accounting are occupations reserved to Europeans. In New Guinea the Co-operative Registry has recently initiated the first elementary training schools for bookkeeping. It is false to blame the lack of such techniques upon lack of awareness on the part of the entrepreneur, or upon sociological factors which make him improvident and unreceptive to accounting. Reciprocal obligations are an important aspect of every primitive and peasant society, and in by far the majority of cases such societies have developed techniques for keeping accounts (in memory if not on paper) of these transactions. Such methods are inappropriate to modern commerce, and it is an important function of the educational system to teach new ones. And if such elementary procedures are lacking, how can we expect entrepreneurs to emerge in situations where they find it necessary to contact the banking system, or write commercial letters around the world?

It is necessary to bear in mind that entrepreneurial behavior as I have defined it is only one among many possibilities for leadership in underdeveloped communities; that leadership roles are in some sense competitive. In one Melanesian group I studied, I found that the successful business leader was often similarly successful in ceremonial pursuits. He had the wealth and the interest to take the initiative in ceremonial exchange. There also existed a different type of business leader, who was not interested in ceremonial, and who recognized it only when it was necessary to his purposes. In another Melanesian group, this time even more subject to Western influences, I found that for mainly historical reasons the people were almost entirely dependent upon wage-earning for their cash needs. Their independent initiative went almost entirely into ceremonial, which attained a high degree of complexity and used many sophisticated techniques, for instance of accounting. The people were technically competent to become skilled entrepreneurs, but they had more security as wage-earners. Their subordinate position did not strike them as involving a lack of independent creativeness because ceremonial provided an entrepreneurial-style outlet.

Entrepreneurial development may be retarded by another kind of competition. Business enterprise is often concentrated in alien hands in the early stages of Western commercial impact. Chinese middlemen in Melanesia and Indonesia, Indians in East and Southern Africa, Europeans in most colonial territories, gather the threads of commerce into their own hands, largely as a result of superior overseas contacts and because their very migration may be traced to their initial desire to make money. The more entrenched they become, the more difficult it is for the indigenous people to break into these fields of enterprise. It becomes increasingly difficult for them to keep abreast of new techniques. Further, the role of entrepreneur becomes institutionalized as belonging to aliens; the indigenous group finds it unnecessary to initiate because the function is already performed by others. And the social stigma that attaches to impersonal commercial operations becomes reinforced as the commercial group is identified as alien, making it even more unlikely that a self-respecting native will behave in similar ways.

In considering the movement and resistances of so-called primitive societies under the influence of industrial society, a number of writers have made use of the psycho-anthropological term "basic personality structure." The concept has its important uses: it is in fact a shorthand signifying that, as a result of cultural, biological, and ecological factors, there is produced, particularly in small-scale societies, a set of values, norms of behavior and institutions; and that personality characteristics are typically congenial to these and derived from them. Modal reactions can be abstracted as representing a basic personality which underlies and reflects normal behavior. The concept, when properly handled, does not deny the possibility of aberrent and nonconformist behavior or of social change.

Nevertheless the concept does tend to focus attention on modal behavior, and overconcentration on modal behavior tends to distort the role of personality in situations of change. This kind of argument is sometimes presented: that there is a basic personality type in a primitive society; that the forces of change must deal with these personalities; but the personalities are resistant to change, and hence change must fail or at least run into very serious obstacles.[7] Up to a point the argument can be valid. But even where the basic personality is not receptive to change the number of people who vary slightly or greatly from the basic type may be considerable or they may exert an influence on behalf of change that would make them, for instance, the real spear-head of entrepreneurial endeavor. Further, the ranks of adults are continually being renewed by recruitment from below; young people may have new ideas and represent altered emphases in the emerging basic personality structure. Those who have developed the concept would recognize these points; some who have followed have not always done so.

The upshot is that when we characterize societies as being customary or static, and write social accounts in these terms, we are writing only relatively, or else misrepresenting the facts.[8] All societies change, however slowly, and this implies some difference and originality in the point of view of initiators. The rapidity with which society is prepared to change is a variable that Rostow has brought into economic analysis with the phrase "propensity to innovate."[9] Responsibility for this propensity may well lie in the hands of people who are not representative of the society's basic personalities—who indeed, as in the case of the Jews at certain periods of history, may be regarded by society as obnoxious subgroups.

It may well be that the question of personality enters into the problem at a slightly different level; namely, in given circumstances, the successful entrepreneur may show significant personality characteristics, and any given social system will require certain personality characteristics of its entrepreneurs before they can be effective. So that the investigation of the personalities of entrepreneurs is certainly worth-while. But from the point of view of setting the problem firmly in its social and cultural setting it is perhaps best to operate with concepts such as "cultural pattern" or "the structure of action and value system," which, however vague they may be, at least focus attention on significant variables rather than probably insignificant uniformities.

Various stimuli have prompted the emergence of entrepreneurs in Oceania. Among the earliest examples were some of the laborers who were forcibly recruited in the New Hebrides and Solomon Islands for work on the plantations of colonial Queensland during the nineteenth century. At the turn of the century, those who remained alive were returned to the islands, sometimes to their own groups, sometimes to alien ones. On their return to the islands they brought with them new values. They introduced new food habits. In their search for social prestige they supported the introduction of Christianity, and accepted roles in the Church. Many of them set up small stores, and pioneered the native ownership of peasant cash crops and cattle herds. Today, this generation has almost died out; but ten years ago it was still possible to pick out returned Queensland laborers by their entrepreneurial behavior, and the values they expressed in conversation, despite the fact that their childhood had been completely traditional.

A similar state of affairs occurs in respect of Melanesians who have been brought up as children in European households. I have in mind, for example, a man who is now a policeman in the Solomon Islands, who had been brought up in a European family, and who had gone to primary school for a few years in Sydney; and another in New Guinea who was brought up in the family of a white school teacher, who had a lengthy schooling in Australia, and who returned to his home village as a teacher. In both cases the individuals concerned are markedly innovators, who are intent upon leading (though in different styles), and who retain many Melanesian values along with the new ones they have learned.

Such stimulation towards new activity on the basis of a selection and amalgamation of new values received considerable impetus from the impact of the war which directly influenced almost every Oceanic community. Western values and organization were dramatically revealed, and entrepreneurs obtained followings. Sometimes they felt that they had a social as well as a commercial mission; sometimes they organized relatives into small individual enterprises; sometimes they led confused religious cults with strong materialistic objectives.[10]

IV

I now wish to pay some attention to the forms of business leadership and to the kinds of organizations that non-Western entrepreneurs direct. In this discussion it is advisable to stress the point of view that entrepreneurs are leaders, and that it is necessary for them to direct the behavior of groups in much the same way as political, religious, or even recreational leaders. The attention that modern business executives now pay to such matters as the "technique" of handling board meetings and of training lower rank supervisors in matters of personnel relations is evidence of a growing realization of the point.

It would be a grave mistake to think that successful business leaders of Melanesian groups, even in the culture contact situation, would find it useful to behave in the same way as Western firm managers to achieve their objectives. In the first place, the objectives themselves would not be the same—particularly, though not solely, in the case of labor.

The researches of Lippitt and White and others have suggested that, in unstructured groups of Western origin, the most effective leadership is of a "democratic" kind. Thus, for instance, it has been shown in an experimental situation that children who wished to lead groups of hitherto unknown playfellows were most successful in doing so after they had observed the play values of the group, had gained the confidence of its members by demonstrating ability to lead towards the same objectives: only then, after this confidence had introduced an element of structure into the situation, acting to modify the play values and behavior towards new ends. Would-be "autocratic" leaders, who wished to dominate play from the outset, met with strong resistance and simply caused friction until they had learned their lesson. The principle is basic to leadership.[11] It is the corollary of the principle that individuals joining new groups, such as Officers' Messes, rapidly conform to the canons of behavior, and largely conform to the expressed values, of the group they enter.

But a completely unstructured group is rare to find, and every element of structure implies that there is a modification of the type of leadership that is most successful. The "democratic-autocratic" pattern is a simplified model, to which other variables must be added in other situations. In all cases there is a cultural heritage of the group that sets its values, and which may be institutionalized—that is, have a strong functioning relationship with other aspects of culture and hence a tendency to continue as custom or habit—or internalized—that is, be so deeply entrenched in individual personalities that there are deep unconscious resistances to change. Perhaps at a less extreme level there is the "past history of decisions" (to use Bishop's phrase) which influences the current pattern of behavior in a firm, even as to the possibility of making new ones. And then, once an entrepreneur or leader has gained acceptance by democratic methods, the very fact of his acceptance enables him to lean more towards structured or autocratic devices.

Awareness of the intimate relationship between leadership and the structure of social organization and values leads us to examine a number of propositions that have been put forward on this subject. Barnett, for instance, in his recent examination of innovation,[12] has set forth as statements of fact (a) that dependence upon authority negates innovation and hence cultural change, and (b) that the competition of rivals is highly conducive to innovation. Both these propositions seem to be founded in current American folklore rather than in the structural analysis of varying social situations. The authoritarian structure of dictatorships by no means implies ossification for, in many modern instances, dictatorships have included scientific research and social change as part of their ethos and organization. Whatever else it was, the act of liquidating kulaks was innovation. The history of underdeveloped societies under the impact of industrial powers offers many instances of the way in which socially stratified societies as in Polynesia and East Africa succeeded in changing their beliefs and behavior much more quickly and completely than did other unstratified societies in comparable circumstances.[13] Leadership was more effective and centralized than in, say, Melanesia, and if the chief and his entourage decided it was more politic, rewarding, or personally satisfying to adopt Christianity or to market the cash crops of the common people, then the appropriate changes quite frequently resulted. If they did not, this was because of the limitations of authority rather than "undue dependence" upon authority.

Similarly, it is not necessary to consider the competition of rivals to be an innovative factor, in Barnett's sense, though it does involve enterprise, as I am using it in this essay. For competition may be a socially standardized practice, or may be limited to well-worn traditional forms; it is solely the administration of resources in a society which has "do more than thy neighbor" as part of its ethos.

A question allied to those put by Barnett is the role of the innovative entrepreneur in a perfectly integrated society. Moore holds that "To the degree that a particular society approximates the model of perfect integration, the established and normatively sanctioned patterns" (which I here call social structure) "are internally consistent and self-perpetuating. It follows that an innovation in the organization of production and the means of gaining a livelihood will initially encounter resistance approximately proportional to the integration of the established structure."[14] The confusion arises here because of three possible uses of the word "integration." In the first place, it may correspond to what I have elsewhere called "social equilibrium."[15] That is, the forces within society, including values, environmental pressures, and optimum economy (given knowledge and resources) are in balance, and *ipso facto* there is no tendency to change. This I think is Moore's meaning.

But "internally consistent and self-perpetuating" may have a different implication. It may imply that tensions as between individuals and groups within the society are so minimal that they do not result in conflicting behavior. Society is perfectly united. This definition postulates *within itself* nothing about social change, except insofar as it removes *one* possible source of change—conflict between individuals. But one can conceive of societies united on the very issue of change—this indeed is the assumption that lies behind schemes of "community development." And it is also legitimate to describe these as "integrated," in a third sense.

Such a possibility points up a role of the entrepreneur that ought not to be overlooked. It is easiest for Westerners to regard the entrepreneur as an individual operating on behalf of a privately owned firm. But he also has a role as a community leader, and may be found at the head, or even in the middle ranks, of socialized enterprises. In underdeveloped areas he may be the manager or committee member of a cooperative, or the energetic leader of a native local authority. Public service may be as important an objective in his make-up as private gain. Those of us who have been brought up on the notion that Western advances have been based upon the tremendous opportunities for private profit that existed in the nineteenth century may tend to overlook the fact that in Oceania or Africa many leaders of initiative are motivated by their concern to raise the level of living of their own people, and to provide a more promising future for their children and grandchildren.

So far I have argued that the behavior of the entrepreneur will be conditioned by the social structure in which he lives. This is always true: but, of course, as Toynbee has demonstrated, the consequences of change are not always foreseen.[16] Thus a change once initiated may result in quite unexpected breakdowns in the social structure; the entrepreneur may find himself operating in an atmosphere of greater freedom than he expected; and eventually he may help to create a totally different kind of social structure. One of the clearest cases of this has been described by Hawthorn.[17] He shows that the technical demands of dairying, which the Maori adopted from general New Zealand practice, involve patterns of work, reward, and authority that are quite foreign to traditional culture. According to report, change has proceeded much further than was the case when Hawthorn made his observations: it may well be that the new social and geographical mobility owes its origin to the demands and possibilities of dairying, as well as to other factors.

The entrepreneur operates with and in relation to sets of values which have two main fields of significance—as determining objectives, and as governing the type of organization he can use. The first point is sufficiently obvious,[18] though I will need to refer to it again at length in the next section. The second point is too often ignored and needs fuller treatment.

There are very few published studies of the internal structure of enterprise in noncapitalist countries; but the mounting evidence leads us to expect considerable variations (within the criteria of financial and productive efficiency) from the known patterns of Western firms; and we know that the early history of Western enterprise made use of organizations which differed considerably from those we know today. In the main, these differences can be related to the relevant social structures, and in some instances to technological advances which have made technical requirements more easily adaptable to the requirements of society.

Thus, for Japan, Allen writes that "The internal organization itself of the great business houses is infused with a spirit peculiar to Japan; for it shows marked traces of both the Japanese family system, with its widely ramifying claims and loyalties, and also the emotional dispositions associated with the lords and their retainers under the old regime." Uyeda has shown that the industrial changes had less disastrous results than was at one time feared because electricity as power made fewer demands on organization than did steam. Moore has characterized the Japanese organization, based on traditional forms, as being wasteful in many respects. This may be true in a sense, but it may well be an unnecessary value judgment, because the kinship consumption patterns are an essential part of production motivation; it does indicate, however, substantial differences in approach. Similarly, Fitzgerald has briefly referred to the ways in which Chinese banking operated through a kinship system.[19]

I mention these cases of relatively advanced enterprise in this paper because it seems necessary to demonstrate that success in commerce and production need not necessarily be based on Western precepts of organization. Indeed, in some cases it might well be argued that the failure of entrepreneurs to develop successful organizations might in many instances be traced to contempt or ignorance of local institutions which would have supported them and served their ends, at least in the early stages of development. This is notably the case where wage-earning offers an easy alternative to enterprise, involving fewer questions of administration and insecurity. Kathleen Gough, for instance, documents the social disorganization which has accompanied the adoption of wage laboring in Malabar. There have been considerable migrations to towns and estates, and an increase in social and geographical mobility. Kathleen Gough relates this to "the accumulation of capital and the progressive development of a machine technology, entailing urbanization, occupational specialization by individuals, and a market economy."[20] My point is that these are not *necessary* connections. The example of other parts of India and of Japan shows that, conceptually, the accumulated capital might have been spread through the provision of electric power and different styles of machinery, and that the lineage principle could have been supported and amended by a different organization of enterprise, thus permitting local initiative to develop. This might be unrealistic in Malabar for reasons other than those stated.

Similarly, in Fiji, until recently the Administration has supported a policy of developing individual peasant farming among Fijians. Fijian social structure is highly corporative, with a strong sense of local unity. It is now generally recognized that the policy of developing individualists by this direct method has been a failure. The alternative of encouraging enterprise on behalf of communities also has its difficulties because of the entrenched position of chiefs, but it may offer more realistic possibilities.

Even where the community as a whole does not become incorporated into a cooperative or firm, traditional ramifications of social structure are important. Tobin has shown that paramount chiefs and lineage heads in the Marshall Islands have important entrepreneurial functions, receiving shares of copra sales in return for administrative services. My own researches in New Guinea have revealed examples of individuals who depended entirely upon the support of lineage members for the supply of cash capital, for labor, and for specialist services such as marketing.[21] Indeed, in many cases the entrepreneurs found their incentives precisely in this sense of association with and leadership of a kinship group and in ceremonial obligations that accompanied it. The traditional values could now be satisfied through the use of cash and production to obtain cash; if this had not been the case, the entrepreneurs would not have been interested in organizing production.

V

It is not always easy to assess the success of an enterprise or its contribution to economic development, for a mixture of practical and conceptual reasons.

Lamb has drawn attention to the way in which Western entrepreneurs, particularly in small communities, are guided by a complex of motives, including an interest in placing their families in a leading position in an expanding community.[22] There are of course many subtle variations on this theme, and although it is certainly valid, nevertheless it is usually still possible to consider the maximization of profit as a means toward such ends. This is not always true, or at least it is often hidden in the data, for other societies.

Profit, even if its definition were agreed upon by economists and accountants, and even in the case of a non-Western entrepreneur who has its maximization as an objective, is often difficult to use as a criterion of individual achievement. The relevance of a rate of profit may vary considerably with the size and nature of the enterprise. The state of accounts usually permits only a rough appreciation of the position. This has two aspects. A field investigator or a statistical branch may be seriously handicapped because the entrepreneur does not have accounting techniques, or because the categories of accounting are meaningless to him. Or in the day to day administration of his affairs his domestic and his business expenses may be indistinguishable. Are the expenses of a family food supply to be included as business expenses? Many entrepreneurs in Oceania, and even among Indian fisherman of the northwest coast of America, would answer "Yes." All their monetary transactions are a part of their business administration. Similarly, they may regard the entertainment of relatives and guests as operating expenses, or even capital investment, for those relatives and guests may produce raw materials, labor, and cash as they are required. Westerners are apt to regard lavish hospitality or gifts to relatives as wasteful; such a judgment should not be made without very careful analysis of what the entrepreneur obtains in return.

Sol Tax has described a situation in two types of Middle American community—the larger towns which have material wealth but few religious ceremonies and the smaller towns which have little material wealth but considerable proliferation of religious fiesta ceremonial. He characterizes the first as rich and the second as poor.[23] Such usage is justified by custom. But one is inclined to press further and ask (a) whether the profit motive would be a sufficient criterion for establishing the success of an entrepreneur in the smaller towns, and (b) whether we are justified in drawing a distinction between rich and poor in these terms. One would, I think, need to know whether the people of the smaller towns *regarded themselves* as worse off than their materially minded neighbors, and whether their income was in truth lower or merely used to achieve different satisfactions. It is certainly the case that many entrepreneurs in Oceania obtain their wealth, not for purposes of personal material consumption, but for ceremonial lavishness of a semitraditional kind: this, not the accumulation of goods, is their objective for making money.

An allied criterion, which bypasses some of the accounting and motivational difficulties, is the rate of expansion of the enterprise, which may be related to the rate of reinvestment in it. (I have already used the criterion of expansion to define enterprise in this essay.) Expansion may be observable, in general terms, even when the rate of profit is obscured. We can assume that an enterprise which expands steadily without drawing upon capital reserves is making a good profit on turnover.

Another criterion of success is to review the entrepreneur's own objectives and to judge whether or not the enterprise is meeting them. A field observer must bear in mind the point I have continually tried to emphasize in this essay, that the objectives are likely to be so widely different from our own that they have to be searched for and recorded, not assumed. It is just as likely that the objective will be the disbursement and distribution of proceeds, rather than its accumulation in the hands of formal "owners" of the enterprise.

There is a wider criterion which may be useful on some occasions; this is the degree to which the social and financial costs of the undertaking contribute to the general and financial well-being, either of the participating group, or of the neighborhood society of which it is a part, or of the political unit—state or colony. In bringing facts to bear on this criterion, it is necessary to place the activity of the entrepreneur in an extremely wide and full cultural and institutional framework, in order that credit and debit may be assigned in the "ledger" of social accounting. It is also necessary to bear in mind that this aspect of social economics cannot be described by means of quantification alone, but that it is quite necessary to take into consideration many other factors of a qualitative kind.[24] There is no adequate arithmetical answer to the question: how successful, from the point of view of society, is an entrepreneur?[25]

The Small Industrialist in Japan

JOHN PELZEL

THIS BRIEF PAPER[1] should not be taken as an attempt to characterize the Japanese entrepreneurial group as a whole. Its scope is more limited, being confined to the presentation of a case study of a group of small metal manufacturers whose industry dominates an industrial town suburban to Tokyo. Before considering this case, however, it may be useful to remind the reader of certain background features of Japanese economic history and of the process of industrialization in that country.

It will be remembered that the legal class system which endured in Japan until 1872 defined hereditary class status in terms of broad occupational categories—the military-political elite, the small farmer, the industrial artisan, the merchant, and certain lower professional groups. An hierarchical relationship among statuses, to which individuals were assigned ascriptively, and with differential powers, rewards, and prestige to match, was characteristic of this system. It is sometimes a little difficult to see how people raised to it could have taken on even the productive aspects of modern Western culture with such ease. One must assume an overriding sense of community, akin to our nationalism, among the Japanese, and a rational realization of both the threats and the opportunities of the industrial West. One must also suppose that the habit of hierarchy invested the leading elements with an authority that translated their rational estimate of the situation into effective modernization, participated in by the masses of the people. I have no quarrel with this view, which seems to me the correct one. There

This article is reprinted, by permission of the author, from *Explorations in Entrepreneurial History,* 7:79–93 (December 1954).

are other elements, however, that must be incorporated into this explanation.

A fundamental emphasis of the Japanese system was a thoroughly organic conception of society. As the predominant view of human relations, this goes back deep into Japanese history, and was given ideological expression in the Shinto *représentations collectives,* in various Buddhist doctrines, in Tokugawa Confucianism, and in modern nationalism. It also obtained practical expression, in spite of frequent fierce contentions for leadership of the community, in the Court, in the class system, Shogunal controls and unified fiefs of the Tokugawa period and, during the modern era, in the oligarchic nation-state.

On this view the important thing is the functioning unity of political society. In the context of the whole, there is an honor about each legitimate social status and no class has more or less value than any other. Tokugawa ideology, following Confucianism, classified the political elite, farmers, and artisans as the legitimate society. When, after Meiji, competent authority redefined all occupational statuses, with minor exceptions, as valuable, samurai and farmers could flock to the artisan and merchant roles with no such *arrière-pensées* about the intrinsic disrepute of these callings as, for example, characterized the Chinese reaction prior to 1949.

Hierarchy and differential privileges were pronounced features of this society. I should be the last to maintain that the value of hierarchy was here merely the value of its function in performing society's work. Hierarchy, *qua* hierarchy, was and still is strongly evaluated by Japanese. Leaders enjoy their perquisites, and moreover have been keenly aware of the need to monopolize force; they have ruled as lions, not as foxes. Followers have on the whole accepted their position and could even rationalize hierarchical might as right. Equally, however, hierarchy was not merely a matter of differences in privilege and force among individuals or families.

The idea has been pervasive that hierarchy is a matter of rank among social statuses which individuals or families only happen to occupy, and the most important privilege is possession of a status that gives control of others through political, and not through personal or property, ties. A basic feature of the Tokugawa class system was its emphasis upon politico-military power within the territorial unit. The real class cleavage was that between the rulers and the ruled, not that among occupational groupings. The feudal aristocracy, it must also be remembered, did not own the lands of its fiefs; these were effectively in the hands of individual farm families. What the lords controlled was the political machinery and the right of taxation. It is sometimes said that the feudal system was based on personal loyalty to one's lord, but when there was mobility into and out of control positions, as in the case of hundreds of daimyo and innumerable samurai, Japanese almost universally quietly gave their loyalty to the current holder of the status. Over any short period, of course, family inheritance of both political control positions and their privileges has been pronounced, and ascription was a fundamental formal feature of the Tokugawa system. Nevertheless, this is a system of primogeniture, younger sons are typically disinherited, and families have consistently acquiesced peaceably in the loss of their perquisites when they have lost their political positions—witness the samurai of late Tokugawa who ceased to be employed, and the whole feudal aristocracy at the time of the Meiji Restoration.

It is consistent with this view of society as an organic hierarchy of statuses that all statuses are more heavily defined in terms of responsibility than they are of privilege, and that recruitment for them has been at least as much a matter of rigorous training and selection for the ability to meet these responsibilities as it has been of ascription. Ruth Benedict has emphasized the heavy load of responsibility that pertains to social roles among the Japanese and the general theme need not be elaborated here. One should only add that this burden of duty, far from falling most heavily upon subordinates, in whatever relation, is perhaps most weighty for superiors. No one in Japan was, or is today, more overworked than her entrepreneurs, government officials, and other elite groups, who in this respect resemble their American opposite numbers, though for somewhat different reasons.

With respect to recruitment, there is abundant evidence that ever since Tokugawa times at least the selection and advancement of individuals in occupational as well as in wider social roles has been very strongly influenced by the demand for achievement. It is true that the Japanese are great formalists, and the formal requirement in premodern times was for succession and enjoyment by ascription, through primogeniture, not only of general class status, but of specific group and job status as well. However, it is known that even headship of the small farm family household often did not go by primogeniture where the first son was, in his elders' opinion, disqualified; one recent study reported that the eldest son had been passed over in about a quarter of the cases. In nonhousehold industrial plants, though jobs were formally to go by inheritance, all artisans nonetheless had to pass through and succeed in an intentionally rigorous course of apprenticeship training; in the process many first sons failed and were replaced, by younger sons or by distant kinsmen or even by outsiders, the successful trainee then being adopted by the artisan he was succeeding in order to satisfy the formal ascriptive requirements. Birth, then, merely qualified one for first chance at training for a position. Training tended to be rigorous, and where the preferred applicant failed, what Marion Levy has called the "family civil service" was resorted to; moreover, it extended far below the ranks of the samurai and rich merchants. This is, I suppose, closely related to the Japanese devotion for hard and unrelenting work. It also, I believe, helps to explain the ease with which, once freed of legal restraints upon mobility, Japanese moved horizontally into the achievement-oriented world of modern industry and commerce, and vertically into the new entrepreneurial and control positions thrown open to capture.

The role of government[2] since modernization began in 1868 is of especial interest. The modern Japanese economic system, of course, has developed strongly to the ends of state power and of national —though not, as we define it—social welfare. This truth, taken alone, however, has led many Westerners to misconceptions about the nature of the relation between government and business. For one thing, state capitalism has been relatively unimportant. Government has not since the 1880's owned or operated much of the plant or, except temporarily before 1890 and again during the late 1930's, directly provided much of the investment capital. Private industry has done the job, and government's essential contribution has been to permit and encourage the mobilization of private resources of all kinds in ways that policy makers deemed desirable. Moreover, even government regulation has been exercised in only very slight degree except during the war decade of 1935–1945, and the totalitarian economy, in the Western sense, was a new and, to date, a brief development.

It would be misleading to say that, otherwise than as specified, Japan's modern economy has grown in the free capitalistic mode. On the other hand, if the Japanese conception of society outlined here is at all near the truth, deviations from this mode relate more to the premises for economic activity and do not perhaps need to be striking at the level of day-to-day operation. Government, through national policy, of course dug the channels within which it was profitable for enterprise to flow, but more by determining directions and gross measures and by providing a nutritive milieu than by direct execution of its decisions. The economy served state policy as faithfully as it did, it seems, because the Japanese shared in a remarkable consensus with the bureaucrats and oligarchs the convictions that state power and national welfare are indeed overriding goods, and that they can be attained only through unity of effort led by competent authority.

A striking characteristic of Japanese is their assumption that a whole host of evaluative opinions about the world in which they move are, so to speak, status-linked opinions; only expert opinion is worthwhile and only competent authority can have an expert opinion. Refreshing as this view of things might at times be in America, it has meant that the Japanese businessman has usually accepted the political leader's definition of the situation and has bent with a will to translating his decisions into action, often perhaps because he agreed with them, but probably often too because he accepted it as within the bureaucrat's, and not his own competence to make them. He has also kept his disappointments with government policy to himself and has done relatively little, even at the level of big business, I believe, to put pressure upon policy makers. In this environment, big business has not really been the servant of government, for each has worked with considerable independence toward a shared end. Nor has it been the full partner of government, since the definition of the end has been primarily government's responsibility.

The position of small business vis-à-vis government, however, seems clearer. Where bureaucrats have taken a direct hand in the economy they have dealt almost entirely with big business, and even government regulations binding upon the small enterpriser have been translated to him through communal organs composed of his own peers. Small business has received precious little consideration, one way or another, from the bureaucracy, and has had little direct contact with it. Within the broad limits of the kind of society that I have tried to outline, the day-to-day operations of the small businessman, at least, seem to have been conducted in the spirit of a remarkably free enterprise.

Turning from these general points to the case at issue, it ought to be remarked at the outset that, quite apart from the question of the representativeness of any case study, the one chosen here can at best stand for only one of at least two distinct classes of Japanese enterprise. A chart of Japanese industry in terms of many important criteria shows a strongly bimodal curve, with big business at one extreme and medium and small industry—small business—at the other. Big business tends to operate out of a few very large plants, and turns out the lion's share of the product of its industry. Its operations are modern, its equipment usually comparable with ours, and its personnel drawn from the group with the most advanced Western training. Its ownership is heavily concentrated in the hands of a few small groups, often organized as family holding companies, and through its private banks and the preferences it receives from quasi-official banks it controls a good part of the nation's available capital. Small business, on the other hand, comprises a multitude of quite independent firms and enterprisers—usually over 90 per cent of those in the industry nationally—employing fewer than 100 persons each, the vast majority fewer than 30. Most of the workers and most of the employers are engaged here, but small business ordinarily turns out considerably less than half the total product. Its plants operate with relatively poor capital equipment, and can attract only those personnel with the simplest and most nearly traditional training, very often drawing them directly from the farm. Its firms are almost always owned in simple form by individual owner-operators who have access only to the most meager of personal and commercial credit sources. Big business, then, is sovereign with respect both to resources and its power to influence major trends in the industry, and is a principal concern of government. Small business scurries about in an overpopulated world of cutthroat competition where it seems to have little effect upon its industry, largely disregarded by big business and government alike. And there is relatively little between the two.

In the case reported on here, only five or six of the 1000-odd plants of the community employ between 100 and 1000 workers apiece and only two of these are very minor affiliates of the national combines. Ninety-five per cent of the total plants, employing 85 per cent of all workers, have fewer than 30 employees, and are actively managed by their individual owners. This is a case study, then, of small business.

In other respects the local industry does not seem unrepresentative of Japanese development as a whole. Modern manufacturing did not get well under way until about 1890 in Japan. Up to the end of World War II, however, output rose steadily and steeply, two particularly remarkable spurts of growth occurring during the first World War and again during the 1930's. In the latter period the economy shifted sharply towards heavy industry. Throughout this growth, however, average plant size did not increase appreciably, development occurring rather in product and in the appearance of multitudes of new plants, and in the case of small business, of new enterprisers.

The growth of the industrial community reported here almost exactly duplicates that of Japan as a whole. In the 1880's the metal-working establishment numbered 16 tiny, part-time, casting shops, most dating from Tokugawa times, and producing items of daily household use—pots and skillets, in our terms—by traditional handicraft techniques. Early in the modern period these products were joined by simple industrial items like pipe and plow parts, and this complex has continued important, giving the industry before 1930 an almost total bias toward the production of a few standardized goods, simple and rough in design, manufactured by hand techniques and without much capital investment. Capital equipment consisted minimally—and a large minority of even the present-day enterprisers started with no more than this minimum—of a few master molds, everything else being rented from established plants. Even average equipment, however, consisted in addition only of a shed, a simple coke furnace, hand mold forms and rough polishing machinery. The largest plants alone had more production equipment, and even these usually lacked—and still lack today—the expensive service facilities so essential in American culture. Most factories, too, do not have the management overhead that larger size or fuller participation in a complex industrial society requires.

Starting during the first World War, however, and particularly since 1930, a steady change has come about in the character of production. Machine work grew to be much more profitable than the old product, and casting plants have become heavily involved in turning out machine and precision castings. Concurrently a new type of plant, devoted to machine manufacturing, has grown up. By the end of World War I the local industry had increased to over 200 plants, and by the end of the recent World War, to about 1000. Although the largest plants in the community were founded after 1930 and a few of the older factories grew slightly then, the local industry today shows almost exactly the same size range and percentage of plants by size category as it did before World War I.

The government, during the period of direct regulation prior to 1945, treated local establishments as belonging to two entirely distinct industries, casting and machine manufacturing, and channeled its contacts with enterprisers through two control organizations largely mutually exclusive as to membership. In its classification, about half the present metal shops are casting plants, stemming from the old industry, and the other half machine plants, both showing about the same distribution of plants by number of workers, but the machine shops using more production equipment and advanced technical skills and turning out a more valuable product.

From the point of view of enterprise, however, there seems little reason to treat the two industries as quite separate. Machine production offered a wide range of opportunities, from the designing and assembling of completed machinery, through the manufacture of complex new machine parts and work in nonferrous metals, to the production of goods that, though of new design, were simple enough to be turned out in the old-style plant. Enterprise responded to these opportunities with great adaptability and diversity. Of the many new plants that grew up between the wars, some were entirely divorced from the old industry while some devoted themselves completely to the traditional work. Old plants converted some to a greater, some to a lesser degree. Most enterprisers, however, old or new, engaged in some combination of both types of work and have remained highly convertible to this day, in good measure, it is clear, as the result of a conscious policy of diversification.

Moreover, though some new, predominantly machine-producing enterprisers came into the community and have little or no identification with the old casting industry, the leaders of the latter who converted to, entered, or invested in the new enterprise came to control a very considerable share of it, certainly the greater share if one disregards the few large, outside-owned plants. With some additions and a few subtractions, the old entrepreneurial group controlling local industry, and enjoying the highest social prestige and greatest political power in the community, managed to accommodate itself to the production change and so blend in with the new entrepreneurial group. It was only after World War II that any sharp change in the status of this persistent group began to threaten, and this change took the form, immediately, only of a challenge to its political hegemony, presented by politically-organized labor.

Nevertheless, in the process of a transition that at first sight appears to consist in little more than a diversification of production, an increase in its numbers and wealth, the local business group also suffered certain changes in its style as entrepreneurs and communal leaders. The total range of its roles grew. Certain individuals today do not act out any very wide portion of this range, it is true; some of the casters, old and new, who did not keep up with the times, form an enclave of traditionalism, while some machine manufacturers who have no connections with the older portion of the industry represent a different extreme. Probably most operators, however, span a considerable portion of the range and it is they who set the style here. I should like, in the following, to consider the older entrepreneurial role, concluding with some remarks on the changes of the last twenty years or so.

The casting enterpriser—i.e., the typical entrepreneur before the 1930's—was very much the artisan. Production, and production alone, was his job, and his reputation and view of himself were determined very largely by such qualities as superior skill in his technique, and productivity. This definition of the enterpriser's role made considerable sense in Tokugawa times. Full-time artisans were largely concentrated in the administrative castle towns or in isolated industrial establishments. In the former case they usually had the assured and hereditary patronage of the upper class and belonged to self-regulating guilds that, under government charter, strictly controlled their behavior, occupational and social. In the latter case they were dependents of a merchant capitalist or of the officer of a local feudal aristocrat. Commercial and capitalistic orientations were consciously denigrated, and were not in fact very important to the functioning of the artisan class itself, though they were vital to the merchant creditors and the samurai officials of the aristocratic employer or patron of fief enterprises. Even with the latter, of course, enterprise was not purely capitalistic, since industry served merely as one tool for the well-being of a territorial economic community, but it seems more than coincidence that the upper class, which in government and private enterprise spearheaded the post-Meiji modernization, should have been the group with most experience before Meiji in the management of industrial undertakings.

The artisan role of the pre-1930 casting enterpriser was consistent with his personal background. For one thing, most of today's casters have come from artisan or farmer families. In the case of 40 per cent, the incumbent's father was also in casting work, though only 30 per cent of the total have in fact inherited a family enterprise as well as an occupation, and a certain proportion of these are adopted, not real, sons. Another 35 per cent of all of today's casting enterprisers have come into this work and made their ways up the ladder to entrepreneurial status from farm families. Only 25 per cent of all entrepreneurs had fathers who were in commerce or other industrial occupations.[3] These proportions are, incidentally, quite close to those found for persons engaged in modern occupations generally in a recent study of the six large cities of Japan,[4] so that the phenomenon observed here can be taken as more or less typical, at least of urban conditions.

For another thing, over 60 per cent of the casters have had eight years or less of formal schooling, and fewer than 20 per cent have been exposed to higher education, either technical or in the liberal arts. Again, this situation seems likely to prove typical for Japanese enterprisers as a whole. The recent metropolitan survey, for example, revealed that a survey class which included enterprisers, managers, and government officials had somewhat less than ten years of formal education, the average for urban dwellers generally, and very little more than industrial laborers; one would expect that the official, and possibly the manager component, of this survey class had considerably more than an average education, and that the urban enterprisers consequently were not much better educated than the casters whose case is being reviewed here. It is also of interest that, among the casters, there is no correlation at all between amount of the entrepreneur's formal education and size of his enterprise. Success has been in practical terms, a conclusion which individual case studies further illustrate. The largest owner in the community, for example, a man who is also its leading politician, former Mayor and present Diet member, did not complete primary education, and came to this city penniless from a poor farm family in one of the most backward, starvation regions of Japan.

In pre- and early modern Japanese society training for almost all specialized occupational statuses was in terms of on-the-job apprenticeships. This training closely parallels that of an earlier Europe in its general character, and so does not need to be described here. What ought to be emphasized about it, however, is that apprenticeship was training for a way of life and a total social role, not alone for a limited economic role. Apprenticeship gave the artisan a new and more important family and a community in which to spend his life—that of his master's plant. The rewards and ethics of this factory-society underline the same compromise between ascriptive hierarchical values and the achievement virtues of superior skill and productivity that have already been mentioned.

In sum, the enterpriser himself was first of all defined as a workman. Owners even today, in the pictures of themselves they and their older employees emphasize, are evaluated in terms of their technical prowess. Management, they say, consists equally in fulfilling the traditional patron's role of head of a tiny territorial community and in work leadership by example. As work leader, the master cannot control his workmen if he cannot prove his superiority to them at their own or more demanding production jobs. It was moreover essential twenty-five years ago for the owner to work alongside his employees much of the time, and this is still the practice in most small (10 or fewer employees) and even many medium-sized (10 to 30 employees) plants today. This evaluation of technical skill is so pervasive that it is taken as a general criterion of leadership of any form in the factory society; it is said that even leaders of the union movement must be superior workers if they are to attract any kind of a following, and it is a fact that most of the labor leaders in these plants today do have this reputation for skill.

Certain other qualities or interests that one might think essential to the role of enterpriser, however, have not been absorbed very well. Commercial skills, for example, have continued to be depreciated, and the small artisan-enterpriser typically wants as little as possible to do with merchandising and finance. In a market and money economy, of course, he has had to suffer the consequences of this attitude, consequences that include a hand-to-mouth existence with respect to both orders and capital, and dependence upon personal relations and merchants.

Merchandising in the casting industry has been left almost entirely up to the wholesaler. Less than 10 per cent of the largest producers have direct sales outlets of any type, even today, and very few more have a brand name for their products, most wares being known in the market by the house name of a wholesaler. A producer is fortunate if he can persuade a wholesaler to give him fairly steady orders; most often he has to engage in an extreme form of competition with other producers in what is typically a wholesaler's market.

The financial situation of the caster has always been bad both for operating and for investment capital. He has found it usually hard to get more than very limited amounts of money. Banks, moreover, have been of little use to any but the tiny minority of large and established firms. There have for long been branches of the large central private banks in the community and their numbers have increased in recent years, but it is a fact that they lend little to the local industry, their main function apparently being that of mobilizing savings locally for use nationally.

Beyond his personal savings the small-and medium-sized enterpriser has usually had recourse only to relationships with capital sources that had been, or that subsequently became, extra-economic. For one thing, there is much evidence of aid by kinsmen. Successful establishments have often been built up in good part through the use of extended family resources—the family farm under an elder brother's control, for example, and a younger brother's iron-casting trade. Very much more important than kin ties, however, have been relations that were, or that grew to be, those of patron and client, in the Mediterranean sense.

The patron-client relation is a traditional and formal one in Japanese society. It is typically established between a person with power, of whatever sort, and one who needs access to that power. Teacher and student, master and artisan, political leader and follower, are only a few of the many roles it is used to relate to one another. The bond between patron and client is hierarchical, of course, but it is also ideally that of nurturant and dependent, and is diffuse, or total, in its application. A patron, for example, is expected to help his client in economic, political, personal, and a host of other matters; a client is expected, in return, to follow his protector's direction in whatever matters the patron chooses to undertake. It is significant that in the more popular forms of this relationship patron and client refer to one another as "father" and "child." Much of the work of Japan has gotten done, and still gets done, through relations of this sort.

The community reported on here is dominated by small industrialists perpetually in need of capital. The two principal immediate sources of this capital have been, and probably still are, a few of the largest industrialists and the few large wholesalers. The industrialists have helped a number of weaker enterprisers, and have in consequence been readily and gratefully accepted as patrons. The wholesalers, however, have been at least equally important as sources of capital. Raw material wholesalers supply goods on credit, and finished product wholesalers make advances against future production or purchase wares in slack seasons; both kinds of wholesaler, moreover, have made considerable capital investments in the metal plants. From the producer's point of view, merchant capital is more an evil than a good, and enterprisers are usually in private quite bitter about their dependence, but they admit that when they are hard up they usually "run to the wholesaler like a small child." And though, in contrast with the bond through credit to the large industrialist, that to the wholesaler is looked at wryly, it too leads to a powerful patron-client relationship in fact.

The immediate economic advantage of the tie for both patrons and clients has undoubtedly been great. The relation, however, allows the extension and diversification of the patron's powers and the client's opportunities beyond those with which it may have begun. For one thing, in this society the relationship has traditionally been an ideal one, and so it gives the patron more prestige and the client more security than a specific and contractual relation could provide. For another thing, an organic view of political society and a tradition that assigns highest prestige and power to the holders of political status tend to make such status the final goal for the upwardly mobile. Until perhaps the first World War, and again during the recent war period, the top status was that of the bureaucrat. Filled earlier by those of aristocratic lineage, and later increasingly from a developing upper class defined by breeding, education, and previous access to political power, such positions have at the same time been assigned and manipulated in terms of patron-client relations. When Japan enacted universal manhood suffrage thirty years ago, political parties first became fashionable, a style that lasted briefly into the early 1930's and that has reappeared since the last war. Parties also acquired considerable power during these periods at certain levels. They did not, and do not today, have much real influence in the rural countryside, where I think it is safe to say they are still considered to be among the more unpleasant excrescences of modern life. Nor were they very important at the national level during the first period they were in fashion. In the sphere of urban power relations, however, and particularly in the smaller cities, they became a convenient focus for local patterns of influence. Businessmen, from large industrialists to shopkeepers, generally considered it *de rigueur* to become politically active, and aimed through this means at both local and national bureaucratic and elective positions. In party matters too the patron-client relation has been heavily employed.

Thus, whatever the political machinery in vogue, the patron-client ties in the factory society have been vital. In them, moreover, economic and political considerations have reinforced one another. Capital-rich patrons avid of political positions have become the cynosure of smaller enterprisers, who find in the relation both economic advantage and a foothold on the political ladder for themselves. Small enterprisers, in their turn, control large numbers of clients among their workers and the citizenry. Once established, moreover, such political controls seem to produce further economic advantage. Most enterprisers contend that it is essential for their businesses that they have political affiliations, and it does appear to be a fact that every large industrialist and wholesaler who did not play politics after 1930 has gone bankrupt, or at the least lost economic leadership. This situation, I suppose, has somewhat the same causes it has had in the United States during the last generation, but the relationship between political access and economic well-being has probably been even closer in Japan. Apart from a few scandals that have appeared in the press, my data do not allow me to say that undue favoritism has been shown in the economic relations of government and business, but one would not expect them to have been influenced by party considerations between 1935 and 1945. Nevertheless, during the 1930's and the war period, of course, the government was a direct source of orders for both big business and the largest factories even within the ranks of small business, while much of the rest of small business lived on subcontract work.

In the event, the patrons upon whom small enterprisers depend for capital dominate the local political scene. It has long been the contention of the Socialists that the association of casting enterprisers is nothing more than the headquarters of the local conservative party—Mr. Yoshida's Liberals today—and no one who knows the community would deny, however one might evaluate, the charge. In this organization, moreover, the largest local industrialist, who has invested heavily in many other plants of the community, holds undisputed and open sway, ably seconded by a number of lesser industrialists. Most such patrons operate through party organizations, but the capital-providing relationship is effective for political purposes even without a party organization as is well illustrated by the case of the largest wholesaler. Though respected, this man does not seem to be overly popular. He is reputed to have active investments of some sort in over 200 plants today, and has occupied a somewhat similar position for twenty years. He was Mayor—a prestigious and powerful position in Japan—during the late 1930's and war years, when parties were moribund or prohibited. Though purged by the Occupation, and affiliated with no party, he recently decided that he would like to be Mayor again; all opposition immediately vanished and the man easily achieved his wish at the polls.

One of the more interesting features of Japanese enterprise has been the permanence of a sharp division between big and small business, and the failure of small firms to grow. Reasons for this fact, I suppose, include the already predominant position of big business, the capital and merchandising situation in which small business finds itself and which it does not really attempt to alter, the pressure of a rapidly-expanding population well trained to minimum modern economic skills but with very slight access to advanced knowledge and experience, and so on. Along with these reasons, however, many enterprisers themselves cite others.

The local entrepreneurs, even the largest ones, count their independent status an extraordinarily precious thing. Growth through partnership or stock sale, and submission to outsiders in management, has been to them a very distasteful prospect. In fact, almost no partnerships have been entered into, or lasted long, in this community. Patrons, moreover, have confined themselves to the supply of capital and to preference in orders, and only within the postwar years has one of them—the largest wholesaler and Mayor—tried openly to take over any part of the management of the plants in which he has large investments.

I do not pretend to know why independence of entrepreneurial status should be so universally evaluated when it entails a loss of the chance at bigness, or even at a real economic independence. Producers rail continually at their bondage to merchants. Bigness is very highly rewarded in Japanese culture generally—e.g., in big business and big government. Growth might even come from the exercise of the strongly cooperative ethic to which Japanese pay even more constant lip service than do we—an ethic, moreover, which is consonant with their organic view of political society.

Some of the reasons for their attachment to independence, I suggest, however, lie in the very backgrounds and artisan-farmer orientations of today's enterprisers. The traditional economic unit for persons of these classes has been the real or simulated household of father and son, or of father-figure master and his dependent workers. Larger size, moreover, could be achieved only through the use of skills that—like the commercial—are still consciously deprecated or—like those in finance and rational management—are not included in the training of the typical producer. It may be important in this connection also to recall an earlier remark about the Japanese view of competence, as status- rather than individual-linked. The sense of general social class is still strong, though informal, in Japanese life. Bigness in business, and the entrepreneurial qualities it calls for, have hitherto been monopolized by those of upper-class backgrounds (samurai in the earlier modern period; those with advanced Western training in recent decades). Most small entrepreneurs are keenly aware of the shortcomings, by contrast with this upper class, of their own backgrounds, and the tendency to keep their own station in life has, I suspect, helped to discourage many small businessmen from the attempt to move into another class world.

It also seems true that Japanese have little aptitude for cooperation among equals in what is defined as an individualistic or profit-oriented situation. They are excellent at cooperation between leader and follower, once status and power differences are clearly recognized. They are also outstanding at cooperating with equals in any form of activity directed overwhelmingly to the ends of a supra-individual, solidary, group, as in the cases of kin and territorial communities. The Tokugawa farmer, *qua* farmer, however, was a largely independent agent, and so too were most artisans. This tradition, I suggest, has remained strong. It is symptomatic of these orientations that the government first tried to guide medium and small business, in the late 1920's and early 1930's, by encouraging voluntary self-regulation of a local industry through enterpriser associations. This attempt failed miserably to attain any degree of order or concert, even in the enterpriser's struggles during the depression period with the unions. The government thereupon backed the associations by its own directives, and to this clear definition of hierarchical authority enterprisers reacted with a remarkably ready and efficient acquiescence.

One should also remember that many positive values that can drive men toward entrepreneurial bigness in the West cannot be as effective in Japan. The businessman, even the big businessman, has not been able to compete with either the intellectual elite or the government functionary as an ideal type of this culture, and for the practical man wealth and sheer economic power have not given the general communal prestige or final effective power that political position bestows. This is apparent elsewhere in Japanese society and I believe is the best single explanation for the fact that local entrepreneurs in pursuit of real prestige and power have used their economic controls as a means to the attainment of political status. Again, even the by-product of wealth, consumption power, has not been as real a lure as in the West, for conspicuous consumption by individuals has been improper in this, on the whole, ascetic culture. Thus one can cite many deterrents, as well as the lack of many positive impulsions, to business growth to add to those economic and legal restrictions that have inhibited the true Western capitalistic orientation towards bigness.

At least some suggestion of the changes that have occurred in the local enterpriser's role during the last generation ought to be put forward in the short space I have left myself.

The enterpriser has been led away from the floor of his factory and from a close identification with his workmen, in part by changes in the character of the entrepreneurial demands laid upon him after 1930. Machine production, for example, required a higher level of skill, and so more time and interest devoted to mastering complex abilities. The greater use of machines to do the work of a plant unquestionably led to a gradual devaluation of hand techniques, to the point where there is today a strong movement among even producers of the simplest traditional products to try and convert to a more mechanical form of manufacture. Most of the work during the 1930's and war years was contributory to machine manufacturing. Virtually all of this production was carried on under subcontracts from large factories, in this community or elsewhere. Subcontracting required that the enterpriser learn, and conform to, the specifications of others, and spend a great deal of time in liaison with his contractors. The need to know government regulations and to submit a flood of government reports, and work in liaison conferences dictated by government intervention, became for the first time important to the small entrepreneur, took up an enormous part of his time and energies, gave him much more sophistication in paper work and in management problems, and made him deeply dependent on a somewhat better-educated clerical and managerial staff. In consequence of these sorts of management changes, the entrepreneur was given a sense of problem and a set of concerns that led him to a divorce from his own workmen and from participation himself in the production process.

At the same time, of course, most producers were freed from any immediate concern about orders and credit. They had usually in the past shifted responsibility in these matters to others, but they had had nonetheless to worry about such problems continually. Prosperity during the years after 1930, however, made them secure in these fields. Most had more orders than they could conveniently fill, and advance payments from large contractors and from government supplied them with easy capital. Great profits were made, moreover, and these were liberally reinvested—before the end of the war in setting up new plants or adding to the capital equipment of old ones; after the war in buying the land and buildings they had usually previously rented and in repairing the rundown wartime plant. After 1948, moreover, a significant positive advance in the field of credit came about through the development, by a number of the leaders among small and medium enterprisers, of a usable lending society. In this society the average producer for the first time has secured access to a relatively impersonal source of short-term operating loans, specifically designed so as to be helpful to the local industry.

In spite of all improvements in his sales and credit situation, however, the average producer has not been fundamentally freed from dependence on the patrons of his community. With great astuteness the largest producers and wholesalers managed both to acquire and retain control of the political machinery—even more important economically between 1930 and 1945 than formerly—and to become one of the principal channels through which work for subcontract was made available in the community. Before 1945 it is my impression that these patrons had been able to gain control of a portion of the local industry that was absolutely many times what it had been previously, and relatively certainly no smaller. The position of the patrons was moreover maintained even during the postwar years, when orders were few and far between, because of their investments and continued control of potentially key positions; and apparently because no producer really believed that a prosperous and free economy, in which he could stand alone without patrons or political connections, was possible in Japan. The same patrons who for a generation have controlled most of the community's economic and political life are today, it seems to me, in as strong a position as they have ever occupied, vis-à-vis producers at any rate, and both they and most other enterprisers explicitly agree with this conclusion.

It may be of interest at the end, as at the beginning, of this paper, to suggest some of the features of contemporary industrial society and of Japanese society generally, that, after the changes of the last generation, form the context for today's entrepreneur.

The old patron-client relation among entrepreneurs has not broken down, but it has steadily changed its character with the general commercialization and modernization of Japanese society and with the local changes of the postwar years. Thirty years ago the personal, the familistic, and the sentimental aspects of this bond seem to have emphasized more than the economically functional features; the reverse is true today, and a tie that could once be rationalized as a valuable expression of social solidarity now has to be interpreted in terms of power and economic rationality. Without predicting what this change may lead to, I should like to point out that the same process has also gone far in the relations between the enterpriser and his employees, with results that clearly point to a kind of industrial society.

The tie between the artisan-enterpriser and his artisan-workmen has become attenuated as a result of the changes in the entrepreneur's role already noted. The process of separation had begun much earlier, however. The old apprenticeship system, with its correlate, the master-artisan plant community, had begun to break down during the first World War, with rapid industrial expansion and the chance for quick profits. At the same time, ideological Marxism and the union movement had come to Japan from one direction, and Western democracy, with its stress upon egalitarian relationships, had made its first deep impression from the other. The combination has led to many cross-currents and compromises. Lengthening terms of compulsory schooling, the spread of higher technical skills, increasing spatial and occupational mobility, the Depression, and a number of other factors in succeeding years dealt this system still further blows. Nevertheless, hierarchy in human relations has been progressively devalued, even where it has continued in fact to exist, and in the 1930's the otherwise often reactionary Japanese Government legally abolished the traditional apprenticeship system. Thus, the old social system of the factory had, by the late 1930's, begun to come to pieces, and to enter upon a process of replacement by a set of factory relations more nearly like our own.

In the course of these and other changes the general position of the member of industrial society, whether entrepreneur or worker, has risen, at least temporarily, and especially in the post-war period. This period has seen the bureaucracy sharply deflated, and so has provided an empty spot into which the entrepreneur could rise. Political parties have taken over many of the former functions of officialdom, and in the parties businessmen have long experience and strong controls. Moreover, the accumulated strength of egalitarianism and what I believe is a more nearly equal distribution of income have seriously undermined the old sense of hierarchy and specifically the self-depreciation in which persons of lower status held themselves. Keeping one's place in terms of even an implicit general class system is no longer so important. A remarkable piece of evidence on this point is the universal respect, amounting to adulation, with which what is known as "culture" is pursued. Local businessmen have opened their tills to the tune of hundreds of millions to build schools, to install sanitary facilities, and modern utilities and to prettify their city. Suddenly too they have freed themselves from their old, often squalid, living conditions at home, and since the war have pushed their girls into fashionable finishing schools and their boys into better liberal arts and technical universities. Presumption is the order of the day, and though this may lead to economic and political consequences of debatable value, it does to my way of thinking indicate a marked further step toward emancipation from the Tokugawa habit of mind.

This process might perhaps be summarized as follows: industrial society a generation ago consisted of an indefinite number of small groupings, each centered around a factory and bound together by tight quasi-familial ties among master and workers. Employer and employee shared a common membership and way of life, and were alike lower class in terms of an implicit general class system. Such groupings stood relatively independent of one another, finding their relationships with the wider society through the ties of the master himself and through a general devotion to the political community. In the industrial society today, however, the factory has ceased to be a community of interest or action save on economic matters, and here the times tend to define the ends of employer and employee as fundamentally antagonistic. Management, the opening of the political arena to the businessman, and the loosening of general class divisions pull the enterpriser away from the worker into an expanding upper class. The worker, for his part, leads a life that is newly distinct from that of his employer and is tempted into new organizations, the union and the labor party, consciously contending with the upper class for leadership of the political community. The emergent differences between employer and employee are defined as symbolic of the existence of two new classes—"Capitalist" and "Worker"—seen to stem from a power differential that no on can any longer fully justify. Large numbers on both sides of this fence view the separation and the definition of the separation with enormous distaste, but in the country as a whole both sides are powerfully organized and their contention is the most important single fact of the political climate today. It seems to me however that neither side is really willing to abandon the organic conception of political society, so that no matter what the outcome of the struggle may be the prospect for an economic milieu even moderately individualistic by our ideal standards is quite slight.

French Business and the Businessman: A Social and Cultural Analysis

DAVID S. LANDES

WHEN THE FRENCH MISSION of the European Recovery Program totted up its results at the end of the first year of operation, the discovery was made that the contribution of so many new machines plus so many tons of coal and raw materials had not added up to the sum of products anticipated. This deficiency cropped up again and again in the case of firms which had apparently had the benefit of every facility and incentive to efficient production. And yet our economists and technicians had presumably taken into account all the variables involved. What was wrong?[1]

It was soon clear that one very important element had been left out of the equation, the imponderable "human factor." The whole thing simply boiled down to this: given the same machines and the same funds as an American, the French businessman will not use them in the same way or for the same ends.[2]

The peculiarity of the French entrepreneurial pattern, this problem of aims and attitudes, is by no means new from the point of view of historiography.[3] The French have long rather felt than understood it.[4] Foreign studies of the French society and economy have sometimes been aware of the problem to the extent of a few lines, or perhaps even several pages, which usually treat more of symptoms than of the disease.[5] And of course, there is always the convenient or, in all justice, the indispensable fare-thee-well that runs roughly, "But this consideration takes us beyond the scope of the present work . . ."

This article is reprinted, by permission of the publishers, from Edward M. Earle (ed.), *Modern France: Problems of the Third and Fourth Republics* (Princeton: Princeton University Press, 1951).

leaving the reader with some uncooked and well-nigh indigestible food for thought.

This is understandable. Subjects like this are somewhat disagreeable, for they lend themselves little, if at all, to a precise, statistical approach. Yet the significance of the "human factor" is such as to outweigh considerations of congeniality. As our government's representatives have empirically discovered, the effort to study it must be made. And while I do not think that a short essay of this nature can possibly do justice to so complicated a subject, a brief analysis of the role, actual and potential, of the French entrepreneur should prove enlightening and useful, if only for heuristic purposes.[6]

I

Consider first the structure of the firm, the fundamental unit of business activity. It is widely known, to the point of being almost a truism, that the typical French business is small.[7] What is less often realized is that most businesses are family-structured in a way that has generally been associated with precapitalist economies. They are inextricably united economically in the sense that business treasury and household purse are simply one, just as national treasuries were once inseparable from the king's personal fortune. In such a firm it is standard operating procedure for each of the partners and often all the relatives who so wish to leave their disposable funds with the business, just as Americans would deposit their money in a bank. An interest of 5 or 6 per cent is generally paid on these more or less current accounts, while the "depositors" pass by the cashier whenever they need money, even though it be only petty change to cover some daily expense. Each has his account book, duly kept up with all the other records by the apparently overworked accountant. In the nineteenth century, when the franc was still a franc, it was not unusual to draw eighty centimes for postage or ten francs for food, all carefully entered in the ledger. Nowadays, of course, the wife may take ten or twenty thousand francs for her week's expenditures, but the system remains the same.[8]

Such economic unity exists because of the profound social ties of family with firm. The latter is the material basis for the prestige and status of the former, just as the domain was the material foundation of status in an earlier age. The business is not an end in itself, nor is its purpose to be found in any such independent ideal as production or service. It exists by and for the family, and the honor, the reputation, the wealth of the one are the honor, wealth, and reputation of the other.[9] The word *maison* has retained business connotations long since lost by our word "house." It is this bond that accounts for the astonishing solidarity shown by French families when the integrity or the stability of the firm is imperiled; even today, the social register or family tree is often a better credit reference than the most profitable series of annual statements.[10]

To be sure, the industrial development of the past 150 years has inevitably affected the structure of business enterprise, giving rise to large, impersonal corporations in certain sectors of the economy, notably public utilities and heavy industries like metallurgy. But even in such fields, the role of the private firm remains impressive. Thus in the steel industry, where the requirements of production encourage, indeed impose, concentrations of capital beyond the means of most family fortunes, the largest company of all, Les Petits-Fils de François de Wendel, the biggest toolmaker, Peugeot, and perhaps the leading specialist in alloy steels, Holtzer, are all family businesses. And the greatest company of machine builders and engineers, Le Creusot, despite the fact that its shares are actively traded on the exchange, remains a partnership in which the active partners have been drawn for over one hundred years exclusively from the Schneider family. The very business form of which Le Creusot is one of the outstanding examples, the *commandite par actions,* is proof of the desire to get outside capital without yielding personal and family control and responsibility.[11] It should be noted, moreover, that the nationalization of the strongest groups of corporatively organized business—the big banks, the coal mines, gas and electricity, and the railroads—has cut down considerably that portion of the sector of free enterprise that falls outside the family-type firm.[12]

In such a system, the compulsive urge toward growth inherent in business for the sake of business is either diluted or absent. The family firm, large or small, is run like a household or, more specifically, a bourgeois household. The primary concern is to live well within one's means, saving as much as possible. Translated into business terms, the main objective is to avoid use of credit and to make the highest rate of profit possible on a given turnover; to amortize expenses rapidly and build up huge reserves; and to finance expansion out of such reserves, or by what the French call *autofinancement.*[13]

The retardative effect of this emphasis on conservation and consolidation is reinforced by an all-overriding concern for family independence. The French entrepreneur is inclined, in anything, to postpone possibilities for development, simply because expansion might sooner or later compel recourse to outside capital and seriously, if not definitively, compromise the exclusive character of the enterprise.[14] For the same reason, profits are often sacrificed to an overintegration extremely harmful to efficient production—the manufacturer does not like to rely on outside help or cooperation. The system of subcontractors and suppliers that creates in American industry a sort of division of labor on the factory level is still relatively neglected in France.

There is even a tendency in some cases to turn down chances for growth outright, on the theory that the firm is earning enough and that additional profits are not worth any additional effort. This particular variation, by no means uncommon, is quite alien to the thinking of most Americans, as indicated by the standard reaction of the tourist: "But don't they want to make money?" The answer is, of course, that they do, enough to give them what they want in life. "As for making money just to make money," says the pretty *charcutière,* "and giving yourself so much trouble that you have no time for pleasure later on, good heavens, I'd rather fold my arms . . ."[15]

To be sure, the entrepreneurial pattern just described has its compensations. The French family firm, when successful, is, if I may be permitted two contrasting images, as solid as the rock precisely it is almost drowned in its own liquidity. It can hold its prices and survive all but the most severe depressions, a fact reflected by the comparative flatness of the cyclical curve of French business activity. Throughout the nineteenth century, the literature abounds in references to France's good fortune in not being subject to the acute crises that periodically swept England and the United States.

Unfortunately, the knife cuts both ways, and this excessive prudence, this overwhelming concern with security, means less initiative and dynamism on the upswing. Confronted with an expanding economy, the French producer still does not go out and find or make new markets; he waits for them to come to him. Prior to 1914, this drawback was not nearly so critical as it proved to be later. Once the World War had permanently changed France's economic problem from one of conservation and leisurely growth to one of reconstruction and replacement, this lack of dynamism became a force for retardation and strangulation. This was the more true because the simultaneous collapse of the franc, after over one hundred years of stability, was utterly demoralizing in a society whose greatest economic virtue was thrift.

II

The survival and prosperity of the family type of enterprise imply in themselves a certain relationship between this traditional sector of the economy and the sector composed of corporations. The latter, generally possessed of superior financial resources and controlled by technicians whose kinship ties and family problems are totally divorced from the management of the firm, theoretically should long since have driven many of these obsolete family units from the field and forced the others to convert to forms better adapted to the needs of modern business.

Yet such has obviously not been the case. An analysis of business concentration in France clearly reveals the coexistence within most industries of (1) a few powerful firms employing a substantial portion of the labor force, and a veritable swarm of small units often occupying well under half the total men in the field; and (2) a few modern regions characterized by bigger plants and more efficient techniques, and many more or less backward areas in which the small workshop and semiartisanal methods still hold sway. This friendly cohabitation of lion and lamb suggests that these supposedly natural enemies have somehow found a remarkable *modus vivendi,* or—to put it into economic terms—that the time-honored mechanism of competition has been less than effective in France.[16]

The explanation of this *modus vivendi* must be sought in a combination of several factors. To begin with, the nature of the market accessible to the French producer is in many respects decidedly encouraging to small enterprise, and consequently limits severely the extent to which big business can throw its weight around. This market has always been relatively restricted to the home population, a population that to all intents and purposes has remained static for the past one hundred years. French businessmen are quick to remind critics that much of America's rapid economic development simply reflects the demands of a rapidly growing mass of consumers.[17] There is certainly justice in the argument, but even more important in the case is the pattern of consumption of the forty million people the French entrepreneur must satisfy.

In the first place, at least two important sections of the French population are not in a position to buy anything more than the barest essentials: (1) the vast majority of workers—industrial, commercial, and agricultural—who earn less than $40 a month in base pay[18]; and (2) those self-supporting farmers whose small plots provide little surplus to exchange for manufactured goods.[19] In other words, those people who would unquestionably provide the best market for cheap, well made standardized articles, are largely unable to buy them.[20]

In the second place, the average Frenchman buys far less in proportion to his means than his American counterpart. Quantitative conspicuous consumption,[21] for example, is an anomaly in a country where taxation has always been calculated on the basis of *signes extérieurs de richesse*,[22] and where it is not uncommon to find a millionaire more or less comfortably ensconced in an apartment building or home of the most impressively unprepossessing appearance. Indeed, the waste characteristic of American life is by French standards almost immoral. No Frenchman will ever understand how an American can trade in last year's car simply to have a later model.

Moreover, the very idea of living standards governing expenditures, of borrowing against the future to obtain even such semi-necessities as furniture, is heresy in a country where the proverb defines a man who makes $5,000 a year and spends $5,001 as poor, and one who makes $5,000 and spends $4,999 as rich. Nor should it be thought that this attitude is confined to those whose incomes permit the luxury of such abstinence and virtue. The worker who makes $35 a month is, if anything, more fearful of debt than the businessman earning ten times as much, as those enterprises who have tried to introduce installment buying will testify.

Finally, it would be hard to overestimate the effect of the structure of retail trade in France. As is generally known, it is highly fragmented. On the one hand, there are generally far too many outlets for a given type of merchandise—the café is the best example. On the other, there is dispersion of what would form in this country the stock in trade of a single store—the American corner grocery or delicatessen equals *épicerie* plus *crémerie* plus *charcuterie* plus *boulangerie.* In France the small shop fills a vital role: as a symbol of independence and the most convenient ladder between *peuple* and *petite bourgeoisie,* it is the great ambition of thousands of salaried proletarians. The mercery clerk, the butcher's assistant, the apprentice baker, even the great professional cyclist (who holds approximately the same place in France as an all-star outfielder here), all save toward the day when they can have their own *boutique,* with the husband to work and the wife to help with the counter and handle the cash drawer. *Le petit commerce* is thus an indispensable mechanism of social mobility, and hence, paradoxically enough, of social stability.[23]

This situation, however, has inevitably imposed higher costs of distribution, hence higher prices, on the French consumer, not only because of the inefficiency mechanically inherent in excessive dispersion, but at least equally because of the spirit of the sales process. The small shop in France is a sort of caricature of the family firm already described, with the objective of high profits on a limited turnover carried to an astonishing degree. There are haberdashers who try to live on the sale of three shirts a day, restaurants which serve six meals at noon. This effort to make a lot of a little is closely associated with a short-sighted philosophy of exchange wherein each transaction is considered a unique opportunity to make money. Take while the taking is good. The customer is not there to be served, cultivated, courted, persuaded to buy what he needs, and even more, what he should need or does not need. He is there on his own initiative to satisfy self-felt wants and should pay for this satisfaction as dearly as possible. He is simply a walking purse.[24]

It goes without saying that under such conditions, the techniques of creating a market are conspicuous by their absence. There is an art to selling, but the very word "merchandising" does not exist in French. Advertising is poor and limited in scope; price-leaders are nonexistent; sales, few and feeble. Confidence between buyer and seller is seriously compromised by the refusal of the latter to accept responsibility for the quality of his merchandise—in case of dispute, the customer is always wrong. *Caveat emptor!*

This picture, to be sure, is unfair in the sense that it gives only the dominant pattern. It would require a long digression to analyze French retail trade in all its forms and nuances. There are certainly enterprising merchants who do not proceed in the typical fashion. The fact remains, however, that to an American accustomed to commerce as conducted in the United States, most French shops are a delightful or an exasperating anachronism, depending on one's mood or point of view. Even the Parisian department stores, which once pioneered modern sales techniques, not only in France but in the world—the Bon Marché was the first *grand magasin* of all—have sunk into an inertia that has chased thousands of customers back into the small specialty shops.[25]

This traditionalistic, habit-ridden, tight-fisted system of selling acts as an effective damper on the economy as a whole. The merchant who insists on exaggerated profit, who abuses the consumer in a sellers' market and would rather let his stock lie than take a loss and clear his shelves in a buyers' market, is the bane of the manufacturer.[26] It is surprising how quickly the clogging of this multitude of small outlets can back up the stream of merchandise until the very sources are dammed. Modern mass production demands turnover above all, and French retail trade turns very slowly.

III

Of course, in all fairness, the French merchant is up against a very difficult customer.[27] In this relationship of producer, middleman, and consumer, qualitative factors are just as important as quantitative ones: the French public not only buys less than the American; it buys quite differently.

Most important in this respect is the simple fact that those people who are in a position to buy have never been completely willing to accept the standardization implicit in mass production.[28] There is no need to labor the French emphasis on individuality, especially in clothing, where the *couturière* is a sacred institution and even the poorest and most overworked housewife prefers to buy fabrics—which must themselves be something different—and sew her garments to her own taste. The French do not joke about the stock American situation of two women meeting at a party or dinner wearing the same dress; it is nothing to joke about.

As a result, the entire textile industry, which is still the most important in France in terms of labor employed, and wool and silk particularly, is compelled to distribute its efforts over a fantastic gamut of new designs and materials. These fabrics, often launched by fashion and decorating houses, compete from season to season on the highly fickle basis known as *"la mode."* In such a situation, the advantage is all with the small firm. Everything is uncertain, and woe to the producer who places his trust in big factories and mass production. It is too easy to guess wrong and starve amidst the plenty of an unsold inventory. In other words, the sort of irrational structure found in the United States only in the higher reaches of the ladies' garment industry is characteristic in France of much of the manufacture of the cloth itself.[29]

Nor is this attitude limited to light, semidurable products like textiles or leather goods which lend themselves to a certain amount of differentiation. As regards automobiles, for example, the reproach most frequently addressed to American cars is that they are all alike. From a person accustomed to choosing between front engines and rear engines, front-wheel drive and rear-wheel drive, among motors ranging from two to twenty-six fiscal horsepower, and a remarkable variety of body styles, such an observation is not surprising. The comment generally made when comparing the mass-produced Cadillac with the custom-built Delahaye which costs two or three times as much, is: "Not everybody can have your Delahaye."[30]

From one point of view, therefore, France has her conspicuous consumption, but it is fundamentally different from the American. In its stress on individuality, it is aristocratically directed toward a personalization of the relationship of producer and consumer. The former works not so much for a large, amorphous market, as for a specific client or clients. There is a hint of servitude in all this: this dress was made for *me;* this car was made to *my* taste.[31] As a result, a significant portion of French effective demand is oriented toward the products of artisanal and semiartisanal as against mass-production industry.

As already implied, this notion of difference is closely related to one of quality, both presuming extra attention and effort. The ideal of quality is almost a fetish in France, and has always been greatly stressed as a sort of compensation for the inferiority of her techniques of mass production. So much so that business and social prestige depend on it to a significant degree, and French firms will perpetuate outmoded hand techniques in order to achieve utterly trivial gains in this regard. It is an important fact that throughout the history of the French textile industry, the coarser types of cloth, which would best lend themselves to efficient large-scale production, have always been left precisely to those backward centers in no position to take advantage of these possibilities. The prosperous districts of the North and Alsace have always concentrated their efforts on the middle and higher quality lines. One could even point to firms in these areas that made their success in some less expensive article, only to abandon it when the responsibilities of wealth demanded a shift to finer things.

Furthermore, the general standard of living in France—and this is true of all classes—is far more heavily biased in the direction of services than our own. For the American, such material comforts as good plumbing, electrical appliances, and even a car, are almost necessities; if not universal, they nevertheless represent idealized needs toward which people direct their efforts. In France, that part of the income left after provision for food, shelter, and clothing is channeled not so much into durable goods as into such things as vacations, domestic help, the café, and entertainment. Service and time are too cheap to make the Frenchman buy those machines and conveniences that would represent an important field of expansion for manufacturing industry.[32] Even in the case of such a necessity as clothing, the evidence tends to show that the Frenchman not only buys less than the American, but wants far less in proportion to income.[33]

IV

The influence of this pattern of consumption on the productive process, especially the emphasis on differentiation, is greatly intensified by the family structure of most firms as described above. Since one of the primary *raisons d'être* of such a business is its stability, the tendency is to put the eggs into as many baskets as possible by turning out an abnormally wide variety of goods.[34] The shoe manufacturer will make men's, women's, and children's footwear of all types. The textile producer will turn out all sorts of weaves and mixtures, often shifting so frequently that no one type is run long enough to yield any economy of factor costs.

It might be pointed out, moreover, that this excessively mixed output, which so seriously limits the possibilities of efficient mass production, is not characteristic only of the light industries producing consumers' goods for a differentiation-conscious market. Such considerations would hardly account for the output of one hundred types of rails, joists, plates, etc., by a given steel firm. Here—and this is the second factor involved in this *modus vivendi*—another phenomenon must be taken into account, the resemblance between the entrepreneurial techniques of the large, impersonal corporation and the modest family-based firm, to the point where one is sometimes tempted to describe the former as the latter writ large.

Nor is this surprising, when one recalls that all the normative standards of good management and successful operation are derived from traditions established when the family-structured firm was almost alone and unchallenged. For the one, as for the other, the virtues have always been prudence and a sense of proportion, and the end has remained security and solidity. From the start, the prosperous corporations have amortized assets as quickly as possible, often writing the largest items off to profit and loss, and hoarded enormous reserves against the day when a depression might make it necessary to compress sales far below the break-even point in order to maintain prices. Like the small partnership or individual firm, they have always used obsolete equipment side by side with the latest devices and warped their price structure to cover both.[35] And also like the former, their ultimate goal has been and is the highest *rate* of profit rather than the biggest profit.

To be sure, inflation and new taxes have compelled certain modifications. No firm writes its books as it did in the good old days, nor is it possible to build up cash reserves with what is still a weak currency. Such conditions, however, have only strengthened the pressures for extraconservative management. More than ever, the French businessman wants security. He cannot hoard franc notes, but one of the biggest manufacturers in the field can still stock wood and coal stoves against future price rises at a time when the demand is insatiable. And if this expedient is closed to the weaver of wool or cotton, exposed as he is to frequent changes in fashion that might leave his stock worthless overnight, there are still ways and means to invest money in the colonies or abroad.[36]

V

Of course, everything is relative. It would be possible to point to similar signs in American business, a new concern with security, a desire to play it safe and eliminate so far as possible the elements of risk and competition. But where, in our case, such policies represent a marked departure on the ideological level from the optimistically liberal economic doctrines that prevailed almost unchallenged only a generation ago, in France—and here we have the third major element in the accommodation of big and small enterprise—these policies are the logical continuation of centuries of entrepreneurial tradition. The concept of free enterprise as developed in the England of the nineteenth century and transplanted to the United States, with its postulate of a competitive struggle for markets and drastic penalties for failure, and with its emphasis on earning more and more through producing more and more for less and less, has never really been accepted in France. Instead France—the reference here is to the prevailing current of opinion—has continued to cherish the precapitalist ideology that underlay the guild organization of the pre-Revolutionary period. This ideology may be summed up briefly as follows: every man has his place in society, should produce enough goods and services of quality to maintain his place, and has a right to the living earned in this manner. In other words, the justification of survival lies not in the ability to make a profit, but in the correct performance of a social function. In the days of the guild system, these concepts were translated into concrete measures to establish the rules of correct performance and to restrict competition and undue growth on the part of overenterprising producers. These measures, of course, were formally abolished during the Revolution,[37] but the ideas behind them proved less vulnerable to legislation and decree. One little story may well convey the idea better than a dozen paragraphs. An executive of one of the leading textile firms in France—Dollfuss, Mieg, et Cie, the internationally known DMC—discussing the consideration and respect generally accorded the successful businessman in American society, had only one comment to make: "Do you mean to tell me that you can respect a man who has become wealthy through the ruin of a dozen or more competitors? Such a man is a menace to society."

The result of this "sanction pattern" has been to create an environment hostile to the development of a capitalistic business structure. But more important for our present purpose, it has formed to a significant degree the mind of the businessman himself, who has never fully accepted the principles of risk and competition that are at the root of a free-enterprise system as we understand it. As regards risk, there is no need to elaborate here on the oft-criticized French dependence on government protection and help, which, in its almost infantile presumption of social responsibility for the prosperity of the individual firm, is to be carefully distinguished from the predatory attitude so often characteristic of American enterprise. As for competition, one of France's largest steel manufacturers, asked why no one there had established a continuous strip mill in the 1930's, when the new technique was revolutionizing the production of sheet steel in the United States, replied briefly and to the point: "It would have been pretty expensive, to begin with; but even if the money had been available, the creation of such a mill would have entailed the closing of most of the plants producing sheet steel by the old system. The public would not have stood for it, the government would not have stood for it, and that sort of thing just isn't done in French business."

Under the circumstances, it is easier for big business to live and let live, even to protect the small, marginal producer. In the protected, comparatively noncompetitive domestic market, it is the latter that sets the prices, prices which are necessarily especially favorable to the more efficient units. The same consideration holds true for those foreign firms operating in France whose resources might permit them, if they so desired, to destroy home competition. Here, moreover, the normal pattern is reinforced by political considerations, since the government and the people are even less likely to accept such a monopoly in the hands of foreign capital. It is this consideration that explains a recent reference in *Le Monde* to the "sportsmanlike" behavior of Unilever in the French soap market,[38] and the policies of such companies as Ford or Standard Oil and Shell.[39]

Here a word of caution is in order. I would not give the impression in all this that France has never produced businessmen who in imagination and spirit of enterprise bear comparison with the greatest of our so-called "robber barons." A mere list of names like

Péreire, Talabot, Schneider, Boucicaut, Révillon, and more recently, Michelin, Renault, Citroën, Coty, and Boussac is enough to show the absurdity of such an argument. France has always produced pioneers, but as one observer wrote, she has an equally extraordinary talent for putting such men in their place.[40] The point is, the innovator may innovate all he wants. He may build great factories, install whirring machines, turn out standardized goods, introduce new techniques of distribution. But he must not upset the applecart of vested interests. For controlling or rebuking those who refuse to abide by this simple rule, there are ways and means. In the nineteenth century, the Péreire brothers were the most famous victims.[41] In this century, the best example is probably André Citroën. And in those fields like retail trade, where the powers-that-be are too fragmented to furnish any real resistance on an economic level, political pressure is at least as effective.[42]

This *modus vivendi,* this compromise between big and small, modern and traditional, has been and is a crucial factor in France's economic evolution. For not only does it create a superficially Alice-in-Wonderland situation in which the laggards more or less set the pace,[43] but in the last analysis, it places a premium on cautious and conservative as against daring and innovative enterprise by giving all the chances of survival to the former. Why take risks and make money faster, when you can follow at a safe distance, earn less to be sure, but still be there when the front runners have long since faded? "You see, cher Maître," says Larsonneau to Saccard, "you're very good when it comes to making it rain gold pieces, but you don't know how to pick them up."[44] It is no coincidence that most of the key positions in French economic life are held today by a small group, most of whom laid the foundations of their fortunes a century or more ago and have nursed them carefully and discreetly ever since—this through a period of unprecedented political, economic, and technological change.

VI

Given this human factor and its inhibitive influence on economic development, what, then, are the prospects for future improvement? Much, of course, can be done within the entrepreneurial pattern described. A recent, unpublished survey by representatives of our own

Bureau of Labor Statistics indicates that an appreciable increase of productivity could be achieved with a minimum of expenditure simply by reorganizing production so as to eliminate waste motion and time. Such waste is in itself largely a reflection of the lack of competitive pressure, but since its removal is to some degree a question of education, and since it will not hit the businessman too hard in his most sensitive point, his pocketbook, much may yet be accomplished along these lines.[45]

As for changing the fundamental pattern, that is another story. The destruction of two wars, the inflation of the past thirty-five years, and the great depression of the 1930's with its sequel of labor discontent and political instability, have if anything intensified the quest for security. Where once gentlemen's agreements more than sufficed, cartels and *syndicats* have made their appearance and, what is more, with popular and governmental blessing. French capital, labor, and government—for a desire to increase productivity does not necessarily imply a desire to increase output—are all generally committed today to a neo-Malthusianism that prefers to limit production and spread the profits and work. The businessman wants to make sure of his market; the worker wants to make sure of his job; the government wants to make sure of its votes.[46]

This new effort on the part of the entrepreneur to formalize the live-and-let-live pattern has received its most important expression in the Conseil National du Patronat, the French equivalent of the American National Association of Manufacturers. The primary aim of this organization is to establish a system of interprofessional local committees and intraprofessional *syndicats* that are essentially eighteenth-century guilds in twentieth-century dress. Such groups, of course, would make some important contributions to the improvement of French industrial and business procedures. They would disseminate technical information, promote research, study foreign methods and pass the findings on to French manufacturers, regroup production so as to eliminate some of the excessive product-mix described above. They have appointed a committee on productivity to tackle this crucial problem from the employers' point of view. But all these accessory objectives will not conceal the primary aim of assigning quotas and markets in such a way as to provide security for all but the most inept units.[47]

In answer to the objections and fears of American representatives on this score—and one of the major purposes of our European aid program is to eliminate just that sort of thing—M. Georges Villiers, president of the Conseil National du Patronat, points to the social upheaval that would probably result from an all-out competitive shakedown of the type logically implied by our conception of free enterprise. Probably he is right. If the hand of big business were really forced, the carnage would be sad to behold.

In the last analysis, whether or not the CNP succeeds in organizing a businessman who is notoriously averse to formal organization, especially in those fields where the family firm predominates, the traditional entrepreneurial pattern will continue to prevail in more or less undiluted form. For what is involved is a whole way of life, the values and standards of a people, a way of life embodied in the word *civilisation*. The Frenchman can and does point with pride to those traditions of leisure and quality, of individuality and taste, to the *goût*, that *raffinement* inseparably connected with an economic system as yet unperverted by mass production and standardization. Can the one be changed without sacrificing the other? After all, it takes all kinds to make the world, and it has yet to be proved that a world formed in the image of the United States would be an improvement.

The only difficulty is that this is a very hard world, and that those finer things that are the pride of France and French civilization unfortunately weigh little in the balance of power. France—and this is the heart of the matter—had neatly solved prior to 1914 the conflict between old and new, between the traditions and norms of an aristocratic culture and a petty-bourgeois economy and the iconoclastic energy of modern industrial capitalism, by the *modus vivendi* which it has been the aim of this paper to describe.[48] The only exception, and a most important one, was the increasing conflict between a new proletariat and the rest of society, but even this might well have been resolved and the worker integrated in the whole had France been able to work out its problems in some sort of splendid isolation—in other words, had France had time.

This, of course, was impossible. The development of the Industrial Revolution in the rest of the world, the rise of modern Germany, the growth of a politically conscious labor movement of an international character, and most recently, the nightmarish upsurge of a Communist Russia, all these have brutally posed the incompatibility of *la doulce France* with a new iron age, of aristocratic culture and petty-bourgeois values within, with industrial capitalism without. In a new atomic world, time is the most strictly rationed commodity of all. Thus the urgent, the critical dilemma hangs over France today: To change and, in changing, die; or not to change, and risk a swifter death.

PART IV

THE ENTREPRENEUR AS AN INDIVIDUAL

The Entrepreneur as an Individual

RECURRENT PROBLEMS at the Research Center stemmed from our habit of personifying the concept that was the subject of our inquiries. No great sophistication of argument was needed to show that no person could be an entrepreneur all of the time, that a great variety of persons acted as entrepreneurs some of the time, and that if we were going to devote our energies to arguing over who was an entrepreneur and who was not, the result could only be frustration and dissension. Far better, surely, to abjure all talk of the entrepreneur as a real person and concentrate on entrepreneurship as a category of action. Yet, resolve as one might to speak only of "entrepreneurship" as a function or as a social role, the sheer convenience of the phrase "the entrepreneur" gave it a secure place in the everyday language of our discussions. Our *Hamlet,* it seemed, had to have its Prince.

This habit was reflected in the contents of the Center's journal, and not only as a kind of convenient shorthand. Particularly in the earlier volumes, studies of entrepreneurs as individuals appeared very frequently. The explanation is to be found partly in the fact that, at a time when no general theoretical framework had been devised or accepted, the biographical approach held out the prospect of yielding useful information without requiring that the writer commit himself to any specific theoretical point of view. Beyond this, it was congenial to most of us. It was a traditionally proper way to write history. The source materials were often readily available in the form of collections of letters, autobiographies, diaries, and the like. And to the prospective author of a doctoral dissertation it had the advantage that the final product could be neatly packaged.

A careful historian of the Research Center's work, however, would point out that the predilection for the biographical approach had deeper roots than these. Fundamental in the thinking of the pioneers of the subject had been a desire to re-emphasize the human element in economic change. Reacting against the increasing impersonality of economic theory, they were concerned to stress that economics is, after all, the study of what people do, and that sometimes what a particular individual decides to do in a particular set of circumstances can have very important consequences. What was involved was not a repudiation of the direction in which modern economic theory was moving, but an attempt to redress the balance a little, to make of the individual something more than part of the error term in a regression equation. This attitude, this cast of thought, would have been apparent no matter what the particular topic of inquiry had been. But in its application to the study of entrepreneurship it acquired new point and vigor, for the analysis of entrepreneurship was inextricably tied in with the analysis of change, of innovation, of the why's and how's of individual differences.

This being the case, the study of individual men who could by some reasonable criteria be classified as entrepreneurs was a natural and obvious approach to the problem. A difficulty that could not long be ignored, however, lay in the fact that, in the absence of a theory of some kind, conclusions drawn from individual cases could not be generalized. Sole reliance on the biographical approach held out no more constructive prospect than the indefinite accumulation of particular facts. To investigators who thought of themselves as social scientists, this was hardly adequate. The obvious way around the difficulty lay in the construction of a theory that could make the mass of biographical data comparable and intelligible. This was one of the objectives of the Jenks-Parsons social role theory. Other alternatives were tried, of which perhaps the most fruitful were the comparative studies of career data carried out by William Miller and his associates. But it would be idle to pretend that, by the time the Research Center ended its career, a solution to the problem had been found.

From the many available studies of individual entrepreneurs, four have been chosen for presentation here. The criterion of selection is partly the probable interest of the subject matter, but partly too the fact that each of these four was written with a sense of problems to be solved. The concern of the authors, in other words, was not only to answer particular questions about particular individuals, but also to exemplify, test, or call into question hypotheses suggested to aid the solution of problems of theoretical importance.

Harold C. Passer, in his brief but content-packed article on Thomas Edison, analyzes one of the major innovations of the late nineteenth century—the central station electric lighting system—and in the process offers a useful corrective to conventional notions of what it takes to make an innovation successful.[1] Edison, it is clear, modeled his electric light distribution system on the existing gas industry. His aim was to "sub-divide the electric light." This involved radical departures from the technology and business arrangements characteristic of the only electric lighting system that had at that time proved its feasibility: the arc light. But it involved also, in Edison's hands, detailed and deliberate imitation of gas lighting systems, and it is in this sophisticated imitation of a competing system that Passer finds the key to Edison's success.

The essential element in Edison's innovation is sometimes said to be the incandescent bulb, sometimes the central generating plant. Passer's analysis makes it clear that these interpretations are superficial. What Edison did was create an electric analogue of gas lighting systems. The particular devices introduced are relevant only because they were necessary for the system as he designed it. From this point of view, the innovation consisted of the introduction of a system of light supply that rested on a technological base different from the gas light but replicated the particular elements of gas light systems in detail.

The inventive aspects of Edison's genius hardly require new emphasis. His genius as an innovator has received less attention. In the case presented here, the elements that stand out are his clear appreciation of the economic context of the innovation and his desire to minimize the consumer's perception of radical change. In combination, these elements implied a concern with imitation of the established and the familiar. Equally remarkable was Edison's ability to discriminate between relevant and irrelevant models: his refusal to be distracted by the technical and commercial features of arc lighting systems, which on a superficial view might have seemed to offer valuable precedents, and his determination to take as his exemplar the very system that his innovation was designed to supplant.

Novelty, as Abbott Payson Usher has frequently stressed, is a matter of degree, and the radical innovation merges gradually into the minor departure from routine. Innovations in management, precisely because they involve changes in the behavior patterns of a going concern, are less dramatic than innovations in technology and typically leave less adequate records for the historian, but in the process of economic growth they are of the first importance. Dennis Chapman's study of William Brown, owner of a Scottish textile mill in the early nineteenth century, directs attention to this somewhat neglected aspect of entrepreneurship. Brown is a little-known figure in the annals of economic history; his importance lies in the light his writings throw on the thinking and practices of a small-scale manufacturer during the industrial revolution. How far he was ahead of his time, to what extent he was typical, and to what extent a pioneer—these are questions impossible to answer in the present state of our knowledge. Certainly his ideas have a distinctly "modern" air about them; Frederick Taylor and William Brown would have understood each other.

Particularly noteworthy in Chapman's account is his emphasis on Brown's systematic approach to the analysis and solution of managerial problems. Practice was to be based on careful observation and experiment; findings were to be recorded and made freely available to interested inquirers. If this was not in the strict sense "scientific" management, by Taylor's definition, it was the next thing to it. The historian of management will note in particular Brown's integration of record-keeping with planning and control and—in Marshall's mill at Leeds which Brown visited, though apparently not in the Dundee mill—the combination of printed job instructions with extreme division of labor. Some of the innovations we associate with Taylorism had, it is clear, antecedents that Taylor did not recognize.

Brown's "enthusiasm"—his single-minded devotion to spinning—did not imply innovation for innovation's sake. Prudent management demanded above all that the mill remain profitable. "A spinning mill," Brown noted, "is a complicated and ticklish kind of concern." In the circumstances, a sound rule of thumb was to make "the fewest possible changes in every respect in the management." This point of view would have appealed to Sir Ambrose Crowley, the subject of Michael Flinn's essay, who would also have insisted, no doubt, that if changes were to be made, he and he alone would make them. Crowley, as Flinn depicts him, is not an attractive or appealing personality. It is not for his charm that he is included in this portrait gallery, but for his organizational and administrative genius. That he could run, by personal correspondence from London, an extensive ironworks in the north of England and build in the process one of the largest and most successful industrial enterprises of the eighteenth century, is ample testimony to this side of his character.[2]

Crowley's life and work, according to Flinn, was "a constant struggle against dishonesty and idleness." Analysis of his methods should remind us not only of the perennial difficulties involved in controlling an organization from a distance but also of the fact that the industrial virtues, so-called, were still alien to the England of Crowley's time. His minute and detailed orders, his surveillance of everything his employees did, whether on duty or off, his insistence on prompt and particular reporting, his use of committees to minimize the trust that had to be placed in any single individual—these are reflections not only of Crowley's censorious and suspicious character, but also of the human resources he had to work with. If, to our eyes, the *Law Book* of the Crowley ironworks seems archaic and perhaps a trifle ridiculous in its infinitely detailed absolute orders, the reason may be that few of us have faced the problems of building an industrial enterprise in a preindustrial society. Crowley, for reasons connected with the marketing side of his business, chose to maintain his residence and head office in London. This decision made it impossible for him to rely on the kind of direct personal supervision normal for manufacturers of his time. The alternative was to develop and enforce a code of law. The remarkable detailed complexity of this code suggests that Crowley could rely only to a very limited extent on the self-discipline of his employees and their willingness to merge their own ambitions with those of the organization.

In the articles on Brown and Crowley, the principal objective of the authors is to shed light on the early development of industrial management. Technological innovation as such receives little emphasis. McLaughlin's essay on the steam automobile, on the other hand, focuses on a problem in the history of technology. He presents the case of the Stanley Steamer, in which entrepreneurial concentration on technological improvement spelled neglect of finance and marketing and resulted in the premature disappearance of the firm and its characteristic product. The Stanley brothers, as entrepreneurs, contrast sharply both with the autocratic industrial government practiced by Crowley and with the systematic experimentation and observation of William Brown. Personality differences provide the key. Essentially the Stanleys were inventors, tinkerers, ingenious craftsmen. Their primary interest was in the product itself, in its mechanical perfection and simplification. Their orientation was not to the market place, but to the world of metals and tools.

Yet the contrast can be overdrawn, for the word "enthusiasm" that so fittingly describes William Brown's attitude to the manufacture of textiles, and might equally well be applied to Crowley's compulsive devotion to orders and rules, is appropriate also to the Stanley brothers and their long love affair with the steam automobile. They had a fine machine—one whose essential characteristics, as McLaughlin points out, have had to be imitated by the gasoline-powered car at the cost of great ingenuity and complexity. Their final defeat came not from any defect in the product but from their own neglect of finance and marketing. The Stanley brothers, McLaughlin argues, had no real interest in seeing their car come into general popular use. They preferred that their business remain small. They had no more interest in the mass production of their cars, as Detroit understood the word, than they had in the mass production of their violins.

Few pieces of machinery have generated such affection among their owners as the Stanley Steamer. Its place in American folklore seems secure, and to those Americans unfortunate enough to live in smog-filled cities, its early demise is a matter for legitimate regret. As a case study in entrepreneurship, however, the career of the Stanley brothers is important because it underlines emphatically the essential distinctions between inventor, innovator, and entrepreneur. As inventors and innovators the Stanley brothers were remarkably successful. As entrepreneurs they were failures. The basic reason for their failure as entrepreneurs was their inability to reconcile the technological requirements of the product with the commercial requirements of the market. Many other examples of failure for the same reason could be found. With Edison, as Passer's article shows, both sets of skills were combined in one man. More typically, perhaps, in the modern world complementary skills are contributed by cooperating individuals in some form of multiple entrepreneurship. But somehow or other the reconciliation must be made, and the effectiveness with which this is done is one key to successful entrepreneurship.

As was emphasized earlier, case studies of individual entrepreneurs, however interesting and informative in themselves, do not lend themselves readily to generalization. Yet the four presented here are more than entertaining anecdotes. They emphasize, first of all, the continuity of entrepreneurial problems, and in particular the problems of grappling with technological change and controlling human organizations. They bear witness to the variety of human types that have, at one time or another, played entrepreneurial roles, and the variety of motives and philosophies that have inspired them. And, implicitly, they serve as warnings against easy assumptions and premature generalizations. Perhaps this last is not the least important function that biographical studies can serve, for it is easy for general theories of entrepreneurship to lose themselves in the rarefied air of abstract concepts and simplifying assumptions. The challenge of explaining and understanding the behavior of such men as Edison, Brown, Crowley, and the Stanley brothers provides a useful corrective.

The Electric Light and the Gas Light: Innovation and Continuity in Economic History

HAROLD C. PASSER

I

WHEN THOMAS ALVA EDISON gave the signal to start the dynamo in the Pearl Street Station, New York City, on September 4, 1882, a new system of light supply had its commercial beginnings in the United States. The development of the American economy during the nineteenth century with attendant industrialization, urbanization, and new methods of transport, had greatly enlarged the demand for light. To meet this increasing demand, methods of lighting had slowly changed. Candles had been replaced by oil lamps, oil lamps in turn by kerosene lamps, and finally, in the larger cities, gas had become the accepted means of illumination. But gas, too, was to be supplanted as an illuminant. The central station incandescent lighting system which replaced it is one of the major innovations of the nineteenth century.

The obvious fact that the electric light differs from the gas light in important respects will not be of prime concern in this paper. Rather, I shall stress the continuity in the development of the business of selling light and how the electric system evolved out of the gas system. The striking similarities between the two systems serve as the main focus here. Edison's clear and complete understanding of the gas industry gave rise to his desire to design a method of electric light supply as much like it as possible. This choice of goal is the principal reason for the very substantial and early success achieved by his electric lighting ventures.

This article is reprinted, by permission of the author, from *Explorations in Entrepreneurial History,* 1:1–9 (March 1949).

The first electric light to be of commercial importance was not Edison's incandescent light but the arc light. This light is produced by an arc formed between two carbon rods inserted in an electric circuit. The arc light was fairly satisfactory and in many ways a great improvement over gas. It flickered considerably, however, and the carbon rods, which gave off ill-smelling fumes as they burned, had to be replaced frequently. But its chief disadvantage was its intensity. Nobody had been able to make an arc lamp of less than 1000 candlepower, which meant the light could be used only in outdoor areas or in very large rooms. Beginning about 1878, arc lights were used as street lights and in factories, hotels, and auditoriums. In nearly all these cases, the dynamo and the lights were owned and operated by the light consumer himself. In the case of street lights, a separate company was usually formed to operate them under contract from the municipality. Arc lights were series-connected and hence had to be all turned on or off at once. But this was no great handicap because they were only used in places where it was the usual desire that all the lights be burning at once. No meter was needed in the arc light system because in those few cases where the owner of the equipment was not the consumer of the light, a contract for specified hours of lighting was easy to arrange. The system was thus very simple and elementary—no meters, no fuses, and almost no accessories were needed.

Edison first began experimenting with the electric light in 1877 but he soon laid it aside to perfect the phonograph which occupied him until the middle of 1878. At that time he turned again to the electric light. The arc light did not interest him, however, because of its unsuitability for domestic and office illumination. Edison knew that ninety per cent of the gas industry revenues came from interior lighting and that the really profitable electric light would be one of small candlepower, suitable for the home. His problem, therefore, was to "sub-divide the electric light"—a problem considered by many respectable scientists to be as incapable of solution as the invention of a perpetual motion machine.

Edison first made a very careful study of the gas industry. He is quoted as having said in 1878, "I started my usual course of collecting every kind of data about gas; bought all the transactions of the gas engineering societies, etc., all the back volumes of the gas journals. Having obtained all the data and investigated gas-jet distribution in New York by actual observations, I made up my mind that the problem of the subdivision of electric current could be solved and made commercial."[1] Edison's conception of the problem before him is shown by entries he made in one of his notebooks (no. 184) about this same time. "Object, Edison to effect exact imitation of all done by gas so as to replace lighting by gas by lighting by electricity... Edison's great effort—not to make a large light or a blinding light but a small light having the mildness of gas."[2]

Edison's basic plan, which is suggested in the above quotations, was to imitate the gas system as closely as possible. He believed that the methods, devices, and practices which had gained wide consumer acceptance in the sale of gas should be used in an electric lighting system wherever possible. His goal was to develop a system of light supply which would differ from gas only in that it provided a superior and hence more desirable light.

II

The similarities between the Edison system and the gas system can be analyzed from both the technical and commercial points of view. The technical features common to the two systems stem directly from the fact that Edison was looking for an electrical analogue to the gas system. It is hard to appreciate how revolutionary an idea this was. To refuse to consider as relevant the technical aspects of the arc light system, which was the only electric lighting system known, and to see instead an analogy with gas was truly remarkable. At that time electrical phenomena were very imperfectly understood. Edison stands out as a scientist who had grasped the fundamental laws of electricity and thus was able to make sound comparisons between electrical pressure and gas pressure and between resistance to the flow of electricity and resistance to the flow of a gas.

Edison decided on a system of central supply with mains (copper conductors) carrying the electric energy to the lights in the houses. This is exactly how gas was distributed and entirely different from the isolated plant method which had so far been used in arc lighting. The novelty of Edison's approach is emphasized by the opinion of Sir William Preece, the most prominent English electrician of that period, who wrote in 1882 that each house would have its own dynamo driven by a gas motor and that "it is in this direction that the practical illumination of houses will be carried out."[3] That Preece was wrong and Edison right can be attributed to Edison's perception of the gas system analogy.

Edison decided to put his conductors underground like the gas mains instead of on poles like the telegraph, telephone, arc light, and fire alarm circuits of that day. He realized that the similarity between his conductors and the gas mains was far greater than any similarity between his conductors and the common electrical conductors. When questioned about putting his mains underground, Edison replied, "Why, you don't lift water pipes and gas pipes up on stilts."[4] The decision to put the mains underground necessitated that the Edison Electric Illuminating Company be incorporated under the gas statutes of the State of New York for only then could it have the power to break up the streets. Designing and installing the underground mains was a difficult, expensive process but the essential wisdom of this method is indicated by the fact that within ten years no overhead wires were permitted in New York City.

Gas was distributed under constant pressure with each jet controlled independently of the others. Likewise, in Edison's system, the electric current is delivered at constant pressure (parallel system) and each light can be controlled independently. This is in sharp contrast to the arc light systems which were series systems and which had a different voltage at each light. And, as mentioned above, the arc lights were all turned on and off together with no independent control.

The gas consumption of each user was measured by a meter located on his premises. Edison decided that his system also should have a meter. Here is another instance where the extent of the novelty of Edison's idea is hard to imagine. At that time, electricity was a mysterious force which could be measured only crudely and imperfectly in the laboratory. To suggest that this force could be measured in some simple, reliable, and inexpensive way seemed fantastic in the extreme. Yet such measurement was necessary if electric light were to become a commodity.

The gas meters had a dial mechanism where pointers indicated the cubic feet of gas consumed. Edison realized the advantages of such a direct-reading type of meter from the consumer's point of view. He tried to perfect an electric meter which was direct-reading and measured electricity used in cubic feet (like gas) but failed.[5]

The meter he finally worked out fulfilled all the requirements except that it was not direct-reading. It was a chemical device and contained plates which were removed each month and taken to the central station where they were weighed. The customer could learn nothing about his consumption of electricity from the meter and had to trust the company to be accurate and honest. For this reason, these chemical meters were never completely successful and eventually were replaced by direct-reading, mechanical-type meters.

As to the candlepower of the electric light in the Edison system, it is sufficient to say that it was designed to produce 16 candlepower which is equivalent to the standard gas jet of the 1880's.

The thinking of Edison in developing the technical features of his system is brought out very clearly when his reasons for rejecting the storage battery are examined. It was thought by some electricians that the most practical system of light distribution would involve storage batteries in each house to be charged during the daytime by the central station dynamo which could then supply current to other lights—say street lights—at night. This method has the following advantages: 1. while the battery would be discharged at a low voltage suitable for inside a home, it would be charged at a high voltage—thus reducing the energy lost in transmission from the central station; 2. the central station could have a much steadier load and therefore lower cost per unit of electrical energy.

Edison was interviewed on January 28th, 1883 by a *Boston Herald* reporter and made the following remarks on the storage battery: "In 1879 I took up that question and devised a system of placing storage batteries in houses connected to mains and charging them in the daytime, to be discharged in the evening and night to run incandescent lamps."[6] Edison went on to say that he found this system unworkable.

The reporter next asked, "Then you consider storage batteries wholly impracticable? Is there no hope for their doing good, legitimate work?"

Edison replied, "None whatever. Except in a very limited number of cases, storage of gas could be made analogous to storage of electricity. One of the principal outlays of a gas company is for pipes. The average diameter of their mains is five or six inches. But under pressure greater than they now force the gas through their mains, an inch pipe would answer under the storage principle of having a small gasometer in every house. The difference saved to the company by this arrangement would be about $15 for pipes from house to house, 25 to 30 feet apart. But the gasometer would cost a great deal more in each house than the 25 feet of pipe buried in the street. Besides, gasometers might not be just the thing in the hands of the public; there might be explosions; some of them might not have room. The gasometer would require some little mechanism to reduce the pressure down to a limit where it could be burnt. Now, these little mechanisms are uncertain."[7]

Edison's reasons for rejecting the battery method, apart from technical difficulties which might have arisen from batteries as such, were based, therefore, on his analysis of why the gas companies had never adopted the corresponding method in gas distribution. Considerations of safety, reliability, and convenience applied equally to both. The reservoir of gas in each home would be a potential source of fire or explosion just as the battery, especially its high voltage side, would be a potential cause of fire or personal injury. The gasometers and the batteries were both costly and unreliable to the extent that any savings in cost of gas pipes or electric conductors would be more than offset. If there would be inconvenience to a household in having space occupied by the gas reservoir, there would also be inconvenience in having space occupied by the coffin-sized battery.

With the conception of the electrical analogue to the gas system in his mind, Edison and his associates worked for nearly four years designing the components of his system and perfecting the details. In essence this meant inventing a suitable dynamo; a system of underground mains; switches, sockets, and junction boxes; a fusing device; and, of course, the incandescent lamp itself. What Edison finally achieved was a system of light supply vastly superior to the gas system from a purely technical point of view. The light was of much better quality. It did not flicker or vitiate the atmosphere or give off a noticeable amount of heat. The system was much safer, too, in that there was no open flame, no danger of explosion or suffocation, and almost no chance of personal injury or fire. The Edison meter was extremely accurate and marked a great improvement over the gas meters which were, at times, notoriously inaccurate.[8]

III

Commercially, the Edison system showed the same similarity to the gas system as it did technically. The estimates of the demand for light in the area of New York City chosen for the first central station were based on the number of gas jets in use. Edison had men thoroughly canvas the district to obtain information on the number of gas jets burning at each hour up to three in the morning. A house-to-house survey was made later which provided complete data on exactly how many jets were in each building, the average hours of burning, and the cost of this light to consumer. These estimates served as the basis for determining the size and quantity of electrical equipment needed.

The Edison electric light was priced to equal the price of gas light. In one of his surveys, Edison asked the gas consumers whether or not they would take the electric light if its price were the same as gas. All but 850 of the 16,000 gas users answered in the affirmative.[9] There remained the question of exactly how much these consumers had paid for gas light with the price of gas at $2.25 per 1000 cubic feet. To determine this, Edison collected some 24 books containing gas light bills of consumers in the district.[10]

On the assumption that a 16 candlepower jet consumes 5 cubic feet per hour, the price of 16 candlepower-hours of light, when gas is $2.25 per 1000 cubic feet, is 1.125 cents. The price of light supplied by the Edison central station was set at 1.2 cents per 16 candlepower-hours (with the central station supplying the light bulbs as well as the electric energy). Thus the price of the electric light was almost exactly the same as the price of gas light, the commodity it was designed to replace.[11]

Edison was aware that if his system were really effective, the gas companies might conceivably reduce the price of gas. In an 1882 interview,[12] he explained that he had calculated that the cost of the gas which sold for $2.25 per 1000 cubic feet was 90 cents—of which 45 cents was variable production cost and 45 cents overhead. Even if the price of gas were reduced to $1, Edison was confident that he could get one-half of the lighting business in the district by setting the price of electric light equivalent to gas at $1.50. With their volume cut in half, the gas companies would find their cost to be $1.28 and Edison did not consider them strong enough to sell below cost for very long. By the time several years had elapsed, the Edison people became more confident and expressed the belief that the electric light customers could be held at the existing price no matter what happened to the price of gas. They made the comparison with the success of the gas companies in retaining their customers in the face of lowered kerosene prices some years before.[13]

In the business methods adopted by the Edison Electric Illuminating Company, every effort was made to simulate the practices and terminology of the gas companies. Monthly bills were rendered and the Edison lights were often referred to as burners. The consumer was billed for light-hours instead of for electric energy to avoid confusing him with mysterious terminology and to stress the fact that he was buying light.

Edison did not expect to find much of a market for light distributed from a central station in communities too small or too poor to support a gas company. The areas of the nation which were considered as possible locations for Edison central stations once their commercial feasibility had been demonstrated in the New York district were those chosen with reference to the gas industry. Here again can be seen Edison's hesitation to depart very markedly from the business practices of the gas companies.

IV

The similarities between the Edison central station light supply system and the gas light supply system indicate how closely Edison was able to achieve his goal—the electrical analogue of the gas system. But the impact of the gas industry does not end with the conception and design of the electric light system. Once this system had been placed in operation in the New York City district, the Edison company had to take account of the gas companies in its policies and decisions. In this section I shall discuss the actions and tactics of an innovating firm in view of the competition from the product that the innovation is designed to replace.

The location of the first central station was so chosen (by accident or by design) that gas was placed at the greatest quality disadvantage possible. At a time when water-gas (as against coal-gas) was forbidden by law in New Jersey and Massachusetts, lower Manhattan was furnished with this poisonous, inferior gas. The *London Journal of Gas Lighting,* December 12, 1883, contained the following comment: "One thing that will operate in Edison's favour, when he gets to work in earnest to light the downtown district, is that this section of the city is supplied with water-gas. This gas gives a great deal of trouble by causing the burner tips to become stopped up with carbon; the result, of course, being a miserable forked flame. Further, people are beginning to realize that carbonic oxide is not so harmless a substance as they have been led to believe. The truth is, the number of deaths caused by water-gas in New York City alone, during the past few months, is simply appalling. The *Sanitary Engineer* stated that 14 deaths have occurred in the city in the consequence of the use of this gas, since the 1st of July. If there is to be a fight between gas and electricity, this is a heavy load for the gas industry to carry to the conflict."[14]

The proposition that Edison chose lower Manhattan because of the water-gas use there cannot be proved on the basis of available evidence. He could hardly have chosen it on the grounds of a large lighting demand, however, because even in 1882 lower Manhattan was a business district where most buildings were dark after 6 P.M. There are some indications that Edison may have chosen the Wall Street area in order to impress the prominent capitalists at first hand. Whatever the reason for the choice, the electric light was able to demonstrate its superiority over water-gas much more easily than if it had been competing with coal-gas.

The advertising and sales efforts of the Edison company in trying to expand the use of incandescent lights were directed almost entirely toward showing its superiority over gas. In the Bulletins of the Edison Electric Light Company and the Edison Company for Isolated Lighting which were published every month or so during the years 1882–1886, explosions, fires, and deaths due to gas in New York and elsewhere were reported with monotonous regularity. Incidents of gas supply failure were cited to give the impression that gas was unreliable. The reader of these Bulletins learned that the heat given off by a gas light was uncomfortable and impaired the acoustical qualities of theaters; that the gas light was sooty and grimy; and that the clean, cool, steady Edison light had none of these disadvantages. The gas light was pictured as inconvenient and limited in use because it required a match to be lighted, could not be turned on from a distance, could not burn inverted, and could not burn in a wind.

In one Bulletin, a comment was headed "The Electric Light Cures Shortsightedness" and an English journal was quoted as follows: "Remarking the number of students who are afflicted with short-sightedness, Professor Pickering has lately examined some physical causes that may bring about this abnormal condition of the eye. He finds that it is not the light so much as the heat that is mainly concerned in the developing of prejudicial effects . . . Ordinary gas burners give out a considerable amount of heat by the energetic combustion of hydro-carbons and hence their injurious effect. In this respect, the electric light is not open to the same objection, for although the light may be rendered as intense as desirable, still there is very little heat produced."[15]

V

The relationship between a new product (the incandescent electric light) and the product it displaces (the gas light) is seen to have two important aspects. How is the new product like the old and how is it different from the old? The similarities between the two express the continuity in economic development; the differences are the discontinuities, the abrupt changes, in economic development. From the standpoint of the innovator, the time to be especially conscious of the continuity elements is in the period when the new product, its production, and its marketing are conceived and worked out. The time to be especially conscious of the differences is when the new product is marketed and is facing the competition of the old product.

One of the key factors in Edison's success in the New York City electric lighting venture was his ability to select from the gas system those elements which could serve in his system. His original conception of an electric analogue for gas carried him to exceedingly sound judgments in the design of his electrical light system. How sound they were is proven by the test of time. The size of the area he chose for one central station is still used for distribution purposes although now the immediate source of electric energy in each such district is a sub-station which contains transformers and converters. His choice of voltage (110 volts) and the constant pressure parallel system are standard throughout the United States. The bamboo filament of the Edison light has been replaced by a metallic filament and the glass is commonly frosted now, but the physical size of the incandescent light, its electrical characteristics, its life, and other features are not radically different from the originals of 1882. Edison's decision to put the conductors underground and his original work in the accessories of the system—the fuses, the switches, the underground mains, the sockets—were also correct anticipations of the future course of the industry.

The meter, it will be recalled, was satisfactory except that unlike a gas meter it was not direct-reading. Inventions in the late 1880's and the early 1890's made possible a mechanical-type direct-reading meter which replaced nearly all the chemical meters by 1900. The one important respect in which Edison failed to imitate the gas industry turned out to be a source of consumer complaint which was not remedied until a gas-type of direct-reading meter was finally perfected.

William Brown of Dundee, 1791–1864: Management in a Scottish Flax Mill

DENNIS CHAPMAN

THE ECONOMIC HISTORY of Great Britain has been enriched by a number of monographs describing the technical ingenuity, the enterprise, the foresight and the energy of such pioneers as Samuel Oldknow in cotton, Peter Stubs in toolmaking, and Benjamin Gott in the woolen industry. But these accounts, like the nineteenth-century biographies of Samuel Smiles and others, tell us little about achievements in the art and science of management. The study of the firm of Boulton and Watt by Erich Roll, the essays of Robert Owen in his *New View of Society,* and Charles Babbage's *On the Economy of Machinery and Manufactures* suggest that the subject was not altogether neglected, but much less is known about the development of management than about the more spectacular advances in technology and trade.

The account which follows is of a pioneer in industrial management, William Brown of Dundee in Scotland. It is based almost entirely on Brown's own writings: two editions of a small pamphlet entitled *Reminiscences of Flaxspinning* (1st edition, 1861; 2nd edition, 1862) which he published anonymously after he had retired; an account book, "The Day Book of Messrs. W. & J. Brown, 1816–1821"; and his manuscript *Essays in Flaxspinning,* written between 1819 and 1823. Brown was a retiring person and avoided public life, so that little can be learned about him from contemporary sources, but occasional references in the *Dundee Advertiser,*[1] in the reports of Factory Commissioners, in Warden's *The Linen*

This article is reprinted, by permission of the author, from *Explorations in Entrepreneurial History,* 4:119–134 (February 1932).

Trade Ancient and Modern,[2] and in Norrie's *Dundee Celebrities,*[3] confirm the impression given by his own writings.

I

William Brown was born in Cononsyth in the year 1791. His father was James Brown, one of the first mill spinners in Scotland, who operated Trottick, Friockheim, and Arrot Mills, and who in 1806 erected the first "modern" mill, the West Ward Mill in Dundee. William was one of four brothers, all of whom were successful in the linen trade. His eldest brother, Andrew, born in 1784, was associated with his father in the West Ward Mill and later took over its direction. The other brothers, James, born in 1785, and John, born in 1790, were both originally partners with William in the East Mill. In 1817, however, John "not being employed in the East Mill," ceased to draw an allowance for his services, although he continued to hold a third of the capital. He later ran a mill of his own. James (junior) and William continued the business, James managing the mercantile part of the firm and William the spinning mill. In all public affairs James was to the fore, William being in no way a public figure. James was Lord Dean of Guild in 1824, a Justice of the Peace for Forfarshire, and founder and first President of the Dundee Chamber of Commerce from 1835 to 1837. He was again President in 1845 and Provost of Dundee from 1844 to 1847.

How much William Brown and his brothers owed to their father is hard to assess, but it may be noted that, according to the evidence taken by the Commissioners inquiring into the employment of children in 1834, a similar policy was followed in the three separate establishments on such matters as discipline and punishment, while the employees in each spoke well of the humanity of their masters.

William Brown had little formal education and at an early age assisted his father at Trottick; by the age of eighteen, in 1809, he was managing his own concern. His first two years in business were difficult, and the mill was closed in the autumn of 1810 and spring of 1811. Thereafter the firm entered upon a period of unbroken success which continued throughout his working life. He began with one small mill with a single engine of twenty horsepower and with 698 spindles, and lived to see his business grow to be one of the largest spinning firms in Scotland. As a manager, he based his practice on systematic observation and experiment. The titles of a few of his essays will illustrate his method of work:

> Thoughts on Accidental Fire at Mills.
> Expense of Fuel for Steam Engine.
> Experiments on Breaking and Scutching Flax.
> Performance of East Mill from Whit to March 3rd, 1819.

There were also numerous essays on that most intractable problem, "Carding." Every change in management, in machinery, in building, or in technical operations was recorded so that his experience would be available for future reference. Brown worked out, recorded, and practiced a complete system of management. As his success became known, he was asked for advice by other mill owners, thus becoming one of the earliest "management consultants."

The personal qualities of William Brown can be best conveyed by quoting two of his Essays, the first being the Introduction to the volume, the second his "Apology" which appears near the middle of the series. The Introduction contains an appraisal of the extent of technical knowledge in flax spinning and illustrates Brown's essentially scientific attitude to technical and managerial problems. It reads as follows:

> The chief object of these Essays is to improve the Author of them in the knowledge of his business, and to acquaint him in the management of it. They are meant to be composed of such circumstances, occurrences, rules, descriptions and hints for improvements at East Mill as may appear useful to be printed or remembered afterwards. It is evident that by means of such essays much useful information will be preserved which would otherwise be lost, and when it is considered that in the flaxspinning business nothing can be obtained from books, all from observation or enquiry only, the reading or writing of essays must be particularly useful to exercise the understanding and to refresh the memory. Without essays or something similar one's knowledge must necessarily be limited, but with them there can be no bounds to knowledge, and he who makes a right use of them will learn more in a few years than he who does not will learn in a lifetime. Surely all managers of extensive well-conducted works must write much, otherwise they could never establish order and discipline among their Hands, nor improvement and regularity in the construction and arrangement of their machinery. These Essays therefore will embrace everything of importance relating to the management of the East Mill, and show not only a comprehensive state of it at different times, but likewise many

little circumstances regarding every-day's transactions, whether respecting machinery, hands, operations or flax. If any thing be wanting to make them either useful or entertaining it is a taste in the author for carrying on, or a clear head for describing.

The second essay, entitled "Apology for my Writings," takes up the theme of the last sentence of the Introduction:

If this book should ever fall into the hands of persons given to literary criticism, but unacquainted with the business of spinning, the just probability is that they will despise it as low and vulgar, and call me everything but learned. To such persons I must here address a few words. My writings in point of style and composition I readily admit are inferior to most books given to the public by learned authors. To acknowledge this I account no dishonour as I never intended my writing but for private use. Had I been a man of leisure I should have considered myself highly reprehensible for not producing something better, but as I am my case is different, my education when at school was at best but scanty, not costing more than fifty pounds and ever since my 18th year I have been always closely occupied toiling in a ruinous mill.

As a businessman, Brown emerges as an honest and direct dealer, hating the "higgling and prizzing" of the market. At a time when secrecy was the rule, he allowed potential rivals to visit his works, and he was willing to give young men at the outset of their careers as well as less successful spinners the benefit of the experience which he had acquired from years of systematic study. Nor was his search for knowledge restricted to his own works, for he made a habit of journeying far afield in search of improvements—to Aberdeen, to mills in Fife and Forfarshire, as well as to Leeds and Darlington to visit the mill of Porthouse and Kendrew, inventors of the "mill or machine, upon new principles, for spinning yarn from hemp, tow flax or wool"—and he encouraged his subordinates to do likewise.

Brown was a humane, even a kindly man, but his outstanding characteristic was probably his enthusiasm, his single-minded devotion to spinning. In a "Note" which establishes among other things his debt to Owen, he says:

To become eminent in one's business one must in great measure be an enthusiast. Managers of mills are in general not enthusiasts, but slaves in their business; they are urged on more by necessity than choice, and are utter strangers to the delights and advantages of enthusiasm, which it would be their interest and happiness to cultivate. The brightest examples in the spinning profession are Marshall, Haddon, Leys, Owen—all of whom became eminent by their enthusiasm, rearing up immense mills and creating for themselves amazing fortunes, devoting their whole souls to it, and bringing their concerns to the greatest perfection and extent.

It may be noted that the account of Brown's career given by Norrie, which is based upon the obituary in the *Dundee Advertiser*, stresses the same point.[4] "William Brown, an eminent flax-spinner of Dundee, and who, at the time of his death, was the father of the trade, was descended from a flax-spinner, and in his boyhood became a spinner also; and never, during his long lifetime, did his enthusiasm for his favourite trade falter or flag."

II

William Brown acquired a considerable reputation as a mill manager in Dundee. His essays show that he was consulted on particular problems by other spinners and that for one of his customers, Messrs. Bell and Balfour, he made an inspection of their mill and, in an essay of some fifteen pages, reported how it should be run. Casual reference in another essay discloses that for a time he managed Dudhope Mill and "visited" a mill in Lochee regularly. The former was probably North Dudhope Mill which in 1822 was owned by Mrs. John Scott, and from references to "John Scott's Sequestered Estate" and "the late John Scott's Trustees" it would seem that Brown was managing the mill on behalf of creditors, of whom he was one. The reference to Lochee is obscure; there were only two spinning mills in this village adjacent to Dundee, one of which, East Mill, was owned in 1822 by "Watt and Brown."

Brown's theory and practice of management contains several elements which warrant separate treatment. These are the personal qualities of the manager, his technical and business knowledge, his administrative ability, and the social skills with which he carried out his functions.

As might be expected, the more tangible matters like technical and administrative procedures are fully described in the essays, whereas the personal factors rarely appear except incidentally.

Reference has already been made to Brown's belief that "to become eminent in one's business one must in a great measure be an enthusiast." In the same essay he also notes that a manager of a mill should be "chaste, temperate, modest, and devout, scrupulously just in his administration and severely exact in the discipline of his hands; upon which he should know his glory and his success in a great measure depend." There is every reason to believe that Brown modeled his life by these precepts, but, as we shall see, exact discipline did not imply inhumanity.

William Brown's main responsibilities lay in the technical and production side of the business, but he was not without knowledge of the mercantile aspects as well. This knowledge he acquired during his brother's absence from the mill, during which time he did the work of both men, and incidentally drew both salaries. He described his experiences in an essay "On Business":

> In addition to the spinning department of the East Mill concern I have for the past six months had the sole management of the Mercantile Department. Now, however, circumstances having relieved me of this, I feel desirous to explain in writing some of the benefits I have derived from it.
>
> Before entering upon it I was alike ignorant of markets, of customers, of accounts and of book-keeping. Now I have a tolerable idea of all these; I am now pretty well acquainted with the method of finding out prices, of buying and selling flax and yarn, the respectability of merchants and manufacturers, the method of keeping books and accounts, of handling money, and of avoiding errors, disputes, and careless promises.
>
> I have likewise had the satisfaction, by perseverance in fairness and candour, of gaining the confidence of most people I have dealt with, though to my vexation, some were inclined to be rather suspicious. Prizzing and higgling I detested and seldom practised. Other advantages are my peace of mind will not now be disturbed with groundless fears and apprehensions respecting my partner's exertions in his business, and the state of the Companies [sic] affairs—formerly when I was ignorant of these things, I could not help often thinking the worst of them.
>
> My acquaintance with the mercantile department would also be a considerable help to me in the management of the spinning, for in conversing with my partner on business, I will now at once comprehend what he means, and what he wants, and will be at no loss, how to tell him what I mean and I want.

Besides these advantages in the way of business, I have likewise profitted by having got acquainted with many of the merchants, manufacturers and others, few of whom I knew or was known to before. I shall now conduct the mill with less trouble than formerly for having been necessarily limited in my attendance, I learned to become more effectual. I shall now likewise possess an agreeable feeling of independence, which I was a stranger to before, for however well affected my partners and however little the chance of separation, still there was a probability in my being thrown upon myself unprepared. Having thus in some measure become acquainted with the business, I will now do well to use such means as will be effectual to retain it. For this purpose I must occasionally in the market place make the whole round of the shops and warehouses I am acquainted with, enquire into the prices and sale of goods, examining the qualities, and hear opinions.

This experience so impressed Brown that he returned to it in a miscellaneous essay entitled "Facts, Maxims, etc" in which he stated:

The management of East Mill is vested in two of the partners, one for the mercantile dept. and another for the spinning. Their powers for managing are chiefly discretionary and each acts from his own personal sense of duty. The partners repose great confidence in one another's [judgment], dictation and control being out of the question. In all matters of importance however consultations are held and advice taken. The exertions of both are required to make the common good; the neglect of but one to make it bad. If both perform their duty well both are fairly and equally concerned with their respective departments. If one perform it ill he not only deprives his partner of due profit, but throws an additional burden of management upon him. As for instance if the spinning manager should mis-size the yarns, making it too coarse, or with too much waste the mercantile manager is burdened with difficulties and vexations in disposing of the yarn which do not arise from his neglect but from his partner's. And, on the other hand, if the mercantile manager becomes negligent, provide bad flax, small parcels, or unsuiting qualities, the spinning manager is burdened with difficulties and vexations in his department which would not have occurred had the mercantile manager done his duty.

The same essay discusses "good character" (or, as we should say, good will) in relation to the quality of yarn. In describing the different methods adopted he concludes, "Some use great endeavours to manage well and provide good hands with old machinery and some treat and flatter the manufacturers hence it follows that many attain the same ends by different means." He continues:

Contemplating upon the state of the spinning frames of East Mill I have often thought how it is possible for me with those old complex things to compete with my neighbours nowadays most of whom have nothing but simple and substantial new ones. My reflection has been not a little satisfying.

The system of management worked out by Brown was to divide the works into departments and to study each department according to a definite plan at set intervals. Part of the supervision of the works was delegated to an undermanager whose duties, rights, and responsibilities were set out in a letter. This letter is very informative: it specifies in detail the functions of each operative, in the style of a modern job description; and it stresses (as does the report to Messrs. Bell and Balfour) the importance of allowing a manager complete authority in his area of responsibility. The general plan was described in these terms:

The first and great object to be aimed at by the Manager of East Mill is PROFIT. The chief requisites to profit are—a good quality of yarn—large quantity—little waste—moderate expenses—and a good state of the machinery. To ensure all these as far as possible it is necessary that the manager lay out his business into twelve different departments, each of which, from its peculiar nature, requires its own separate portion of attendance and consideration.

Departments

Warehouse Department	Heckling Department
Flax preparing Department	Tow preparing Department
Tow spinning Department	Rating Department
Mechanic Department	Storehouse Department
Improvt. or Alteration Department	Sundries Department
Countinghouse Department	

In the warehouse department the various things that have to be daily investigated by me as manager are as follows:

1st. *The Undressed Flax:* as to what different parcels are on hand—whom they belong to—probable quantity in each parcel—kind—colour—quantity size of yarn intended for—fitness or unfitness for that size—picked out of coarse or damaged heads—quantity of pickings—stuffings—tare of mats, ropes, etc.
2nd. *The Drest Flax:* as to what different parcels are on hand—whom they belong to—probable quantity in each parcel—kind and quality.
3rd. *The Tow:* as to what different parcels are on hand—whom they belong to—probable quantity in each parcel—kind and quality.

4th. *The Yarn:* as to what different parcels are on hand—whom they belong to—what made from—whether correctly spun to size.
5th. *The Ropes, Strings, Waste, Empty Matts:* as to what different parcels are on hand—quantity in each—whom they belong to—why not disposed of—likewise whether the management of the various articles in the different warehouses be neat, regular, and distinct, and if the warehouse be kept clean.

In investigating this department I must be accompanied by the Heckling overseer to assist and inform me as to the different things to be examined; and I must always endeavour to acquaint myself well with the quality of the different parcels of flax and tow I have to spin—the same being essentially necessary to my directing aright, without chance of blunders, the general affairs of the work.

In the course of his notes on the heckling department he observes: "Occasionally I must acquaint myself as to the number of workmen employed—their character—their attendance—the current wages the state of heckles—order of heckling house, etc." His reference to the flax preparing department, the flax spinning department, and the reeling department are brief, for, as he explains:

The conducting of these departments being submitted to an Assistant manager, I, as principal manager, have only to investigate them in a general way. My plan is—to call my assistant daily into the counting house at a stated hour to examine his books and slates, question him concerning them, talk with him, give him further orders, and, if necessary, visit with him any part of the work that may be suspected deficient. Occasionally I must read over with attention the Instructions for the Assistant Manager, see page 42—the same being calculated to bring to my mind every particular of his duty.

The tow preparing department was under Brown's personal supervision and he therefore gives a full description of his procedure:

In this department the following things require my daily investigation, viz:

1st. *The Towrooms:* as to what different parcels of tow are on hand—the kind and quality of each parcel—and what picking, mixing or moistening they require.—Also if the different parcels of tow be properly kept separate, so as not to be carelessly mixed, if each gets its due proportion of waste and brokage, and if the room be kept in good order throughout.
2nd. *The Feeders' work:* as to correctness of weighing—and evenness and neatness of feeding, to be examined both on the cloth and in the slivers—very important.

3rd. *The Slivercarrier's work* at front and back of all the cards and breakers: as to—the handling and piecing of the slivers—brokage of slivers—filling of canns—placing of same at the machines—and cleaning of rollers, brushes & conductors. Each hand separately.

The rest of the work of this department, the tow spinning department, the mechanic department, and the storehouse are described in a similar way. Two further departments—the "Improvement or Alteration Department" and the "Sundries Department"—are of sufficient interest to warrant quoting Brown's notes on them. Of the first Brown wrote:

As the art of Flaxspinning is still improving and improvable it is necessary that every mill manager devote a portion of his time to the cultivation of improvements. Should this be neglected the consequences must be disagreeable as one must necessarily be left behind his neighbours. Improvements may be made in two ways: either by invention or adoption. If invention is to be tried the best way of proceeding is to understand the present machinery well, to be familiar with its imperfections, and to remedy them accordingly. If adopting is to be tried, the only way is to visit improved mills, to acquaint one's self with the nature of their improvements, and to adopt accordingly.

At present I have no particular method of proceeding with improvement farther than attending to the above hints. One thing however I require to keep in mind, and that is—that the success of a mill depends much more upon keeping the machinery in good order and managing well on the present plan, than upon pursuing and looking after what are commonly called alterations and improvements.

Of the "Sundries Department" Brown observed:

Most of the things classed under this head do not require daily or even weekly investigation. The bare reading of them over once or twice a week is sufficient to keep me in mind of them. In reading them I must observe to give each its due thought and enquiry as I go along. The different things are as follows:

1st. Accidental Fire—Insurance etc.
2nd. Pilfering—Nightwatching—Dog etc.
3rd. Fastening of doors, windows, gates, etc.
4th. State of mill hard, water channels, ponds, etc.
5th. State of houses, roofs, floors, doors, windows, etc.
6th. State of necessaries.
7th. State of scales, weights, etc.
8th.

This last item was left blank to accommodate an afterthought which apparently did not come.

The letter to the under-manager to which Brown referred is of considerable interest, containing as it does not only instructions of a technical nature but also principles for maintaining good relations between the manager and the under-manager. The letter is some eighteen pages long, so that it is impracticable to quote more than a little of it.

To John Reid. East Mill, Jan. 3rd, 1818.

As you are about to enter upon the management of a department of the work I think it proper to state a few things to you on paper that you may have an idea how to conduct yourself so as to ensure good management, and to prevent misunderstanding betwixt us.

The following are the principal things that I mean to put under your charge:

First, the steam engine.

Second, the operation of the flax preparing and spinning.

Third, the mechanics [sic] workship, as far as relates to the repair of the machinery to be under your charge; and also as to the cutting out and working the different kinds of wood required in the work for bobbins, wheeves [?], rollers, etc.

Fourth, the providing, engaging and managing of all the hands necessary for your department, and the purchasing of all the articles and materials required for the mill except the following which I am to attend to myself, viz: coal, oil, tallow, lists and greenwood. I am also to attend to the management of the tow preparing and spinning operation with which you are to have nothing to do unless at any time required.

The work of every operative in the under-manager's charge is described and procedures for the care of every part of the plant laid down thus:

4th. The doubler's work,—as to the number of slivers in the boxes whether they be regularly and carefully put in so as to come out again easily; whether sufficiently pressed in the boxes so as to make them hold as much as possible, and whether the ends be neatly pieced.

5th. The frame minder work at the front of the bell carriage, as to the shifting of the canns precisely when the bell rings and marking them the proper number with chalk; as to the pressing of the sliver carefully down into the canns and as to the keeping of the frame clean.

. . . .

10th. The oiling of the machinery especially the feet, necks and tops of the spindles, and the axles and journals of the drawing rollers which are apt to get dry if not attended to. The axles require oil in proportion to the pressure on the levers and the feet of the spindles in proportion to the tightness of the belts. Both of these must be carefully attended to, and every means taken to make them, and every other part of the machinery as easily driven as possible, by keeping the different parts clean, rightly set, oiled, and in proper repair.

Brown likewise gave a detailed explanation of causes of "variations in the weight of yarn" and the means of correcting such faults. He then proceeded to lay down certain general principles of management under five headings (hands, machinery, production, improvements, and administration) in the following words:

For your further information the following is a general plan on which I wish the work to be conducted.

1st. To keep up a set of as good hands as possible throughout the work. This I wish particularly observed in regard to the spinners, to whom I would always be willing to give liberal wages; others to be kept as moderate as possible consistent with the state of the trade, and the plentiness or scarcity of hands. Every one to be held strictly at duty, and no one of bad habits allowed to remain longer in the work than she can be replaced with another. An outlook must always be had for new hands, both learned and unlearned, and before taking them in particular regard must be paid to their habits and character. Care must be taken to keep them always under engagement to the work, and no engagement ever allowed to run out before being either renewed or a fresh hand provided. At present the set of hands in the mill is very good, most of them are under engagement till the end of the year, and all are tolerably satisfied with their situation. Under your management I trust the set will not be allowed to fall off nor any dissatisfaction to take place.
2nd. To keep the machinery constantly in the best state of order and repair . . .
3rd. To endeavour by every means to obtain a large quantity of yarn from the frames daily . . .
4th. Concerning alterations or improvements in the management, machinery, or operations of the mill, I have only to say that you will make it part of your business to bring everything to as much perfection as possible, consistent with the convenience of the work, and the expenses attending it. It will be highly proper for you to take frequent opportunities of seeing what your neighbours are about in the way of spinning, and making yourself acquainted with all their proceedings, especially such as are reputed good managers. And if you may think at any time to gain anything at a distance I shall be glad to let you away for a few

days, paying your expenses, and managing for you till you return. As to alterations and improvements, however, they must always be *second in consideration* to the keeping of the mill in good order, and managing well upon the present plans.

The general instructions on administration are interesting examples both of the "exact discipline" advocated by Brown and his understanding of the causes of tension:

A desk to be placed in the reeling room and a new book begun for keeping the accounts of the spinners, and reelers work and waste, the weight of the yarn, the quantity spun, etc. The overseer with your assistance will daily attend to it, and it will be highly beneficial for you to spend a portion of time with it every day, examining and considering the state of the different hands work and waste, comparing the one with the other, yesterday's with today's, and making yourself intimately acquainted with all their performances.

As it will be proper to have as distinct a separation as possible in the management of the lint and tow department it will be necessary that neither you nor I interfere much with one another's hands. If any of yours come to me for redress of grievances, I shall refer them to you as their proper manager. I shall have no more to do with your hands than merely paying them their weekly wages which I, as clerk, shall do every Friday morning as usual. Observe that I shall be in the counting house regularly every forenoon at 10 o'clock, and that this is the time that you must bring forward everything you may have to say about the work. If any hands are to be engaged, any disputes settled, any money advanced, or any proposals made, the same must be brought forward at 10 o'clock and at no other time of the day.

In Brown's memorandum to Messrs. Bell and Balfour he divided his advice in much the same way between the specific and technical and the general administrative procedures. His general remarks are in line with his letter to the under-manager:

There are some things I should yet mention regarding the welfare of the mill, which will depend entirely upon yourselves, and over which the manager can have little control. I think it as well to mention them, though it is possible you may be partly aware of them already. A spinning mill is a complicated and ticklish kind of concern, and however nicely arranged and anxiously cared for is extremely liable to fall into disorder. It ought therefore to be subject to the fewest possible changes in every respect in the management, consequently it will be necessary never to have more than three different kinds of yarn making at a time.

I also take it upon me to say that your own attendance on the work should be subject to regulation. It will be proper that one Partner only take any charge of the mill, the other visiting it but seldom and never interfering with the manager in giving directions, making inquiries or passing opinions. One Partner being appointed, it will be necessary that he have a stated time daily of visiting the work. The most suitable time for the manager would be every forenoon at 10 o'clock, but any other hour will do if that is not convenient for the Partner. One hour a day I would reckon sufficient for the Partner's attendance, at least after a proper manager is set agoing; a visit in the evening might sometimes be useful. Should things be put upon this footing it will be indispensable to have a small counting house fitted up in some convenient place near the small door. In this the manager and clerk must both have desks for their convenience in keeping accounts, engaging hands, and doing the other business of the mill. The Partner in his daily visits must resort to the counting house, calling the attendance of the manager and clerk, examining over all the accounts of the preceding day's performance, and making such inquiries and remarks and giving such instructions as may seem necessary; then he may go over all or any part of the work as he may think fit, accompanied by the manager, and making such further inquiries and remarks as may appear proper. Then, leaving the manager, he should see through the whole of the warehouses and heckling houses, accompanied by the heckling overseer, and making such remarks to him as the state of things at the time may demand.

It must be observed by the Partner that the manager be allowed full scope and power in managing, so that not only the hands may look upon him as their sole manager, but that he may be allowed the whole merit of conducting the work. A manager, if on such a footing, will do a great deal for his own personal character and credit. The Partner should never need to speak to or have any thing to do with the hands, excepting in the case of prosecution. If any of the hands apply to him for redress of petty grievances, he must just refer them back to the manager, who, they must be informed, has full power to settle all their differences.

Brown applied his systematic approach to the business side of the administration of East Mill, and integrated record keeping with the planning and control of the works. Describing the counting house department, he wrote:

The different books kept by the manager of East Mill, besides the business books, are as follows, viz:

First, the daily work book
Second, the wages book
Third, the petty expense book

Fourth, the advance and deposit book
Fifth, the agreement book
A clerk is employed to keep the most of these books, but everyone of them requires careful examination at set times, by myself.

The "advance" book was probably the record of small loans made to his operatives, for in another part of the Essays he noted:

Of about 90 hands employed at East Mill there are generally from 8 to 12 in debt to their employers. The sum given to each at a time never exceeds 20/-, seldom even 10/- and none ever get any but on known pressing occasions. The money is repaid at the rate of 1/- or 1/6 per hand per week and the whole sums advanced are never allowed to exceed £10. Were I to advance money to every hand that calls for it I would soon be out of pocket more than £100 and almost all the hands in the mill would be in my debt in a short time, but in place of giving them money when they ask it I generally tell them that they ought to provide beforehand for any contingency by allowing 6d. or 1/- a week of their wages to remain in my hands by way of stock. This however few of them attend for I have never yet at any one time had more than 9 or 10 of them in arrears.

He concluded the essay on the counting house thus:

The great business of the counting house dept. does not consist merely in attending to these few books. It is in the counting house that I must think, consult, and mature in my mind everything of importance that is done in the work; it is here that I must arrange all my plans, make all my bargains and agreements, settle all disputes, grievances, difficulties, etc. And for the more regular conducting of these matters I must make a point of being always personally in the counting house from 10 till 11 o'clock in the forenoon; at which time and at no other the people of the mill must be taught to bring forward their affairs so that during the rest of the day I may have nothing to interrupt me when engaged at the other departments of the work.

Brown's interest in and systematic practice of management was evident in the account he gives of his visit to Leeds in 1821. This gives a detailed description of the industry as a whole, the mills, steam engines, water supply, yarns spun, the level of technique in every department, and the cost of production. In addition, he has this to say about the "management of Hands":

In general the hands in Leeds are not under better discipline than in Scotland. Excepting Mr. Marshall's and a few more, the others are under no sort of methodical arrangement whatever. Marshall's have very particular printed instructions set before them, which are as particularly attended to. I tried to procure copies but could not succeed, so strict are the instructions that if any overseer of a room be found talking to any person in the mill during working hours he is dismissed immediately —two or more overseers are employed in each room, if one be found a yard out of his own ground he is discharged. No overseer is allowed to touch a tool or shift a pinion with his own hands, on pain of dismissal— everyone, manager, overseers, mechanics, oilers, spreaders, spinners, and reelers, have their particular duty pointed out to them, and if they transgress, they are instantly turned off as unfit for their situation. Not so with the other mills—there, few rules are laid down and as few attended to—the hands are allowed to roam about from place to place, and from window to window without control,—the overseers are lazy and the manager and masters ineffectual. In Marshall's every man chases his business—in the others every man's business chases him. The result is striking—Marshall has made hundreds of thousands—the others, excepting two or three, have become bankrupts, and are leading their life in the midst of dust, waste, confusion, and discontentment.

III

We have now summarized William Brown's systematic observations on management. There remain, however, a number of incidental remarks which illustrate his thoughts and methods. These notes describe such matters as morale, giving orders, resolving conflicts, wages, and labor relations.

In 1823 a number of alterations to buildings and improvements to the mill yard created so much disturbance that Brown set down the events in an essay entitled "Disorder in Business," describing the effect on morale in these vivid terms:

The bad consequences of such a combination of things on work soon becomes considerable, a falling off gradually takes place in the quantity of yarn spun—the frames begin to go ill—the quantity gets further reduced—the weight of the yarn gets too high—the waste increases—the wages and expenses swell up—the best of hands begin to leave the work through disgust and accidents take place—fire breaks out, pilfering is practised—machinery is broken, hands are hurt or torn to pieces, and in short everything soon falls into total confusion; and work which had previously been doing well is, by the silent operation of neglect, and the bearing-in of disorder, reduced from step to step to an unprofitable or ruinous concern. I do not say that such was the case with the East Mill in the fullest extent; I only say that the evil was begun, and that from the cause ceasing to exist, the evil in time began to abate.

His attitude to employees clearly owes much to Robert Owen:

Hands in a mill should always be kept busy. The more closely they are held at their work the more comfortable they are. If allowed to leave their places they are continually sighing after something they have no business with. It is a mistaken humanity to indulge them in ease, idleness, or play. When in fault they should be reprimanded, first calmly, then seriously, then sharply—great care should be taken to point out faults—explain duties—to young ones or beginners especially. There is scarcely any one so backward or corrupt that may not be improved by unremitting attention.

In contrast to this, his essay on the art of giving orders is quite original and modern in its ideas, despite its archaic literary style:

The giving of orders and directions to servants is a thing that has to be practised in a mill several hundred times a day and ought to be well understood; yet notwithstanding its importance, most people pay no attention to the manner of it. In giving orders, no apology should be made, however hard the order; but great care should be taken not to demand anything that is ill-timed or unreasonable. If orders are given in a sensible, reasonable sort of way, the servant will likely do his utmost to fulfil them; but if given in a rude ill-humoured sort of way he will likely do but bare justice. Masters reap great benefit from having the art of making their servants interested in their work, being responsible in character for what they perform, enjoying their own merit, and not being depressed or offended by sulky looks or harsh expressions. Masters who are properly up to the management of their hands, are always welcome among them, and their presence is agreeable; but those who rule by wrong methods are disliked and their absence is always earnestly wished for.

Between January 1821, and May 1823, a night shift was worked at the East Mill. This experiment, which proved highly profitable to Brown but ruinous to those of his competitors who tried to follow suit, was described in an essay "On the Conclusion of Night Spinning" and gave rise to some of the most acute human problems which Brown had to face. During this period, in pursuance of his policy of delegating full authority to his manager, Brown limited his intervention to "a single hour per night, spent chiefly in the Counting House with the manager. My presence frequently in the mill I considered improper, as the manager was vested with full authority to manage. This authority would have been injured by my presence." Many conflicts arose between the day and night shifts, particularly over the responsibility for errors in the size of yarn. "Sometimes it was scarce possible to discover whether the faults were occasioned by the night or day hands, and the overseers when questioned were apt to be very crusty on the subject, readily attaching blame to each other in place of themselves. Indeed misunderstandings sometimes came to such a height between the overseers of the carding room that they secretly took means to lead each other into errors in the size, merely for the purpose of venting their own petty revenge on one another and shewing their own performance in a better light." Brown goes on to list the numerous "little tricks they practised, and attempted to practise on each other in this way to the great annoyance of the work and vexation of the manager," and comments "It required no common exertion of prudence [?] and forbearance to counteract and rectify them. The best course I generally found was to say little to them on the subject, far less to rage against them, but to manage as vigilantly and direct their attention as carefully as possible to what most obviously applied to themselves."

Brown's attitude to wages and labor relations does not appear to have been unusual. He seems to have paid piece rates where possible, with an incentive bonus of "extra wages" to spinners, spreaders, and others who exceeded their "stint," and a similar bonus to overseers. He apparently considered, but did not adopt, a system he found in "some English mills" where

> the overseers of rooms find hands for themselves, paying them out of their own pockets, and making the best bargain they can with them. On this plan they drive economy of hands to the utmost pitch, employing and teaching many new cheap ones, squeezing down wages to the lowest fraction, and giving each hand as much work as she can possibly do, and enforcing the most rigorous attendance and attention; thereby doing the business of a room not only at lower rates of wages, but also with a considerably less number of hands. On this plan masters have much less trouble themselves and nothing can more effectually tend to keep down the rates of wages in general.

His policy on wages appears to have been planned in consultation with his fellow spinners in Dundee and neighboring districts. Thus in his account of a strike and lockout of hecklers[4] Brown states:

> Owing to the badness of trade, the little prospect of a revival, the plentiness of hands, the highness of wages, etc., a reduction was some weeks ago meditated by the mill spinners of Dundee, and was last week to

come into effect. Wages during the bypast two years have been gradually advancing, not so much on account of good trade, or a scarcity of hands, as of improvements in the operations of spinning, thereby causing an increased quantity, from which proceeded an increase of wages, as the hands were all on piece work, and the rate never altered.

From the rest of the account it appears that the reduction of wages for some operatives was made by increasing the number of spyndles[5] to be spun before the extra wages were paid. The reduction did not cover all workers. "The carders, covers, shifters, etc. could bear nothing as their wages were already moderate."

IV

This paper has so far dealt with some of the elements which made for the success of the firm of W. & G. Brown: the enthusiasm of its manager, his technical and mechanical skill, his understanding of social and administrative procedures, his frugality, the investment of profits in the business, and the careful study of competitors. There remains one more factor: Brown's humane treatment of his workers.

Evidence of this appears in the Factories Inquiry Commission on the employment of children in factories, to which we have already referred. Brown's evidence shows that, unlike many of his contemporaries, he was in favor of a reduction of hours. His opinion, he stated, "is decided, that the hours of labour, as well with a view to the interest of the mill-spinner as of the workers, their health and education, should be limited to eleven hours each day, and ten on Saturday; that he does not think that, by such an arrangement, the cost of production would be materially affected, as he thinks the work would be better done." Brown's manager gave evidence that no corporal punishment was employed in the mills, although James Scott, a ten year old boy, asserted that a foreman, his uncle, "gives him a slap in the face when he falls asleep or does anything wrong." From the same source we learn "that two school rooms, one for boys, the other for females, attached to the mills . . . are provided by Messrs. Brown and Company, with two good teachers, for the workers, who have the privilege of education there, as soon as the mill work is over, every day but Saturday; that most of the young workers attend the school, and can read, but all cannot write."

Consideration was also given to the needs of the older employees. A report in the *Dundee Advertiser* stated that a room with newspapers was provided for adult workers, one of their number being appointed to read aloud for those who could not read for themselves. The manager also reported that the machinery was "with very few exceptions, well boxed in; that every year, since he came here, improvements in this respect have been made; and that his employers have hitherto approved of every suggestion he has made." In later evidence he described the working conditions, stating

> that seats are provided in all the three mills in the spinning rooms, and also partly in the preparing rooms; that there are thermometers and timepieces in each of the mills, and that great pains are taken to ventilate the rooms, by opening the large windows and the doors, and by sprinkling water as well through the day as at night, on the floors . . . and that there are passages in two of the spinning-rooms, four feet wide, between the walls and the frames.

Two women operatives, Ann Mackay and Elizabeth Porter, after complaining of the fatigue and disability caused by long hours, went on to speak in glowing terms of the employers. One of them asserted "that there cannot be better masters than Messrs. Brown and Mr. Cooper [the manager]; that nobody has a word against them, and it is reckoned a good thing for a worker to get into their mills; that she is often absent from indisposition and her place is kept open for her." Elizabeth Porter gave the final accolade, stating that "she believes Messrs. Brown the finest masters in this town, and she would not like to leave them, that she knows plenty of the workers to whom he has given the means of living when they were unwell."

Sir Ambrose Crowley, Ironmonger, 1658–1713

MICHAEL W. FLINN

THAT SIR AMBROSE CROWLEY was one of the most outstanding figures in the history of British industry has long been recognized by economic historians. He has received, and continues to receive, honorable mention in textbooks of modern economic history, where reference is usually made to his remarkable compilation, the *Law Book of the Crowley Ironworks.*[1] These accounts of Crowley have usually tantalized us by their failure to tell more than the briefest of details concerning the life and character of the creator of this complex code. Paucity of source material has been to blame for this brevity, and although a few writers have tried to probe a little deeper than the *Law Book,* their results have been disappointingly meager.[2]

Many of the laws in the *Law Book,* which is a closely written manuscript book of 382 folio pages, govern the preparation of returns, reports, journals, and minutes, and order the keeping of an infinite variety of stock books, day books, log books, and accounts; and it seemed reasonable to expect that some portion of this vast collection of business records should have survived to provide the foundation for the model business history. But these hopes were destroyed in 1887, when a Newcastle journal, referring to Crowley's register of workpeople, reported that this, "along with other valuable business documents of the firm, was cast into a furnace and destroyed in 1862 at the command of the then proprietor."[3] The failure of subsequent investigators to bring any of the records to light lent authority to this report, with the result that "the greatest ironmaster of the seventeenth century"[4] is still little more than an enigma to students of industrial history.

This article is reprinted, by permission of the author, from *Explorations in Entrepreneurial History,* 5:162–180 (March 1953).

The present account, which is in the nature of a preliminary report, draws on manuscript sources not previously used by those who have so far investigated Crowley's life and work. These sources are contained in four main collections: two series of family and business letters, one in a collection known as the "Lloyd Mss." at the Library of the Friends' Meeting House in London,[5] and the other in the private possession of a descendant of the Crowley family, Mr. Humphrey Lloyd of Marlow;[6] a large mass of legal and other documents in the "Ashburnham Collection" at the Suffolk County Record Office in Ipswich;[7] and an immensely valuable series of administrative instructions from Crowley in London to the staff at his ironworks in County Durham in the North of England: this series, bound together into a single volume, is in the possession of the Society of Antiquaries of Newcastle-on-Tyne.[8]

II

Sir Ambrose Crowley's origins were by no means as obscure as has been suggested: he did not begin his working life as a common smith. He was born in Stourbridge in the county of Worcester in February 1658, the son of a prosperous ironmonger of the same name. Ambrose Crowley senior, who was a prominent member of the Society of Friends noted for his generosity not only to the Society and its poor but also to his personal friends, gave his son a sound start in life by apprenticing him in 1674 to a freeman of the Drapers' Company in London. Clement Plumstead, to whom Crowley was indentured, was an ironmonger of Great Minories in the City of London.[9] Crowley served his apprenticeship with exemplary diligence (so he tells us himself), and acquired the freedom of his company in 1684. "I never asked for one Hollyday all my time of apprentysshipp except when my Father was in towne . . . My dilligence in my apprentyship raised mee severall Freinds who was allways ready to assist mee in every thing that was needfull."[10] In what capacity he remained in London at the end of his term of apprenticeship it is not yet possible to say: it is known, however, that at about this time he started a factory for the manufacture of ironware in the north-east coast town of Sunderland. The date traditionally associated with the foundation of his ironworks at Sunderland is 1682, but the only direct evidence so far discovered suggests that this date is too early. One of the earliest descriptions of Crowley's factories in County Durham names 1684 or 1685 for the foundation of the enterprise in Sunderland.[11] There has also survived, fortunately, a remarkable document of the year 1685 in which the young Ambrose explained his reasons for establishing a factory for the manufacture of nails in Sunderland, giving the impression that the factory was only in course of erection in that year. Furthermore, from the year 1684 onward, Crowley began to take apprentices.[12]

From a letter to his father dated 10 February 1684/5,[13] and addressed: "Brother,[14] deliver this to my Father seal'd up. To bee broake up at my Fathers discretion in the presence of none but considerable Ironmasters that principaly trade in or near Birmingham," it seems clear that by this time Crowley was trading in ironware on his own account, and, not having entered the manufacturing side of the business, depended upon Midlands suppliers for his purchases of iron. The Midlands ironmasters were to be present at the reading of this letter because Crowley considered that they had treated him unfairly and he had decided to cast himself adrift from dependence upon their doubtful goodwill. Without apparently reckoning upon the caliber of this youth in London, they had goaded him to the point where he threatened to manufacture nails on his own account on a scale and at a price which would drive them out of business. But he was ready to give up this project if the ironmasters would buy him off at the cost of £10,000, or two years' purchase of his estimated profit of £5,000 a year, on which condition he would be prepared to "put a stop to my naill trade in those parts, but tell I have an assurance of the sd. 2 years purchase I shall proceed with all immadgenable resolution and diligence."

In this letter he explained his reasons for the choice of Sunderland as the location of his "intended mill." He had observed that Tyne colliers returned from many south and east coast ports in ballast, and that for negligible freight rates he could have rod and bar iron from Sussex, Kent, and Yorkshire (via Hull) carried to Sunderland; in Sunderland coal was cheaper than in the "nail country" (Worcestershire and the Black Country); "vitals is above ⅓ cheaper than in the present nail country"; and finally, cheap labor was abundant around Sunderland.

Unfortunately the reply of the Midlands ironmasters to this impertinence is no longer to be found, and it can only be conjectured that they refused to be blackmailed, for Crowley went ahead with his plans at Sunderland. At this early stage, however, his confidence outran his fortune, for in Sunderland his affairs did not run as smoothly as he had anticipated. He imported foreign labor either to instruct the north country workers in new skills, or simply to make good an unsuspected shortage of suitable labor. These workers came from the Liège district, and their Roman Catholic religion offended the Protestants of Sunderland.[15] To avoid further trouble, Crowley decided to move his mill some miles to the north-west, to the decayed hamlet of Winlaton, five miles from Newcastle. Once settled at Winlaton, he evidently managed to dispense with foreign workmen, for neither the parish registers nor lists of his employees contain more than isolated names which could possibly be of foreign origin.[16] It is usually stated that Crowley moved his works from Sunderland to Winlaton in the year 1690, but evidence from two sources indicates that the move was probably made in 1691. In that year he took a lease of property in Winlaton from Sir Thomas Tempest:[17] in July 1694 Crowley agreed with the Corporation of Newcastle for a fixed yearly payment of £6.13s.4d. for exemption from toll, making at the same time payment for the three previous years.[18]

Although Crowley chose the North of England as the most suitable location for his factory, this merely remained one branch of his business. His head office, chief warehouse, and his own residence were at first located together at the sign of the "doublet" in Thames Street in the City of London.[19] His business at first was concentrated on the manufacture of nails,[20] and specialized in the production of sheathing nails used in shipbuilding. The market for this type of product was not centered in any particular locality, and in establishing his head office and warehouse in London, Crowley was clearly thinking in terms of a nation-wide sale for his products.[21] By 1704 the business had evidently expanded to a point where the Thames Street accommodation was no longer adequate, and Crowley looked for more commodious quarters. "I have brought a howse at Greenwich wher I am now just a goeing . . . designing to build a very large ware howse their."[22] The house, which remained the head office of the Crowley business until its dissolution in the nineteenth century, was evidently a fitting house for a wealthy merchant. It was said to have contained an interior court, paneled rooms, and a fine carved staircase.[23] The old warehouse in Thames Street was still retained, and other warehouses at the Gulley Hole in Thames Street, in the "Coal Harbour," "at the Waterside," and in Suffolk Lane, were later added to the accommodation in London.[24]

The additional warehouse accommodation in London was planned to cater for the increased output of the extended factories in the North of England. In the early days of the nail factory at Sunderland and Winlaton, Crowley bought his rod iron, the raw material of the nailing industry, from slitters in the Midlands. Once again, dependence upon outside suppliers for raw materials irked Crowley, and about the turn of the century he extended the manufacturing side of his business to include another process—that of slitting. A slitting mill needed water power, and Winlaton lay on the top of a hill: Crowley sited his new slitting mill—"Mill No. 1" as he called it—a mile to the east of Winlaton in the valley of the River Derwent, at a point now rather confusingly called "Winlaton Mill." Plans for the new mill were drawn up in London, and sent to the north, where the construction was carried out under detailed postal instructions from Crowley.[25] By this time production in the factories was no longer confined to nailmaking: a very wide range of wrought iron goods was produced and a beginning made with steelmaking for which the Crowley works later became well-known.

In 1702 and 1703, three partners, William Bayliss, Edward Harrison, and Thomas Wood, set up what appears to have been a rival ironworks, making similar smithware at the nearby village of Swalwell.[26] In 1704, Crowley received information from Winlaton that "many of his nailers and patten-ring makers had left his service at Winlaton and gone to work for Mr. Edward Harrison at Swalwell."[27] Some time after this, possibly in 1707,[28] Crowley took over these works at Swalwell, developing them until they became the principal center of his manufacturing business. Here, later, were made the great chains and anchors for which the Crowley ironworks became famous, and here was established the famous "Square," a model community which in some respects anticipated the social experiments of Robert Owen.

After manufacture, such goods as were not sold in the immediate vicinity of Newcastle were brought to Greenwich or London by a small fleet of ships belonging to Crowley. After the death of Sir Ambrose's son and successor, John, this fleet numbered four ships named after members of the Crowley family. The *Crowley* itself was a vessel of 270 tons; the *Ambrose,* the *John,* and the *Theodosia* were smaller, of about 150 tons.[29] From the Thames warehouses, goods were distributed to subdepots in different parts of the country. Crowley maintained five of these warehouses, at Blackwall in Essex, Ware in Hertfordshire, Wolverhampton and Walsall in Staffordshire, and Stourbridge in Worcestershire. The latter warehouse was also used as a storehouse for bar and rod iron from the Stour valley forges. To complete the organization, Crowley kept a manager at Newcastle whose duties included the supervision of the unloading of ships bringing raw materials from other parts of England and from Sweden, and the loading of the Thames-bound coastal vessels. Upriver from Newcastle, transport was by keel, and a shuttle service of keels carried goods between Newcastle and Crowley's staith at Blaydon-on-Tyne, the nearest point on the river to Winlaton.[30] Here Crowley maintained another warehouse, for although Winlaton was but one mile from Blaydon, this mile was often impassable in winter.[31]

Perhaps the most remarkable aspect of this unique organization was that it was controlled by correspondence from the head office, first in Thames Street, and later in Greenwich, at a time when postal services were notoriously slow.[32] Crowley's visits to his factories in the North of England appear to have been rare.[33] A great deal of Crowley's working time must have been devoted to the writing and dictating of correspondence.

The main stream of letters was directed, of course, to the factories in the North. These letters, of which an incomplete series covering the years 1700 to 1702 has survived, dealt with every aspect of the day-to-day running of the factories. They display an astonishing mastery of detail. Nothing was too trivial or unimportant to merit his attention, nor was any omission or error on the part of his employees too small to avoid his censure. Indeed, the shortcomings of his workpeople at work and at leisure seem to have been the greatest of Crowley's preoccupations. Each "Council Instruction," as these letters were called, was numbered and divided into paragraphs or "Verses" headed and numbered separately: cross reference was therefore easy, and was a feature of the correspondence. Many of the instructions contained in these letters became subsequently embodied in the *Law Book*. In reply to these letters, Crowley required the weekly submission by return post of detailed accounts, reports, journals, and minutes: these he evidently scrutinized in closest detail so that he was able to detect any idleness or dishonesty amongst his employees 300 miles away.

A second stream of correspondence was directed to his buying connections in the ironmaking districts of the Midlands. In particular, Crowley maintained a close relationship with his brother-in-law, Sampson Lloyd, the Birmingham Quaker ironmaster, supplying Lloyd with many of his products. "I hope yow have taken care to hasten the 15 ton of Mill barres now at Budley [Bewdly] to Storton [Stourton] beeing I am in want of it."[34] "I thank you for the account you give me of Mr. Richd. Knights[35] Best Tough Rods. I shall keep private what you mention of the price."[36] "The steell you had last year from me I am sure is good but only tis too high converted for severall uses. But that sent you this year you'll find is lower as the numbers increase. If you prevail with the most knowing workmen to try it you'll find it will be in great reputation."[37] "I am now providing Steel for the next cheap land Carriage and desire you to let me know what Quantity of Broad and Narrow and Rod steel, and the respective Sizes of each will be a sufficient sortment for the whole year. Pray yor answer to this with speed."[38] These extracts are typical of much of the surviving correspondence between the two brothers-in-law. In a trade where there was a great deal of dishonesty (at least this is the impression gained from a study of Crowley's business correspondence), this connection with his Quaker brother-in-law was no doubt valued by Crowley.

A third series of letters dealt with family affairs, for Crowley played the role of benevolent despot in his family circle. This became particularly clear in the last few years of his life when his father retired from business, suffering from loss of memory. His father had carried generosity to an extreme which grieved the son, and when infirmity prevented his father from recovering many outstanding loans, for the most part to fellow Quakers, the son took his father's affairs in hand.[39] His action was characteristically vigorous, but hampered by the interference of other members of the family. His father, too, got his knuckles rapped for lapsing into further acts of charity. "When your age and your decay thereby is considered, there is none but Rogues and villains worse than Highwaymen that would ask you to enter into any obligation or to lend 'em money now, being you are past helping your self, and if it please God to give you long life, I don't see how you can avoid utter ruin...

but those that love you will first see that you be provided for, that you may be secured from ending your days in a gaol. I want words to express the trouble I am under for you, for since your memory has fail'd you, I find you have not resolution enough to withstand the temptation of rogues and villains who comes to involve you in your old and helpless age, in such trouble that you will never be able to get out of. I, as in duty bound, have made it my chief study to preserve you and your family from ruin, but if you do continue to lend money and be bound for people, it is out of my power to preserve you, and if you do it again, you can't expect my assistance, for if you will, before I can end one broil, run into another, it will be in vain for me to attempt to preserve you."[40] His younger half-brothers, who clearly lacked his ability and application to business, strayed from the strait and narrow path only at the cost of incurring his displeasure. "You have now an opportunity to serve yourself, and if you show yourself ready, diligent, and carefull, you will not want my advice or assistance. If you slight it now, you will not easily obtaine it hereafter."[41] "If you serve your time faithfully you shall not want my advice nor assistance (a rowling stone gathers noe mosse). You have beene guilty of that that hath rendered your self unsteady and to retrieve that you ought in an extraordinary manner to show your stedfastness in business, in nothing wavering, or disobedient to your Master, and desire no time to spend in folley."[42]

Both the *Council Instructions* and the *Laws* suggest that Crowley's work was a constant struggle against dishonesty and idleness, vices which drew from him a wonderful flow of abuse. In a Council Instruction of 1702 he arraigned and finally dismissed an erring official. "Whereas I have found him to be very negligent, careless and extravigant, so that he hath run out much, and in all things hath been put upon, hath either omitted it or done it by halfs. He hath made a jest of business and hath not onely slighted it himself, but hath disturbed others in the prosecution of their part . . . Such a drunken sott never undertook any business, for let him be upon the greatest business immaginable, if a drunken companion appear, if his absence wad be mine and his ruin, business must be kept undon, and sotts caressed and waited upon. A jest he maketh at the most searious business, and a game att all those that discharge a good conseince in doing the business they are paid for."[43] In another of the same year he condemned in round terms a project to alter one of his most rigid rules concerning workmen's stocks. "Hell and the most mischievous Angells therein contained could never have struck at soe much ruin in soe few words as in this project; consider the consequence—the Poor ruined, the work destroyed, and things brought into confusion; a harvest for rogues and thieves."[44] Responsibility for supervision rested, in some respects at least, on committees rather than on individuals, and it has been this use of committees which has given the impression that Crowley was an early exponent of democracy in industry. Nothing could be further from the truth: never was a business more autocratically controlled. The words "for remedy whereof I do therefore order . . ." occur in almost every verse of every law or instruction. The use of committees rather than individuals was a device to avoid relying upon the doubtful integrity of one man. Only after the business had been working for some years did Crowley find men whom he could trust. Jonathan Story in Winlaton was the first to become a responsible manager:[45] later, John Hanmer, who remained in Greenwich, emerged as the key man in the business. His integrity and worth reaped their reward in the handsome salary of £400 a year, increased to £450 a year on Crowley's death.[46] Hanmer outlived both Sir Ambrose and his son, John, before dying in 1730. He was succeeded by John Bannister, whose knowledge of the iron trade was such that he was called to give evidence before a parliamentary committee of 1737.[47] Bannister gave way to Abraham Alleyne in 1740.

Crowley never apparently felt at ease with the committee system of control, as the elaborate nature of the precautions against independent action by members of the committees showed.[48] Nevertheless, the committee system was retained in the North, and it is to this form of organization that we owe the *Law Book*, which was simply the codification of all the instructions issued from time to time from London and Greenwich for the guidance of the members of the various committees—the "Council," the "Committee of Survey," the "Committee of Aggrievances," the "Arbitrators," and the "Governors of the Poor."

The aspect of Crowley's organization which has attracted most attention in the past is that of industrial welfare, but as this aspect has been discussed fairly fully by earlier writers it is not proposed to say much here.[49] It was in this respect that Crowley was probably most in advance of his time. Every aspect of communal life was thought of: there was a parson, a doctor, and a schoolmaster, a superannuation scheme, and a health insurance scheme with compulsory contributions graduated according to pay and deducted at source (with similarly graduated employer's contributions).

London was chosen as the headquarters for the organization for more than one reason. It was, firstly, the natural center of a business which imported raw materials from several overseas countries, sold its finished products in all parts of Great Britain, and (in John Crowley's time, at least) exported to the West Indies and the mainland of North America. At all times, the most important single customer of the Crowley business was the Royal Navy. One of the principal dockyards was at Deptford, on the south bank of the Thames, adjacent to Greenwich. It was possibly the convenience of proximity to this dockyard which decided Crowley to move from the city to Greenwich in 1704. A list of debts due to John Crowley at the time of his death in 1728 included Navy Bills drawn on the dockyards at Deptford, Woolwich, Plymouth, Sheerness, and Chatham, amounting to £2,949.5s.4d.[50] In 1740 there were goods worth £563.3s.4d belonging to the Crowleys at the naval dockyard at Deptford.[51] During Ambrose Crowley's lifetime there were often much larger sums outstanding against the Navy.[52] John was evidently more successful in handling the Navy Office than was his father. On the other hand the Navy in the reigns of William III and Anne was notoriously dilatory in the payment of its debts,[53] and the accumulation of debts made Sir Ambrose an important government creditor. In the financial crisis of 1711, when Harley persuaded government creditors to accept shares in the newly projected South Sea Company in settlement of their accounts Crowley found himself the largest single shareholder and a founder-director of the Company. In his will of three years later there were bequests of South Sea Stock amounting to £56,000. The contact with government circles established through the Navy Office in the first instance was thus reinforced by this connection with the South Sea Company.

Crowley's wealth and position as a freeman of one of the London Livery Companies had already drawn him into an active and distinguished part in city politics. As early as 1697 he had entered the city government as Common Councillor for Dowgate Ward. In 1706 he was Sheriff of London, and it was whilst serving in this office that he received his knighthood.[54] In 1711 he became an Alderman, and in 1713, only a few weeks before his death, he successfully contested the parliamentary borough of Andover, defeating Thomas Pitt ("Diamond" Pitt, former Governor of Madras).[55] Unfortunately he died in October 1713 before Parliament assembled, and the House of Commons was deprived of a member who would no doubt have served the interest of the iron manufacturers with characteristic vigor and color.

But though Parliament remained for a time without a representative of the iron industry after Sir Ambrose's death in 1713, the great business he had founded continued with little change. Ambrose's only son, John, was twenty-four when his father died, and proved himself to be a very able successor. John not only emulated his father, in that he became an Alderman of the City of London, and a Member of Parliament first for Okehampton and later for Queenborough (1722–28); he also developed the family business and laid the foundations of a considerable estate by which the Crowley family climbed into the ranks of the landed aristocracy. In 1715 he married Theodosia Gascoign, daughter of a Rector of Enfield, Middlesex, and her marriage portion of £8,000 included the manor of Barking, near Ipswich, which later formed a nucleus around which a considerable estate in the County of Suffolk was formed.

John and Theodosia had six children, and on the death of John in 1728, the business passed into the hands of Ambrose his eldest son. This Ambrose, born in 1718, was a minor at the time of his father's death, and the business was continued by John's executors until Ambrose came of age in 1739. Ambrose died unmarried in 1754, as did his only brother John in the following year. After this date the business remained under the nominal control of Theodosia, whose widowhood lasted 54 years. On her death in 1782, the estate was inherited by the second Earl of Ashburnham, who in 1756 had married Elizabeth, daughter of John and Theodosia. By this time the family had apparently withdrawn from active participation in the business, leaving the management to the successors of Hanmer and Bannister. In 1782 the manager was Isaiah Millington, who instead of drawing a salary for his services, retained an agreed proportion of the profits of the business—two elevenths. Millington occupied the great house at Greenwich, and the business was now conducted under the name of Crowley, Millington and Company. The last half-century of existence of the business remains wrapped in obscurity, and further research is still needed.

III

It should be clear from the foregoing that Sir Ambrose Crowley was an uncommonly successful entrepreneur. In a business career of less than thirty years he built up what has been described as the largest ironmonger's business in Europe and amassed a fortune running well into six figures. This was achieved at a time when joint stock and other forms of corporate enterprise were becoming commoner. In the metallurgical industries, for example, two of Crowley's close neighbors in County Durham were corporate businesses—the Ryton Company, formed in the early 1690's, was a lead-mining partnership,[56] and the Hollow Blade Sword Company was a chartered company which set up a sword-making business in 1691 a few miles further up the valley of the River Derwent than Crowley's works.[57] In the coal-mining industry of the Tyne valley, partnerships were becoming increasingly common in the late seventeenth and early eighteenth century.[58] Sir Ambrose, however, was not unique in rising to fame and fortune as a result of his own unaided enterprise: in this respect he was typical of a group of merchants of his day which included, amongst others, William Cotesworth, merchant of Gateshead;[59] Charles Duncombe, goldsmith and financier of London;[60] and William Stout, merchant of Lancaster.[61] Crowley's unique achievement was the building of a substantial business which survived him by 150 years.

To accomplish such a feat called for unusual qualities, and it is worth while to consider what these special attributes were which made Sir Ambrose the entrepreneur *par excellence*. In the absence of a partnership bringing together varied resources, the entrepreneur who works on his own must possess a whole range of qualities, and it is perhaps the diffusion of his genius over the many qualities of an industrialist and merchant which brought success to Ambrose Crowley. As an iron manufacturer[62] he was master of all the techniques and processes employed in his own works; as a business man he displayed a sound judgment in monetary matters; and as the sole director of a nation-wide organization he built up an administrative system unique in the history of British industry.

It has sometimes been asserted that Crowley started life as a common smith:[63] had this been the case there could have been no cause for surprise at the extent of his technical knowledge. It is known, however, that he served his period of training with a London merchant, and he is therefore unlikely to have come into close contact with the actual manufacturing processes. As a boy in the industrial Midlands he may well have been familiar with some of the processes, but he left Stourbridge for the metropolis at the age of sixteen. In spite of this lack of experience of the manufacturing side of his trade there is ample evidence from his letters and orders that he was as conversant with the details of all the processes employed in his business as were his own foremen. Indeed he regarded such a mastery as indispensable to the equipment of the master of a business, large or small. One of his clerks wrote in 1712 to James Crowley, one of Sir Ambrose's young half-brothers, "I perceive it is very pleasing to Sir Ambrose to hear that you stick so close to your business, and that you work so hard in the Forge your self and indeed you are un[doubtedly] in ye right of it, to make yourself a perfect master of the business, it's not only the wages you get or save by working your self, but you save twice the value in the wast of the steel and good management, of the forge, and will be master for ever afterwards of your workmen when they know you understand it."[64]

Crowley was constantly writing to his officials in the North on matters of detail relating to manufacture. "The furnaces about London: the bars are not above one inch square, 7 foot long, 18 inches broad above the seeges. The seeges stand in at least 3 inches and are the breadth of a brick or a brick edgeways above the barrs, the Furnace 18 inches high above the Seeges. A man in half a day putteth in fresh seeges, the vents are from 5 to 6 inch square and at the mouth of the Furnace."[65] "You must melt thus: take a large melting ladle and line it with loome, and fix it in one of your harths under the Tueiron and then fill the ladle full with charcoale, and putt 3 bricks round the ladle to keep up the charcoale, and then light it and blow it up. Then putt your quantity of brass and Pewter with more charcoales upon the fire till all the mettle be melted in the ladle, and then poure it into the mould."[66] He was as familiar with the details of the construction of new mills and forges as he was with the manufacturing processes themselves. "By the draft now sent you will see where I shall build my plateing forge.[67] The wheeles and ladles I shall send yow ready made.[68] Conduit 1 is to be for the wast water. Conduit 2 to carry the wheeles. Note Conduit 1 must be boarded over, and I shall contrive the gates soe that when one is shutt, the same mocion shall open the other, soe that my slitting mill wheels shall not be disturbed with back water . . ."[69] Sir Ambrose has been credited with the introduction of new methods of steelmaking into England.[70] It is quite clear from his correspondence that he was collaborating with his father in experiments in steelmaking, but from the evidence at present available it is not yet possible to say whether or not he was an innovator in this respect.

On the other hand, in matters of finance Sir Ambrose has long been recognized as an innovator. Swift first drew attention to notes for small denominations ranging from twopence to twenty shillings issued by Crowley to overcome the shortage of small coins, "which passed current in all shops and markets, as well as in houses, where meat or drink was sold."[71] Token coins were quite commonly issued by tradesmen during Crowley's lifetime. These issues, however, were largely confined to the reign of Charles II[72] and careful enquiry has failed to reveal their use by Crowley. The issue mentioned by Swift, however, was not of token coins but of notes. Crowley displayed much intelligent ingenuity in the issue of paper in an effort to circumvent the "want of money." This paper appears to have taken two forms. The first was the issue of what Crowley called "Tickets." Almost all the raw material for his ironworks at Winlaton had to be transported overland from his staith and warehouse at Blaydon-on-Tyne. There was therefore constant employment for a small army of "carriagemen." To avoid the complications and unnecessary labor involved in paying for individual journeys, Crowley devised a system of credit notes in accounting for carriage: these credit notes, or "Tickets," were payable at fixed times. It is possible that the convertibility of these notes would have given them some local circulation.[73]

It is, nevertheless, more probable that it was not to the "Tickets" that Swift was referring, but to Crowley's "Current Bills." These were an interesting combination of bills of exchange and banknotes. They were definitely designed by Crowley to remedy the shortage of coin, and were, in fact, not to be used by his Cashier "if he hath any money to pay the party that demandeth a Reckoning."[74] Moreover he envisaged a circulation for his Current Bills which would be more than local. They were to be issued as a form of cash payment within the Crowley organization (i.e., in payment of wages, etc.), but they were also to serve as normal Bills of Exchange in the payment of Crowley's external debts. The Current Bills were issued on printed forms from books with counterfoils: both bill and counterfoil were to bear "numbers and other characters," so that the book must have borne a close resemblance to the modern cheque book. From the first, Crowley resolved that "they may be vallued in all places better than money," and confidently required his staff to seek a premium on them whenever possible. With sound judgment he recognized that free convertibility was of first importance and he resolved "not to give out any of the Currant Bills till money be first laid by, and secured for the punctuall payment of them. I will order constant attendance to be given to pay them at the very first demand without any delay whatever, and not oblige the receiver to come at particular times." The Bills could be cashed either at the works in County Durham or at the London offices. Every effort was to be made to render the Bills commercially attractive—"the said Currant Bills shall be paid in Specie and not by Bank or Goldsmith notes without desired." The Bills, which were payable to Bearer, were so designed that they could be issued payable after date or sight. They were assignable by endorsement. It seems clear that they were not issued for specified round sums, as is suggested by Swift's account, but for particular amounts. Whilst the Current Bills and Tickets answer only partly to Swift's description of Crowley's notes, they are the only note forms to which reference has yet been found. This does not preclude the possibility that there was a third type of note for fixed round sums issued later in Ambrose Crowley's lifetime, or even by John Crowley.[75]

Above all, Crowley followed the precept "take care of the pence and the pounds will look after themselves." Many of his sales were of small quantities of goods to scattered buyers, and the utmost diligence was needed to ensure that these multitudinous small debts did not drain away his profits. There is a characteristic instruction of 1702 listing small debts in the Newcastle district: appended to the list were two draft letters in graduated terms of severity demanding payment. Each debt was marked "A" or "B" according to which letter was to be sent to the debtor.[76]

Space does not permit a full analysis of Crowley's administrative system. It was immensely complicated and a thorough understanding of it is obscured by Crowley's terminology. To understand fully the many laws and instructions governing each branch of the administration of the business requires a glossary of expressions which Crowley adapted to particular uses. Such a glossary can only be compiled by detailed examination of all available evidence. Words such as "claim," "cheque," "auction," "assessment," etc., are given particular meanings by Crowley to which their normal meaning unfortunately gives little indication. Although this administrative organization was clearly built up "ad hoc" (the Council Instructions provide evidence of day-to-day amendment and additions to existing orders), it justified the name of system. The whole was designed to function with the minimum of interference from above: this was necessary where a large business was to be controlled by a single entrepreneur. At the same time each part of the system had to function, as it were, in a glass case, so that its working could be examined at any time. Authority was delegated but control was retained. The striking of such a fine balance was achieved only by the regulation of every detail. The reader of the *Book of Laws* or the *Council Instructions* is impressed mostly by Crowley's marvelous grasp of detail. Nothing was left to chance; every contingency was foreseen and catered for. Control was assured by the weekly presentation of accounts and journals by every official, and such was Crowley's complete mastery of the detail so presented to him weekly, that the slightest deviation from the normal caught his attention and an explanation was demanded by return of post.

Sir Ambrose was possessed of a very great talent for the management of a large and complicated business, and knew it. This recognition of his own ability must have rendered him odious to members of his own family, who were constantly being made aware of his superiority. His young half-brother, James, for example was censured for poor handwriting—"I have yours of the 1st instant, and am sorry to see you write such a sprawling bad hand and do desire you as you respect your own good to get some good round hand copies, and at spare times write after with care and deliberation till you have brought your self to write a more firm and plain hand which you will find will be greatly to your advantage."[77] Even his father was treated with scant respect—"I thought you and my Bro. Benj. had known me better than to have thought I wo'd have laid down rules to be shaken by every puff of wind. I desire you that you would immediately order that impudent fellow Tho. Shuerd to be dunn'd for the £30 and if not instantly paid to sue him, that it may be a terrour to such bloodsucking rogues from coming a near you."[78]

Nor is it easy to conceive that he could ever have been popular with his employees. Although in many ways a model employer, his constant suspicions of their integrity, however well founded, and his elaborate provisions for inquisition into how his employees spent their leisure hours, were hardly calculated to promote good relations between master and servant. In a verse of a Council Instruction of 1702 delightfully headed "Clerks' Ruin," he set out in detail how the moral welfare of his unfortunate clerks was to be supervised. "I doe order and require the Treasurer to make it his business to pry and enquire into the actions of all clerks whatever and if he findeth any guilty of the said vices to inform me . . . In case any of my Clerks and Servants what ever shall any wayes lay out or spend more than their sallaries let their pretences be what it will be sure to inform me. When any Clerk or Servant shall make a frequent practice of goeing much abroad perticularly to Newcastle which hath been the ruin of severall, to inform mee . . ."[79]

There is more than a hint in many of his directions of his Quaker upbringing. Crowley's father, it has already been noticed, was a prominent Quaker in Worcestershire, but Crowley himself joined the Church of England after his arrival in London. His marriage in 1682 to Mary Owen, daughter of a Shropshire squire, took place in the parish church of St. Bartholomew the Less. By 1712 he was sufficiently well recognized as a member of the Established Church to request the Earl of Oxford to be included in the list of commissioners for the building of the fifty new churches of London, "being very desirous to have Greenwich church built with all prudent speed.[80] In about 1703 Crowley made arrangements for the accommodation of his workmen in a special gallery in the parish church of Ryton, three miles distant from Winlaton.[81] In 1710 a newly built chapel was opened in Winlaton.[82] Sir Ambrose, it seems, abandoned his father's faith as a young man, for persistence with membership of the Society of Friends must have closed many doors to him. Certainly he could never have achieved distinction in the city and at Westminster as a Quaker.

In his favor it must be said that he achieved the greatest of all human distinctions, that of originality. In essence, his business was similar to that carried on by a score of ironmasters and merchants in England at his time, but on this orthodox foundation he built a superstructure the breadth and originality of which scarcely found an equal in British industry in the succeeding two centuries. Every detail of the organization bore the stamp of his personality, for he made it his business, to an extent which demands the admiration if not the emulation of modern industrialists, to make it clear that his will was law. "I would have you all know that the orders I have made . . . are built upon such a rock, that while I have my understanding it shall be out of the power of Satan and all his Disciples to destroy them."[83]

The Stanley Steamer: A Study in Unsuccessful Innovation

CHARLES C. MCLAUGHLIN

AT THE TURN of the century automobile manufacturing was ready to take its place in the Census of Manufactures as an important branch of the carriage-making industry. Nevertheless, the question as to what the proper motive power for the horseless carriage should be had not yet been settled unanimously in the minds of its makers. The three candidates—steam, electricity, and internal combustion—still had to prove themselves acceptable to the general public. This meant that the winner had to be cheaper to operate, more reliable, safer, and more convenient than the horse and buggy. An economic, as well as mechanical, *coup d'état* had to be staged before the horse could be replaced by mechanical power. The automobile had to duplicate artificially the general availability, use, and standardized maintenance and fueling (if we may call it such) of the horse-drawn vehicle before it could become a necessity instead of a luxury. Thus in examining the process of choice which was to end in the selection of the gasoline engine for the automobile, the innovations in production, distribution, and servicing which accompanied the various forms of power must be given their due weight as well as the mechanical advantages and disadvantages which attached to each one.

The problem of explaining why the internal combustion engine was selected over its rivals is interesting not only because some people still doubt the wisdom of the choice, but also because any attempt at a solution of the problem is likely to illuminate the broader question of the nature of technological choice in a rising industry and its effect on our civilization.

This article is reprinted, by permission of the author, from *Explorations in Entrepreneurial History,* 7:37–47 (October 1954).

The assumption that in a young industry in the early twentieth century the technological choices were made by experts, properly qualified and not to be questioned by inexpert historians, will not stand examination. There were no experts in the present-day sense in the automobile industry in 1900, but only inventors and promoters who had more faith in than knowledge about the merits of their innovations. If there were any experts at that early time, they were narrow specialists not likely to consider many alternatives for long. Thus the other factors already mentioned—new ways of distributing, producing, and servicing, and even accidents of time, place, and personality—must be given consideration.

In 1900 no public standards had yet been developed as to what the automobile ought to look like and how it ought to be powered. Although the electric motor vehicle was to have its advocate in the Studebaker Company until 1904 and was produced on special order by Detroit Electric as late as 1930, it was eliminated as a practical form of power for light road vehicles for what were apparently sound mechanical reasons.[1] In spite of its smooth, quiet performance, the weight of the batteries required and the constant need for recharging them made the electric car less convenient than its rivals. Speeds as high as sixty miles an hour were possible in specially designed racing machines, but the qualities of responsiveness and rapid acceleration which the electric car possessed could not be sustained over long distances or for long periods of time because of the size and weight of the batteries.[2]

The steam vehicle shared the advantages of the electric car: its simplicity of control, smoothness, and flexibility admirably adapted for a road vehicle. To these advantages were added a greater range of operation and greater power and speed than that of the electric car. But in spite of the fact that there were probably more light and maneuverable steam buggies on the road at the turn of the century than any other kind,[3] the steam engine was considered by many, as it had been in Europe earlier, to be inherently unsuited to power a small, light road vehicle. The stereotype of the steam engine as a ponderous and heavy machine liable to boiler explosion, requiring slow-moving heavy machinery, and using very bulky and dirty fuel and large amounts of water apparently dominated the thinking of many experimenters. Only a few of them seemed to note that the light little Mobile steamer of 1900 could beat the best European gasoline cars at races and hill climbs.

The gasoline-fueled internal combustion engine, however, seemed to hold out the possibility of a lighter and more compact power package once its operation and mechanism had been refined and perfected. But, as with steam propulsion, there were many problems yet to be solved before the internal combustion engine could be considered a reliable and flexible form of power. The adaptation of the Otto four-cycle gasoline engine to the varying load and speed requirements of a highway vehicle was inevitably a difficult task because it necessitated many compromises with the intrinsic nature of an internal combustion engine. Once the difficulties of accommodating the precisely machined interior of a piston-actuated engine to the timing and resultant stresses of a rapid succession of powerful explosions had been met, perhaps the most irksome difficulties still remained. To operate without stalling, the gasoline engine had to turn over at a rate of at least 900 revolutions a minute, and to gain maximum efficiency it had to run at three times this speed.[4] The transmission of this power at a controllable speed to the wheels of the vehicle became a complex problem. To add to the complications of having to gear down a high-speed engine and allow it to "idle" at almost 1000 revolutions per minute, there was the fact that the gasoline engine runs only within a narrow speed range, because of its need for a large flywheel to keep it moving through its unpowered strokes. The larger the flywheel, the narrower the speed range; if the size of the flywheel is reduced to gain greater possible speed variation, the danger of stalling or running the engine too fast is increased. Of course, the proper compromises were in fact made to adapt the internal combustion engine to the automobile, but only at the price of a mechanical complexity and need for close tolerances in machining not shared by either of the alternative forms of power. The process of refining the details of the engine and transmission design continues even today.[5]

The 125 firms (a minority of all the companies) which chose steam instead of gasoline in the early 1900's[6] were probably dissuaded from adopting internal combustion mainly because of its internal complexity and the delicate precision required for its manufacture. Problems already solved in the case of steam would have to be tackled anew for internal combustion; timing, valving, and carburetion were to command a great deal of ingenuity for fifty years to come. The various chores required of the driver of the car perhaps discouraged them as well. Starting required many adjustments, such as cylinder priming, advancing the spark, and the dangerous business of cranking. Besides attending to the steering and enduring the noise and vibration of the engine, the driver had to shift gears and operate the clutch—a feat which, at that time, required considerable dexterity. Even Ransom E. Olds, whose company made gasoline engines, started his automotive experiments with steam.[7]

With a small high-pressure fire tube boiler and a two-cylinder double-acting steam engine, it was possible to have a vibrationless and quiet ride. The engine, lubricated with special cylinder oil fed into it with the steam, required far less attention than its gasoline counterpart, because it was running at a much slower rate of speed and hence did not wear out so fast. A steam engine had to be propelling an automobile at sixty miles an hour before it reached the slowest possible rate of revolution at which the internal combustion engine could run without stalling: 900 revolutions a minute.[8]

Unfortunately, although the engine itself posed no problems, the early automotive boilers and burners required a great deal of adjustment and attention and posed a multitude of technical difficulties for the manufacturer. This was one of the reasons why Olds decided to use his company's gasoline engines. To be sure, there were adequate safety devices available at the time, and Rollin White had already invented a flash boiler in 1899,[9] but trouble-free automatic controls had not yet been invented to match the simplicity of driving the steam car. Actually, completely satisfactory steam generators were not in use until after the steam car had lost its battle with internal combustion. The Doble steam car, built in the late 1920's and early 1930's, was unsurpassed in trouble-free operation and performance by any car at that time,[10] and the Vapor-Clarkson steam generator for train heating, to be found on Diesel passenger locomotives today, is considered remarkable for its extreme compactness and completely automatic controls.[11] Nevertheless, it seems safe to presume that the difficulties of the earlier steam generators were no more annoying than the hand-cranking and arduous gear-shifting of the gasoline car up to 1925.

The electric automobile, as we have already mentioned, seems to have lost out to its two rival forms of power because it could not fit the requirements of a self-propelled road vehicle. Any study of what happened to the two remaining alternative forms of power should probably be mainly concerned with the companies which manufactured them for the longest period of years. In the steam automobile field, the two companies which remained active the longest were the White Motor Company of Cleveland, which continues today as a small manufacturer of high-quality gasoline-powered trucks and buses, and the Stanley Motor Carriage Company of Newton, Massachusetts, which ended its career in 1925. Of these two, the Stanley Company had the longest record of continuous manufacture of steam vehicles, ending its production of this type of automobile fifteen years after the White Company had shifted over to the making of gasoline cars and trucks. The gasoline automobile companies which started at roughly the same time as the White and Stanley Companies were located at Detroit and grew into the large companies which we know today. Two of the most important of these which have continued from the time of the first Stanley and White steamers were the Oldsmobile Company (now a branch of General Motors) and the Ford Motor Company.

The Stanley brothers had a remarkable range of interests and abilities, even in comparison with such inventive contemporaries as Henry Ford and Thomas Edison. Originally from Maine, the two brothers had taught themselves to whittle violins at an early age. Later in life they were the first to apply manufacturing principles to violin assembly.[12] Although considered a trifle rough as to finish, these violins, when they appear on the market today, are considered good in comparison with other manufactured violins.[13] After the Stanley Company ceased production of its cars, F. E. Stanley and his cousin, Carleton F. Stanley, went back to violin-making, and C. F. Stanley has continued in that business ever since.[14]

When the Stanley twins moved from Kingsfield, Maine, to Newton, Massachusetts, they perfected a photographic dry plate on which they managed to make substantial profits until they sold their patents and process to the Eastman Kodak Company. Even their automobile factory, when it was built, was something of a novelty, being one of the first reinforced concrete structures in New England. Long after the building was completed, architects and engineers came to consult them about this new type of construction. Both the brothers had a flair for mathematics and taught school as young men. One of them tried college for a week but did not like it. Both were sufficiently educated in the science and electronics of their day, however, to invent and patent various kinds of X-ray apparatus.[15]

The Stanley brothers entered the business of making automobiles as an experiment to see whether they could make a car which would out-perform the car they had seen at a fair in Brockton in 1896.[16] In this they were completely successful. In building this experimental car they ordered the boiler and engine from a local foundry. Unfortunately, the boiler and engine proved much too heavy and bulky to mount in an ordinary buggy. Instead of rebuilding the buggy to fit the propulsion machinery, which was perhaps the more obvious solution, they worked out boiler and engine designs radically different from conventional practice, achieving finally a power unit which could be fitted easily into the light horse carriage of the time. Thus, instead of turning from the heavy and bulky steam equipment of the day to the comparatively lighter gasoline engine with all its complications, they were confident that they could make the steam engine and boiler light enough to fit the requirements of the road vehicle and thus retain all the advantages of a form of power which did not require a complicated transmission to adapt it to varying load and speed requirements. The boiler they devised, although it was safe at a pressure of 600 pounds per square inch, weighed only ninety pounds, while their engine weighed only thirty-five.[17] With each new model of their car, the Stanley brothers simplified the mechanical design, ending up by reducing the number of moving parts to thirty-two, including the four wheels. Thus the steam car, as perfected by the Stanleys, contained no more moving parts than did the self-starter alone of a gasoline car.[18]

At the urging of their friends and from an understandable interest in making their inventions earn them money, the Stanleys in 1899 decided to produce enough cars to satisfy the enthusiastic market which the success of the experimental model had generated. When they had enough parts on hand to produce their first two hundred cars in July of that year, thereby becoming the first to manufacture automobiles in any appreciable quantity, they were bought out by John Brisben Walker of *Cosmopolitan* magazine for the sum of $250,000. The Locomobile Company, formed by Walker, produced several thousand steam cars in 1900 using the original Stanley design and patents. Meanwhile, however, the Stanleys completely redesigned their car and developed improvements so important that the Locomobile was rendered obsolete. In 1901 the Locomobile Company decided to switch to the gasoline automobile and gave up its control of the Stanley patents and factory for $25,000.[19] Whatever the reasons may have been for the Locomobile Company's switch to gasoline, the Stanleys were happy to get back into manufacturing. They did not suffer from lack of a market until the 1920's, about the same time that the Locomobile Company went out of business.

Despite the constant improvements and simplifications which they lavished on their product, the Stanley twins did little to improve their methods of production, financing, or selling. During this period they never had to worry about getting customers, and they were not interested in making any more money than they did. In consequence, they fell behind the industry as a whole not only in average production per firm, but in managerial techniques also. They gave little attention to reducing costs of production or to building up sales all over the country. In short, they were not really interested in seeing their car come into general popular use. This was, however, a concern the industry as a whole had to have if it was to survive and if the automobile was to replace the horse and buggy. Nevertheless, until 1914 the Stanley Company encountered no difficulty in earning a comfortable profit. They had by this time abandoned the buggy-type vehicle and successfully followed the demand for a larger and heavier kind of car. The heavy and expensive car lost favor after 1908, but the Stanleys went right on producing them and still managed to make money by selling their car in the upper ten per cent of the general price range.[20]

Encouraged by the success in selling their 1914 model for $1,400, the Stanley Company planned to produce 500 of this type in 1915. But in this year their passion for simplification and their hand-to-mouth financing procedures at last produced a serious crisis. The Stanleys had never given much thought to the problem of equipping their cars with water condensers. The White steamers had been condensing from the beginning, but the New England company regarded condensers as a needless and unnecessary complication. In the New England region there were plenty of horse troughs and adequate supplies of soft water. The Stanley steamer could travel forty miles on one tank of water, and this was considered by its manufacturers an ample cruising range.

Stanley owners from the earliest days had made use of the ever-present horse trough to slake the thirst of their steamers. In 1914, however, watering troughs were being removed from the roadside in an effort to control an epidemic of the hoof and mouth disease. The limited range of the Stanley cars fast became a serious inconvenience. A rival company, also located in Newton, the Doble Steamer Company, advertised that their cars (not yet in independent production, but using Stanley boilers) would travel for 800 miles on a single filling of water. Further incentive to the Stanley Company to switch over to a condensing model was provided by notices from the cities of Chicago and Boston informing the company that their cars would not be allowed within city limits unless measures were taken to control the clouds of exhaust steam which billowed out behind the steamers, especially in damp or cold weather, seriously curtailing visibility for the traffic behind them.

The need to experiment with condensing systems before their next model could be brought out necessitated a sharp cutback in production from the 740 cars produced in 1914 to the 126 which they managed to make in 1915. The Stanley Company was no longer in the favorable position which it had enjoyed in 1900. In 1914 they had no surplus capital, since they had continued the hand-to-mouth financing procedures that had long since been abandoned by the industry in general, and they were very reluctant to borrow. Other smaller producers, such as the Packard Company, were dependent on large supplies of outside capital to pull them through bad years or through periods of retooling or experimentation.[21] The Stanley Company had no such resources.

By 1916 the Stanleys had evolved a condensing system for their cars which worked effectively in spite of the fact that there was no oil trap to catch the cylinder oil in the steam before it went on to clog the condenser or form scale in the boiler.[22] They managed to make a profit on the 250 cars they built that year and planned to build 500 cars in 1917. Unfortunately their lack of capital resources placed them at the mercy of events when they were prevented from maintaining or increasing their production.

The cutback in production during 1915 returned to plague them in a new way in 1917. Wartime restrictions permitted them to turn out only fifty per cent of the average yearly production of the three previous years, or 194 cars. In 1918, too, one of the Stanley brothers was killed in an automobile accident on the Newburyport turnpike. The remaining brother was forced to give up active management of the Company because of poor health, at a time when experienced guidance was especially needed.

The government then restricted automobile manufacturers to one-half of the steel they had been using in the second half of 1917. The Stanley Company started looking for some kind of war contracts and succeeded in securing a contract for 160 mobile water heaters. The test model of the heater performed excellently, but the company was unable to fill the order before the war ended and the contract expired. This was perhaps a reflection of the inability of a small firm with old-fashioned production techniques and limited capital resources to convert rapidly to the quantity production of a new, though similar, product.

In the hope of recouping the losses incurred during the war, the Stanley Company raised its prices in the immediate postwar period, since they did not consider it feasible to produce their cars in much larger quantities. For a time this policy proved successful; one half of the wartime losses were recovered by selling Stanley cars at from $4,250 to $5,000 each in 1919.[23] Other producers, such as the Pierce-Arrow Company, also thrived by selling cars priced at $4,000 and over, as the demand for distinctive and exclusive-looking automobiles in this period of prosperity seems to have been relatively large, perhaps a reaction against the standardization of automobile design taking place at this time.[24] On March 15, 1920, the Stanley Company had the biggest backlog of orders, in terms of dollar value, in its history. Deposits on the orders had already been paid, and it looked as if the company would be able to make up all its losses by the end of the year. In May, however, the onset of a sharp recession resulted in the cancellation of orders and forfeiture of deposits before all cars could be sold. The Company's inventories of parts had been bought at the high prices commanded just before the break, and the cars were now so expensive to produce from the materials on hand that the Company could not drop its prices below $2,700 per car and still meet expenses.[25]

The automobile industry generally had been rapidly expanded between 1918 and 1920 to meet the demands of a four million dollar market which had been confidently expected but which did not in fact materialize. The twenty-two firms which, attracted by the prospect of high profits, had entered the field of automobile manufacture in 1920 found themselves in 1921 competing desperately for survival with eighty-eight older firms. By the end of 1923 twenty-three firms had withdrawn from the industry.[26]

The Chicago Investment Company, which had bought the Stanley Company at the time of its last difficulties, unloaded its unprofitable purchase onto the newly formed Steam Vehicle Corporation of America. The Newton plant was sold, and headquarters were transferred to Allentown, Pennsylvania, in 1925, but no cars were ever produced there.[27] The Stanley Company, like other small companies lacking productive capacity and capital resources, had priced its product out of the market. Two other famous eastern automobile manufacturers passed from the scene at the same time. The fact that they were producing gasoline-powered cars did not make either the Locomobile or the Stevens-Duryea companies immune to the pressure of Detroit competition. Both of these firms, like the Stanleys, were selling small quantities of high-priced cars and lost their place in the market when prices fell.[28] The technical merits or defects of the steam car do not seem to have been a major factor in the demise of the Stanley Company; the Company was caught with high-cost inventories in a period of rapidly falling prices and, for lack of financial resources, was unable to weather the storm.

The state of Michigan had assumed leadership in the production of automobiles in 1905, just at the time when the market had shifted significantly to gasoline cars. The Detroit manufacturers almost from the beginning were specialists in large quantity production of gasoline cars. This concentration on one type of car and on high-volume production was made possible not only by the early training of the Detroit entrepreneurs and inventors, but also by the characteristics of the available labor force, the market they intended to serve, and the availability of raw materials. In all these respects the situation of the manufacturers in Detroit differed significantly from the situation of manufacturers in the east, especially of those in New England.[29]

The Detroit entrepreneurs had turned quite naturally to the gasoline engine to power their vehicles. Gasoline engines were already being manufactured in Detroit by the Leland and Faulkner Engine Company and by the Olds Motor Company to power launches on the Great Lakes—a purpose to which the constant speed gasoline engine was well adapted since there was no serious transmission problem. R. E. Olds, although at first attracted by the possibilities of steam, turned to gasoline because he was eager to make use of the engines manufactured by the Olds Motor Company. "The gasoline engines were our bread and butter business," he said, "and most people thought that the car was just a toy, but I knew that the car was the big venture."[30] The early Oldsmobile, which was energetically promoted all over the country, apparently set the pattern for the rest of the industry springing up around Detroit. What the Stanley brothers in Newton referred to contemptuously as "an engineering fashion" established itself as the norm in Detroit. Other companies, such as the Studebaker firm in South Bend, Indiana, the Locomobile Company in New York, and Colonel Pope's Electric Vehicle Company in Hartford, Connecticut, switched to gasoline. The White Motor Company of Cleveland acknowledged the arrival of the "gasoline era" when they abandoned the manufacture of their fine steam car in 1910.[31]

In the field of production techniques, the Stanley Company was actually handicapped by the ready availability of skilled workers, because they made it all too easy for the company to continue to rely on handicraft techniques and discouraged interest in radical labor-saving methods. This factor, combined with the unadventurous desire of the Stanley brothers to keep their business small, prevented the adoption of new production, distribution, and financing techniques. The automobile manufacturers in Detroit, on the other hand, were compelled to adopt many innovations in production and distribution, not only because they wanted to sell their products to a wide market, but also because of the nature of their labor supply and the economies of consuming readily available raw materials in large volume. The unskilled farmers, immigrants, and lumberjacks that Henry Ford hired forced him to simplify the productive process with as much inventiveness and ingenuity as the Stanleys had put into simplifying their automobile.[32] In contrast to the mechanical standardization and specialization of the Ford assembly line, the assembly of Stanley steamers took place in separate departments. Each gang of workmen knew its job and had its own distinctive way of doing it. The wheel-base of a Stanley car could be changed to suit the demands of particular owners, and the boilers would be piped in differently, as a matter of course, depending on which gang did the work.[33]

High volume output not only lowered the production costs of the Detroit manufacturers; it also resulted in easier maintenance and servicing. Henry Ford visited the Stanley factory some time before 1914 and learned that it was producing 650 steamers a year, a feat which his own factory equaled in a single day. His Model T had captured a quarter of the Massachusetts market by 1915, and the 25,900 owners of Fords must have found it considerably easier to get service and parts from the 118 distributors throughout the state[34] than the approximately 778 Stanley owners. It must be said, however, that although the Model T was the popular favorite, the Stanley steamer ranked eighteenth in popularity out of the 947 different makes of car on the road in Massachusetts in 1915.[35]

In the middle 1920's Abner Doble, impressed by the mechanical excellence of the steam automobile, attempted to break into the automobile business with an improved steamer, incorporating all the automatic devices which had been perfected for domestic oil burners. He planned to manufacture his car in Detroit, hoping to take advantage of all the innovations in production and distribution which the Stanleys had neglected and to have readier access to parts, supplies, and raw materials. But the attempt to market an improved steamer came too late. Although the Doble-Detroit Company boasted of a network of a thousand dealers and at its beginning spoke of having twenty million dollars' worth of advance orders, it failed to weather the depression. By this time the steam car, as a marketable product, was dead, although the Germans used Doble-engined trucks, buses, and official cars when gasoline was in short supply in the 1930's.[36]

The automobile industry, through quantity production and distribution, made an institution and a tradition of the gasoline car. To the disenchanted steamer advocates the defeat of their favorite could be ascribed to a conspiracy of various "interests" to push the steam car from its rightful place as the family automobile. But, if we take the oil companies as representative of these "interests," the fact of the matter is that gasoline prices rose steadily, while the price of the kerosene that the Stanleys came to use in the middle 1900's and the furnace oil that the later Dobles used remained at attractively low levels.[37] Even the invention of the self-starter could not be blamed for the eclipse of the steamer. The flash boiler, invented in 1899, and the pilot light principle, devised by the Stanley brothers, precluded any lengthy wait to build up steam pressure. The Doble boiler was under a full head of steam in three minutes,[38] while the Stanley steamer, if the pilot light were left on, could be started instantaneously. The principal factor responsible for the demise of the steam car was neither technical drawbacks nor a conspiracy of hostile interests, but rather the fact that its fate was left in the hands of small manufacturers. Even White and Stanley, the most prominent makers, failed to introduce the innovations in production and selling which would have enabled them to survive in the face of Detroit competition.

Ironically enough, however, steam automobile performance, perhaps at its best in the Doble steamer, has remained the ideal for any car. The chore of shifting gears almost became accepted as normal and inevitable during forty years of automobile history, but not quite. Automobile manufacturers can now safely advertise the joys of shift-free driving without running the risk of sounding as old-fashioned as the catalogue of the Stanley Motor Carriage Company for 1902, which claimed the same advantage for the steam car. Years of research, starting well before the disappearance of the Stanley steamer, have evolved the complex and expensive automatic transmissions of today which were explicitly designed to recapture for the gasoline automobile the performance of the steam car. S. O. White, engineering chief of a gear division of the Borg-Warner Corporation, one of the companies that developed the automatic torque converter transmission, put this point succinctly:

> If the money and effort that have been put into the gasoline engine had been concentrated on the steam engine, its boiler and controls, we would not now be discussing automatic transmissions. The gasoline engine is so firmly entrenched that we must have some kind of multi-speed transmission to make up for its deficiencies. We can only use the steam car performance as an ideal we would like to attain.[39]

It cannot be argued with any confidence that the final adoption of the internal combustion engine as the standard engine for use in private automobiles was solely or even principally the result of its inherent superiority as a form of motive power. More likely it was the result of the fact that those automotive engineers who decided to adopt the internal combustion engine decided also to introduce at the same time a series of radical innovations in production engineering and in distribution. In this case at least the relative success of the rival innovations depended as much upon the managerial abilities of the entrepreneurs responsible as upon the technical merits of the alternative forms of power.

PART V

HISTORICAL VARIETIES

Historical Varieties

FIVE STUDIES OF entrepreneurial types make up the final section of this book. Each can safely be left to speak for itself with a minimum of editorial introduction, for the methods and assumptions of this sort of research are not complex. What is involved is simply the attempt to describe a group of entrepreneurs, selected according to some relevant set of criteria, in the hope that in this process of aggregation the random idiosyncracies of individuals will cancel out and the common characteristics become apparent. Much depends, of course, on the way in which the group to be studied is selected and defined.

It is interesting to note, in the articles which follow, the caution with which the authors approach this matter of classification. Walter Minchinton, for example, dissects with nice precision the notion that the merchants of eighteenth century England formed a "class" in the sociological sense of the word. Emphasizing that the term "merchant" was at that time used quite loosely, he argues that on a national basis class solidarity was virtually nonexistent, whatever may have been the case in particular localities. Similarly Bernard Bailyn, in his study of the New England merchants, is as much concerned to show the emergence of diversity and differentiation as he is to demonstrate the presence, in the colony's early years, of very marked similarities in social origin.[1] And Peter Mathias, analyzing entrepreneurship in the English brewing industry in the eighteenth and early nineteenth centuries, stresses internal diversity as the fact with which understanding of the industry must begin.[2] There is no tendency here to assume a greater degree of homogeneity than in fact existed; the inclination of the authors is to be highly skeptical of the conventional categories.

To a large extent this is, of course, the normal scholarly reaction to the simplifications found in textbooks and popular histories. But entrepreneurial historians seem to show an unusual reluctance to accept even the most obvious systems of grouping. The reason for this may lie in an uneasy suspicion that the classification systems acceptable for other types of research may not be appropriate for the study of entrepreneurs. One has to know quite a bit about a population before one can begin classifying its members sensibly—and "sensibly" in this context means by criteria relevant to the explanation of entrepreneurial behavior. Critical theoretical problems underlie even such an apparently simple matter as classification.

A few words of explanation are called for in connection with the article by John Habakkuk. After much heart-searching, I selected this single essay to serve as representative of a sizable group of articles that appeared in *Explorations* in 1953 and 1954 on the general theme of the European aristocracies as sources of entrepreneurship. The inspiration for this collection of articles came from Dr. Fritz Redlich, and it is much to be regretted that no suitable essay from his pen on the subject could be included in this volume, for the opening-up of this area of research was not least among the Research Center's accomplishments. Redlich began with a strong hunch that the contribution of members of the nobility to the early economic development of Europe had been seriously underestimated. His own subsequent research, reinforced by the findings of other scholars in Europe and America, has fully supported his initial intuition. In the meantime the significance of this line of inquiry has been broadened very considerably as a result of the growing appreciation of the role of social elites in promoting or inhibiting economic development in the contemporary world.[3]

Fascinating though the potentials opened up by Redlich's suggestions certainly were, it has proved no easy task to make a general appraisal of the entrepreneurial performance of the European aristocracies. The evidence at hand is sufficient to rule out of court any simple or unqualified interpretation. But it does not, I think, justify a complete reversal of our former conceptions. Habakkuk's careful scrutiny of English landowners in the seventeenth and eighteenth centuries, for example, leaves him skeptical: "The main point about landowners—in England at least—is that they did not acquire their land in order to develop it, but in order to enjoy it. . . . Some landowners did perform the functions of genuine entrepreneurs, and these have caught the limelight. But it would be odd if these were at all common." Habakkuk is prepared to admit that the landowning classes of England may have made a critically important contribution to economic development. If they did so, however, it was not because they acted as entrepreneurs, but because they could borrow easily on mortgage—a fact which introduced a bias into the capital market and distorted the allocation of funds in favor of agriculture.[4] Much the same problem arises in connection with other countries that have been studied. If we wish to appraise the contribution of noble entrepreneurship to economic development, we have no alternative but to discuss the issue in relative terms. So far the progress of research has turned up an unexpectedly large number of cases of aristocratic entrepreneurship, but it has not unearthed evidence strong enough to justify according to aristocratic entrepreneurship a developmental role of major importance. Research on the subject continues, however, and it may be premature to suggest a verdict at this date.

Henry Rosovsky ends our survey with his essay on the serf entrepreneurs in Russia. Of all the articles contained in this book, Rosovsky's is probably least in need of editorial introduction. Suffice it to say that the initiative for this line of research, as for research on aristocratic entrepreneurship, came from the disciplined brain of Dr. Fritz Redlich. Rosovsky's findings for Russia are interesting in themselves, but no less worthy of attention are the hypotheses of more general relevance that he suggests in his conclusion. No social class, he maintains, can be dismissed offhand as incapable of entrepreneurial activity; the requisite skills and attitudes are widespread and not restricted to any particular social stratum. No environmental matrix, however seemingly hostile, can prevent the emergence of entrepreneurship of some sort, although it may indeed restrict its range and limit its impact on the economy as a whole. This is an intellectual emphasis rather different from that with which entrepreneurial studies began, but as a springboard for research in the future it has much to commend it.

The Merchants in England in the Eighteenth Century

WALTER E. MINCHINTON

THERE IS GENERAL agreement that the dynamic element in English economic life in the eighteenth century was provided by the merchants. They were, in Addison's phrase, "the life, spring and motion of the trading world." It was their commerce which was "the prime source of national wealth." Possibly at no other time in English history did they play such an important part in English life not only economically but also politically and socially. Yet while something is known of their economic enterprises and of some of their political activities, studies of individual merchants or merchant firms are disappointingly few and there has been little discussion of the merchants as a class.[1] To quote one definition:

> A social class is composed of individuals who, through common descent, similarity of occupation, wealth and education have come to have a similar mode of life, a similar stock of ideas, feelings, attitudes, and forms of behaviour and who, on any or all these grounds, meet one another on equal terms and regard themselves, although with varying degrees of explicitness, as belonging to one group.[2]

How far can it be said that the merchants were a class in this sense? What did merchants have in common, the term "merchant" being used in the eighteenth-century sense of the word, to cover not only the wholesale trader in distant markets. but also the stock jobber, loan contractor, exchange broker and bullion dealer? And if the merchants were a class, was this of economic significance? These are the questions which this paper sets out to answer.[3]

This article is reprinted, by permission of the author, from *Explorations in Entrepreneurial History,* 10:62–71 (December 1957).

I

With the expansion of trade, the number of merchants grew in the eighteenth century. According to various estimates, there were 2000 eminent merchants at the end of the seventeenth century, 2900 in 1750, and 3500 in 1812,[4] but there is no means of knowing how accurate these figures are. So much depends on definition. Moreover, men did not confine themselves to wholesale trade but carried on other forms of economic activity as well. A man could be described as "merchant and manufacturer," "merchant, dealer and chapman," he could own property or farm land. Since specialization was not yet far advanced, the term "merchant" described a function rather than an occupation. Moreover, by the eighteenth century, there were no institutional barriers to prevent a man engaging in trade. In consequence, there was great diversity of origins. Men became merchants by many routes.

The formal method was by apprenticeship. Boys entered upon their training in the counting house about the age of thirteen or fourteen. In the majority of cases they served seven years but in some the term was as long as nine and in others as short as five. As a great number of the merchant houses were family businesses, it was customary for the youths to be apprenticed to their fathers or their relations: to choose a few examples at random from Bristol, William Weare, a Virginia merchant, apprenticed all four of his sons to himself; John Powell, a Guinea merchant, his five sons; while William Sedgeley was apprenticed to his uncle, Andrew Pope.[5]

Then, since trade was "far from being inconsistent with the character of a gentleman," the younger sons of the country gentry and even, in a very few cases, of peers, entered trade. As Sir Lewis Namier has described it:

> the eldest son inherited the family estates, the second, third, or even fourth, were placed in the Church, in the army or navy, at the bar, or in some government office; but the next had usually to be apprenticed to a merchant, and however great the name and wealth of the family, the boy baptised Septimus or Decimus was almost certain to be found in the counting house.[6]

But the greater number of recruits came from the other classes in society, from the sons of parents in a wide range of urban occupations and rural employments. In the eighteenth century three-fifths of the Newcastle apprentices came from within the town and the proportion in Bristol in the last years of the century was rather higher. Most of the remainder came, as might be expected, from the surrounding counties. So Newcastle drew most of its apprentices from Northumberland and Durham, and Bristol from Gloucestershire, Wiltshire, and Somerset; but in each case a few came from further afield, to Newcastle from Cumberland and Yorkshire, to Bristol from South Wales, Devon, and Cornwall.[7] The size of the area of recruitment for each port was affected by the prospects in that particular port and the other opportunities available in the region. Was it, perhaps, a comparative assessment of the commercial futures of Exeter and Bristol which led Sir John Duntze, the Exeter merchant, to apprentice his ward, Samuel Munckley, in Bristol?[8] And over-all, there was the influence of London which attracted apprentices from all parts of the kingdom, the wealthier Newcastle merchants, for example, preferring to send their sons there rather than have them trained in the home port.[9]

Within the family it was usual for an apprentice to be taken without fee but premiums were usually charged for those having no blood relationship. In the sums demanded there were great variations. At the beginning of the century, between £150 and £210 were being asked in Bristol, about £130 in Liverpool, and upwards of £500 in London. At the end of the century while premiums of over £1000 were being paid in London, between £10 and £300 in Bristol, and little if anything in Liverpool.[10] Further, not all merchants took apprentices. When a Newcastle man was trying to place his son in London in the 1740's, he was told "the most eligible merchants are determined never to take any apprentices . . . The difficulty lies when they are out of their times, how they are to begin in the world."[11] Thus variations in the amount of the premiums were determined partly by economic factors such as the demand and supply position and partly by personal considerations. As an institution, however, apprenticeship was in decline in the eighteenth century but there was considerable variation between ports. In Bristol, where the number of apprentices fell in the course of the century and men became merchants without fulfilling the formal requirements, apprenticeship retained some importance not economically but politically, since it was one way in which the freedom of the city, and hence the right to vote at elections, might be obtained. In Liverpool, by contrast, apprenticeship continued to be a common method of entry into the world of trade. As yet there is too little evidence to show what effect these differences had on recruitment.

At the same time the expansion of trade provided opportunities for men to become merchants by other routes. A few rose from the ranks, as clerks in merchants' counting houses. William Daling was in the employ of Lascelles & Maxwell before he was taken into partnership with Daniel Lascelles in 1763[12] and Thomas Thompson of Hull graduated from the counting house to membership of the firm of Wilberforce & Smith, later Smith & Thompson.[13] But a greater number came from adjacent occupations, from shipbuilders, retailers, and manufacturers. Beginning by taking a share in a ship and its cargo, they increasingly devoted more of their attention to what had been but an extension of their main activity. And masters of ships, having accumulated some capital through trading, made use of the contacts they had made while at sea and came ashore to establish themselves as merchants. Such were the initial steps in the careers of Anthony Bacon, of Sir Samuel Standidge of Hull, of Nathaniel Wraxall of Bristol, and, so it is said, of Bryan Blundell of Liverpool.[14]

The popular archetype was that of the self-made man who by his own efforts acquired a sufficient competence to set up as a merchant and died fantastically rich. According to the legend,[15] William Miles, later a prominent Bristol merchant, came to the city with three halfpence in his pocket, worked as a street porter, apprenticed himself as a shipbuilder, saved fifteen pounds, and sailed to Jamaica as a ship's carpenter. There he bought a cask of sugar which he sold in Bristol for a large profit. With the proceeds he bought articles in huge demand in Jamaica, repeated his former investment and, in this way, soon became wealthy. Although it is not possible to check all the details, the literal truth of the story is suspect. William Miles began his career not in poverty but as an apprentice to a hooper at the age of thirteen; he married the daughter of a substantial Bristol merchant, probably benefiting from her dowry, and it has been suggested that he was already established in Bristol before he went to Jamaica.[16] Further, while money could be made by the sale of sugar in Bristol, there was little profit in and only a limited demand for English products in the West Indies. It is not to be denied that given good luck and reasonable judgment, fortunes could be made in trade but the men in the best position to do so were those already in the possession of capital and not those with none.

Because a smaller sum was usually required, it was easier to set up as a merchant overseas. John Baker, a director of the Royal Exchange Assurance Company, for example, wrote to a Newcastle correspondent: "had I a son of my own, I should be very much puzzled how to dispose of him. I should first think of sending him abroad," suggesting Lisbon as a possible place for "there a young man may begin busyness without any assistance from his master."[17] Whether for this reason or in order to gain experience, a number of Bristol merchants spent a period abroad: Jeremy Innys in Virginia, Samuel Brailsford in Carolina, William Gordon in Jamaica, and Thomas Daniel in Barbados to name but a few.[18] From Hull, youths usually went to the Baltic, while Exeter merchants usually sent their sons to their regular customers in Germany and Holland. And in certain trades, young men from London went abroad, those concerned in the Dutch trade, for example, serving for a time in established houses in Amsterdam.[19]

That the merchants were drawn predominantly from the middle ranges of society is clear, neither the aristocracy nor the very poor making any appreciable contribution to their ranks. Overwhelmingly the greatest number lived in London but how they were distributed between ports is not known though Bristol, Liverpool, and Newcastle predominated among the outports. What appears to be the case is that the sources of recruits varied from port to port. In the seventeenth century, Roger North had written of Bristol that "all men that are dealers even in shop trades launch into adventures by sea chiefly to the West India plantations. A poor shopkeeper that sells candles will have a bale of stockings or a piece of stuff for Nevis or Virginia &c."[20]

And it remained true in the eighteenth century that it was from retail trade—an inferior group socially—that most of the merchants came. In Newcastle, the merchant *per se* was a declining force in the coal trade which was increasingly dominated by the territorial magnates from whose ranks the new recruits came.[21] Of Liverpool it was said that "no town in England has so many merchants in it who rose from Saylors."[22] And in Whitehaven immigrants from Ireland and the younger sons of gentry appear to have predominated in the merchant community.[23] In London, where the range of recruitment was wider, the largest single source was stated to be the younger sons of country gentlemen.[24] More detailed work is required before such assertions can be made with confidence but they suggest that recruitment was affected by the stage of development of the particular port, the character of its hinterland, and the alternative opportunities for employment.

The composition of merchant communities was also influenced by the movement of men already established as merchants. First, there was the movement within the United Kingdom. London received the largest augmentation in this way; Anthony Bacon came from Whitehaven;[25] Lionel Lyde, John Coghlan, and others from Bristol;[26] Robert Newman from Dartmouth;[27] and Francis Baring from Exeter.[28] In similar manner there was movement between the outports, William Kennaway going from Dartmouth to Exeter,[29] Isaac Hobhouse from Minehead to Bristol,[30] and Joseph Daltera from Bristol to Liverpool,[31] whose rise as a seaport is reputed itself to have been the result of the settlement of merchants from London in the 1660's.[32] On a much smaller scale, some merchants left Boston for King's Lynn.[33] In general, having accumulated some capital and gained some experience merchants moved from a smaller or declining port to a larger, growing port in search of wider opportunities. Then, merchants came from Ireland and Scotland. In Liverpool, there were few Scots, apart from the Nicholsons, until the end of the eighteenth century[34] but the Gordons and Baillies were established in Bristol rather earlier.[35] In Bristol, too, the greater part of the Irish trade was in the hands of men who, like Patrick Mullowney, had come from Ireland.[36] From farther afield came men who had been engaged in trade in India and in the American colonies, or as planters in the West Indies. Most of them settled in London but in Bristol were to be found at least five from America—Joseph Farrell and William Randolph from Virginia, and Henry Cruger from New York—and others, like John Pinney, from the West Indies.[37]

Finally, there were the aliens. For centuries they had made their contribution to the economic life of London and they continued to be influential in the eighteenth century. The French colony, prominent amongst whom was Thomas Papillon, was reinforced following the Revocation of the Edict of Nantes by Huguenots of the second migration. Of the 543 London merchants who signed a petition in 1745, 82 were French.[38] The close contacts with the Netherlands were reflected in the substantial Dutch community, including Sir Joseph Vanneck, the Neufvilles, van Hemerts, and Muilmans.[39] Finally, there was a significant expansion in the number of Jews in London at this time, Goldsmit from Amsterdam, da Costa from Spain, and Montefiore from Leghorn.[40]

Outside London, Bristol and Exeter had the most cosmopolitan merchant communities. In Bristol, the Huguenots were the most numerous, names like Bonbonous, Casamajor, Laroche, and Peloquin betraying their origin. But there were other nationalities also, among them Lambert Schimmelpenning and Diedrich Mayerhoff who came from the Baltic and Edward Neufville from the Low Countries.[41] In Exeter, there were Germans, like Duntze Katenkampf and Baring; Swiss such as Mandrot and the Passavants; Hirtzel and others from the Netherlands; and the Cosserats who were of Huguenot origin.[42] A Huguenot, Isaac Minet,[43] was the leading merchant in Dover early in the century and there were others, notably Theophilus Daubez in Falmouth.[44] Less is known of the merchants of Liverpool in the period but names such as Beeckmann, Busigny, and Zuill suggest their owners were of foreign birth.[45] As far as is known, no alien merchants settled in Hull, Newcastle, or Whitehaven. Thus, while chance may have determined the choice of a few, alien merchants usually settled in ports which traded with Europe, enabling them to make use of their connections and knowledge. They made their mark because they were commonly amongst the more vigorous of their countrymen.

II

As merchants differed in their origins so they differed in the extent of their education. Although information is often lacking on this point, it has been commonly held that many merchants had only a fairly rudimentary education. Of Liverpool it was said that "a few of the merchants have more education than benefits a counting-house"[46] while in Bristol "lost to all learning, elegance and sense"[47] it has been held that the merchants "apart from the minimum requirements of business were substantially illiterate."[48] And similar statements were made about the merchants in London and most of the other outports. But such criticism overstates the case. In the course of the eighteenth century, a growing number of merchants, especially those of the second generation, had a more systematic education. Of 361 merchants who find a place in the *Dictionary of National Biography,* 110 were educated at grammar schools, 77 at public schools, 64 at private schools, 62 at home, and 44 at dissenting academies. A number went on to the Universities.[49] Or to take a particular case, of the 155 pupils at Bristol Grammar School between 1710 and 1717, 53 were intended to be merchants or mariners.[50] Further, if their letterbooks and accounts may be called in evidence, many merchants were not illiterate in the twentieth-century meaning of the term. Their libraries, too, confirm this view.[51] Often their education seems to have been judged by the wrong criteria. The measured period and the considered classical quotation had their place in the House of Commons but they were not necessary to the conduct of business. There is some force in the reply of Michael Miller, a Bristol merchant, to David Hume, who while in employ as a clerk, criticized the style of his letters. Miller told Hume that he had made £20,000 by his English and would not have it improved.[52]

More to the point was the criticism voiced by some contemporaries that the classical education then given in the schools was inappropriate for intending merchants. The reform of the curriculum was therefore proposed, the following being typical of those put forward at the time.[53] A merchant's education, it was said, should ensure, among other things, that:

> He has the command of his Pen . . . not crampt up to a set Secretary like a Scrivenor's boys nor scrawling long-tails like a Wench at a Boarding School but a neat charming mixture of Roman and Italian flowing with a kind of Artificial Negligence. He is well-skill'd in . . . the Science of Numbers . . . he is expert in the Nature and Form of Charter-Parties. He understands the Customs, Tolls, Taxes, &c. Particularly as the Owner or Part-Owner of ships he has an insight into the Goodness of Prices of all Materials. By his frequent voyaging he becomes skillful in navigation.

Knowledge of modern foreign languages was also often regarded as necessary.

To meet the demand for a mercantile education along these lines there were three developments. First, a number of old grammar schools situated in commercial centers, notably Christ's Hospital and the grammar schools at Newcastle, Manchester, and Hull, reformed their curricula along these lines.[54] Secondly, a number of the dissenting academies, though by no means all, followed the same course. Prominent amongst these was the Warrington Academy to which some of the Liverpool merchants sent their sons.[55] But the leadership of the Dissenting Academies has been overstated. Some of them continued to provide the kind of classical education which Thomas Mortimer criticized as unsuitable for intending merchants since it produced "pedantic blockheads." Richard Champion, the Bristol merchant who earned fame with his manufacture of porcelain and his friendship with Burke, was educated at one of these. "Even at the age of seven years," he once said, "I had made a tolerable proficiency in Latin: and read a chapter in the Greek Testament."[56] Unfortunately his career provides little support for the contention that this form of education better fitted him for business. And thirdly, there were a number of private academies which grew up particularly in London but also in the other seaports such as Bristol and Newcastle to provide a mercantile education. The master of one of these, Thomas Mortimer, advertised that he was willing to instruct ten young gentlemen of fortune in the accomplishments necessary for a merchant for the sum of one hundred guineas per annum.[57]

But education has never been merely a matter of vocational training; it had at this time, as it still has, its social aspect. The sons of the wealthier merchants were sent to public schools or educated by private tutors as were the sons of the gentry into whose ranks they hoped to enter. In Newcastle, for example, where the links with the land were particularly close, the sons of merchants were sent to public schools like Sedbergh and Eton and then to Cambridge.[58] As they grew in wealth, so in behavior the merchants came closer to the landowning classes.

III

In religion as in education, the importance of Dissent has been exaggerated. Certainly many merchants were Dissenters, the relative importance of the various sects varying from port to port. In Liverpool and Exeter the Unitarians were the leading dissenting group;

in Whitehaven and Bristol the Presbyterians were the most numerous. In the latter city, according to one estimate, nearly one-half of the merchants engaged in the West India and American trades in the 1760's and 1770's belonged to this denomination.[59] The Baptists and Congregationalists also numbered merchants amongst their congregations in Bristol but, despite the fact that it was the center of Wesley's activities, no Bristol merchant was a Methodist. And there were Quaker merchants not only in Bristol but also in Falmouth, Hull, Lancaster, Liverpool, and Plymouth.[60] In addition, the various alien communities, where they were numerous enough, maintained their own religions. Most particularly was this true of the Jews who established synagogues in London but there were also Huguenot churches, for a time at least, in Bristol, Dover, Plymouth, and London.[61]

For technical reasons, particularly because their numbers were small and there was a positive test of membership, the activities of dissenting traders and industrialists have been fully described. But this should not be allowed to obscure the fact that most merchants, like most Englishmen, adhered to the Established Church. In Bristol where Dean Tucker preached and it was said "the very parsons talk of nothing but trade and how to turn a penny," a substantial number of merchants including the Hobhouses, the Frekes, Henry Cruger, John Noble, and George Daubeny were members of the Church of England; in Liverpool, Bryan Blundell and the Cunliffes; in Whitehaven, the Kelsicks; and in Hull, the center of Evangelicalism, almost all the merchants belonged to the Established Church.[62]

In the course of the century, there were three developments which affected this position. First, since adherence to the Church of England carried, as it has continued to carry until recent times, a social value, some Dissenters, anxious to consolidate their ascent of the social scale, became Anglicans. The Gales and Lutwidges of Whitehaven, for example, were originally Dissenters from northern Ireland but later generations became members of the Church of England; Sir John Barnard was the son of Quaker parents but he joined the Established Church in 1703; and there were others.[63] Secondly, the Quakers, while remaining of importance in banking and brewing, suffered defections amongst their mercantile members. With a stricter code of behavior in economic matters than the other sects, the Society of Friends condemned bankruptcy, participation in privateering and the slave trade, and certain worldly pleasures. In Bristol, for example, the Quakers "disowned" William Reeve, Thomas Frank, and Joseph Berrow for bankruptcy and proscribed others, including Nehemiah Champion, for taking part in privateering ventures. Further, Joseph Harford was reprimanded because he supported the establishment of a theater in Bristol.[64] And thirdly, with the growth of radical opinion, some of the other nonconformist denominations gained ground amongst merchants later in the century. About 1800 in Liverpool, the Heywoods, Harveys, Nicholsons, Holts, and Booths were prominent amongst the dissenting families.[65]

IV

For the ambitious, thrusting merchant politics provided the means to greater wealth and the route of social advancement. As Sir Lewis Namier has told us:

> the Government contracts were usually held with a seat in the House of Commons, while baronetcies, the crest over the profits, had invariably to be gained by service in the House; and a generation or two later, provided the money was preserved, the trade discontinued, and a seat in the House retained, a coronet was within the reach of the children or grandchildren of the successful government contractors.[66]

So James Lowther, the descendent of a Levant merchant, became earl of Lonsdale, Edward Lascelles, of the West India house, earl of Harewood, and William Bouverie, the grandson of the immigrant merchant, earl of Radnor.[67] But such cases were exceptional. The more usual reward was a baronetcy—as with James Laroche, Ellis Cunliffe, Samuel Fludyer, and others—or less frequently an Irish peerage such as John Henniker, Joshua Vanneck, and William Mayne obtained.[68] And for financial favors membership of the House of Commons was equally necessary. Of the fifty or fifty-one merchants returned to the Parliament of 1761, at least thirty-seven can be proved to have had extensive dealings with the government. Of these Brice Fisher is the best-documented example.[69] But other examples, Anthony Bacon among them, can be found from other Parliaments in the eighteenth century.[70] When Henry Lascelles was elected, his partner commented "we expected no sort of disappointment after being chosen for Northallerton."[71] But, because the consolidation of their businesses demanded the full attention of merchants in their early years, they entered politics later in life than those drawn from the landowning classes, their average age on entry being forty, almost six years higher than the national average.[72] In addition to the question of personal advancement, representation in Parliament was, as has been discussed elsewhere, important for the merchant community since it was through political action that commercial interests could be protected abroad and fostered at home.

The merchant class was headed by a comparatively few great and wealthy merchants, whose influence was widespread. They were directors of the Bank of England, of the East India Company, and the other trading companies; they were prominent in insurance and finance as well as trade. In wealth and ostentation they vied with the aristocracy. The picture is a familiar one. When they had accumulated a substantial fortune, they bought estates and settled as landed proprietors. Some of them married into the gentry or aristocracy to consolidate their ascent of the social ladder.

But upward social mobility was not confined to London alone; it was also in evidence in the outports.[73] Newcastle is clearly a special case since "thanks to coal there was always a greater degree of fusion of landed and merchant interests in those parts than elsewhere."[74] But the same process can be illustrated from Bristol. First, with the separation of the counting house from the dwelling, entries like "William Miles, merchant, Queen Square and Clifton-down" appeared in the Directories.[75] Then came the erection of a house farther away from the city. A number of Bristol merchants built fairly modest houses at Stapleton or Frenchay; others like William Miles at Kingsweston, Thomas Farr at Blaise Castle, or William Reeve with Arno's Court, built in more splendid style.[76] Such was the achievement of the richer, more successful merchants.

But their number should not be exaggerated. The experience of the majority was different. As Miss Sutherland has written, "it is important to bear in mind the cleavage between the rich merchant and financial classes and the lesser men. Most of the latter lived lives entirely circumscribed by their urban traditions, a seat in parliament was quite outside their ambitions. They neither considered that their richer fellow citizens who obtained seats in the House represented them nor that they represented the commercial interest with which they were concerned."[77] They had limited goals, were locally centered. In their own ports they enjoyed a status higher than they did in the nation at large. To be a merchant in an English provincial town in the eighteenth century was still to be a member of the group which dominated its economic life and controlled its government. These merchants were bound together less by common origins or education than by economic interests. Their common outlook found visual expression in the houses they built. The terraces of eighteenth-century merchant houses can still be seen in Bristol, Liverpool, Exeter, and elsewhere. And meeting together in the Exchange, in coffee houses, in their clubs, and in each other's homes, they developed common social attitudes and forms of behavior: by intermarriage they became knit together as a group. Perhaps less prevalent in London, though three of Sir Ambrose Crowley's five daughters married merchants,[78] examples abound of mercantile intermarriage in the outports. Two examples from Bristol will suffice. Michael Miller married Mary Elton, the daughter of the merchant and banker Isaac Elton (whose sister had married Peter Day). Elton's son, also named Isaac, married Sarah, the daughter of Samuel Peach, linen draper and merchant, whose second daughter, Ellin, married Henry Cruger. So five Bristol merchant families were linked together. On some occasions, the connections were forged between ports. Henry Bright of Bristol married Sarah, the daughter of Richard Meyler, also of Bristol, and their son, Richard Bright, married Sarah, the daughter of Benjamin Heywood of Liverpool.[79] If intermarriage is a good test of social cohesion, then the merchants were effectively a group.

Because of the fluidity of English society, the absence of rigid barriers preventing movement between classes, no merchant caste, no mercantile patrician class formed. As a result the composition of the merchant community was constantly changing. Whereas the landed gentry "were educated at the same schools; know one another's family name from boyhood; form a society; are the same kind of men; marry the same kind of women,"[80] this was less true of the merchants; they were a more motley race. They were diverse in their origins, their education, and their incomes. Between the great London merchant and the small provincial merchant there was a great gulf. Rarely did they meet on equal terms nor did they have common ideas and interests. On economic matters, the London merchant was not infrequently at loggerheads with the merchants in the outports. Thus as far as the whole country was concerned the merchants formed not a class but an occupational group. Locally, within particular ports, the situation was different. Common interest, a fairly high degree of intermarriage, a measure of self-recruitment, often common religious beliefs, and an acquired community of outlook gave the merchants in a particular port a considerable degree of cohesion as a class.

V

These social aspects of the English merchant class in the eighteenth century were of economic significance in a number of directions. First, they influenced the mobilization of capital. "To say what sum of money will enable a Person to commence as a merchant is difficult but it certainly can be no small matter" was a contemporary opinion.[81] For this reason it was held that "youths who have or are like to have good fortunes are the fittest for this station of trade."[82] Some capital could be amassed by hard work but rarely more than enough to permit operation on a small scale. Assiduity and enterprise were not the only avenues to business success. There was no adequate machinery for mobilizing capital, the banks being of small importance[83] as yet so that the source of capital was personal, whether for the individual merchant or the partnership, inheritance and marriage providing the main means. Edward Norris was enabled to set up as a merchant in Liverpool when he was left 87,000 rupees on the death of his brother;[84] Jonathan Ivie of Exeter left his son, George, £1,000 stating in his will "if possible I would have him drive the Irish trade with it either in Exeter, Torrington, Bideford, or Barnstaple."[85] Arthur Heywood of Liverpool acquired capital with which to carry on his business by his marriage to Elizabeth Ogden, the granddaughter of John Pemberton;[86] and an important contribution to the Baring fortunes was made by the marriage of the first John Baring to Elizabeth Vowler, the daughter of a wealthy Exeter grocer, and of his sons, John and Charles, John to Anne Parker and Charles to Margaret Gould, daughter of a wealthy landowner in Devon.[87]

Secondly, the basis of business was to a large extent personal, being influenced by bonds of friendship and consanguinity. The history of William Braund shows, for example, the way in which his relatives and connections were concerned in his business enterprises.[88] Sons, younger brothers, or relations had their place in the counting house or acted as agents for the firm overseas. In the European trades, like that with the Low Countries, merchants met as frequently as possible.[89] In the Atlantic trades, the merchant often spent some period overseas making contacts. The use made of this period abroad might well determine the degree of success enjoyed by a merchant when he returned to England. "The close friendships which George Maxwell formed in Barbados" Professor Pares has written "no doubt brought the House a great part of its business."[90] Sometimes the obligations so incurred might prove a source of embarrassment. In this case Professor Pares adds "they were also responsible for some of its most serious scrapes for Maxwell did not like to refuse a loan to an old friend." And the scope of business was expanded by personal recommendation. A correspondent in Montserrat wrote to Isaac Hobhouse of Bristol:

> I am therefore to assure you that the Colonel is a very honest man and one of the fairest fortunes in this Island and that there is no risque in advancing for him: but that it may be not only of advantage to him but to you likewise for I assure you his interest here is considerable.[91]

Further, the English merchant relied on the judgment of his overseas correspondent for the purchase of the homeward cargoes and for advice about the state of the local markets.

It was here that religion was of some importance. Except in the case of the Quakers, whose mercantile membership was declining, the doctrines of the various religious bodies to which merchants in England belonged were of negligible economic significance. Nor does it now appear that the education afforded by the dissenting academies was necessarily more suitable for the intending merchant than that provided by other institutions. The importance of membership of a particular religious body from the economic point of view lay in the sense of social cohesion which such membership afforded. Within a port it was to be expected that members of a particular sect would deal with each other and the same was often true of trade between ports. The more so when such economic contacts were often strengthened by intermarriage. "It was wholly natural," Professor Tolles has written, "for Quaker merchants to carry on the major part of their mercantile business through correspondents of their own religious faith . . . The merchants in London with whom the Philadelphia Friends had business dealings were almost exclusively Quakers: Henry Goldney, Daniel Flexney, Sampson Lloyd, David Barclay, Andrew Pitt, John Askew, Joseph Hoar, and Isaac Hunt."[92] And the Quakers were not peculiar in this respect. Similarly, "London Jew dealt with Amsterdam Jew, London Christian with Dutch Christian."[93]

Such links of religion and family facilitated trade. Did they also limit competition? It has been suggested that Bristol merchants were less aggressively competitive than their rivals in other ports because they were so closely interconnected. Professor Pares has written:

> it would not have been very genteel for fellowmembers of a small dining club connected together by the inter-marriages of their children to wage war to the knife by cutting freight rates or instructing their captains to snatch consignments from each others' ships or to utilise some of the other weapons in the armoury of competitive enterprise.[94]

Not until more information is available will we be able to say whether this was more generally true.

Lastly, the attitudes and aspirations of merchants affected the life of the merchant house. The ease with which money could be made in trade gave the merchant a less cautious attitude to wealth than the landowner. Samuel Johnson once observed "with what munificence a great merchant will spend his money . . . whereas you will hardly find a country gentleman who is not a great deal disconcerted at an unexpected occasion to lay out ten pounds."[95] Further, while landowners used the principle of primogeniture to maintain their estates, the merchants in the eighteenth, as in the sixteenth, century tended to disperse the greater part of their capital in legacies.[96] After the death of Henry Lascelles, for example, the firm was "much weakened financially for only one-third of his fortune descended to Daniel Lascelles (to carry on the business) and even that seems to have been held for him in trust."[97] The remainder went to establish the noble house. Merchants were "commonly ambitious of becoming country gentlemen," not of perpetuating their businesses.

Other factors could menace the continuance of the family firm. On how many occasions must the absence of a male heir or the death of a son before his father have brought the firm to an end in the direct line? A single instance will suffice. For two generations the Blacketts had been prominent in the Newcastle coal trade but the Blackett of the third generation had no male heir. He willed his property to his illegitimate daughter on condition that she should marry her cousin who should adopt the name of Blackett. And this was done. But of this union there was no male heir so the line came to an end.[98] Further, while fortunes could be made in trade, such was not the inevitable outcome. There was no habitual round of business, trade was often hazardous and speculative, and much depended on the flair and ability of the individual merchant. So through bad luck, inadequate knowledge, and poor judgment, fortunes could be lost as well as won. The responsibility of personal character for changes in the family fortune should not be disregarded. Finally, the absence of appropriate institutional arrangements militated against the persistence of the merchant firm. For these reasons, the majority of merchant houses were short-lived and the number that lasted beyond three generations was small. Or to quote Professor Habakkuk: "there were wealthy merchants but few mercantile dynasties."[99]

But there were some exceptions. The most notable was provided by the wine trade. Kennaway's of Exeter, founded by Robert Kennaway who turned from cloth to wine, dates from 1743; Hunt, Roope and Company of London from 1679, to give but two examples.[100] In other cases where the merchant business was combined with shipowning the firm survived, so Brocklebanks of Liverpool[101] continues and the Bristol firm of Charles Hill & Co. is the descendant of James Hilhouse & Co.[102] The firm of Skilbecks, drysalters, provides an example of the third category where merchanting involved stockholding.[103] Finally, the firms established by merchants who turned from trade to finance continued to exist. But these examples show that either the assets had to be held in tangible shape or in the form of obligations which could not easily be realized for the merchant house to survive. It may even be that difficulty in securing the rapid settlement of debts may have ensured the continued existence of a firm for at least a period. But, with these reservations, it was unusual for a merchant house to be long-lived.

VI

By the end of the eighteenth century, the position of the merchants as a class was changing. In 1700 they were rivaled in wealth only by a few lawyers and civil servants; by 1800 they were flanked by a growing number of professional men—doctors, estate agents, as well as lawyers—and, more important, by a growing number of industrialists. As a result they were no longer the dominant representatives of the commercial classes. The specialization of function and the growth of impersonal institutions also played their part in altering the composition of the merchant class. Much more work needs to be done in investigating the position of the merchants in particular ports and in plotting the fortunes of merchant families before we shall be able to speak with assurance about the course of events in the eighteenth century. The purpose of this paper has been to suggest some of the directions in which inquiry is necessary.

Kinship and Trade in Seventeenth Century New England

BERNARD BAILYN

By THE END of the colonial period of American history the merchants were among the acknowledged leaders of the northern commercial provinces. Their business enterprises dominated the economic life of the port towns; their voice was powerful in provincial politics; their social position pre-eminent. An imposing occupational group, the merchants have seemed to historians to have formed an unmistakable social unit. Wherever we turn in colonial historiography we find the merchants referred to as a "class"—a word which, though its exact definition is disputed by sociologists, yet conveys a sense of unity of interests, social role, and style of life. But when we cut beneath the surface of this supposed social unit and reach the hundreds of particular men who comprised it, we find our assumptions disturbed. The group ceases to appear unified; social differences seem to outweigh common interests.

The merchant group, seen not as an abstract social entity with a life of its own but as a number of specific men engaged in a particular type of enterprise, is worthy of close examination. Much of importance for the understanding of colonial society lies hidden in the folds of its history. Certain characteristics of the development of the merchant group in seventeenth century New England may serve to illustrate this fact.

There was, to begin with, no desire on the part of the founders of New England to create the business community that actually came into being. Early New England society was dominated by religious

This article is reprinted, by permission of the author, from *Explorations in Entrepreneurial History*. 6:197–206 (May 1954).

members of the lesser English gentry who shared a suspicion of commerce. Many of them, like John Winthrop, had lost their stability in a rapidly changing world and like him had become convinced that in England "trades are carried soe deceiptfully and Vnrightusly as yt is almost impossible for a good vpright man to maynteyne his charge and to liue comfortably in his profession."[1] The influential Reverend John White expressed an aversion to the life of trade characteristic of many settlers when he wrote to the Puritan governor,

> I heare shopkeeping begins to growe in request amongst you. In former age all kinds of retailing wares (which I confess is necessary for mens more convenient supply) was but an appendixe to some handicraft and to that I should reduce it if I were to advise in the government . . . the common good . . . is not furthered by such as drawe only one from another and consequently live by the sweat of other mens brows, producing nothing themselves by their owne endevours.[2]

Yet the first generation leaders, being, in John Hull's phrase, "noe Babes nor windy-headed men," knew the importance of trade and the need for a firm economic foundation for their new commonwealth.[3] Their purpose was not to prohibit trade, but rather to place it within a structure whose proportions had been drawn by the hand of God. In part to accomplish this they set up, while still in England, what was called the "Undertaking," a subcompany of ten men which took over the debts of the Massachusetts Bay Company in exchange for half the beaver trade, the sole right to manufacture salt in the colony, to transport goods and immigrants, and to establish a "magazine" of goods to retail to the settlers. But nothing ever came of this wide franchise. The Undertaking failed to exploit its imposing monopolies.

During the first few years the ownership of goods in the Massachusetts Bay area was acquired by individual settlers going directly to the sides of the occasional ships that arrived with freight, and negotiating with the captains or the ships' merchants for parts of their cargoes. This primitive method of obtaining goods, which gave the advantage to the settlers with the most ready cash, was clearly unsatisfactory. It did not provide for resupplying the same men's stock: those who bought goods from one ship might fail to replenish their stores from the next. Competitive buying at the dock helped force prices up and gave to those who bargained successfully with the ship captains the possibility of engrossing needed supplies. The dangers of such a possibility were palpable, and the Massachusetts government soon asserted its right to control this aspect of the economy for the public welfare.

Drawing on familiar English practices the Puritan magistrates in March 1635 attempted to deal with the problem by creating what would have become an exclusive guild of merchant-importers. The General Court awarded to nine men representing nine towns around the Bay the exclusive right to board incoming ships, examine the goods, decide on the prices, and "acquainte their p[ar]tners therewith." These men were given the right to buy the goods, which were to be stored "in some maggasen" near the ship and to sell them to the inhabitants of the several towns at five per cent profit "& not above."[4]

Such a restriction of access to incoming goods, however appealing it might have been to the Puritan magistrates, reflected more clearly the traditional English method of controlling trade by placing it exclusively in the hands of a responsible group whose rights and obligations were defined than it did the realities of life in New England. A law that demanded of other buyers that they stand idly by while nine fortunate individuals made comfortable middlemen's profits could not be enforced. Moreover, the buying of goods sufficient to satisfy the needs of a whole town required ready money in amounts above that possessed by the nine assignees. And was it realistic to hope that supercargoes and sailors who had goods to sell would limit sales to these men when others on shore would pay more? Within four months of its enactment this law, which might have affected the society and economy of New England significantly, was repealed. The magistrates had to content themselves with licensing both wholesale and retail dealers and reserving for the government the first choice of any incoming cargoes.

Thus the origin of the merchant group in New England lay neither in the original subcompany Undertaking nor in the merchant importers guild that might have been created by the General Court. In the same years as these attempts to institutionalize control of the business community failed, trade quite unsupervised took root and before the end of the second decade of settlement the merchant community was flourishing. How had this come about? By what process had independent trade emerged? What conditions set the limits to membership in the merchant group? What effect did these limitations have on the later development of the business community?

The survival of certain documents, particularly notarial and court records, permits us to locate the precise moments when a number of individual strands of trade were woven. In these documents lie clues to the answer to our questions.

Thomas Lechford, in his *Note-Book* covering the years 1638–1641, kept a copy of a letter he wrote praising the prospects of a young man named Henry Gray. Gray's future, he suggested, was bright, for "His brother also, a citizen of London, hath promised to stock him with 100£ worth of commodities from time to time, if the Lord keepe open the way, and he is to have half the profit which may be of especial advantage."[5] Henry Gray thus started in trade on the basis of a loan from his brother, presumably a London merchant, who supplied him with his first shipload of goods. This document is suggestive. Were such family business arrangements commonplace? Do they apply to other, better known first generation New England merchants?

John Cogan, according to Winthrop, was Boston's first shopkeeper. Notarial records reveal that this early merchant dealt with a certain Humphrey Cogan, a tradesman of Exeter, England, who turns out to have been John's brother. Valentine Hill, a leading Boston merchant from the time of his emigration in 1636, drew bills of exchange on his brother John, "mercht at the Angell & Starre in Cheapside," of London.[6] Joshua Hewes, brought up by his uncle Joshua Foote, a member of the London Ironmongers Company, began his business career shortly after his arrival in 1633 by selling cutlery and ironware, and then branched out into general merchandise which he received in large shipments from his uncle. Foote himself became so interested in the trade that he sent over his son, Caleb, and used the cousins as factors in his own transactions. Henry Shrimpton, who called himself "a Brasyer" upon his arrival in Boston in 1639 and who left property worth £11,979 at his death twenty-seven years later, drew continuously for credit upon his brother Edward, a London merchant. Like Joshua Foote, "Eds. Shrimpton & Companie" soon sent over goods on its own account and became a specialist in exports to New England.[7] The Hutchinson family, which produced a remarkable number of early

New England merchants, looked for business authority to the elder William's brother Richard, a flourishing Cheapside ironmonger, and perhaps also to another brother, John, a woolen draper in the native town of Alford.

But the importation and distribution of goods was only one of the enterprises of the early merchants. The exportation of fish was at least as important for the establishment of merchant families. A typical document of the first years of the fish trade is a bond recorded in the Aspinwall Records by which a certain Robert Houghton, of London, pledged to two London merchants that Robert Sedgwick of Charlestown, Massachusetts, would load on their ship, *Mary,* 1500 quintals of fish within twenty days of its arrival in Massachusetts. Robert Houghton, the key man in this transaction, was Robert Sedgwick's brother-in-law.

What about the commercial traffic to the Wine Islands, the continent of Europe, and the West Indies? The Massachusetts Hutchinsons had started in trade by selling the goods sent them by their kinsman Richard Hutchinson of London. By the end of the Commonwealth period they had extended their interests into the Bay Colony's hinterland, south to Rhode Island, and into the Caribbean. The pivot of these new extensions was Peleg Sanford of Portsmouth, Rhode Island, who was Richard Hutchinson's nephew. Peleg ran the Hutchinson's Rhode Island cattle farms and exported their horses and provisions to Barbados where they were handled by his own brothers, the Barbadian merchants William and Elisha Sanford. Similarly, the Winthrops became involved in commerce in the first years of settlement when John Winthrop, junior, became the American partner and distributing agent for the exporting undertakings of the interrelated Winthrop-Downing clan. Eventually, the Winthrops had family commercial representatives in Rhode Island, New London and Hartford, Connecticut, Teneriffe in the Canaries, and Antigua in the West Indies. The famous Boston mint-master merchant John Hull built up his many-sided business not only with the help of his uncle Thomas Parris and his cousin Edward Hull, both London haberdashers, but also with the assistance of still another relative, John Parris, a planter in Barbados.

Business arrangements like Henry Gray's were not, then, unique. They were, in fact, the mechanism which permitted a considerable number of first generation New Englanders to begin commercial operations. The conditions of trade help to explain why this should have been so.

Overseas commerce in the seventeenth century was capricious, uncontrollably affected by the accidents of sailing. The chance arrival or loss of single, well-laden vessels created local gluts and famines. At best, where there were well-established markets and reliable factors, it was difficult to invest shrewdly on the basis of information months old regarding a situation that might change many times before the investment took effect. But the American markets were not well-established, nor were there reliable factors. The initiation of trade demanded credit. But potential creditors lacked the means by which to judge the reliability, resources, and business acumen of strangers in America. They could rely only on personal ties to men in New England. Blood relationships were the most useful bonds of all. Lacking these, prospective New England importers must themselves have had previous experience in business and to have left behind friendships and reputations which they could draw on in attempting to finance their new ventures.

A consequence of the limitation of entrance into the import trade was the striking homogeneity of the earliest merchant group in New England. The first New England merchants who dealt in goods and provisions were almost to a man recruited from petty tradesman and shopkeeper families of London. None of them had been leaders of guilds. None of them had held municipal office. None could have vied in prestige and power with the City aldermen. Not only were the first New England merchants drawn from the same social group, but even from the same locality. For the most part the first exchange of goods was carried on between men in the Bay Colony and their relatives and close friends clustered in the Cheapside-Cornhill-Leadenhall district of London. This area had been the scene of continuous agitation in the 1630's as intensified tax collection had touched off a series of panics. Many of the boldest or the most desperate of the local tradesmen, already affiliated with the radical Puritan movement, had joined the hundreds of uprooted East Anglian cloth workers and husbandmen from all over England in their exodus to the New World.

Once in America they sought to recreate the life they had known at home. Congregating in the towns around Boston Bay, in Salem, and in New Haven, they saw many of the same people with whom they had pushed through the crowds of Cheapside a few years earlier. From the first they called the main thoroughfare of Boston Cornhill, and along it and the intersecting King Street, which led to the wharf, many established their residences. The list of property owners on Cornhill between Milk and Dock Streets during the first decade reads like the roster of expatriated tradesmen and shopkeepers of the old business district. The mercantile community of New Haven was composed almost entirely of ex-inhabitants of Coleman Street, the extension of which, Old Jewry, led like the stem of an inverted T into the junction of Cheapside and Cornhill.

Since commerce was so much a matter of personal relationships, this group of ex-London tradesmen, scattered now among the seaside villages of New England, found themselves in an advantageous position at the establishment of the Commonwealth government in their home country. Their relatives and friends in England rose to positions of power, and their trade was favored. In 1644 Parliament exempted the commerce of New England from the English import and export duties. The expedition of 1655 that captured Jamaica was largely provisioned in New England and the naval purchasing agents became important buyers of New England produce during the campaign. War threatened England's supply of naval stores from the Baltic and, fearful of being denied these essentials of sea warfare and transportation, the English government placed enormous orders for New England tar, timber, and turpentine. Some of the New England merchants felt circumstances so promising that they returned to England themselves and reached for power and influence. Some achieved their goals. Robert Sedgwick, the Charlestown merchant, became a Major General in charge of part of the Jamaican expedition, and Edward Hopkins, the London "Turkey merchant" who had moved from Massachusetts to Connecticut, returned to England in 1651 where he became Member of Parliament, Commissioner of the Navy, Warden of the Fleet, and Keeper of the Palace of Westminster. And Nehemiah Bourne, the New England shipwright and ship captain, after having been made "Rear Admiral of the Fleet of the Commonwealth of England and Captain of the St. Andrew" for his part in a sea battle with the Dutch, became one of the first Commissioners of Trade.

But the closely-knit tie between the New England merchants and the new English authorities could not withstand the pressure of events. It was torn apart at the Restoration. Overnight England and particularly London took on an aspect different from that which had become familiar to the colonials during the Cromwellian period. Passage through governmental and commercial circles was no longer eased for the New England merchants by kin or friendships; they now confronted closed doors guarded by clusters of courtiers, hostile functionaries, royal hangers-on of all sorts. This was the world of Samuel Pepys, dominated by cliques of powerful men to whom patronage and nepotism were guiding principles of political preferment and sinecures the reward for loyalty.

But if England's aspect changed for the New England merchants, so also did that of the Puritan colonies alter for the new men of influence in the home country. To them the New England settlements, which once to some had seemed outposts of spiritual enlightenment and social and religious reform, appeared to be distant, troublesome dependencies, hotbeds of the nonconformist fanaticism that had convulsed England for two decades. But dependencies still, fruit ripe for the plucking. The result was that the New England merchant group after the Restoration began to be recruited in part from a different portion of English society. The growing economic promise of New England began to attract men intent on careers in trade who were not only strangers to New England orthodoxy but to Puritanism itself. Adventurous Englishmen seeking their fortunes, they brought with them the spirit of a new age. Unlike the first generation merchants whose origins had been in the petty tradesmen class, these newcomers, royalists Anglicans for the most part, were commercial imperialists who went to New England as fortune-hunters in the almost untouched area of colonial commerce. There was nothing petty or pious about them. Men of large ambitions and broad visions, they had in varying degrees the "imagination, power of organization, courage in taking risks, ability to inspire, confidence in prospective investors, driving force, tireless energy [and] optimism" attributed to the most famous of them, Richard Wharton.[8]

Like Wharton, also, the majority of this group quickly made a place for themselves in the growing society of the port towns. Their presence greatly influenced the eventual character of the merchant group.

By the end of the first decade after the Restoration an important development was taking place in the organization of the merchant group. The American-born sons and grandsons of the first generation tradesmen were beginning to feel a sense of distinctiveness their emigrating forebears had never known. Not only did they find a community of interests in the needs of trade, but the pursuit of these interests led them into a series of disputes with the governing Fathers which strengthened this sense of group identity. Moreover, their involvement in the world of Atlantic commerce committed them increasingly to attitudes and a style of life alien to the established mores of the Bible Commonwealths. The feeling of uniqueness among the merchants, heightened by their exclusion from political power above the town deputy level, grew slowly, but by the end of the third generation it had made itself felt with great force in a most important way.

Family records disclose an extraordinary degree of intermarriage among the children and grandchildren of the successful first generation tradesmen. They intermarried so consistently that it may be said that eligibility for marriage was effectively restricted to children of other merchants and of ministers. By the third generation the merchants in each locality formed what amounted to a single interrelated family. Thus, for example, by the marriages of the ten children of the immigrant brothers William and Edward Tyng those venerable merchants became related to the Bradstreets, Whartons, Brattles, Dudleys, the Searles of Barbados, the Savages, Ushers, and Gibbonses—all merchant families. Winthrop junior's children married into the Palmes and Corwin families, the latter already connected to the Browne, Lynde, and Wolcott clans. Elizabeth and Charles Lidget, children of the mast merchant Peter Lidget, married respectively John Usher, son of Hezekiah, the book-seller merchant, and Bethiah Shrimpton, daughter of the immigrant brazier Henry Shrimpton. Through the Ushers and the Shrimptons, the Lidget family gained kinship association with the whole Tyng tribe as well as with the Hutchinsons, Breedons, and Stoddards.

The speed of this group consolidation may in part be accounted for by the frequency of remarriages by widows and widowers. Thus, for example, Richard Wharton, in the course of his thirty years in New England, married successively daughters of the Tyng, Higginson, and Winthrop families. By the last two of his four marriages Lawrence Hammond, the Charlestown merchant, became related to the Willoughby and Gerrish families. Nor was Samuel Sewall, the diarist, one to enjoy a solitary life. Shortly after the death of his first wife, Hannah Hull, when he was in his sixty-eighth year, he took to wife one Abigail Helyen, twice a widow, who died within a year and was succeeded in Sewall's ménage by Henry Shrimpton's daughter Mary, the relict of the merchant Robert Gibbs.

If this process had proceeded undisturbed the merchants would, no doubt, have emerged by the end of the century as a "class," in the common meaning of that term. But the altering structure of power which introduced important divisions within them and the related influx of new merchants prevented that development from taking place.

The arrival of these newcomers coincided with the settlement in the colonies of official representatives of the home governments, men whose duty it was to draw the distant colonies closely into the empire by enforcing the regulation of trade and by guiding provincial politics. These high officers, civil and military, became the nucleus of a group of Englishmen new to the colonies: customs functionaries, lesser bureaucrats, fortune hunters in official positions—all men seeking careers in the quickly expanding colonial administration. The social importance of this officialdom group quickly became evident, for not only did it represent cosmopolitan fashion and political influence, but in its access to those who controlled the weapon of customs regulation it offered great economic opportunities. Toward this group moved every colonial with ambition and hope of success. And none were more successful in linking themselves to officialdom than the post-Restoration *arrivés,* already connected to influential people in England. At the same time as they secured their positions with the governors and customs officials they also made connections with the native merchant group. By the late 1660's it was already evident that the newcomers suffered no social liability in New England for their Anglicanism or royalism. It became a normal social procedure for ambitious young Englishmen making careers for themselves in trade to marry the heiress daughters of nonconformist colonials. The royal Commissioner who said in 1664 that the New Englanders "will marry their children to those whom they will not admit to baptisme, if they be rich," had exaggerated, but he had exaggerated the truth.[9]

These newcomers, men of influence in Restoration London business circles, in touch with colonial officialdom, and now linked to the older commercial families, were instrumental in shaping the social character of the merchant group. By the end of the seventeenth century it was clear that in New England the merchant group was no longer socially homogeneous; it was by no means an undiversified social unit. The merchants, despite their common interests, now formed not a singular social entity, but a spectrum; not a clearly defined bloc of like-minded individuals with similar attitudes and styles of life, but a combination of people as different as Richard Wharton and Samuel Sewall.

To Sewall, as active a merchant as New England could boast, Wharton and his friends lived in a superior world, linked closely to the powers that ruled in America and England, an elegant, mannered society of government. Next to them Sewall, born into a Puritan family of humble status, was provincial. To him they were the *haut monde,* living lives of frivolous and wicked extravagance. He was not invited to their dinner parties, nor they to his, and he concluded his description of the pomp and ceremony of Humphrey Luscomb's funeral with the remark, "None of our family were invited."[10] Their fashions revolted him, and none more so than the wearing of those symbols of Restoration sophistication, perriwigs. To Wharton and his friends they were important articles of dress which they carefully selected and proudly wore. But to Sewall they were the height of artificality and unnaturalness, and he had no hesitation in saying so. It was a fitting end that came to Mr. Clendon, the Boston barber and perriwig maker, Sewall wrote in his *Diary,* who died "being almost eat up with Lice and stupefied with Drink and cold."[11]

The scale of merchant types descended from the high-church officialdom group, to the well-born natives with less wealth and poorer overseas connections but with equal social ambitions, to the successful first-generation merchants like John Bray of Kittery and Andrew Belcher of Boston, who were still part of rural, provincial frontier society, to the lowest reaches of the group where tradesmen, peddlers, shop-keepers, mariners, and fishermen gathered together their resources, invested in a few voyages overseas, and gradually came to think of themselves as merchants. The base of the merchant group was hidden in the obscurity of occasional voyages in small ships, the jumbled shops of port towns, and the isolated trading shacks of backwoods Connecticut. There were no distinct boundaries of the merchant group.

By the early eighteenth century the occupation of trade, though it defined an area of common interests, did not delimit a separate stratum of society in New England as it did in England. It was not a way of life so much as a way of making money; not a social condition but an economic activity. It was the most important vehicle for social ascent. By the wealth and connections it offered, as by nothing save the ministry, one could traverse the slope of colonial society.

Time and time again obscure families rose through trade to affluence and power. By the mid-eighteenth century the pattern was clear. An unknown, hard-headed colonial tradesman, sailor, or even farmer becomes a successful merchant, competes for the political and economic favors of the official group, attains a position on the colonial Council, creates friendships with influential people in England, and passes on a fortune to his son. The heir grows up in a different society from that of his father, solidifies the family position in Anglican officialdom, uses his family connections to advance in trade and to receive important political appointments, and becomes a colonial member of the British ruling class. Having reached through different channels the social and political position of the Englishmen who left the home country for careers in the colonial government, he is tempted to end his career in the English countryside. But what is a return to his colleagues is an arrival for him, and most often he prefers to end his career as a colonial merchant prince.

So it was with the Belchers, whose lives illustrate the pattern of mercantile ascent with classic perfection. At what point did Andrew Belcher become a merchant? The son of a Cambridge settler, he started probably as a country peddler or innkeeper, progressed as an inland provision wholesaler, and, inheriting some money from his wife's father, bought a vessel and became an independent shipmaster-merchant. The economic upheaval of King Philip's war offered him the opportunity to branch out into large-scale commerce in provisions. Gradually he inched upwards across the surface of colonial society, finding a few firm footholds in successful voyages, slipping and stumbling on poor risks and hard luck, dashing through the open stretches of political favors. The measure of his success was less his eventual wealth or the fact that his equipage at the governor's reception in 1702 included a Negro footman, than that twelve years after serving as master on one of Samuel Sewall's vessels he had become the main provisioner of the royal ships that touched at Boston harbor.

At each stage in the process by which the merchant group assumed this ultimate character, kinship played a vital role. Kinship goes far in explaining the initiation of overseas trade in New England and the recruitment of the first New England merchants. Study of the family relations in the second and third generations reveals the consolidation of these early mercantile families. And in the kinship ties secured between the established merchants and the post-Restoration commercial adventurers one may observe the final construction of the merchant group.

The Entrepreneur in Brewing, 1700–1830

PETER MATHIAS

I

Recent study in economic history has, in several ways, sought to explore the diversities existing within national aggregates and generalizations. Research makes plainer every year that the eighteenth-century industrial entrepreneurs were far from belonging to a single ideal type in class, creed, or attitudes.[1] When the industrial structure itself was so differentiated—as to such matters as the size of plant, the level of technique, or the relationship of enterprise to the ownership of landed estates or to foreign trade—it is no wonder that noble coal-owners, landed canal and railway projectors, wealthy merchants like the Findlays of Glasgow or the Reynolds of Bristol should qualify for the compliment of this title equally with the traditional élite of the type—Quaker ironmasters, Unitarian cotton spinners, or even the dissenting yeoman turned industrialist. In turn, single industries which were virtually nation-wide, like textiles or brewing (or even, in a different way, farming) possessed within themselves, at the same point in time, a complete spectrum of industrial organization from household production through cottage workshop to powered factory. Such industries show, in consequence, as diverse a collection of business leaders, of entrepreneurs and non-entrepreneurs.

In 1750 there were 996 Common Brewers in England and Wales, and 48,421 Brewing Victuallers—that is, almost a thousand people who brewed only for sale to publicans and private customers away

This article is reprinted, by permission of the author, from *Explorations in Entrepreneurial History*, 10:72–80 (December 1957).

from their breweries, and over forty-eight thousand, who, like Peter Stubs of Warrington, brewed mainly for their own inn, but also for distant customers.[2] In London alone, where production had been dominated since the seventeenth century by Common Brewers, there were 165 of them, who together produced about one quarter of the entire national output for sale. The differing roles of the entrepreneur in such an industry have, therefore, to be related to the several diversities contained within this national aggregate of firms. Only then will the common features, as well as the differences, become historically significant. Most entrepreneurs in the eighteenth century were opportunists—even if opportunists with vision to see opportunities not apparent to others equally anxious to get ahead, and with determination to organize things in such a way that potential opportunities become actual ones. Effectively controlling the relevant factors of production, for example, could enable them for the first time to gain effective control over the product and so design it for a particular market. A similar flair in trading might discover, develop, or create a new market—success usually involving elements of all these three activities. As individuals they made a positive step by seeing opportunities for profiting in enterprise in a new way. But the more one emphasizes the degree of opportunism involved, then the more importance one must attach, by implication, to the circumstances which conditioned their response, and offered them the possibility of success. These "circumstances," of course, make up collectively the emptiest box one could wish to fill—the assorted factors within it ranging from technological invention to new transport, a changed law or a change in fashion—but such an approach has the merit of relating "entrepreneurship" to its objective context, to the actual problems and opportunities facing the business man. To develop hypotheses and concepts of "entrepreneurship" in the abstract, uncontrolled by concern with the limitations put upon the actors by real factors, is a temptation to arbitrary theorizing unsupported by historical experience.

Here there is space to look at only a few of the contrasts and common features in the brewing industry. Four have been selected: as contrasts, the nature of the enterprise over the country, and the kind of person entering the London porter market at different times; as common features, trading skills and social positions.[3]

TABLE 1

NUMBER OF BREWERS, 1700–1799

	Brewing Victuallers[4]		Common Brewers	
Year	England and Wales	London	England and Wales	London
1700	39,469	—	746	174
1750	48,421	—	996	165
1799	23,690	—	1,382	127

II

There is firstly, of course, the vast gap in size between the few giants in London, where perhaps half a dozen were brewing over 100,000 barrels (all of porter) by 1800 (the greatest of these double that amount) and the anonymous multitudes of humbler producers in smaller towns and villages.[5] The story of most of these as brewers, if not as entrepreneurs, may be summed up by saying that they prospered upon and were limited by their local markets. Clearly, for a commodity of such low "value density" as beer, high transport costs set strict boundaries to the possibilities of expansion as a brewer, save in special circumstances. John Smith of Oundle, for example, first seized his chance to develop from a brewing victualler when the prisoner-of-war camp was set up at Norman Cross; while John Gardner of Cheltenham and John Palmer of Bath enjoyed the patronage of the visiting élite who took ale as well as the waters.[6] For them, a metropolitan market, so to speak, brought itself to their localities each season. In other small towns another special factor channeled the response of persons eager to take what business opportunities were available to them as brewers. Francis Cobb, for instance, who established a brewery at Margate in 1760, became so dependent upon naval demand that he bought a second one at Deal to be closer to his market.[7] Heavy dependence upon public contracts survived the establishment of naval breweries at all the admiralty dockyards for many brewers in the south coast ports.[8]

The limitations of the local market gave the entrepreneur an incentive to employ his capital and his energies in other directions, ambition for enterprise necessarily overflowing from its source, unlike the situation in London where the market for the brewer was large enough to satisfy the ambition and absorb the capital of those most aggressive in expansion. Although this characteristic was by no means universal in London by the end of the century,[9] the decades of most rapid expansion after 1740 certainly saw it, and as will be apparent below, nonbrewing wealth and enterprise became associated with the industry precisely because the need for capital in brewing became so urgent, and on such a large scale that it could not be produced fast enough from the profits of the firms.

The Burton brewers had no demand on such a scale at their doorstep. They were mainly dependent upon selling to the Baltic until Napoleon, by closing the ports in 1807, forced a rapid deployment in the English market on them.[10] Their traditional market demanded a very strong and expensive ale to survive both the journey and the transport costs, its profitability being always dependent upon the fact that most vessels cleared to the Baltic from Hull in ballast. Owners and skippers were looking for any cargoes outward to replace the bulky inward freights for which the voyage had primarily been made. A very short brewing season, therefore, had to be sandwiched between January and May: that is, starting in preparation for the year's Baltic sailings but ending before weather became too hot to brew with safety. The greatest Burton brewers, Benjamin Wilson, Thomas Salt, Worthington, and Bass, brewed not more than 5,000 barrels annually at this time—even though their product was widely known for its quality—but their initial sales of beer formed the basis for a pyramid of transactions, with trading margins being taken at every stage to supplement already comfortable manufacturing profits. The shortness of their brewing season was useful, too, in giving them the time to profit by other enterprise.

Through the lack of a mass market in England, and through the need to accommodate the Baltic merchants to whom they sold ale, they were drawn into dealing in Baltic produce by ledger-barter and complementary purchasing of timber, staves, iron, flax, and hemp.[11] They dealt in London as well as through Hull and the vale of Trent. One group, at least—Benjamin Wilson and his sons—concentrated mainly on timber and staves at Burton, which was a distributing center for their region of the Midlands. In addition, they owned parts of ships and were willing to take a profit by speculation and trading when buying any of their raw materials for brewing ale and in all the goods gained with the credits they piled up from selling it. Until the expansion of brewing in Burton in the next century, when the railways opened up London and the national market to them, little of their accumulating surpluses went into fixed capital for brewing, but was put out in these ways to other enterprise. The majority of them were amplifications and extensions by trade of the central business. Less linked to brewing was one further venture. Benjamin Wilson became a partner in a cotton mill near Lichfield in 1784. All this activity lay apart from his investments in those fields where "enterprise investment" merged into "status investment" and his motives included a desire for rentier profits—real estate, canal shares, government stock.

Parallels to this situation may be seen in Samuel Palmer of Bath developing two theaters, a tallow chandler's business, and a spermacetti factory; Sir Edmund Lacon in Yarmouth investing heavily in malting for sale and in ships; the Cobbold family in Ipswich, and brewers in the north-east coast becoming prominent on the east coast as corn merchants, merchants in foreign trade, and as shipowners.[12] These last two, amongst numerous other instances of the same link, also illustrate the widespread connection between banking and brewing.

The move by country brewers into banking in small towns may well have been an entrepreneurial response, the objective being to profit from the status which wealth brought and from funds it was less profitable (or less possible) to reinvest in brewing, as well as being a useful adjunct, seasonally, to their breweries. All things considered, for such businessmen as these, limited by the narrowness of their local markets for brewing, the distinguishing mark of the entrepreneur was nonbrewing activity, the unenterprising being content to slumber peacefully as brewers or rentiers in a traditional market in a traditional way.

III

The leaders of the industry were, generally speaking, not the first technical innovators. Here the pattern is that of Arkwright and Crompton, rather than such as Abraham Darby (or Bessemer), who made their fortunes on their inventions. The great quickly adopted

TABLE 2
Brewers and Bankers

Provinces			
Family	*Place*	*Family*	*Place*
Simonds	Reading	Bireham and Fox	Reepham, Norfolk
Oakley	Deal	Weston	Norwich
Cobb	Margate	Dowden and Lee	Alton
Smith	Oundle	Mildred and Sampson	Diss, Norfolk
Gardner	Cheltenham	Crabb	Hitchin
Ramsbottom	Windsor and London	Lucas	Hitchin
Hector	Petersfield	Ashby	Staines
Greenall	St. Helens, Warrington	Searle	Saffron Walden
Christie	Hertford	Gibson	Saffron Walden
Lacon	Yarmouth	Hollick	Cambridge
Weston	Norwich	Angove	Falmouth
Wells	Biggleswade	Threlfall	Liverpool
Cobbold	Ipswich	Billingsly and Jillard	Oakhill, Somerset
Worthington	Burton	Baldock and Rigden	Canterbury
Tollemache	Ipswich	Farr	Beccles
Tawney	Oxford		
Clinch	Witney		

London			
Family or Person	*Brewery*	*Family or Person*	*Brewery*
Bevan	Barclays	Shaw-Lefevre	Whitbreads
Barclay	Barclays	Clutterbuck	Whitbreads
Hanbury	Trumans	Wilshere	Whitbreads
Gurney	Barclays	Hoare	Hoare
T. Brown	Whitbreads	J. Cripps	
Hobhouse	Whitbreads	J. Curtis	

This list is by no means complete, but it is sufficient to show the intimacy of the connection between brewing and banking. Each case listed is of a person being brewer and banker, or partner in a brewery and a bank.

In addition there is a possible, but as yet unproven, connection between brewing and banking in the case of the following, whose names appear separately in directories as brewers and as bankers: Drew (Chichester), Tylee and Gent (Devizes), Wakefield (Kendall), Woodcock (Halesworth), Burdon (Newcastle on Tyne), Slocock (Newbury), Deane (Reading), Embury (Tewkesbury), Wells (Wallingford), Sanders (Witney), Dawes (Warwick).

Much of this table has been composed from banking rather than brewing evidence, and for this I am indebted to Dr. L. S. Pressnell of University College, London, and Mr. C. N. Ward-Perkins of Pembroke College, Oxford.

innovations perfected by brewers, it is true, but brewers who were and remained in a small way of business. An obscure London brewer, Harwood, supposedly first brewed porter in 1722, the stability and efficiency of which made the mass-production plant a possibility in the industry: but he did not rise to industrial eminence himself.[13] It was almost the same with Michael Combrune and the application of the thermometer, James Baverstock and Thomas Richardson with the hydrometer, similarly with the attempts to introduce an attemperator for controlling the speed of fermentation.[14] All these innovations are scarcely technical inventions in the sense of Wyatt's roller spinning, Watt's separate condenser, or Hackworth's steam blast. They are more the quick-witted adaptation to industrial use of instruments already known in scientific circles, to achieve exact "measurement control" of processes which were traditional (and of which the chemistry remained unknown).

Other important changes involved merely a simple alteration in a process of manufacture without any new device: such as making black porter malt by "high drying" on the malt kiln, varying the hop rate with the season to improve stability, or employing the more rigorous extraction methods in "mashing" which porter malt made possible to give more efficient use of raw materials. Only in certain aspects of innovation did the sheer problems of size force the opportunity of increasing productivity to the attention of the greatest, and improvement arrive from the top.

Important efficiencies resulted from planning the brewery rationally, which was being noted as a feature of the "Great Common Brewhouse" in London by the 1730's, and from storage in bulk by vatting.[15] Mechanical innovation is the other field where technical change penetrated through the industry from above but only after the great expansion in fixed capitals was well under way, and as a consequence of steam power. In the 1780's steam engines came to most of the "capital houses" in the metropolis as a more efficient substitute for horse-milling and horse pumps. Once installed the gains from applying the engine to new jobs previously done by men —cleansing casks by steam, hoisting, mashing, rousing—which it had *not* been installed to replace, became as important as its superiority over horses in the functions it *was* designed to perform.[16] Its creative effects, so to speak, proved as valuable as its substitution effects.

IV

With such diversity in the scale of operations and the nature of the market the capital requisite for entering the industry varied correspondingly, and with this the social origins and attributes of the entrepreneurs. At one end of the scale is Isherwood, a Windsor brewer, who, from being a servant in the Christopher Inn at Eton, married some money, established a brewery and left his son between £8,000 and £9,000 a year from the business.[17] In London already the barrier to entry could be high. Ralph Thrale was the son of a farm laborer, it is true, but he had a successful uncle without a son and was enabled to buy his brewery from him for £30,000 out of the profits (over 11 years).[18] By 1736, Samuel Whitbread's apprenticeship cost him £300 and he needed all of his £2000 patrimony as younger son of a prosperous—and dissenting—Bedfordshire yeoman, plus loans from friends at home, plus a sleeping partner, to set up porter-brewing on the competitive scale current in the 1740's.[19] By the next generation in the same market, it needed the resources of the Barclay-Bevan-Gurney Quaker banking clan to put up the £135,000 for Thrale's old business.

With them was the old manager who had saved his way up the salaried ladder of a lifetime to climb into the partnership on his master's death, and he still had to borrow from his master's widow in 1781 to make his stake a respectable one.[20] This man, John Perkins, had been one of the architects of success for thirty years, personifying a new race of men, the salaried entrepreneurs, little known in the brewing industry outside the capital in the eighteenth century. In London, however, they became more important as the unit of production became larger, so demanding greater capital and more partners, some of whom were less intimately associated with day to day control of production. In consequence of the increase in size more articulate management developed with a division of function between buying, brewing and accounting. This path of entrepreneurs from salary to partnership-profits was trodden increasingly. It was one way of overcoming from the inside the increasing barrier of capital required for ownership, feasible by middle age where a senior clerk's salary rose to £1,000 p.a. as it could do in a London "capital house" by 1800. And usually these "department Managers" invested considerable savings (at 5 per cent) in the firms.[21]

TABLE 3
PARTNERS AND CAPITAL

Year	Barrels Brewed	Loans to Retailers and Value of Leases	Number of Partners	Surplus Capital Invested in Firm
		(*i*) *Whitbreads*		
1790	175,000	£ 11,860	1	£ ?
1799	203,000	45,060	4	75,450
1810	110,939	114,500	7	66,000
1830	131,300	355,600	9	297,200
		(*ii*) *Thrale—Barclay Perkins*		
1780	65,460	7,800	1	1,206
1790	126,725	26,570	4	167,740
1800	105,905	39,180	4	139,150
1811	264,165	114,280	8	417,300
1830	231,340	356,050	8	702,864
		(*iii*) *Trumans*		
1780	80,730	18,810	2	2,135
1790	93,715	19,570	2	5,850
1800	101,560	37,970	3	51,050
1810	144,990	121,670	4	90,720
1830	203,530	345,590	6	288,925
		(*iv*) *Meux—Reid*		
1797	95,375	?	5	?
1810	211,010	266,440	20	166,340
1820	159,385	294,370	16	177,190

SOURCES: Rest Books and other records at the breweries.

NOTES: Much of the surplus capital (that is, capital surplus to the joint partnership capital) was invested by the partners themselves, as references to Table 4 (Capital invested in Barclays, 1784–1830) will make plain. There is not enough space here to give a complete analysis of the capital, nominal and actual, of these concerns in a single table, nor is it possible in all cases. These figures have been extracted to illustrate the points made on pp. 316–318.

Gyfford's brewery in Long Acre was bought in 1787 by a typical combination of talent, capital, and kinship. Joseph Delafield moved from being an employee with twenty-three years of technical training and considerable savings behind him as a chief salaried brewer of

Samuel Whitbread. Harvey Christian Combe, the second partner, was his brother-in-law. He was the son of an eminent attorney and landed proprietor in Hampshire, having a rich uncle (who became also his father-in-law) who launched him in London grain markets as a factor. George Shum, the third, was just rich.[22] Rather different pressures were supplementing this growing barrier on entry by 1800. Then a race to tie the trade was on in London and elsewhere so that the already large capitals needed for buildings, plant, horses, drays, and stock were further increased by the necessity of becoming the landlord and creditor of publicans.

Established concerns welcomed into their partnerships bankers and merchants, who of necessity brought in the social and political consequences of vast wealth made in other fields. Shipbuilding and East India profits poured into Meux and Meux-Reid with William Wells, Sir Robert Wigram, and his son; Gurney cadets arrived at Barclay Perkins from Norfolk; Sir Benjamin Hobhouse, Daniel Clutterbuck, Timothy Brown, and William Wilshere brought banking wealth from Bath, Hertford, and London to Whitbreads. Buxton and Hanbury wealth sustained Trumans.[23]

This wave of recruitment, however, sometimes brought in money more than active partners. Managerially, Whitbreads was brought out of the crisis of a reckless second generation by two salaried clerks, whom the elder Whitbread had enabled to become partners in his will, foreseeing trouble from his son. One of these elderly men then succeeded in bringing an independent brewer, John Martineau, and his two sons, who were operating prosperously on a smaller scale in Lambeth, into the declining firm.

John Martineau and his sons had no partnership articles at all for their firm.[24] Where, as with Meux-Reid in 1809, no less than twenty partners were required to provide the necessary capital, the problems imposed by those dissociated from active management became acute. Written into the deeds of partnership, therefore, there was a detailed series of formal, institutionalized procedures to regulate the relations between the managing partners and the passive partners. Within the private world of partners, this mirrors exactly the arrangements between the shareholders and the directors of a public company which became formalized in manufacturing industry during the nineteenth century. The partners owning a fairly small fraction of the joint capital in their hands but enjoying the substantial stipend of a managing partner thus, as entrepreneurs, approach in function the salaried clerks of Whitbreads who have a considerable stake in the surplus capital invested, and whose salaries were often calculated to benefit according to the profits by bonuses. At the end of the spectrum, the only serious attempt to break into the London porter market from outside the established firms and without the backing of great family wealth and influence came in 1804 when two men, W. H. R. Brown and J. Parry, raised £300,000 in the open market for a subscription company.[25] It prospered only for six years. With fixed capitals becoming greater and control over local marketing more complete, established concerns absorbed new entrepreneurs, from employees and rich partners, rather than new entrepreneurs establishing new concerns.[26] The names and families of the breweries operating in London at the present day bear eloquent testimony to this fact, which a commentator remarked on first in 1747,[27] and which was clearly apparent by 1800. The original founder families, too, have shown an astonishingly sustained ability to produce not only sons, but sons who were able businessmen, happy in remaining businessmen and brewers.

Needless to say, in the country at large each sort of person may be found entering the industry, down to the humblest, while such a precociously mature situation existed in the London porter trade, the position varying with the nature of the urban markets across the country. In some midland counties there were very few Common Brewers at all in 1800, household brewing in cottages and brewing victuallers still satisfying local demand in medieval tradition.

V

The importance of kinship in the world of the unincorporated, family or partnership enterprise is a much-told tale, of course, but nonetheless quite fundamental for this industry. The typical success story of John Perkins is, in this instance, more accurately the typical tragedy of the family business without an heir. Johnson's comment is well known but apt: "A son is almost necessary for the continuance of Thrale's fortune; for what can Misses do with a brew-house? Lands are fitter for daughters than trade."[28]

The new cousinhood were the relatives of his wife Amelia, who was the widow of the great Quaker merchant and banker, Timothy

Bevan. While the immediate family was usually the first source for successors to industrial property, capital for it derived from a wider range, still within the personally known circle of relatives, friends, and trusted business associates. The Barclay-Bevan-Gurney-Perkins cousinhood provided both a flow of capital and a succession of able young men which other brewers sorely lacked.

The following pattern might be illustrated at length from several sets of brewers' records: extensive borrowings in the early years of rapid growth, or at purchase, from within the family circle of family

TABLE 4

BARCLAY PERKINS CAPITAL, 1784–1830

		Surplus Capital on Private Account					
Year	Joint Partnership Capital £000	Partners £000	Quaker Banks £000	Family & Friends £000	Others £000	Publicans, "Clubs" etc. £000	Total £000
	(1)	(2)	(3)	(4)	(5)	(6)	(7)
1784	95.0	—	5.0	8.0	56.0[a]	2.0	71.0
1790	135.0	16.5	71.0	22.5	40.0	17.5	167.5
1800	160.0	56.0	17.0	34.5	21.0	10.5	139.0
1811	200.0	309.0	20.0	56.0	16.0	16.5	417.5
1820	200.0	456.0	5.0	10.0	33.0[b]	80.5	584.5
1830	200.0	556.0	—	4.5	—	142.5	703.0

SOURCE: Rest Books at the brewery. (All figures rounded)

[a] This £56,000 includes £51,000 still owing to Thrale's executors from whom the new partners were in the process of buying the brewery.

[b] £32,000 of this total is a loan from Thompson and Co.—in fact a banking-trade debt which paid off with a year or two.

NOTES: The bankers in col. 3 are without exception relatives of the partners: Gurney and Bland; R. Bartlett and J. Gurney; J. Gurney, Gurney and Webb; Taylor and Lloyds; Ketts and Back. The private persons in col. 4 are linked by family and friendship ties as well as by their Quaker stock. They include Timothy Bevan, Priscilla Bevan, Elizabeth Bevan, Elizabeth Kendall, Benjamin Moseley, Ambrose Benning, Thomas Kett, David Springall, S. Fox, Elizabeth Fox, John Freame, Charles Lloyd, Christiana Gurney, Phineas Bond (of Philadelphia); Delaney Barclay, Cadwallader, Rosa Perkins, Mrs. Perkins trustees. Almost all invested above £1000. Col. 5 includes unidentified names, some of which are undoubtedly tradesmen supplying the brewery with raw materials. These latter, in the 1830 account, appear under col. 6. Col. 6 is a "trade list" not given the compliment of being on the "private account" list of personal friends and the families. It is composed of employees of the brewery, publicans bringing the deposits of clubs and friendly societies at their public houses, and, latterly, tradesmen.

and friends; as a substitute for this, perhaps, "external" sleeping partners, these being paid off as the profits accumulated. Then temporary accommodation from the same group, supplemented by credit from tradesmen and banks in a year of crisis or a year of heavy investment. Often bank loans secured on note for a few months became in effect long-term investments running over several years, for when the note was nearing its term the brewer would ask for its continuance for a further short term, and if the bank was not anxious to call in its investments this might occur several times.[29]

Then, in the case of the London brewery, there came the entry of very large capital after 1795 for investment in property. For this only the family nexuses behind Barclay Perkins and Truman, Hanbury and Buxton (which was more explicitly the same clan) were financially and genealogically resilient enough to provide the necessary capital from within, wealth external to the family groups coming into the partnerships at Meux, Reid, and Whitbreads. To sum up on a much divided field: on the whole it was talent of varying middle-class origins that entered the industry. The field of recruitment was so diverse that one can only say that the entrepreneur belonged to a *type* not a *class*. There was, however, a more than average strain of dissenting or Quaker stock there.

Whatever the role played by individual religious consciousness—in particular the renowned dissenting ethos—it cannot be dissociated from the social and kinship aspects of the dissenting communities, manifested in such things as the flow of capital and talented succession to partnerships. Perhaps those conscientious in their dissent were kept more free than others from temptations bad for business, for example in education. Possibly more important was the negative utility of keeping youths free of the entrepreneurially debilitating values disseminated at the ancient universities. The second generation of Whitbreads and Hucks[30] show the ill effects of the dominant value-system associated with a wealthy upbringing in the eighteenth century: the turf, running a pack of hounds, extravagance in building in the country, spending too much time and money in politics, spending too much of both also in the country and the West End rather than in the City. Conspicuous expenditure of money and time outside business, in short, proved inimical to expansion or success in industry. Thrale, too, was thrice pulled back from such disasters of social expenditure of his own making in the nick of time when he attempted, in addition, a reckless policy of expansion to outbrew Whitbread and Calvert, "two fellows he despises."[31]

But equally, there seemed to be as many owners of packs of hounds among the brewers who maintained their status as entrepreneurs, and all became landed gentry as fast as it was prudently possible. In the early days of "heroic" growth, admittedly, the classic virtues of work and thrift and abstinence from unnecessary spending outside the business apply. Whitbread bought no property between 1742 when he entered trade and 1761, commenting when he did begin, "and I borrowed all the money as I could not spare it to be taken out of Trade."[32] He spoke then for all the ideal entrepreneurs in his predicament. Thereafter, he put over a quarter of a million pounds into land before his death in 1796, and acted for most actual entrepreneurs with his opportunities. Even this was not without its direct business utility. These freehold estates over which the brewing families so assiduously rode to hounds stood always ready to serve as security for personal loans when their London breweries were in temporary need for capital. Nor perhaps is it irrelevant to mention that the Whitbread, Hanbury, and Barclay families were rounding out estates in some of the finest barley counties in the kingdom.

VI

Traditional generalizations about the industrial entrepreneur making his name—and his profits—as an organizer, bringing unified control to the management of all factors of production as a manufacturer, and exploiting his markets as a merchant, are fully borne out by the brewing industry. A little has been said above about local markets for the product fashioning the different responses of entrepreneurs in brewing placed in diverse circumstances. Here, a common feature in the success of brewers needs elaboration: it is the importance of merchanting skills in their raw material markets.

The cost of raw materials (malt or barley much more than hops) remained[33] over 50 per cent of the wholesale price charged to the publican by the brewer so that, given the general level of those technical and commercial economies of scale current amongst competitive groups (such as the dozen porter brewers in London or the handful of Burton brewers driving the Baltic market) the margins most immediately variable and vital were those of malt prices and malt quality. In a sense, as productive efficiency improved, and manufacturing costs per unit of production dropped, buying skills and raw material prices became more significant. Certainly, in no quarter could disaster come more quickly than from inefficient buying. When Thrale's business discretion lapsed in the bad years 1772–1773 the most immediate effect was that Perkins found himself £18,000 in debt to hop-men and very much more to malt merchants; hence he was tied to his creditors and, needing long credit, was unable to gain the best terms in the markets.[34]

Much pivots on this issue of merchanting skills and the industrialist. A theme common to all the surviving letter books of Benjamin Wilson, Samuel Allsopp in Burton, Thomas Greenall in St. Helens and Sampson Hanbury in London is their rigid control of the key decisions about the quality of raw materials, the timing and extent of purchasing, and their rigorous comparisons of price and quality between different sources and methods of supply.[35] They held the initiative, sought out the widest range of choice available from samples gathered from widespread regions, were furious and unreconciliable when a consignment failed to conform with its sample. Only very occasionally did they allow a trusted contact to buy a certain quantity at his discretion over price and quality. "None you know but the most surpassing quality will please me; you have had sufficient experience of me to render anything more on this subject unnecessary," Wilson reminded such a correspondent at the beginning of a new season.[36] The main point, that these buying decisions lay at the center of commercial success, was supplemented by the more subtle one that variations in quality were commonly more extreme than variations in price (confirmed by the advent of exact measurement by hydrometer in the 1770's).

In the course of time, the structure of malt marketing developed partly in response to this trading initiative being kept by the brewer. For London porter brewers this search for quality combined with the problem of ensuring vast and increasing malt supplies to encourage bypassing the open markets and independent malt merchants. Independent malt factors in Hertfordshire collected samples from many small makers, sent them to the brewers, carried out their orders for purchases, organized shipments down the Lea in their own barges, and handled the payments. Apart from their commission as factors, they took the profits of providing both the transport and a cushion of credit between the maltsters and brewers.[37] But the initiative in selecting grain was emphatically not theirs, and they had developed as factors primarily because the merchanting decisions belonged to the industrial entrepreneur. It was the same for active provincial entrepreneurs in the barley market. The Burton brewers bought mainly barley, by sample, from agents in a wide arc of country to the South and East, from Oxfordshire round to Lincoln, occasionally up towards York, supplementing their direct choice of local grain.

Further, the porter brewers themselves developed a partial—and only partial—stake in malting, either permanently by buying malt houses, or temporarily by commissioning maltsters, so that, at a time of hardening prices they could ease the strain by moving into the barley markets but in a year of glut take the greater gains possible in buying malt.[38] Hanbury put off a would-be seller of barley in November 1802 with the comment "I can still buy cheaper than I can make." He wrote to his own maltster, John Kemp, "I can buy the best brown at 44s therefore I think it madness to make any . . . you cannot take the same advantages of the Market in buying Barley as Malt."[39]

More generally, of course, the insistence of these businessmen in trading only with those who accepted their own strict standards of dealing was an important factor behind success in a business where returns depended on a multitude of small transactions with many customers and where profits came from the translation of very small margins over vast quantities. Efficient control of buying, with efficient control of accounts, as in any modern mass-production concern, were crucial for success.

VII

A further common factor about the brewers, as true for those leading in growth and innovation as for the conservatives in business, has an important entrepreneurial truth lurking behind it. It is that as businessmen they were usually remarkably active in nonbusiness activities, sometimes, as I have instanced, to the prejudice of business, but not so in the majority of cases. In London and the localities alike there are brewers everywhere as aldermen, sheriffs, mayors, J.P.'s, Lords Lieutenants, governors of hospitals and schools, prisons and almshouses. Between six and a dozen were in the House of Commons throughout the century, Southwark (and to a lesser extent the City) being "brewers' boroughs" for at least one seat most of the time. They were noted for philanthropy, for their patronage, and for splendor of their hospitality. Did not Richard Meux give 200 people a dinner to celebrate the opening of his huge vat—inside the vessel—and Whitbread entertain royalty in 1787?[40] To take but two examples from among the enterprising: Humphrey Parsons, brewing just east of the Tower of London, inherited a landed estate at Reigate and a seat in Parliament from his father, Sir John, who had been Lord Mayor of London in 1703. The son was a member of the Wax Chandlers Company, then the Grocers and Brewers. He was President of the Bridewell and the Bethlehem hospitals, a City Alderman from 1720, Sheriff in 1722, Lord Mayor in 1730 and in 1740, an M.P. continuously from 1722 to his death in 1741. He obtained a duty-free monopoly of beer exports to France, it is said, by presenting his horse to Louis XV at a hunting party.[41]

On the more modest, provincial scale, three successive heads of the Cobb brewery at Margate were consuls to several foreign courts, pier wardens, Lloyd's agents and Deputy Magistrates to the Cinque Port of Dover.[42] The presidency of institutions, as Humphrey Parsons' more explicit horse-trading, implied a direct business *quid pro quo,* of course, but the main point is that, taken together, these other activities were no less importantly if less directly related to business success. The fortunes of the brewing industry, after all, were lapped about by noneconomic (or at least nonbusiness) considerations. Duty rates took up 22 per cent of the wholesale price of beer in London in years of peace (rising to 47 per cent in the French Wars) and taxation at the point of production implied an intricate excise supervision, and legislative control of all processes of manufacture—both aspects of the excise system, making brewer M.P.'s and their allies in the Commons very useful individuals to the industry. Locally, all facilities for retail sales were subject to annual permission for the licensing justices (at which Brewster Sessions no brewer J.P. could sit after 1751),[43] which meant that status in local society could pay important dividends. All this was incidental to the informal advertisement of fame and quite apart from the fact that acceptance of office became a natural consequence of property, wealth, and social position—as it was for brewers in national politics.

The underlying point is, I think, the same, that the study of business enterprise in the eighteenth century—when the operation of most business was as uninstitutionalized as the operation of most politics—cannot be abstracted out as a purely economic or entrepreneurial phenomenon. The business historian is much concerned with the economic consequences of noneconomic factors. Even more, he is concerned with relating the intimate springs of enterprise in individuals to their differing business circumstances and their differing social circumstances. Some few of these relationships, too briefly, have been explored here with regard to the entrepreneur in brewing. Case-studies of single families in the industry would illuminate the general truths more pointedly, and investigations in other industries perhaps contrast their applicability.

To conclude. About the most forthright of the great London entrepreneurs in brewing during the late eighteenth century, those most aggressive, most dictatorial, there lived an air of greater civility, of status to put it no higher, than about most industrialists. It is reminiscent of the elegance more associated with great wealth in foreign trade or banking. Partly, no doubt, it was that the brewer was recognized as belonging to the same club as the landed interest, whose rents he was directly supporting and whose ranks he was rapidly joining. But as an entrepreneur, too, he was fortunate in the nature of his business. No better comments exist than Bagehot's opinion of the London bankers[44] (which are transposed to the terminology of the other mystery): "The calling is hereditary; the credit to the brewery descends from father to son; this inherited wealth soon brings inherited refinement. Brewing is a watchful but not a laborious trade. A brewer, even in large business, can feel pretty sure that all his transactions are sound, and yet have much spare mind. A certain part of his time, and a considerable part of his thoughts he can readily devote to other pursuits."

Economic Functions of English Landowners in the Seventeenth and Eighteenth Centuries

H. J. HABAKKUK

WHAT PART DID the English landowners play in the economic changes of the period between 1600 and 1800? How far were they active agents of agrarian improvement and industrial innovation? No confident answer to these questions is yet possible. The present state of our knowledge of English agrarian history reflects the interests of the founding fathers of the subject who were concerned primarily with the social consequences of change; with the result that we know a good deal about the effect of the enclosures on the peasant, less about the agricultural changes which accompanied them, and very little about their causes. In the next generation such deficiencies in our knowledge will probably be remedied, for not only have historians developed a more vigorous interest in the mechanisms of economic change, but the archives of landowner families, which form the most important single source for our problem, are now reasonably accessible.[1] Until they have been systematically examined, we can do little more than describe the ways in which landowners contributed to development, and give a very general impression of how common such contributions were, and of their importance compared with that of other agents of change.

AGRICULTURE

It is reasonably clear that the landowners as such did not make a very substantial contribution to the discovery of new methods. The men who advanced knowledge—Tull, Bakewell, the two Collings,

This article is reprinted, by permission of the author, from *Explorations in Entrepreneurial History,* 6:92–102 (December 1953).

etc.—were a mixed bag, but if one can generalize about them, they were farmers rather than landowners. This point is not, perhaps, one of great importance, since the increase in agricultural output does not appear to have been due primarily to the discovery of new ways of doing things. The improved methods were the result of the accumulation of a very large number of small adaptations, and while a few of them do sum up to methods which can legitimately be regarded as new (the advances in cattle breeding, for example), the substitution of turnips and grass crops for fallow, the technique responsible for the most revolutionary changes, was already known. That is to say, the increase in output, where it was not merely the result of the employment of more men and land, arose from the spread of the best existing techniques rather than from the invention of new ones. The more important question, therefore, is how far did landowners stimulate the adoption of improved farming methods.

In the traditional version of English agrarian history, at least that of the eighteenth century, the great improving landlords played a central role in this process. There is no doubt that, in this period, many English landowners were interested in agriculture, made experiments, and promoted or supported agricultural societies. A standard source like Arthur Young's *A Six Months Tour Through the North of England* (1770) mentions several landowners.[2] But what the practical influence of such activities was, it is very difficult to say. In the main, landowners exerted their influence through two agencies, the home farm and the lease. The landowners under consideration, i.e., the gentry and aristocracy as opposed to the small owner cultivators, normally let the greater part of their estate to tenant farmers. Many of them, however, had home farms, run predominantly for the needs of the household, and it has commonly been argued that these farms employed advanced methods and spread knowledge of such methods among neighboring farmers. In an amateur way they provided some of the facilities of State Experiment Stations.

The two examples most commonly quoted are those of two Norfolk landowners, Lord Townshend at Raynham and Thomas Coke at Holkham. Some of these home farms were very large; Coke's, for example, was said to be about 3000 acres. To assess the home farms as centers for the dissemination of the new agriculture we need to know how many owners had such farms, and how they ran them.

My suspicion is that such information would show that the importance of the direct agricultural activities of the improving landlords has been exaggerated, and that popular memory has ascribed to them the achievements more properly due to a multitude of unknown predecessors. The verdict which Miss Riches suggests on Coke is probably true of many of the other well-known names—they were not the creators of the new agriculture so much as created by it. There is one general reason for skepticism about the influence of the home farm: it is probable that there was in the working of many of them an uneconomic element; it is unlikely that they were often worked in such a way as to afford a commercial rent. This was indeed one of the circumstances which allowed experiment, but it must also have made the results of those experiments seem of doubtful relevance to the problems of the tenant farmer.

The covenants contained in leases were probably of more general effect. Here again we need more information before we can generalize with any confidence; there were doubtless important variations according to estate, region, and period. My own impression is that leases were not often used to impose new methods upon the tenancy. "Some leases," as Adam Smith observed, "prescribe[d] to the tenant a certain mode of cultivation, and a certain succession of crops, during the whole continuance of the lease."[3] But in the leases I have seen, the elaborate conditions seem primarily designed to specify the division of responsibility between landlord and tenant with respect to such matters as repairs, and to ensure that the tenant did not harm the property. They prohibited objectionable behavior, rather than enjoined behavior thought to be positively beneficial; they kept the tenant up to standard rather than urging him forward. This seems to be true even of most covenants about cropping; their main object seems to have been not to secure the adoption of the most advanced techniques, but to ensure, in the words of a lease of one of the improving landlords, that the tenant cultivated "according to the usual course of husbandry of the country" (i.e., county). Perhaps the most crucial feature of a lease was the length of the term for which it provided. The best opinion held that long agricultural leases were necessary to stimulate the best efforts of the tenants, and it is probable that in many parts of the country there was a tendency, until the Napoleonic war period, for the term of rack-rent leases to grow longer. But in so far as agricultural covenants are concerned, it may well be that leases promoted agriculture more by the covenants they omitted than by those they included; i.e., a detailed study of leases might disclose the progressive omission of covenants designed to maintain the traditional methods of agriculture.

Pressure to adopt improved methods may, of course, have been exerted in less formal ways, for example by the action of the stewards. The stewards were, there is good reason to believe, key figures in the agricultural advance of the eighteenth century; some of the best of the authors of the Reports presented to the Board of Agriculture were drawn from their number, and they may in general have been important disseminators of better agriculture.[4] But so far as the landowners were concerned the estate correspondence that I have seen does not suggest that the landowners themselves were often the pacemakers in agrarian advance. They appear generally to have been interested quite actively in the problems of estate administration, in the collection and proper transmission of rents, the choice of new tenants, the proper accounting by their stewards for expenditure incurred. Their interest in such questions often took them into points of great detail. But they do not, as a general rule, devote much attention to problems of agricultural technique among their tenants. Supervision of estate management rather than the promotion of agricultural improvements was their characteristic contribution. My own impression is that the initiative in the adoption of improved methods is more commonly to be found among the tenants who, after all, knew much more about farming. This is no more than an hypothesis, but, at least so far as the landowners are concerned, it appears to have Adam Smith's support. "It seldom happens," he wrote, "that a great proprietor is a great improver."[5]

The second function of the landowner was the provision of capital. There are some suggestions in eighteenth century literature that permanent capital may have been a smaller ratio to output than in the nineteenth century, but one particular form of improvement did demand, over a short period, relatively considerable investment. The introduction of new rotations did not invariably or inevitably involve much additional fixed capital; it does not appear to have done so in many parts of continental Europe. But in England, for reasons which cannot be investigated here, their introduction did involve—or at least was accompanied by—the consolidation and enclosure of farms. There is little satisfactory evidence about the cost of enclosure before the middle of the eighteenth century; from then on it is relatively easy to calculate the public costs, i.e., the costs of obtaining the Enclosure Act, surveying the land, etc., but still difficult to obtain information about the costs of ancillary improvements, such as the re-siting of farm buildings which enclosure necessitated or invited. It has been estimated that the public costs ranged from three or four shillings to four or five pounds an acre. The Enclosure Acts empowered owners who were life-tenants under family settlements to mortgage their estates up to £3 per acre for the costs of enclosure, and it is reasonable to suppose that the average costs were not a great deal lower than this.[6] These figures should be taken as minima, which might be substantially added to by private improvements. Large-scale land reclamation likewise involved heavy expenditure.[7]

How far was it the landlord who provided the necessary capital? In so far as there was a general understanding on the point, the position in the seventeenth and eighteenth centuries appears to have been the same as in the twentieth—the landowner provided the permanent capital, the buildings, drains, enclosures, etc., and the tenant provided the working capital. From the terms of leases and estate accounts, however, it seems that the division of responsibility between landlord and tenant might differ, not only from estate to estate, but also from period to period. There are several cases of permanent improvements in the eighteenth century, which were paid for by the tenant. It might be argued from the fact that tenant compensation did not become an active issue until the nineteenth century, that such cases cannot have been common at earlier periods, but it may be, alternatively, that many eighteenth-century tenants felt sufficiently secure in their tenure to make improvements despite the fact that the landlord was under no obligation to compensate them if the lease were given up. There are some signs, moreover, that the financial responsibility for repairs and improvements was subject to shifts, and that over the country as a whole the landlord's share of expenditure increased in bad times. An unpublished study of the estates of the Dukes of Kingston in the eighteenth century suggests that on these estates in the second half of the century, as tenants became more plentiful, an increasing part of the liability for repairs was borne by the tenants.[8]

What I have seen of other estates suggests that this happened elsewhere. There is some evidence too that in the years of depression following the end of the Napoleonic wars the cost of repairs tended to shift back to the landowner again. It is difficult to know how far these shifts represent real changes in the liability for repairs. It may be that they were merely alternatives to the rent charges which were warranted by changing circumstances. This is very likely to have been the case in periods when agricultural profits were falling—a landowner might well prefer to assume an increased share of the cost of repairs rather than accept a formal reduction of rent. It is not, however, easy to see why, in periods of rising agricultural profits, a landowner should have found it better to shift the cost of repairs on to the tenant rather than raise the rent. And the possibility remains that the changes are not a mere substitute for rent changes, but reflect the availability of tenants with adequate capital resources. These considerations apply mainly to improvements other than those involved in enclosure. The costs of enclosure were, it seems clear, borne by the landlord either directly, or by allowing the tenants exceptionally favorable terms in their leases on condition that they undertook specified investment.

How often did landowners finance improvements out of income? There is a distinction, on this point, between enclosure and most other forms of government. Most improvements other than enclosure appear to have been financed most commonly out of income. Some figures for the estate of the Dukes of Bedford in the early eighteenth century show that, in this particular case, repairs and improvements accounted for about £2,400 out of a gross annual income of about £31,000, i.e. roughly 7½ per cent.[9] This is not untypical of what might be called 'normal' expenditure under this head. Enclosure and the accompanying charges presented a more serious financial problem and appear most commonly to have been financed out of capital, in many, and possibly even in most cases with borrowed money. But even in the case of enclosure some landowners were able to meet the costs out of current income, especially perhaps the larger landowners, because the enclosure of their estates was usually piecemeal. There is probably also a distinction to be drawn between landowners who had savings (who tended to be the recently established owners) and those who had not. It was Adam Smith's judgment of the mere country gentleman (as opposed to the merchant who had bought land) that "if he improves at all, it is commonly not with a capital, but with what he can save out of his annual income." The merchant recently established as a landowner "is not afraid to lay out at once a large capital upon the improvement of his land, when he has a probable prospect of raising the value of it in proportion to the expense."[10]

Finally, the landowner was the agent of the institutional changes necessary for the rapid introduction of the improved methods. Enclosure, the creation of compact farms, affected so many complicated property rights that it normally could not be carried through without the initiative and compulsion exercised by the gentry and aristocracy. It has been noticed that unenclosed villages tend in some regions to have a high proportion of owner-cultivators, and this has sometimes been interpreted as evidence that enclosure is inimical to small owners; the correct deduction is more probably that small owners are inimical to enclosure. The large owners by purchasing the property of small owner-cultivators reduced the number of interests to be considered in an eventual enclosure, and they usually had the authority to obtain agreement among the remainder. The history of the enclosure movement (as also the readjustment to overseas grain in the later nineteenth century) suggests that the English system based on landlord and tenant was much better suited than were many continental systems to make large adaptation to new situations.

NONAGRICULTURAL ACTIVITIES

The division between agriculture and extractive industry, while it is to be hoped excusable as a convenience of exposition, was not at all clear in practice. In England, as the result apparently of a judgment of 1568, minerals other than gold and silver were the property of the owner of the soil. Whereas in continental Europe therefore the exploitation of minerals normally necessitated a concession from the Crown to the finder, in England, in the early stages at least, it was done as a normal part of estate business. There was a close association between the ownership of land and the working of coal and iron. In some cases the landowner himself assumed the entrepreneurial function and worked his minerals directly or through an agent; in other cases, he let the property on a long lease to a capitalist (who might also, of course, be a landowner).[11] We hardly know enough yet to be able to generalize about the frequency of the two methods or about the conditions which favored direct working. Some evidence seems to suggest that direct working by landowners, though it is to be found at all periods, was most prominent in the early stages of the development of a region, and that direct exploitation tended to give way to leasing as the area developed. It may be conjectured too that this development was influenced by the availability of lessees with adequate capital resources;[12] it may be said that, in the early stages, landowners who wished to develop their properties were compelled to work them directly by the absence of any effective alternative. Whichever method was adopted the landlords provided a large part of the initial capital; early iron works, for example, were commonly built by landowners, even when they were subsequently leased.[13]

The role of the landowners in the transport improvements of the period appears to have been more ambiguous. The owner of mineral-bearing properties had in general a firm motive for promoting such improvements, but the position of the purely agricultural landowner was more complicated; on many occasions, for example, the purely agricultural interest was opposed to improvements in river navigation.[14] Landowners did, nevertheless, play a leading part in promoting turnpike trusts and canal construction. What is not yet altogether clear is the reason for their prominence. How often did they provide the real initiative in such changes? How often, on the other hand, was their prominence due to the fact that such schemes involved private acts of Parliament which could best be promoted by the M.P.'s of the area? The most famous of all the "canal-entrepreneurs" was a landowner, the third Duke of Bridgewater.[15] Was he in the economic functions he performed a freak, as he certainly was in his personality?

It is clear that the fact that the landowner owned any minerals under the land had considerable effects on the form which the development of the extractive industries took. What its effect was on the rate of development, compared with that of continental countries, is less clear. Professor Nef concludes that "the private ownership of minerals hardly contributed to the expansion of the coal industry in the sixteenth and seventeenth centuries."[16] A systematic comparison with continental experience would be interesting.

Another field of activity was the develo~ment of urban sites. The development of London properties has been investigated by Mr.

Summerson, author of one of the most informative works on the activities of urban landlords.[17] As a general rule the properties were let on building leases to speculative builders; i.e., the builder took the property on lease for a long period, paid a low ground-rent and often a lump sum on the granting of the lease, and agreed to build upon the property. The builder built at his own expense and at the end of the lease the building became the property of the landowner. A few landowners, also, undertook the development of ports, and sometimes of whole areas, a type of activity which became common in the nineteenth century. One of the most notable achievements of this kind was the development of Whitehaven by the Lowther family in the later seventeenth and eighteenth centuries.[18] Another was the work of the first Duke of Bedford in building docks at Rotherhithe.[19]

There has been some dispute about the merits of the method of development whereby the landowner retained the ownership of the property and let it on long leases to the actual entrepreneurs. It was argued by radicals in the nineteenth century that the possession of so much land by families whose powers of disposing of it were limited by family settlement retarded the development of mineral and urban property; landowners could not readily grant leases of sufficient length to induce lessees to undertake development. To say how much there is in this argument we need further research into the growth of towns; but my own impression is that any hindrance was slight, for owners who were limited by family settlement could fairly easily, by private Acts of Parliament, obtain powers to grant long leases. The second criticism of this method of development was on grounds of equity; the owners were assured of an unearned increment which under the alternative most often considered—outright sale by the landowner—would have gone to the person responsible for developing the site. That the leasehold system did ultimately secure to the landowner any increase in the value of the sites is certainly a fact, but what the economic consequences were it is not easy to say, and it has not yet been demonstrated, though it is no doubt a reasonable suspicion, that the landlords made a less fruitful use of their gains than would, for example, speculative builders. The merits claimed for the system were two. In the first place, the landowner frequently provided some of the capital, even when he did not actually build himself; not infrequently the owners forewent the rent for a certain number of years on condition that the tenant undertook rebuilding or repairs. Secondly, the system did something to ensure a measure of single control in the development of an area; the Bloomsbury property of the Dukes of Bedford was developed in a much more orderly fashion than if it had been sold off in lots.

CONCLUSIONS

There are at least four reasons why we might expect English landowners to have played a more active economic role than those, for example, of France—reasons, that is to say, other than the possibility that objective economic opportunities were greater in England. First, there is their ownership of the minerals on their estates, on the consequences of which we have already touched. Secondly, no disapprobation attached to attempts by landed families to develop their possessions. Thirdly, the greater part of the agricultural income of most landowners was derived from tenant farmers in the strict sense, i.e., from rents which represented (or purported to represent) the full annual value of the property. While therefore the English landowner had possibly a less direct incentive to improve his land than had landowners such as those east of the Elbe who worked their estates directly and lived on agricultural profits, they had a much greater incentive than had such continental landowners as derived their income largely from payments fixed for long periods and often of a customary nature. Lastly, the institutional impediments to the buying and selling of land, though considerable, were probably less than in many parts of the continent; the strict settlement, the legal device by which the succession to the typical English estate was governed and which certainly restricted the supply of land for sale, allowed for greater flexibility than did the *fidei commissa* which performed analogous functions in parts of continental Europe. Nor was there anything in England to correspond to the rule which, in some parts of the continent, limited the ownership of certain classes of land to certain classes of person. The turnover of estates was probably greater in England, and the ranks of English landowners were replenished by men who had made their fortunes in law, the services, or trade.

These are reasons for supposing that English landowners had more incentive to develop their properties than had, for example, the French. But they do not settle the main question. How far were the economic activities of English landowners the result of a positive attempt to develop their resources, and how far a by-product of their noneconomic activities or a response to external pressures?

It has been argued that, at least in the sixteenth and seventeenth centuries, a large number of men bought estates with the specific intention of developing them. For a number of reasons, but primarily because of the rise of prices in the century before 1640, existing revenues on many estates were much below possible revenues. The purchasers of such estates could by "reconstructing" them make considerable gains. They could exploit these opportunities to a greater extent than long-established landowners because they had greater capital and business acumen. We need several studies of individual estates before we can assess this view. *A priori* considerations can be invoked both for and against it. In the eighteenth century, with which I am more familiar, what potential purchasers looked for was a well-run, well-tenanted estate, not one which would yield "reconstruction gains"; there are indeed cases where enclosures were undertaken before sale, in order to make an estate a more attractive proposition to purchasers. Circumstances before 1640 were different in several respects, but my impression is that in the sixteenth and seventeenth centuries also "new men" bought primarily for security and social prestige, and that the discrepancy between actual and potential gains was rarely sufficiently evident to enter largely into their calculations. This does not, however, entirely dispose of the question. For it is reasonable to suppose that, once they had bought, the new men were in a better position to make improvements than the established landowning families. Though many of the improvements of the sixteenth and seventeenth centuries required little capital, the purchase of rights of small owners, which was often a preliminary to improvement, did cost money, and the "new men" tended to have an advantage over old established owners in this respect. There is also something in the point, already considered briefly, that lawyers and merchants who became landowners exhibited more business capacity than "mere country gentlemen," and that in so far as increased revenue was the result of more efficient day-to-day management, as opposed to great structural changes in the estate—and sometimes at least this was a main source of increased revenue—they had an advantage over long-established landowners in this respect too. But where it was a question of a drastic reconstruction of an estate, it is not at all clear that heavy debts were not a greater stimulus than wealth and business acumen. The truth is that we are not yet in a position to say how many landowners were enterprising in the sense that they actively sought out opportunities for developing their properties. Nor can we yet generalize about why some landowners were enterprising and others not; the main explanation may very well turn out to be differences of personal temperament.

My own impression is that many of the landowners' activities which had greatest economic effects were merely the by-product of the pursuit of predominantly noneconomic purposes. Take, for example, the purchase by landowners of small properties adjacent to their estates, an activity which was largely responsible for the diminution in the numbers of the English peasantry. This, no doubt, often had an economic motive, since it might facilitate enclosure or a more profitable arrangement of the purchaser's own land; but on many occasions it was influenced by a desire, for reasons of prestige and authority, to own all the land in a particular neighborhood.

Moreover, in the eighteenth century at least, much of the landowner's more specifically economic activity can be interpreted as a response to pressure from the tenants. Many of the most important developments in English agriculture arose from the growth of the class of tenant farmers and their slow accumulation of working capital and skill. The landowners, as I see them, were not primarily interested in ensuring rapid improvements on their estates, but in seeing that their estates were let to good tenants, in the limited sense of men of good character, ability, and adequate capital.

This, however, involved the landlord in making improvements. In the first place it was a condition of the profitability of improvements that there were tenants with capital and ability adequate to earn a return on them. In the second place, the tenancy positively stimulated such improvements, for the best tenants could fully exploit their abilities only when they had control over their own agricultural operations, and improvements often appear to have been in the nature of bids to attract or retain the good tenants. Not the least important contribution of English landowners to agriculture was to ensure their tenants security of tenure. The action at law which protected the tenants against wrongful ejectment afforded them a security which they would not otherwise have possessed.

But even more important than the law was the landowners' attitude to the tenants. For example, among some eighteenth century landowners there is to be found, at least before the spectacular rise of prices at the end of the century, a reluctance to raise the rents of a sitting tenant. This is typical of a generally benevolent attitude which made some tenants feel sufficiently secure to build even on land held at will. If even a tithe of the stories about the ruthlessness of sixteenth century landowners is true, this benevolence was relatively recent, and it would be interesting to trace its development.

There is some incongruity in investigating the entrepreneurial activities of landowners, since the main point about landowners—in England at least—is that they did not acquire their land in order to develop it, but in order to enjoy it. It was the basis for a certain amount of political and social power and a certain style of life. Some landowners did perform the functions of genuine entrepreneurs, and these have caught the limelight. But it would be odd if these were at all common.

I can perhaps best summarize my impression by considering two divergent views of the economic role of English landowners.[20] The first view is that landowners were essentially a consumer class, who, because land was regarded as the best security for loans, were able to borrow "for spend-thrift purposes." Because the most extravagant section of society was also in possession of the type of asset which was regarded as the best security for loans, a smaller proportion of the national income was invested in productive enterprises than would otherwise have been the case. The other view is that the nature of English landowning facilitated the flow of new capital into agriculture and transport. The landowner had an incentive to invest in his estate, even when the cash returns might be small, for the additional pleasure and prestige which the investment afforded. Secondly, because land was the best security for loans, he could readily borrow money for improvements. In England in the seventeenth and eighteenth centuries there was a developed mortgage market—developed, indeed, mainly to meet the needs of landowners—and, except in periods of exceptional stringency, landowners could borrow at the standard rate; there was no need to devise special institutions to provide agricultural loans. In England, the argument runs, at least in the period under discussion, the investment so encouraged was economically desirable.

English landowners as a whole were a class of consumers, and the greater part of their borrowings were contracted for nonproductive purposes, to provide doweries, to fund short-term debts contracted as a result of extravagant living, to build mansions; the borrowings for enclosures, for example, were usually a small part of total indebtedness. This was Malthus' general view of English landowners and there is little doubt that he was right, though there are, of course, numerous exceptions. It does not follow that the money they borrowed was diverted from productive industry; we do not know how productive enterprise would have responded to the greater availability of funds had landowners' ability to borrow been less. Even if we suppose that the superior borrowing ability plus the extravagant habits of landowners deprived productive enterprise of capital, this would still not settle the question of the value of the landowning class. We should still have to take account of Malthus' argument, which probably had a good deal in it for the eighteenth century, that the existence of such a class sustained effectual demand. Moreover, though a very small part of their borrowings was for productive purposes, it may very well have been of critical importance. Historically, the construction of a transport system has been a prerequisite of industrial advance. It has normally proved difficult for business men, unaided, to provide the necessary capital. The building of the railway systems in the nineteenth century, for example, frequently involved government aid in the form of guarantees of interest or land grants. It might be argued that in eighteenth century England, where the state was in no position to provide such aid, an analogous function was performed by the landowners who placed their power to borrow on the security of their estates at the disposal of transport improvement. Similarly in the case of agriculture. It is at least a plausible argument that, historically, economic advance has been halted by a rise in the costs of food production. If this did not happen in eighteenth-century England, it may well have been because the necessary reconstruction of the agricultural system was facilitated by the advantageous position of the landowners in the mortgage market, by the fact that the imperfections of the capital market, which in many societies have had a bias against agriculture, favored investment in agriculture in England.

The Serf Entrepreneur in Russia

HENRY ROSOVSKY

> Entre l'esclavage et la liberté, entre le mal et le bien, il n'y a pas, il ne peut y avoir de milieu. Si l'histoire de la législation, ou l'histoire générale, fournit peu de lumières à cet égard, c'est que . . . ce ne sont pas les esclaves, mais bien les possesseurs d'esclaves, qui écrivent l'histoire.
>
> N. TURGENEV

ECONOMIC HISTORIANS have not yet succeeded in making many valid generalizations concerning economic development. A notable exception is the widely accepted thesis that the institution of serfdom is a serious obstacle to industrial activity, business enterprise, and economic progress. Pre-reform Russia is normally cited as an ideal illustration of the effects of this retarding factor.

I have uncovered no material which contradicts the accepted theories in an over-all sense. Certainly serfdom is an almost insurmountable roadblock in the path of industrial growth. It weighed on Russia like the dead hand of feudalism in Western Europe. It had to be removed as an institution before that country's rate of growth could become impressive.

But this does not mean that economic activity which took place within the system of serfdom, and particularly economic activity by the serfs, was insignificant and can be ignored. Any serf economy is likely to be very complicated because to hold a large segment of the population in bondage requires many rules and regulations. Wide deviations among the subjected must sooner or later arise; clearly some serfs will be in favored positions, economically and otherwise. Some serfs are likely to occupy fairly important positions

This article is reprinted, with permission of the author, from *Explorations in Entrepreneurial History*, 6:207–233 (May 1954).

in the economy of the country and some may even contribute to the slow advance of industrialization. But we must keep in mind that there is no quarrel with the general proposition that serfdom is a retarding factor.

Entrepreneurial activity of Russian serfs, which is the subject matter of this article, probably strikes the reader as a paradox. The serf and the entrepreneur are rarely coupled, and most frequently orthodox economic theory almost separates them by definition. Serfdom implies a condition which ties the individual to the soil and makes him subject, more or less, to the will of his owner. The entrepreneur is thought of in terms of activity, courage, and enterprise; a Schumpeterian figure, not a carry-over from medieval times.

But the list of paradoxes can be continued. "One of my friends," wrote the well-known Decembrist N. Turgenev "traveling in the interior of Russia, stopped to pass the night in a village belonging to Count Sheremetev. One of the notables of the district, possessor of a two story brick house (a rare thing in a Russian village), offered him hospitality, and gave him a good dinner, during which he served champagne. The *salon* was furnished with lacquer furniture; on the wall hung a portrait of the Count. During the conversation my friend said to his host that he must well love his master in view of the prosperity so evident in the surroundings. 'No doubt,' replied the peasant sadly, 'but I would gladly give him my house and the rest of my fortune of 600,000 rubles, if he would only give me liberty.' "[1] Elsewhere Turgenev relates that the largest manufacturer of hats in the 1830's was a serf resident of Moscow who bought his freedom for 800,000 rubles.[2]

Obviously the above-mentioned cases are exceptions designed to serve as vivid illustrations. The average Russian serf was a poor down-trodden agricultural laborer. But the exceptions do offer important testimony concerning the existence of a serf bourgeoisie and the existence of the serf entrepreneur. Both have been largely ignored by historians.

Shortage of entrepreneurial talent had always plagued pre- and post-reform Russia in the nineteenth century. One need only recall the intense efforts of Peter the Great to create an entrepreneurial class, an effort which was not crowned with notable success. In Professor Gerschenkron's words:

There is no doubt that throughout most of the 19th century a grave opprobrium attached to entrepreneurial activities in Russia. Divorced from the peasantry, the entrepreneur remained despised by the nobility and the intelligentsia. The good life which God intended man to lead implied tilling the land, which belongs to God, and receiving the divine blessing of its fruit. Good life did not mean craving for riches, laying up treasures on earth "where moth and rust doth corrupt." In innumerable adages, fairy tales, and songs, the wisdom of folklore insisted upon the unrighteous origin of wealth. Still entrepreneurial activities went on unchecked.[3]

For these reasons it becomes most important to study entrepreneurship among the serfs, a class facing the largest obstacles, burdened as it was from all sides with economic and spiritual debilities. There is no suggestion here that from the serfs came the greater part of Russian business enterprise talent, nor is there the claim that serf-entrepreneurs represent a vital link in Russian economic development. There is, however, the important hypothesis that three classes—not two, as is usually indicated—led the Russian economy along the road to business enterprise and industrial achievement. The sources of Russian entrepreneurship are: the merchants, the nobility, and the serfs. This paper is concerned only with the last, from 1700 to 1850, a century and a half that proved crucial for the class. I will attempt to show that the contribution of serfs to business enterprise was of significance, and in certain areas outstanding. Economists have a natural predisposition to think of entrepreneurship only in terms of free societies; that this is at least debatable will also be shown.[4]

I

In Russia to be a serf implied membership in the lowest of the six major classes of society, i.e., in order of rank: nobility, clergy, officials, merchants, free city dwellers (*meshchani*), and serfs. Serfs formed the largest segment of the population, 51.5 million people (25 million males) just before liberation.[5] In no significant economic sense did this class form a homogeneous group. It was divided into numerous subcategories which bore little resemblance to each other, especially from the economic point of view.

According to the census of 1858—the "13th Revision"—the basic groups within the serf population were:[6]

Types	*Number (in thousands)*
Palace, royal, and imperial family	2,019
Crown (State) of various designations	18,308
Crown of the mining enterprises	386
Landowners' peasants	20,173
Peasants assigned to private factories	518
Artisans of the Crown mines	230

Of these, crown peasants and private landowners' peasants were the only important groups, being both the largest and the most active in the economic life of Russia. Even within these groups there were subdivisions of importance. Some serfs fulfilled their obligations of servitude through *barshchina* (labor services) and some through *obrok* (quit-rents). Still another segment worked under a mixed system, being charged some *obrok* and having to perform certain labor services for the lord: ". . . almost nowhere did an absolutely pure and clear form [of servitude] exist, being instead complicated by another secondary form of labor exploitation of the serf."[7]

The distribution of these two forms of serfdom depended largely on regional-geographic considerations which made the incentives of the owner vary. *Barshchina* makes good economic sense under conditions of prosperous farming. Where the soil is productive and agriculture profitable, the nobleman will normally desire to remain an active cultivator of the soil, disposing of the labor services of his peasantry as he sees fit. He remains the active agricultural enterpriser in this setting, to the point of actively marketing the produce of his estates. These conditions applied in the so-called "Black Soil" region of Russia, i.e., the southern agricultural belt, also the Volga area and the eastern steppe lands. Here *barshchina* predominated heavily.[8]

When agricultural pursuits are carried on under more marginal conditions the temptation to commute labor services into money rents is great. And when this coincides with the desire of a more urban nobility for money, the pressure for this change cannot be resisted. While this may have been a slow process, and at times devious, the issue did not long remain in doubt. The "non-Black Earth" region of Russia, the industrial north, was in this agricultural predicament at the beginning of the eighteenth century, and *obrok* came to predominate in a ratio of 3:2.[9] It is no accident that the north became the main industrial area, as a closer examination of the development of *obrok* will reveal.

During this period the nobility's desire for money became intense. They wanted luxuries and even subsistence commodities which could only be bought. Since their estates were not, on the whole, very profitable, one of the logical solutions seemed to be the formation of estate industries, the products of which could be sold, thereby satisfying the desire for money.

The basic skills for estate manufacturing were at the disposal of the nobles, particularly in northern Russia. *Hausfleiss* among the serfs was abundant and it could be utilized in small-scale estate manufacturing.[10] What the nobles did, in effect, was to unite the small independent part-time production of the serfs into centralized estate manufactures. Here they produced items which peasants had produced themselves—wool, linen, leather, etc.—somewhat more efficiently. The estate factory developed gradually. Probably started on a seasonal basis to occupy idle winter months, it frequently grew into a permanent institution where the serfs were quartered and fed but paid no wages, and by this time their land had been taken away.[11]

Serfs feared the estate factory "like the plague." Working conditions were poor and they did not like being forced factory workers. More important, the arrangement did not prove productive. Haxthausen, that shrewd Prussian observer of Russia in the early nineteenth century, felt that serfs made very bad industrial workers when their jobs were performed as forced labor services, ". . . *arbeiten sie aber zum eigenen Vorteil, dann arbeiten sie herzhaft.*"[12]

Since the noble estate factory owner had no particular craving for business enterprise and perhaps even disliked being an active manufacturer, the *obrok* system came as an ideal solution. Serf families were obliged to pay a yearly quit-rent, depending in size on location and lord, and were allowed to shift for themselves. Of course this system could be operative only in areas where opportunities for employment existed, and the rising North Russian industry provided these.[13] The nobility had accomplished its purpose, i.e., it was provided with a regular money income. The serf, though burdened with a kind of head tax, had achieved a certain degree of mobility and freedom, and the opportunity to better his lot in some instances.

Obrok did not necessarily come into use through the estate factory. But at the root of the change there was always the desire for money coupled with unproductive agriculture. The feasibility of the system lay in the gradual urbanization of northern Russia which offered serfs employment opportunities.

We are dealing here with two fundamentally different systems of economic servitude. *Barshchina,* as a rule, robs the serf of individual initiative. He is usually nothing more than a farmer with two places of employment: his own land, and that of the lord. To look for signs of entrepreneurial activity among serfs performing labor services is therefore quite useless. At best this type of person could have become a prosperous farmer, a *Kulak,* but he was always closer to the soil than to business. The peasant performing *barshchina* was a serf in the classic sense of the word.[14]

Obrok was already a compromise with the traditional pattern of serfdom. It probably occupied the same place in Russian history as the commutations in Western and Central Europe during the thirteenth, fourteenth, and fifteenth centuries; it was the beginning of the end. After all, the rationale of a serf economy does not include extensive exchange and wide use of money. There is serious theoretical doubt whether a serf economy can absorb the great loosening effect of money without undergoing certain fundamental changes—changes so fundamental that the term serf economy must now cover heterogeneous economic concepts such as *barshchina* and *obrok,* robbing it of much of its analytical value. Wherever commutations are in evidence, generally softer conditions existed for the serf, and one finds a tendency for the peasant to become, in time, a small independent owner or a free worker. The intimate master-serf relationship of the "ideal type" pattern is always lost.[15]

For the individual peasant *obrok* meant a new set of circumstances. His close ties to the soil were cut, and he was allowed to exercise independent judgment about his own fate. A logical development soon followed—logical and almost necessary from the point of view of the entrepreneurial historian. Whereas up to the 17th century serfs represented a fairly miserable mass on a more or less even economic level, we can find, following the spread of *obrok,* some peasants pushing to the forefront. There may not have been many, but there were some, and it is in these that we find the germs of the entrepreneurial spirit. To state the tentative hypothesis: *obrok* was a force that differentiated the peasantry. Those with outstanding abilities were given the opportunity to pull themselves up; the great majority remained at the previous low level, and in some instances became dependent on their brother serfs who became successful entrepreneurs. Under *obrok* the lord divested himself entirely of the entrepreneurial role. His place was taken by others: the merchants, some nobles, the government, and in some instances by serfs.

II

A system of serfdom always tends to be a maze of legal rules and regulations wherein all positions and duties are minutely defined. This was true of Western feudalism and of its Russian counterpart. As always, habit, tradition, and above all custom also played a very important role, and these forces could sometimes contradict each other. When they did it would seem as if habit and tradition, the real kernel of feudalism, won over regulation.

Relations between serf and master were necessarily peculiar under *obrok.*[16] According to serf law, for example, all immovable property in possession of serfs belonged to the lord, and the peasant had no legal right to dispose of his property after death, movable or immovable. At any time that the lord wished, the serf could be switched from *obrok* to *barshchina* and back again. A fairly prosperous serf trader, let us say, could be required to report the next day as a swine herd. An interesting case is mentioned by the Soviet historian Yatsevich, who tells of a nobleman who put his peasants on *obrok,* sent them to St. Petersburg to work and trade, and when they had accumulated some capital called them back, took away the money and put them back on *barshchina.*[17]

In spite of tremendous social tension between serf and masters it is noteworthy that instances of genuine economic conflict were rare. To be sure, there were disputes over inheritances and some spiteful ruinations by nobility of serf enterprise. But these were the glaring exceptions. By and large the nobility actively encouraged the small serf bourgeoisie, realizing that it was their best source of large *obrok* payments. Thus we have a sector of the population making economic advances on a purely permissive basis, even if the nobility was following only the dictates of self-interest.[18]

Another technical-legal problem must be cleared up before we can proceed to the case study of some serf entrepreneurs: it concerns the serf's ability to purchase his freedom, leave his class, and become a member of the merchant or free city dweller class. Generally speaking two broad categories existed. State peasants could, after the eighteenth century, make the transition quite easily by inscribing themselves in a merchant guild. Many did, but many were held back by the financial requirement. Private peasants were at the mercy of their owners and absolutely no clear pattern of action exists. Some bought their freedom very "cheaply", i.e., for a few thousand rubles. Some paid 800,000 rubles and some were turned down when they offered larger sums. There is at least one case on record where a serf purchased his freedom for a barrel of oysters. His owner, Count Sheremetev, was sitting at breakfast craving for this mollusk when the serf arrived from a Baltic province. By sheer chance, the serf brought a barrel of oysters as a sign of good will. Sheremetev liberated the man on the spot and invited him to join the table as a guest. Previously he had turned down an offer of 200,000 silver rubles from this peasant.[19]

Purchase of freedom by a serf was not an act of purely economic significance, being unfortunately intermingled with deep-rooted sociological questions mostly stemming from various types of class prejudice. For this reason, if for no other, one should not expect to find a clear line of policy in these matters. Some nobles refused to sell serfs their freedom because they felt it violated their class beliefs; others capitulated to the economic attractiveness of the arrangement. Nevertheless, a fairly sizable group of serfs purchased freedom for considerable sums. The money must have come from economic activity on their part, and not only from economic but also from entrepreneurial activity.

Even if it were handled rationally, purchase of freedom presented tremendous legal and economic problems. How does one arrive at a price? What happens to the property of the serf, in particular his immovable property, if any? Some owners seem to have made attempts to capitalize *obrok* payments which they received from the serf in question, i.e., they asked for a sum which would give a perpetual return equal to the money rent. Others reached their decision on an opportunity cost basis. Maslov, a member of the gentry when he freed the serf poet Sibiryak, demanded 10,000 rubles, the sum required to buy a first class confectionery baker, the post which the poet had occupied.[20] But, as demonstrated above, generally this was not a problem capable of rational solution. *Ad hoc* considerations were always involved.

Obrok could be levied in three ways: on the individual in the form of a head tax, on a family (*tyaglo*), or on a whole village.

Average Obrok Payments per Person (yearly), in rubles[21]

1760's	1 to 2
1770's	2 to 3
1780's	4
1790's	5
1810's	10 to 14
1820's	30

Wide deviations from the averages cited in the table were not uncommon. *Obrok* payments of several thousand rubles were not unheard of among the wealthier peasants. Over-all, the burden imposed by the poorer gentry was higher than the demands made by the wealthier nobles. The marginal nobility squeezed their serfs much more. In fact there are a number of instances where members of the impoverished nobility actively secured its peasants good jobs so that they could reap higher *obrok* payments.

Obrok also created a series of specific problems for the serf bourgeoisie. Some of its members feared to appear prosperous lest the tax be increased; some made a great show of poverty before purchasing their freedom, and once they had secured it angered their former lords greatly by ostentatious displays of wealth. While the *obrok* of the few really wealthy peasants was rarely commensurate with their ability to pay (the scale was not as progressive as that), these people were frequently forced to take over the payments of serf laborers in their employ. In this fashion some peasants paid *obrok* for whole villages individually, and this could be a sum of considerable size.[22]

III

The scope of this article cannot possibly include a general appraisal of the role of serfs in Russian industry. Serfs were to be found in almost all segments of Russian manufacture and commerce performing very diverse tasks. Usually they were ordinary workers, free or unfree, sometimes supervisors, and sometimes enterprisers. Serfs represented the largest Russian population bloc and were the main man-power pool of the nation. They worked in factories and at home as *Kustars* (handicraftsmen); some were engaged in long-distance trade and others were moneylenders. Many were successful smugglers. It would be difficult to cite a form of economic activity during the period in which serfs did not participate in some form or other.

Our interest in them, however, is confined to one capacity: their role as entrepreneurs. Initially our purpose is to examine not the routine normal, but the spectacular abnormal: the career of the Schumpeterian innovator. We are looking for men who "led the means of production into new channels . . . this element that constitutes the phenomenon of leadership."[23] Still the term "entrepreneur" must be interpreted with considerable catholicity in this instance, and I have therefore tried to avoid many terminological problems justly raised by Dr. Redlich.[24] It would seem as if any serf making a commercial or manufacturing career of magnitude can be considered, on *a priori* grounds, to have fulfilled the entrepreneurial function. "Every step outside the boundary of routine has difficulties and involves a new element,"[25] and practically all serf activity outside the realm of agriculture and house production fits initially into this framework. The pathbreakers who hurdled the environment, quantitatively or qualitatively, were performing the entrepreneurial function.

Before proceeding with the study of some actual cases a few remarks must be made about the economic-historical setting of Russia in the beginning of the eighteenth century, our starting point.[26]

The home industry of the north-Russian peasantry is of very ancient origin, stemming, no doubt, from crafts learned during the middle ages and earlier, and practiced chiefly to fulfill domestic needs. It was an industry intimately connected with agriculture, usually organized on a part-time basis, and under *barshchina* part of the products of the industry was frequently given to the lord as payment in kind. Home production was confined to the general lines of activity normally carried on under such circumstances. Peasants produced a variety of textiles, making both yarn and cloth (mainly woolens), socks, household utensils, soap, spirits, sail cloth, etc. Despite the fact that monetary relations, through *obrok* and general increase in the circulation of money, were drawing peasants closer to the market, home industry remained true to its name well into the middle of the eighteenth century. Large-scale production on the part of serfs for the market was not yet taking place.

Under the mercantilism of Peter the Great (1682–1725) an active policy of encouraging industrial development was followed. We have here perhaps our first example of true serf-entrepreneurship, evidenced in three Moscow factory owners who were crown peasants. Unfortunately very little is known about them except their names and occupations. Zaitsev was a leather manufacturer, Jusnetsov produced buttons and accessories, Luknovskii made linen. Even their exact economic status is not available, although it seems certain that they were paying *obrok* to the crown.[27] But these are untypical and rare examples of a period when serfs were still much too weak and inexperienced to enter into general production.

Slowly, however, various peasant industrial activities began to be felt. Between 1726–1762 more and more items produced by serfs in their homes reached the markets of Russia, and we find among the enumerated commodities wool, leather, hemp, lard, iron, linen—particularly coarse peasant canvas produced in such centers as Yaroslav, Vologod, and Kastroma.

A very good sign of the fact that peasant production was making an impact on the economy is the series of decrees issued by the government from the 1730's to the 1750's, all designed to curb economic activity among the class. For example, in 1732 there was issued a decree forbidding the weaving of broadcloth by peasants; in 1747 a similar decree covered the production of hats; in 1753 peasants were ordered to abstain from gold and silver leaf manufacturing. Promulgated largely at the instigation of the merchant class which felt that their monopolies were being violated, these laws proved singularly ineffective and most of the prohibitions were soon lifted. The fact of the matter seems to be that these peasant-serfs were skillful workers, and significantly merchants frequently accused them of "making the most of local situations,"[28] as if this were an unfair business practice to be condemned by one and all.

In the last analysis very much hinged on the policies of the Russian State. The government never gave wholehearted support to merchant demands and in 1762 opened a general attack on the various monopolies. In October of that year it was decreed that all who desired ("people of all names", i.e., classes) could open manufacturing establishments, except in two cities: Moscow and St. Petersburg. And thus by the time we reach the 1770's a situation of comparative freedom prevailed in the establishment of manufactures. Russian backwardness made the process of industrialization anything but easy, but at least official hindrances had been reduced.

This is the setting in which we must examine the Russian serf as an entrepreneur. In no sense have I attempted to present an analysis of all serfs connected with entrepreneurship over the 150-year period. Here are cited only a few typical examples to illustrate the achievements and problems of the larger group.

1. *Grachev and Garelin: Calico Manufacturers*[29]

Grachev and Garelin were large-scale calico manufacturers in the village of Ivanovo, in the province of Vladimir, about 180 miles north of Moscow.[30] Ivanovo was one of the textile centers of Russia, and probably possessed the largest cotton printing establishments in the country. It was a truly remarkable place, being one of the earliest industrial centers of Russia; the initiative of development was largely in the hands of serfs.

Ivanovo belonged to the Sheremetev family, without doubt the richest nobles of Russia during the late eighteenth and nineteenth centuries. Estimates of the number of serfs owned by them vary; usually figures from 123,000 to 200,000 *male* serfs are found.[31] The character and philosophy of the Sheremetev family must detain us for a moment. Count Sheremetev was exceedingly proud of the economic status of his family, and he was particularly pleased with two facets of his opulence. He boasted of being the largest private serf owner in Russia, and of possessing at the same time the most prosperous serf population in the country. Sheremetev took pleasure in the existence of a serf bourgeoisie and rarely did anything to hamper its advancement.

On the other hand the Sheremetevs were dead-set against allowing serfs to purchase their freedom, thinking it would only serve to lower their own status. We are told of a rich St. Petersburg merchant who offered the Count one million rubles for his freedom. The answer of the Russian nobleman is revealing: ". . . leave yourself your money, since for me there is more blessing in owning a man like you than in receiving an additional million rubles."[32] Contemporary sources interpreted the nobility's motives somewhat differently:

> . . . these iron hearts [the nobles] are proud that among their serfs there are millionaires whose hearts and life they can destroy with one word since these unfortunates completely depend on the whim of the lord and his overseers. They are proud when they see their serfs descend from magnificent carriages, products of their own energy, and kneel down until their foreheads touch the ground. And for all this the nobility only had to take the trouble to be born.[33]

Naturally exceptions were made. After all any number of serfs did purchase freedom. But the above well illustrates the state of mind of the greatest Russian serf owner of the period. Sheremetev had placed the majority of his serfs on *obrok,* assuring himself of a high income which made selling freedom an unnecessary commercial activity for him.

Returning to Ivanovo, we find that at the end of the eighteenth century almost the whole population consisted of *obrok* peasants engaged in printing cotton and linen. These were *Kustars* now slowly expanding their production. Napoleon's invasion of Russia and the burning of Moscow in 1812 proved a great stimulus for the Ivanovo industry. A prime source of competition, Moscow, had been conveniently eliminated by the war, and demand was naturally high in the postwar era. Tugan-Baranowskii placed the profit rate in Ivanovo at 500 per cent for the immediate postwar years.[34] His own words make the setting very clear:

> At the beginning of our century [the 19th] the village of Ivanovo presented a most original picture. The richest factory owners, those that employed more than 1000 workers, were juridically without rights and

in the same position as their poorest workers. They were all serfs of Sheremetev. In reality the serf manufacturers owned not only movable and immovable property (the latter being registered in the name of the lord), but they also owned serfs. Thus Garelin, according to his will, owned the village of Spasskoe with its entire peasant population. Yet another Ivanovo capitalist, Grachev, owned serfs.[35]

And Ya. Garelin, son of one of the serf entrepreneurs we are now examining and semiofficial historian of Ivanovo, said in a revealing if somewhat exaggerated statement: "This was a golden era for the cloth printer, and only the lazy and loose were unable to accumulate some capital."[36] This golden era did not last forever. In the latter part of the nineteenth century the prices of printed materials fell greatly due to large entry into the industry and the wide adoption of printing machines, the circular presses.

Ivanovo had a manufacturing tradition dating back to the sixteenth century. The first real industry, linen weaving, developed in the early seventeenth century when an Englishman, Tames, founded a linen manufacturing establishment in the neighboring village of Tokhma. At this juncture the inhabitants of Ivanovo learned the art of weaving fine linen. Under the guidance of merchants in the early eighteenth century there were built a series of factories specializing in the coloring of linen. Since the skill needed for this process was not too great there soon arose some independent *Kustar* printers. In the late eighteenth century these people shifted to the printing of calico because it was more profitable, the raw material being much cheaper and the demand for cotton goods being much larger. During the Golden Era a number of *Kustars* became independent large-scale manufacturers—those that were touched by the entrepreneurial spirit—and soon were employing workers on their own account. Such men were Grachev and Garelin.

In 1789 there were in Ivanovo 188 printing huts (*Izba*) and 20 factories belonging to the peasantry. Out of the latter, the seven largest factories employed 107 wage workers, all *obrok* peasants who had hired themselves out to their fellow serfs.[37] Printers, both factory owners and workers, were considered the economic aristocracy. Their standard of living was high, and a contemporary observer complained that they spent too much on finery and general debauchery.[38]

Employing 22 workers in 1789 (the first documentary mention of the enterprise), by 1798 E. Grachev was already a considerable calico printer. He used a wide variety of physical equipment and many workers of specialized skills. His plants employed 121 people including 59 master printers, 6 submasters, and 4 apprentices. During the same year Grachev spent 86.5 thousand rubles on raw materials, while his production was valued at 154,000 rubles. Certainly the Grachev enterprise was a fully developed manufacturing establishment not to be confused with *Kustar* workshops. Here there were special buildings devoted to separate productive processes, and a systematic industrial division of labor. Master craftsmen with helpers and apprentices testify to the fairly sophisticated methods of production. There was even a certain amount of innovation taking place in the Grachev firm. In 1792 it introduced calendering machines in Ivanovo, a mechanical method of smoothing cloth which considerably speeded up production. As Meshalin has pointed out, the few large-scale peasant manufactures of Ivanovo could compare favorably with the best merchant and government textile factories, even including the famous government showplace at Schlüsselburg.[39]

One of the most interesting facets of the whole story is that Garelin and Grachev were not only engaged in the cotton printing business. Both were also linen manufacturers of considerable importance. Grachev operated 524 looms, 90 himself and the rest on a putting-out basis; Garelin operated 69 looms, 37 himself and the rest on a putting-out basis. They had both been in this business since the 1750's, taking advantage, no doubt, of local flax production. It should be noted that we have here an example of serf-entrepreneurial alertness. Linen was the older industry while calico was the comer of the future. Grachev and Garelin were active participants in both.[40]

A significant sign of progress of the serf entrepreneur in this area is the number of them that succeeded in purchasing their freedom from (and one must remember this at all times) none other than Count Sheremetev. Grachev was the first Ivanovo peasant to achieve this difficult goal, paying 130,000 rubles in 1795 and then immediately joining the First Guild of Merchants. In this region purchase of freedom became a much more generalized event only after 1828 when Garelin and others made the grade for sums of similar magnitude. Unfortunately the particular arguments which Grachev and Garelin used to sway the Sheremetevs are by now unknown. Peasants habitually complained of their inability to obtain credit, restrictions on movement, and many more general and specific debilities. Serfdom hung around the neck of these manufacturers like a millstone and they tried to move heaven and earth to get rid of their inferior status.

One must not think, however, that serf entrepreneurs did not display much imagination and ingenuity in circumventing the disadvantages of their birth. We find, for example, the occurrence of merchant "front men" employed by some of the serfs. Certain sections of Russia, among them the Baltic ports and parts of Siberia, were by law forbidden territory to serf manufacturers and traders. A holdover of merchant monopoly days, serfs were not supposed to market their produce in these localities. Some of the more enterprising serfs—Grachev and Garelin among them—reached agreement with merchants who supplied only their names behind which the peasants carried on all business activities. Even more interesting is the case of Grachev who apparently held a lot of immovable property under the names of merchant acquaintances. Thus in 1794 Count Sheremetev's nephew and estate manager, Nicholas V. Sheremetev, advised his uncle to grant Grachev freedom since every day he was acquiring more property under false names. Presumably it would have become increasingly difficult to determine his true financial status.[41]

By 1807 the Grachev firm had grown to major standing. Its factories comprised four stone buildings (one of them three stories high) and many wooden structures, among which were seven dormitories to house the workers. Calico was woven on 200 looms producing 178,000 *arshin* per year.[42] They printed 652,000 *arshin* of calico per year buying large amounts of material from the local peasantry. At this period the firm already employed 722 wage workers.[43] Even from the purely technical standpoint this was a very interesting factory. For one thing, Grachev already employed spinning jennies (in fact, he was the first man to do so in the province) and he was also the user of the cylindrical printing press, another new development of the period.

It is not easy to judge the position of men like Grachev and Garelin in the social and economic community of their time. The serf bourgeois of the type here described certainly was disliked by his fellow serfs, or former fellows, and even literature (Leskov and other writers) makes frequent mention of their squeezing tactics *vis-à-vis* their former brethren. That these people soon forgot their serf origin—or perhaps remembered it too well[44]—is evidenced by many happenings. Typical was the action of Garelin in 1846, a free man for only 18 years, who became one of the main opponents of *Kustar* production in Northern Russia, and who pamphleteered vigorously against permitting peasant economic activity. He proposed, for example, that peasants not be permitted to own more than four looms per family, that they should not be permitted to own other types of machines, and so on. It would be interesting, I think, to know what mental processes "Merchant" Garelin went through to conceive these proposals.[45]

There is also little doubt that serfs of the Grachev-Garelin type were heartily despised by the merchants, who feared their competition. On the other hand, most available evidence would lead one to conclude that the merchants, as a class, feared peasant *Kleingewerbe* more than the few great serf entrepreneurs whose successes were more spectacular but over-all probably less significant.[46]

2. *The House of Morosov: Cotton Textile Manufacturers*

The case of Savva Morosov and his sons is usually cited as the "ideal-type" example of entrepreneurial activity and spirit among Russian serfs. His career was a magnificent combination of astuteness, luck, courage, and enterprise.[47]

An *obrok* serf from the village of Zuevo in the Bogorodski District, owned by N. G. Ryumin, Savva Morosov was born in 1770. His father was a fisherman on the river Klyaz'ma, and Savva grew up helping him. Dissatisfied with the poor returns in fishing Morosov decided to become a silk weaver, and as a late teenager apprenticed himself to a fellow peasant, F. Kononov, in that capacity; his salary was set at five rubles per year.

Time soon came for Morosov to perform his military service, an obligation he was most anxious to avoid since by that time he was a married man with children and the term of service lasted 25 years. In order to secure an exemption (*rekrutskaya kvitantsya*) he borrowed a large sum (the exact amount is unknown) from Kononov, and worked for him with his whole family to pay off the debt. This feat Savva Morosov accomplished in two years and in 1800, at the age of 31, he opened up his first small independent business. Savva was the main silk weaver of the enterprise and his wife was in charge of coloring. In 1811, when Morosov was already 41 years old, official sources for the first time mention his enterprise in Zuevo. It is recorded that he was working with 10 looms producing silk and lace valued at 40 to 60 kopeks per *arshin.* The village was located less than a day's journey from Moscow, and Morosov took his own wares to the metropolitan center on foot, walking from house to house, selling the produce of his looms.

The Napoleonic Wars caused temporary reversals in the Morosov fortune. Because of war and invasion he was forced to cut production to four looms, and the whole work was, once again, performed entirely by members of his family. Savva now had three sons of working age in addition to his exceptional wife, Ul'yana Afanas'evna, who throughout her lifetime remained the main coloring expert of the Morosov enterprises.

By 1820 Morosov had rebounded from the effects of the war and had even aggrandized his establishment. He was now using 20 looms and employing 40 workers. This was a critical year for the economic future of Savva Morosov during which he made a number of radical changes in his business which led eventually to the establishment of a great enterprise. Firstly, Morosov started branching out into cotton production, a very shrewd move in view of future market demand, but a move which may also have been fairly obvious at that time. Secondly, he started operating with the putting-out system to supplement his own productive capabilities, that is to say, Morosov distributed cotton yarn to peasants in the Pokrovski District for weaving. Eventually he became an extremely clever manipulator of putting-out production, displaying considerable business acumen. In later years, for example, Morosov took great care to send his raw materials far away from the industrialized Moscow area in order to take advantage of cheaper labor in the more rural sections, mainly the outlying districts of Moscow and Vladimir Province.

Quite naturally, Morosov, who had become a producer of some stature, desired to purchase freedom for himself and his family. Even though he succeeded by paying 17,000 rubles in 1823, Ryumin, the owner, drove a hard and cruel bargain. The landlord sold freedom to Morosov, his wife, and four of his five sons. He retained the fifth son, it is said, because he realized that Morosov was only on the very threshold of his great accomplishment, and that by holding out he could eventually get a much larger sum. The last son's freedom was, in fact, purchased some years later for a "fabulous sum."[48]

Russia's protective tariff of 1822 was highly favorable to cotton interests and Morosov, now a merchant of the First Guild, threw himself with full force into this highly profitable trade. He opened his first cotton weaving establishment in Moscow in 1825, definitely abandoning the silk business, and all the time keeping up his putting-out production. Coloring was always done at the home plant.[49] Shortly thereafter Morosov opened one of the first and largest plants in Russia producing mixed cotton and wool cloth. This factory featured a 16-horsepower steam engine, attached to a drive shaft, which supplied power for most of his machines. It was a period of great expansion for the Morosov firm. Concentrating on fairly cheap items of mass consumption, like cotton and mixed materials, they must have found the market very good indeed. Branch plants were opened, central putting-out offices organized, and systematic business methods widely practiced.[50]

Savva Morosov's children, also born in serfdom, seem to have inherited much of their father's entrepreneurial daring and drive. Even the grandchildren entered the business, and the typical Western European phenomenon of escape into land or the more genteel professions (a problem which even the Fuggers could not solve) seemed to be entirely absent. Of course, the fact that upward social mobility was extremely low in Russia may have been important. Two sons, Elisei and Zakhar, opened "independent" textile businesses with capital borrowed from Savva, but their enterprises always remained under close control of their father.

By the 1840's Savva Morosov's main plants were located in Nikolskoye and Moscow. Both of them had grown into fine industrial establishments. In Moscow the firm occupied eleven buildings and used 240 looms, while 864 looms and 1024 workers were employed under putting-out arrangements all through the province. Again, an inventory of the family enterprise in 1852–1853 revealed the following totals, which do not include putting-out affiliations: 9 steam engines, 456 hand looms, 74 mechanical looms, employment of 2,572 workers, and an annual production worth 1,943,000 rubles. In their Nikolskoye plant alone they operated 632 spinning machines; their possessions in the Pokrovski district alone were valued at 6 million rubles.

This then is a rough picture of the growth of the House of Morosov through the first half of the nineteenth century. Not that their growth was by any means ended even then. A French consular report of 1897, for example, assesses their total annual production at 32 million rubles and credits them with employing 22,000 workers.[51]

The avalanche of statistics may seem meaningless, but studied on a comparative basis, i.e., examining the growth of Morosov against the background of his contemporaries and his times, they testify to a phenomenal career. In Morosov we have, perhaps, the classic example of the serf entrepreneur. Obviously a daring and imaginative spirit, combining business talent with good fortune and a sense of timing, here is evidence of a truly Horatio Alger success. That it should have taken place in backward Russia is further proof of the great ability that Savva Morosov must have possessed.

3. *The Brothers Kondrat'ev: Moscow silk merchants*

The father of the brothers Kondrat'ev (Fedor, Kyril, and Egor) was an *obrok* serf of General Bibikov, who worked in Moscow as a weaver in the merchant-owned Lazarev Factory. In 1758 the factory was transferred to Fryanovo, and Kondrat'ev chose this moment to return to his native village of Grebnovo in the Bogorodski District where, under his direction, he and his sons started operating a very small silk weaving business.

On the first day in which the government Manufacturers' Collegium issued tickets (*bileti*—licenses) to peasants permitting them to take up small-scale weaving on an official basis, the brothers F. and K. Kondrat'ev availed themselves of this newly acquired privilege.[52] In December 1769 they started operating three looms weaving various materials and silk handkerchiefs. This was the humble beginning of the most famous Moscow silk merchants; or at least it was the official beginning.

A number of singular features can be seen in the rise of the Kondrat'evs. For one thing, in their initial period of growth, from 1750 to 1780, they always had the active support and guidance of Bibikov, and, perhaps more important, his protection. It is also noteworthy that barely 25 years after the inception of the enterprise this family, by now merchants and producers of consequence, spent "tens of thousands of rubles" building a temple in their native Grebnovo. This probably was a typical case of "repentant" entrepreneurs, showing quite convincingly that a change in financial status does not need to imply a changed value system.

Another untypical feature of this group was the fact that most of the Kondrat'evs—old man, sons, and grandchildren—were never able to buy freedom. They remained *obrok* peasants until 1861. Apparently the key to entrepreneurial success did not lie solely in the ability to achieve legal merchant status. An interesting social note is the further fact that in the 1880's members of the family were living in the Bibikov palace which they had recently purchased. At the same time it must be mentioned that the really great entrepreneur of the clan, I. M. Kondrat'ev, a grandson of the founder, did achieve merchant status in the 1820's, and it is on him that we will have to concentrate.[53]

Let us now briefly examine chronologically the fortunes of the Kondrat'evs and their rise to power. In the 1770's and the 1780's the three brothers operated sizable silk weaving establishments in two villages, Fryazina and Shelkova. They each operated independently with about 30 looms and used one coloring plant collectively. After the 1780's, strangely enough, we lose sight of Fedor and Egor. There is some mention around 1814 of Fedor's son, M. Fedorov, who produced silk with 60 looms, but this branch of the family never made the all-important transition to large-scale factory production. It is probable that most of them were wiped out between 1810 and 1812, when many serf manufacturers suffered serious reverses due to stiffer competition from larger enterprises. Many peasants, during those years, lost their independent producer status and became mere cogs in putting-out systems.

Whatever the reasons for the demise of this branch of the family, the entrepreneurial spirit was obviously stronger in the third brother, Kyril, and particularly in his son, I. M. Kondrat'ev. Kyril's production, employment, and use of machinery also fell off during the first years of the nineteenth century, but he came back very strongly and never lost his status as an independent producer. By 1820 the firm's growth had again resumed, and some documents relate that I. M. Kondrat'ev was already a merchant of the Third Guild. At any rate he was now in charge of the enterprise. At this point his factory consisted of eight buildings and a separate coloring plant using two ovens; he produced yearly 521,000 *arshin* of material (some mixed) and employed 143 people.

A valuable sidelight on this entrepreneur is the fact that he employed entirely wage labor, and what is more significant, entirely native labor. Kondrat'ev employed no foreign specialists of any kind, and it is said that one of his *muzhiks* independently reproduced an improved Jacquard loom for the factory.[54]

Exaggerated or not, Kondrat'ev's technical know-how must have been on a high level. In 1828 he received a gold medal from the Minister of Finance citing him "for usefulness," and the presentation related that his factories made silk materials of the "latest Parisian patterns" which were so good that they could pass for the imported product. An added inducement was that they sold at a lower price. For his part in the Moscow Exposition of 1831 Kondrat'ev received the honorary title of *Manufaktur Sovetnik* (manufacturing advisor) from the Senate. His acceptance in society seems to have been complete.

The strides made by Kondrat'ev during the first half of the century became even more obvious through his 1841 inventory. He was using over 700 looms of which 431 were of the Jacquard type, employing 1500 workers, and producing yearly 238,000 rubles' worth of silk. It is known that at the London Exposition of that decade his products were very well received. Could there be a greater compliment for an early Russian industrialist?

A few peculiar characteristics stand out in the Kondrat'ev enterprises. Production was always centralized and putting-out never practiced. Also machinery was introduced rather late, but that seems to be true of the silk industry in general.

4. *Ushkov: producer of chemicals*

The contribution of the serf entrepreneur in the development of the Russian chemical industry was much smaller than in the field of textiles[55] Reasons for this are not hard to deduce. Production of chemicals requires a considerable amount of technical know-how in most aspects entirely unrelated to peasant *hausfleiss*. The process of production is also more capital-intensive. These factors are of great importance since they made serf entrance into these fields extremely difficult; they are of importance on a more general level in that they show in which industries we are likely to find serf entrepreneurs and in which they are likely to be absent.

Nevertheless, serf initiative was not absent even in the chemical industry; the most important entrepreneurial story is that of the peasant Ushkov.

In 1850 the first large chromate plant was built in Russia. Its like, by size at any rate, could not be found in all of Europe. Indeed, the production of this plant was so large that it even exported its product to most of Europe.[56] It was founded by a trading peasant, Ushkov, from the village of Bondyugi, whose business frequently took him to Moscow and St. Petersburg. There he had close dealings with the large merchant house of Malyut'in, the owners of which had branched out into the chemical and oil industries.

Ushkov learned from the Malyut'ins in the 1840's that chromate was imported to Russia from England and sold for about 915 rubles per ton, and that the raw material, chromite, was exported to England from Russia. (Chromite was found chiefly in the Ufimski Province.) Being a man of initiative, Ushkov decided to rationalize this inefficient economic organization. He realized that Russia was an ideal place for chromate production.

The main problem seemed to be that Ushkov lacked the necessary capital, and he therefore offered the Malyut'ins a chance to enter into a partnership agreement. They agreed and signed a twelve-year contract, after which Ushkov carried on alone. These events led to the foundation of the Kokshanski Plant in 1850 which, barely five years later, produced 123,000 rubles' worth of chemicals.

A few production figures will indicate the great progress made by Ushkov, now joined by his son, during the 1860's. During that decade their yearly production averaged 3,000 tons of sulphuric pyrites, 1,300 tons of chrome ore, 2,500 tons of kaolin, 1,000 tons of potash, and 160 tons of saltpeter. Ushkov's plants were renowned for the fact that they employed a staff of trained chemists, something of a rarity for the Russia of the 1860's. The firm eventually expanded into other chemicals (among them soda) and became one of the largest chemical enterprises in the country.

There is not much evidence on the personalities of K. Y. Ushkov, the father, and P. K. Ushkov, the son. Mendeleev, the great chemist, described the son as a "modest, progressive, sympathetic worker of the Russian chemical industry, full of strength and *new ideas*."[57] We know that he had traveled widely, had seen many European chemical plants, and felt that his own were in some respects superior.

IV

I have discussed the case histories of only five individuals. There were, of course, many more serf entrepreneurs of the "heroic" type who could have been mentioned. This list was chosen because it seemed most representative.

One more important point must be made concerning this group of people. They rose to power during a critical and difficult period for serfs in general, and for serfs engaged in manufacturing in particular—roughly the years 1750–1850. Especially in textiles, these were the years during which the capitalistic mechanized textile factory finally blossomed. This was not a smooth process and on the whole it affected the peasant producer adversely. Two developments hurt the independent serf producer: the resurgence of putting-out and the large factory. Of the two, the question of putting-out is more interesting mainly because it is less obvious.

The relation between a putting-out system and industrial development is exceedingly complex and does not lend itself to easy generalization. Certainly there are instances when industrialization increases side by side with putting-out, as was the case in Russian textiles, and, while the final victory of centralized factory production is rarely in doubt, the period of transition is apt to be full of difficulties for the artisan. Our period is such a transition phase, and this, more than anything, shows the vigorous spirit of the entrepreneurs whom we have examined. Even the statistics are arresting. Independent peasant textile production in Moscow Province, from 1796 to 1853, *decreased* approximately 86 per cent.[58] Presumably peasants either were forced into putting-out arrangements or became laborers in textile manufactures. But it is precisely during this period that our entrepreneurs achieve their full rewards. This would allow one to conclude, I believe, that entrepreneurial success had little to do with the over-all fortunes of the class. It represents, rather, tough individuality triumphing over a set of adverse circumstances. The idea that the serf bourgeois developed smoothly and peacefully from prosperous independent artisans is a myth. Rather, he rose to power during an unsettled period, and the number of serfs who not only did not make the transition to success but ended in complete failure is very large—much larger than the number that made the grade.[59]

V

I have maintained throughout this paper that entrepreneurial activity takes place on two levels, and it is to the second of these—the "drop in the competitive sea"—that we must now turn. It is almost impossible to assess the importance of this aspect of serf entrepreneurship scientifically. Historical descriptions tend to gloss over the less spectacular achievements and failures, and it is not difficult to see why: there are so many more of them. Yet from the point of view of economic theory one type of entrepreneurial activity may be as important as the other. The cumulative effect of many small actions may be more important than the rare large efforts. The herd effect may be more powerful than the innovation.

In the Russia of our period serfs participated in all conceivable trades and crafts, and *obrok* serfs in particular were independent tradesmen in most sections of the vast Empire. A few examples should make the situation abundantly clear.

The Russian historian Yatsevich has written a fascinating book describing St. Petersburg during the lifetime of the poet Pushkin (1799–1837), paying particular attention to the conditions of serfs. What did he find? He found serf candlemakers and serf tailors with considerable prosperity in both groups. There were serf *izvoshchiki* (free-lance carriage drivers) that paid *obrok* reaching 150 rubles. Many serfs operated fruit stores, and some were locksmiths and shoemakers. Serfs became famous as chefs and sold their services to the highest bidders. Others even operated jewelry stores, and we are told that it was the custom of the nobility to patronize, if possible, shops operated by their serfs. The great majority of the serf inhabitants of St. Petersburg were on *obrok* and had to make annual payments to their native villages. Can one deny that many of these serfs, driven to the cities, displayed considerable entrepreneurial talent, especially if the agrarian value system is taken into account?[60]

But that is still not the whole story. Throughout Russia small trading was carried on by the peasantry. At local markets and at central fairs, such as the famous one at Nizhni-Novgorod, peasants traded their wares. They dealt in rough textiles, wheels, small items, holy pictures, shoes, furs, etc. Sometimes considerable fortunes were amassed even in this fashion. Schulze-Gaevernitz mentions at least one peasant trader of the Nizhni Fairs who had a yearly income varying between 20,000 and 50,000 rubles in the 1820's.[61] Add to this money-lending activities in the villages and smuggling, a refined art at which Russian peasants were past masters, and the importance and pervasiveness of this type of entrepreneurial activity emerge. It cannot, alas, be quantified, but there is ample evidence that the spirit of small-scale business (and by the same token entrepreneurship) was well established.

There are still more facets to this type of business enterprise. We have already discussed the prevalence of the putting-out system. All along the echelons of putting-out there were serfs working in various capacities. Some were subcontractors; some acted as agents representing the merchants. All of these functioned at least partially as entrepreneurs. Residents of Ivanovo, for example, even organized central putting-out offices in various districts of Vladimir Province where elaborate records were kept in the form of "weaving books."[62]

This brings us to the more general question of communal entrepreneurship, more specifically entrepreneurial activities within the *mir,* the Russian village commune. Here we have another area where serfs were involved in business enterprise of the unspectacular kind, and where there are many features of particular interest to the entrepreneurial historian. While the type of enterprise about to be discussed was fairly common, I will confine myself to one example relating to the Province of Yaroslav in the years 1851–1852.[63]

Approximately 10 *versts* from the city of Yaroslav there were five villages with a total population of 400 people, belonging to two estates; one estate was owned by Princess C. P. Obolenski and the other by a Mrs. de Markov. The five villages paid *obrok* collectively to the owners but otherwise had no connection with the landladies. Each group of villages chose a mayor, in addition to which each village chose its own elder. During the summer the peasant inhabitants engaged in ordinary agriculture, and in the fall and winter they worked as carpenters, coopers, and box makers. They manufactured containers for alcoholic spirits, candles, tobacco, and food. Aksakov in a very revealing passage wrote about them:

> No one would register surprise, on the contrary all would find it most natural, if one of the rich peasants had taken charge of the box manufacturing, distributed the work to the peasantry, and then sold the product at a handsome price and profit.[64]

These five villages organized their production much differently in that they formed a cooperative enterprise under the direction of the *mir,* thereby guaranteeing a more even distribution of income, no exploitation by richer peasants, and an easy and certain way of paying *obrok.*

Nearly 150,000 boxes were manufactured by these villages each year, a production valued at some 1,800 silver rubles. During the summer the mayors would negotiate with merchants and accept bids. Later, at a communal meeting of all the villages, contracts would be accepted on the basis of price attractiveness and productive capabilities. Subsequently the mayors and the elders would apportion the productive responsibilities among the separate villages, basing their decision largely on the number of inhabitants. Work was performed individually by families in their homes, and normally one merchant would agree to buy the total production of at least one village, each village specializing in one kind of box or barrel.

The assembly also elected a *Postavshchik*—perhaps best translated as expediter or maybe even entrepreneur—who supervised production in the villages and made sure that orders were delivered on time. The contracts were written documents treated with great seriousness by the peasantry. It should also be noted that no member of the *mir* was forced to take part in the collective effort, and all were permitted to take on outside work once their communal obligations had been fulfilled. We cannot tell how many peasants refused to join the cooperative, but the number must have been very small. Those that did refuse immediately assumed individual responsibility for their *obrok* payments. Profits from manufacturing were equalized by elders and mayors; if one village had a particularly good season it would be assigned additional *tyaglos* (households or taxable units) for which it had to pay *obrok*.

I believe that the above describes a purely Russian form of business enterprise where the *mir* clearly functioned as the entrepreneurial agent. We have seen the "drop in the competitive sea" type of entrepreneur in a number of settings. It would seem as if both Schumpeterian concepts were well represented in Russian serfdom.

VI

There are certain problems in beginning an essay by saying that economists have not yet succeeded in making valid generalizations concerning economic development and then desiring, one's self, to make a few concluding remarks. There is the additional difficulty that some readers may have been too thoroughly convinced by my panegyric and fully expect a conclusion which includes a plea for the reintroduction of serfdom, an event which has, after all, in fact taken place within the Soviet Union. Still I believe that both problems, impudence and exaggeration, are capable of solution and can be brought into sharper focus through these short conclusions.

No eternal truths or ever-valid generalizations can be deduced from such a narrow topic as the serf entrepreneur in Russia during 150 years. Certainly no valid generalizations about economic development where, it seems to me, attempts at abstraction must be prefaced by much more empirical investigation. Two things can be legitimately attempted. Firstly, a few remarks may be made about the serf entrepreneur in Russia and his role in the general development of the country. Secondly, a few strategic factors can be pointed out to economic development theorists, which they may throw about at will, and throw out if necessary. However, it does seem as if the serf entrepreneur raises some points of interest even for them.

1. In Russia city air did not make free, and the whole story of the serf entrepreneur unfolds against a background of archaic institutions that were weakening but that still maintained a strong hold on the population. The question has frequently been asked: why did not the serfs run away, take refuge in the vast interior, and merely escape their servile obligations? Russia during these years, one must

remember, was a fairly efficient police state where travel was restricted and where frontier possibilities, in terms of escape, had largely disappeared. And movement to the cities presented no solution to the basic problem.

The initial thesis that the sources of Russian entrepreneurship are three in number (nobility, merchants, and serfs) has, I think, been demonstrated beyond doubt. If persons of serf ancestry may be counted as stemming from the serf sector of the economy, this contention becomes even weightier. After 1861, and especially during the magnificent Russian development of the 1880's and 1890's, persons whose fathers and grandfathers had been serfs made some of the most impressive business careers.[65]

Serf entrepreneurship took place, as mentioned previously, on two levels. On the large-scale industrial and commercial level it was obviously very restricted and its impact on the total economy could not have been very large. Serf entrepreneurs, like the other Russians engaged in economic pursuits, were hampered by the intense backwardness prevailing during the period. Serfdom itself was the paramount retarding factor and little could be or was done until it had left the scene.

Aside from the general problems shared with the rest of the population, serf entrepreneurs were restricted in other ways. Through the logic of experience they were confined to light industries which bore some connection to activities which they had carried on previously as simple peasants. The prevalence of the serf in textiles of all kinds would bear out this point. More important, they were confined to industries where economies of scale were not such that only the large enterprise made economic sense. In other words they appeared in endeavors where the rate of growth was fairly smooth. That no serf entrepreneurs started their careers by building blast furnaces should cause no surprise. Leaving aside the whole question of governmental statutory restrictions in heavy industries, serfs lacked the initial capital requirements which could only be built up laboriously through trade and production.

The more widespread type of entrepreneurship, the small-scale variety, while it must have been the oil that kept the Russian economy functioning, was of no special significance in the subsequent full industrialization of the country.

What, then, is the conclusion concerning Russia? Commutations of the seventeenth century and later, the result of economic and geographic considerations, made it possible for some serfs to embark on entrepreneurial careers. Considering all restrictions, the results of their efforts are impressive. Also the prevalence of the small-scale entrepreneurs demonstrates that this class was not nearly as dead economically as is frequently asserted. When the great test came in the 1890's this group acquitted itself as well as, if not better than, the other social segments of the Russian people.

2. The serf entrepreneur in Russia was a symptom of disease within the economic system of that country. In the realm of strict logic a serf should not be an entrepreneur; in this sense economic theory is perfectly correct in drawing a sharp distinction between these two forms of economic life. Just as commutations announced the beginning of the end of Western feudalism, so did the *obrok* system, a makeshift bridge between feudalism and a modern money economy, create a situation which became increasingly more unbearable and illogical; in other words, a paradox. Yet the interesting thing is this: if the serf entrepreneur was the symptom of a disease, it was a good disease in terms of economic development. This economic paradox was one sign that serfdom was on the way out and that it would eventually have to be abandoned. I suggest, very hesitantly, that the examination of economic paradoxes might be a fruitful pursuit in underdeveloped countries; among them we might find many of the seeds of future development which could be encouraged to faster growth.

It seems to me that theorists of development are very prone to consider everything in terms of free societies modeled on the American and Western European experience. In these terms tearing up the social fabric of an underdeveloped country (say in the Near East or South East Asia) becomes a necessary prelude to desired growth. While this paper, above all, does not make a case for outmoded institutions, it does seem to show that initially a great deal of fruitful economic activity can take place even in very restrictive societies.

Lastly, one can conclude legitimately that no class should be, on *a priori* grounds, defined as incapable of entrepreneurial activity. The talent for enterprise appears to be widely distributed; at least it is not confined to any one social class. All groups of the population should be closely examined; the result may surprise even the most sophisticated researcher.

NOTES

INDEX

Notes

PART I

AITKEN: ENTREPRENEURIAL RESEARCH

1. For more complete information, see Ruth Crandall, *The Research Center in Entrepreneurial History at Harvard University, 1948–1958: A Historical Sketch* (Cambridge, Mass., mimeographed, 1960).

2. The Committee on Research in Economic History was originally a committee of the Social Science Research Council but in 1950 was incorporated as an independent organization. Its title is now the Council on Research in Economic History.

3. The members of the Committee at this time were Arthur H. Cole (chairman), Edwin F. Gay, Earl J. Hamilton, Herbert Heaton, Harold A. Innis, Edgar A. J. Johnson, Frederic C. Lane, Curtis P. Nettels, and Robert B. Warren.

4. Oscar and Mary F. Handlin, *Commonwealth: A Study of the Role of Government in the American Economy: Massachusetts, 1774–1861* (New York, 1947); Louis Hartz, *Economic Policy and Democratic Thought: Pennsylvania, 1776–1860* (Cambridge, Mass., 1948); John W. Cadman, Jr., *The Corporation in New Jersey: Business and Politics, 1791–1875* (Cambridge, Mass., 1949); Harry H. Pierce, *Railroads of New York: A Study of Government Aid, 1826–1875* (Cambridge, Mass., 1953); James N. Primm, *Economic Policy in the Development of a Western State: Missouri, 1820–1860* (Cambridge, Mass., 1954); Lee Benson, *Merchants, Farmers, and Railroads: Railroad Regulation and New York Politics, 1850–1887* (Cambridge, Mass., 1955); Milton S. Heath, *Constructive Liberalism: The Role of the State in Economic Development in Georgia to 1860* (Cambridge, Mass., 1954); Leonard J. Arrington, *Great Basin Kingdom: An Economic History of the Latter-Day Saints, 1830–1900* (Cambridge, Mass., 1958). See also Carter Goodrich, *Government Promotion of American Canals and Railroads, 1800–1890* (New York, 1960) and Edward C. Kirkland, *Men, Cities, and Transportation: A Study in New England History* (2 vols. Cambridge, Mass., 1948).

5. Arthur H. Cole, "Entrepreneurship as an Area of Research," *The Tasks of Economic History*, supplement to the *Journal of Economic History* (December 1942) pp. 118–126. The other participants in the symposium were F. H. Knight, J. M. Clark, and G. Heberton Evans, Jr.

6. Leland H. Jenks, *The Migration of British Capital to 1875* (New York and London, 1927); *Our Cuban Colony: a Study in Sugar* (New York, 1928); and "Railroads as an Economic Force in American Development," *Journal of Economic History*, 4:1–20 (May 1944).

7. Thomas C. Cochran, *Railroad Leaders, 1845–1890: The Business Mind in Action* (Cambridge, Mass., 1953).

8. William Miller, "American Historians and the Business Elite," *Journal of Economic History,* 9:184–208 (November 1949), and "The Recruitment of the American Business Elite," *Quarterly Journal of Economics,* 64:242–253 (May 1950).

9. David S. Landes, "French Entrepreneurship and Industrial Growth in the Nineteenth Century," *Journal of Economic History,* 9:45–61 (May 1949), and "French Business and the Businessman: A Social and Cultural Analysis," in Edward M. Earle (ed.), *Modern France* (Princeton, 1951) pp. 334–353. John E. Sawyer, "Strains in the Social Structure of Modern France," in Earle, *Modern France,* pp. 293–312.

10. Sigmund O. Diamond, *The Reputation of the American Businessman* (Cambridge, Mass., 1955).

11. Wohl later served as first editor of *Economic Development and Cultural Change,* the journal of the Research Center in Economic Development and Cultural Change at the University of Chicago.

PART II

AITKEN: POINTS OF VIEW

1. Joseph A. Schumpeter, "The Creative Response in Economic History," *Journal of Economic History,* 7:149–159 (November 1947).

2. Leland H. Jenks, "The Role Structure of Entrepreneurial Personality," *Change and the Entrepreneur* (Cambridge, Mass., 1949) pp. 108–152.

3. Thomas C. Cochran, *Railroad Leaders, 1845–1890: The Business Mind in Action* (Cambridge, Mass., 1953); *The Puerto Rican Businessman* (Philadelphia, 1959).

COLE: AN APPROACH TO THE STUDY OF ENTREPRENEURSHIP

1. Edwin Francis Gay, "The Rhythm of History," *Harvard Graduates' Magazine,* 32:12 (1923–1924).

2. Moreover, when the "entrepreneur" had been adopted in English (and American) economic theory, he was a colorless personage, and he remained colorless and unchanged down to Marshall and Keynes, perhaps because economic theorists have known so little economic history, and economic historians have paid so little attention to economic theory.

3. Jean-Baptiste Say, *Catechism of Political Economy* (London, 1816), pp. 28–29. The first French edition appeared in 1815.

4. Jean-Baptiste Say, *A Treatise on Political Economy* (London, 1821), I, 104. The first French edition appeared in 1803.

5. Parenthetically I might observe that quite obviously my analysis does not follow that of James Stauss (and of Frederick Hawley before him), who want to identify the corporation as "the entrepreneur." See James H. Stauss, "The Entrepreneur: the Firm," *The Journal of Political Economy,* 52:112–127 (1944); Frederick B. Hawley, *Enterprise, and the Productive Process* (New York, 1907).

6. Admittedly there is overlapping among these three elements. For example, innovations are possible in the business operations commonly looked upon as management; or innovations may be stimulated by efforts to adjust to external conditions; or some adjustment to external conditions of the cyclical character may become a part of business routine. Yet I believe

the threefold division of entrepreneurial function—innovation, management, and adjustment to external change—to be defensible.

7. Possibly one could use relative to all lines of innovation the apparatus of secondary and subsequent repercussions that Leland Jenks suggested in a recent article pertaining to railroads.—*The Journal of Economic History,* 4:1–20 (1944). As an imaginary case, one might think the creation of a "bargain basement" to have led to the development of a new purchasing policy or practice, and this in turn to an experiment with evening store hours. In addition, there would be cases in which innovations within older branches of business led to the erection of new service institutions.

8. Under this concept, the problems posed by Ripley, Berle, Means, and Burnham become almost side issues. They relate to the pressures and strategies in corporate government—much as pressures and strategies in the sharing of public benefits relate to political government.

9. The responsibility of choice by entrepreneurship among possible innovations applies quite as much to technological changes as to others. After a choice is made, there is the need of adjusting new techniques into a pre-existing system of operation, with possible alterations in nearly all phases from wage scales to marketing.

10. What the relative importance may be among entrepreneurship, technological invention, and the discovery of new natural resources is difficult to say, especially if one function of entrepreneurship be conceded to be that of making practical the new techniques and bringing to market the new resources.

11. We are not directly concerned with theories of profit, which indeed seem too inadequately developed to serve as guides in the exploration of entrepreneurship. Quite obviously, however, my approach derives from that of Joseph Schumpeter, insofar as a theoretical schema is involved. A full-blown theory of profits would need to take into account not merely the phenomena of entrepreneurship (as it has never done sufficiently heretofore), but also the effects of the legal system (for example, patents), monopolistic or quasi-monopolistic positions, conjunctural gains, and the like.

12. Joan Robinson, *Essays in the Theory of Employment* (London, 1937), p. 26.

13. Sir Sidney Chapman, "The Profit Motive and the Economic Incentive," *The Economic Journal,* 56:51 (1946).

14. Harold A. Innis, "On the Economic Significance of Culture," *The Tasks of Economic History* (supplemental issue of *The Journal of Economic History*), 4:93 (1944).

15. The differentiation intended between "stages" and "longitudinal segments of change" is between a word that seems to mean action or conditions in specific periods of time, and a phrase which, it is hoped, conveys the sense of continuing action or conditions throughout a long river of time. Early forms often do not wholly disappear, but they become less wide currents in a stream of experience.

16. Robert Aaron Gordon, *Business Leadership in the Large Corporation* (Washington, 1945).

17. By "ancillary" institutions, I have in mind those that are not directly concerned with the production of consumable goods and services: banks, insurance companies, labor exchanges, advertising agencies, machine builders, and so forth.

18. Chester I. Barnard, *The Functions of the Executive* (Cambridge, Mass., 1938).

19. Thomas C. Cochran, "The Economics in a Business History," *The Tasks of Economic History* (supplemental issue of *The Journal of Economic History*), 5:54–65 (1945).

20. The references here to Robert East and below to Chester Destler are to be found in *Journal of Economic History,* Supplement VI (1946), pp. 16–27 and 28–49, respectively.

21. William T. Baxter, *The House of Hancock: Business in Boston, 1724–1775* (Cambridge, Mass., 1945), p. 159. Actually the years 1757–1759 and 1762–1764 are omitted because of insufficient data.

22. E. Lipson, *A Planned Economy or Free Enterprise: The Lessons of History* (London, 1944).

23. *Ibid.,* p. 86.

24. *Ibid.,* pp. 129, 159.

SCHUMPETER: ECONOMIC THEORY AND ENTREPRENEURIAL HISTORY

1. The difficulty of naming our function is of course greatly increased by the fact that such words as "management" or "administration" from which we are trying to distinguish our function have with many authors also caught some of the meanings that we wish to reserve for the term "entrepreneur."

2. The rate of speed at which competitors follow is another very important point for our research program, as are the means at the disposal of the successful entrepreneur for holding his own against would-be competitors (patents and other practices).

3. It is extremely interesting to observe that for a long time and occasionally even now economic theorists have been and are inclined to locate the entrepreneurial function in a corporation with the shareholders. However little the individual small shareholder may have to do with the actual management or else with the entrepreneurial function in the corporation, they hold that ultimate decision still lies with them to be exerted in the shareholders' meeting. All I wish to say about this is first, that the whole idea of risk-taking in this way takes on a further lease of life and, second, that such a theory is about as true as is the political theory that in a democracy the electorate ultimately decides what is to be done.

4. Thomas C. Cochran, "The presidential synthesis in American history," *American Historical Review,* 53:748–759 (1948).

5. Richard Ehrenberg, "Das Zeitalter der Fugger" (Jena, 1896), 2 vols.

6. Cf. Joseph A. Schumpeter, "Creative Response in Economic History," *Journal of Economic History,* 7:149 (1947).

EASTERBROOK: THE CLIMATE OF ENTERPRISE

1. My interest in enterprise as one aspect of changing economic and political organization arises from a study of international rivalries in the North Pacific. Striking differences in types of organization represented by the various participating powers (Russia and Spain, England and New England, and later the United States and Canada) called for consideration of the significance of, and causal factors at work in, these different forms of

economic and political organization. Again, study of the place of primitive societies in the economic history of the area made it clear that economists' and anthropologists' use of such terms as "capitalism," "trade," "profits," "credit," and so on, had very little in common and that there were here unexpectedly difficult problems of definition and method. And finally, A. H. Cole's thought provoking suggestions on the subject of entrepreneurial history posed awkward problems of terminology for those interested in the study of long-period change. At present, I am at the stage of moving from hypotheses to the fuller testing of these hypotheses. My remarks in the paper are tentative and exploratory and it is to be taken as a preliminary report rather than a presentation of conclusions.

2. Kenneth E. Boulding, "Samuelson's 'Foundations': The Role of Mathematics in Economics," *Journal of Political Economy*, 56:187–199 (June 1948).

3. T. S. Ashton, "The Relation of Economic History to Economic Theory," *Economica*, 13:81–96 (May 1946).

4. The environment of "free enterprise" is discussed in W. T. Easterbrook, "Political Economy and Enterprise," *Canadian Journal of Economics and Political Science*, 15:322–333 (August 1949).

5. Oswald Knauth, *Managerial Enterprise: Its Growth and Methods of Operation* (New York, 1948).

6. Study of writings of social scientists who touch on security in any of its manifestations reveals that, for the most part, attention is focused on those manifestations which present the most immediate and pressing problems in the writer's area or field of interest, with other aspects of security neglected or dealt with only by implication. And it is not difficult to discern interesting correlations between the security conditions of a writer's time and the assumptions, explicit, and more commonly implicit, that he makes about security. In this paper, the problem is that of moving beyond the "sealed compartment" approach to security, in which commonly only one aspect of security is taken into account, to a consideration of the combination or balance of security elements in a given environment. In an incomplete study on the history of enterprise, an attempt is being made to extend this approach to a consideration of "security" in authoritarian as well as enterprise environments.

7. Henry C. Simons, *Economic Policy for a Free Society* (Chicago, 1948), p. 146.

8. "Corporate" here refers to authoritarian forms of business organization. The modern corporation may be entrepreneurial or authoritarian, this resting on the distinctions of power and time referred to earlier.

9. See Louis Hartz, *Economic Policy and Democratic Thought: Pennsylvania, 1776–1860* (Cambridge, Mass., 1948), and review of same by Carter Goodrich in *Journal of Economic History*, November, 1941, pp. 210–213.

10. Because of considerations of time and space this section has been cut so drastically that it may well obscure rather than clarify or add to what has been said to this point. It should be emphasized that geography, technology, and institutional factors are mutually conditioning and conditioned and that each category is noted here only in terms of tendencies favorable (or adverse) to enterprise; and that entrepreneurial action and attitudes interact with this complex. In concrete cases, technological changes affect and reflect the character of economic organization. Again, enterprise is itself part of

the institutional framework and one of the problems of "enterprise history" is to account for the appearance of the entrepreneurial form as a significant, even dominant, institutional factor in certain periods and areas, and its absence (or insignificance) in others. Likewise, the "climate of ideas" influences and is influenced by the status and power of the entrepreneur. In short, the security environment of enterprise is a function of the interaction of the above elements, and enterprise, where present, must be regarded as an integral, interdependent element of that environment, one which may be stressed as particularly significant in itself, but which cannot be treated as an isolated, autonomous, or passive feature of historical change.

JENKS: APPROACHES TO ENTREPRENEURIAL PERSONALITY

1. The entrepreneur is taken as given when he is treated in the same way that an engineer treats the driver in rating the operating efficiency of a car.

2. The total physiological make-up of an individual at any given time.

COCHRAN: ROLE AND SANCTION IN AMERICAN ENTREPRENEURIAL HISTORY

1. Deviant, as used here, means some change in a previous pattern of behavior. The new action, however, may be complementary rather than contradictory to the previous pattern.

2. The examples in this section, chosen mainly from the field of business, do not imply any restriction of the theory to business situations.

3. An implicit theme, an anthropological concept, is an attitude that motivates conduct, but is so completely accepted in the culture that it is only formalized in words for purposes of analysis, or propaganda.

4. See, for example, Theodore M. Newcomb, "Social Psychology," (Prelim. ed.). Ann Arbor, 1948.

5. This may be explained by the cultural remains in Europe of feudal patterns of co-operation as against the more individualistic patterns of American culture.

6. Kenneth Burke points out that, from the point of view of social consequences, there are different types of deviant or new behavior. A small deviation in the direction in which the social role is developing will be readily, perhaps unconsciously adopted. To the casual observer it will appear that the role is developing from the accumulation of imitations. A small deviation, however, that portends a basically new organization for the role will be more readily noticed and is likely to run counter to certain sanctions. In so far as John D. Rockefeller, for example, simply ran his oil company with more efficiency than in other firms, he deviated only in details, such as better cost accounting, that were in line with growth of the existing social role. But in the introduction of the trust form of organization he deviated in a way that threatened fundamental alterations in the role of the leaders of big business, and aroused opposition among competitors, suppliers, and the general public. On the other hand, deviant behavior directly antithetical to the existence of the particular role, or to other allied patterns of the culture, will normally fail to attract imitators and hence fail to produce lasting social effect.

7. It is hard to estimate the extent to which the limitations of a particular market could be regarded as direct social sanctions. If the market was fairly competitive, so that the prices of an individual enterprise had to be adjusted to it rather than vice versa, the situation certainly had an effect on a wide range of entrepreneurial decisions. But this type of constraint is a physical limitation similar to that imposed by the cost of materials, transportation, or special geographical features. A true social sanction would seem to arise where in cases of monopolistic competition, perhaps the usual situation, more or less explicit agreements were entered into to price and sell a certain way. Violation of such an agreement, which was frequent, was unsanctioned behavior that might produce mild social penalties and some internal feeling of guilt.

8. We are not speaking of illegal enterprises such as gambling and smuggling.

9. It is worth noting that the famous statements defying the law were by word of mouth, whereas letters have many references to the wisdom of law observance.

10. See Marquis James, *Biography of a Business, 1792–1942: Insurance Company of North America* (New York, 1942).

11. These changes may be seen from the comparison of executive correspondence in the nineteenth century with present-day studies of the functioning of the large corporation.

PART III

AITKEN: ENTREPRENEURSHIP IN THE COMMUNITY

1. David S. Landes, "New-Model Entrepreneurship in France and Problems of Historical Explanation," *Explorations in Entrepreneurial History*, 2d ser., 1:56–75 (Fall 1963).

COCHRAN: CULTURAL FACTORS IN ECONOMIC GROWTH

1. "The Social History of the Corporation" in Caroline F. Ware, ed., *The Cultural Approach to History* (New York, 1940), pp. 168–181.

2. Norman S. Buchanan and Howard S. Ellis, *Approaches to Economic Development* (New York, 1955), p. 405; Social Science Research Council, *Items*, 14:14 (June 1960).

3. Albert O. Hirschman, *The Strategy of Economic Development* (New Haven, 1958), p. 25.

4. Thomas S. Ashton, *Economic Fluctuations in England 1700–1800* (London, 1959), p. 1.

5. Together with various associates, I have done research in Argentina and Puerto Rico. For Mexico I am relying on the work of Professor John Fayerweather of Columbia University.

6. Arthur Spiethoff, "Pure Theory and Economic Gestalt Theory, Ideal Types and Real Types," in Frederic C. Lane and Jelle C. Riemersma, eds., *Enterprise and Secular Change* (London, 1953), p. 452.

7. As quoted in Thomas C. Cochran, *The Puerto Rican Businessman* (Philadelphia, 1959), p. 127.

8. John Fayerweather, *The Executive Overseas* (Syracuse, 1959), p. 65.

9. *Ibid.*, p. 96.

10. David C. McClelland, John W. Atkinson, Russell A. Clark, and Edgar F. Lowell, *The Achievement Motive* (New York, 1953), p. 329. It is held that "there are limits placed on the development of Achievement by too large discrepancies between expectation and results . . . If the opportunities are well beyond his capacities, negative affect should result, he may develop an avoidance motive as far as achievement is concerned." p. 65.

11. David Landy, *Tropical Childhood* (Chapel Hill, 1959), pp. 238ff.

12. Fayerweather, *Executive Overseas,* p. 26.

13. McClelland *et al., Achievement Motive,* p. 329.

14. Fayerweather, *Executive Overseas,* p. 27.

15. Cochran, *Puerto Rican Businessman,* p. 121.

16. Fayerweather, *Executive Overseas,* p. 19.

17. As quoted in Cochran, *Puerto Rican Businessman,* p. 126.

18. Richard Hays Williams, ed., *Human Factors in Military Operations: Some Application of the Social Sciences to Operations Research* (Chevy Chase, Md.: Operations Research Office, The Johns Hopkins University, 1954), pp. 119–120.

19. Hirschman, *Strategy of Economic Development,* pp. 16–17.

20. As quoted in Cochran, *Puerto Rican Businessman,* p. 123.

21. *Ibid.,* p. 125.

22. Fayerweather, *Executive Overseas,* pp. 164–5.

23. *Ibid.,* p. 32.

24. Archives of SIAM DI TELLA LTDA., Buenos Aires, Argentina. See also Thomas C. Cochran and Ruben E. Reina, *Entrepreneurship in Argentine Culture: Torcuato di Tella and S.I.A.M.* (Philadelphia, 1962).

25. Charles E. Perkins to Thomas Potter, May 22, 1882, as quoted in Thomas C. Cochran, *Railroad Leaders 1845–1890: The Business Mind in Action* (Cambridge, Mass., 1953), p. 86.

26. Much of the time the entrepreneur studied in Argentina was used in cementing important friendships. See also Fayerweather, *Executive Overseas,* p. 70.

27. Evon Z. Vogt, "On the Concepts of Structure and Process in Cultural Anthropology," *American Anthropologist,* 62:266 (Feb. 1960).

28. Paul Lazarsfeld, "Reflections on Business," *American Journal of Sociology,* 65:17 (July 1959).

29. *Ibid.,* p. 19.

30. Cochran, *Puerto Rican Businessman,* p. 162.

31. This statement refers only to the period to 1956.

32. Arthur H. Cole, "An Approach to the Study of Entrepreneurship: A Tribute to Edwin F. Gay," *The Journal of Economic History,* V Supplement VI (1946), 10ff.

33. Social Science Research Council, *Items,* 14:16 (June 1960).

34. John Gillin, "Ethos Components in Modern Latin American Culture," *American Anthropologist,* 57:498 (1955). The reception pattern in the United States applies only to the more industrialized areas. For example, Texans of the land, cattle, and oil period, or roughly up to 1941, showed very little interest in general technical knowledge. Bankers did not try to learn about industrial risks, and Chambers of Commerce advised industrialists coming to Texas to bring their managers with them. See Thomas C. Cochran, *American Business System* (Cambridge, Mass., 1957), pp. 172–174.

35. Cochran, *Puerto Rican Businessman*, pp. 143–144.
36. Fayerweather, *Executive Overseas*, p. 20.
37. *Ibid.*, p. 116.
38. *Ibid.*, p. 119.
39. Small businessmen in the United States are also hard to reach with new information; the difference is one of degree.
40. These durables have also altered culture in the developed temperate areas in ways that cannot be discussed here.
41. Since history presents cases of partial and gradual although increasingly successful industrial development, I cannot altogether agree with W. W. Rostow's description of a take-off stage, or with Yusif A. Sayigh's observation that for sustained development an underdeveloped society must accept "the total challenge with its inevitable logic." W. W. Rostow, *The Stages of Economic Growth* (Cambridge, Eng., 1960); Yusif A. Sayigh, "Innovating Enterprise and Development," Mimeo. for Center for International Affairs, Harvard University, December 17, 1959, p. 3.

BELSHAW: THE CULTURAL MILIEU OF THE ENTREPRENEUR

1. L. M. Fraser, *Economic Thought and Language* (London, 1937).
2. I must emphasize that this definition is appropriate for situations of change only. Where change is abstracted out and the anthropologist is using a functional model, the criterion of leadership in the administration of resources is sufficient.
3. Note particularly the brilliant article by J. Van der Kroef, "Entrepreneur and Middle Class in Indonesia," *Economic Development and Cultural Change*, 2:297–325 (January 1954), in which the author combats the almost standard view developed by Boeke that the Oriental (including Indonesian) lacks enterprise, for cultural reasons.
4. J. S. Duesenberry, "Some Aspects of the Theory of Economic Development," *Explorations in Entrepreneurial History*, 3:63–102 (December 1950).
5. For vivid documentation, see M. Marriott, "Technological Change in Over-Developed Rural Areas," *Economic Development and Cultural Change*, 1:261–272 (December 1952).
6. See the discussion under the heading "African Enterprise" in W. W. Lewis, *Report on Industrialization and the Gold Coast* (Accra: Government Printing Department, 1953).
7. Note the use of the concept "personality pattern" in B. Hoselitz, "Some Limitations of Induced Economic Growth," *Explorations in Entrepreneurial History*, 2:203–218 (May 1950).
8. See Van der Kroef, "Entrepreneur and Middle Class in Indonesia."
9. W. W. Rostow, *The Process of Economic Growth* (Oxford, 1953).
10. See, for instance, W. E. H. Stanner, *The South Seas in Transition* (Sydney, 1953); R. Firth, "Social Changes in the Western Pacific," *Journal of the Royal Society of Arts*, 101:803–816 (October 1953); O. H. K. Spate, "Changing Native Agriculture in New Guinea," *The Geographical Review*, 43:151–172 (April 1953); C. S. Belshaw, "Community Development in Papua," *The Australian Outlook*, 6:50–59 (March 1952); "The Significance of Modern Cults in Melanesian Development," *The Australian Outlook*, 6:116–125 (June 1950); "Recent History of Mekeo Society," *Oceania*,

22:1–23 (September 1951); *In Search of Wealth: The Emergence of Business Enterprise in South Eastern Papua,* Memoir of the American Anthropological Association, 1955.

11. It lies behind Bishops' hypothesis that the attempt to hold the good will of employees may be more important in entrepreneurs' behavior than the achievement of "sheer productive efficiency." P. W. Bishop, "A History of a Business History," *Explorations in Entrepreneurial History,* 2:57–70 (January 1950).

12. H. Barnett, *Innovation* (New York, 1953).

13. See A. A. Koskinen, *Missionary Influences as a Political Factor in the Pacific Islands* (Helsinki, 1953); R. Oliver, *The Missionary Factor in East Africa* (London, 1952).

14. W. E. Moore, *Industrialization and Labor* (Ithaca, 1951), p. 14.

15. C. S. Belshaw, *Changing Melanesia: Social Economics of Culture Contact* (Oxford, 1954).

16. A. Toynbee, *The World and the West* (Oxford, 1953).

17. H. B. Hawthorn, *The Maori: A Study in Acculturation,* Memoir of the American Anthropological Association No. 64, 1944.

18. Good documentation is given in Sol Tax, *Heritage of Conquest* (Glencoe, Ill., 1952), pp. 57–59.

19. See C. G. Allen, *A Short Economic History of Modern Japan* (London, 1945); T. Uyeda, *The Small Industries of Japan* (New York, 1938); Moore, *Industrialization and Labor,* pp. 30–33; C. P. Fitzgerald, *Revolution in China* (New York, 1952), p. 29.

20. E. K. Gough, "Changing kinship usages in the setting of political and economic change among the Nayars of Malabar," *Journal of the Royal Anthropological Institute,* 82:57–70, pt. 1 (1952).

21. See J. E. Tobin, "Land Tenure in the Marshall Islands," *Atoll Research Bulletin,* no. 11, 1952; Belshaw, *In Search of Wealth.*

22. R. K. Lamb, "Entrepreneurship in the Community," *Explorations in Entrepreneurial History,* 2:114–127 (March 1950).

23. Tax, *Heritage of Conquest.*

24. I have given attention to some of these problems of social accounting in Belshaw, *Changing Melanesia* and *In Search of Wealth.* The main discussion from the economist's point of view is in P. Deane, *Colonial Social Accounting* (Cambridge, Eng., 1954).

25. I am indebted to discussions with Professor J. W. Davidson, Dr. W. E. H. Stanner, and Mr. N. Butlin of the Australian National University, and Professor H. B. Hawthorn and Dr. K. Naegele of the University of British Columbia, for suggestions and criticism in the preparation of this essay.

PELZEL: THE SMALL INDUSTRIALIST IN JAPAN

1. Research reflected in this paper has been aided by a grant from the Ford Foundation's Fund for the Advancement of Education and the Social Science Research Council.

2. I am particularly indebted for knowledge of the general role of government to discussions by William Lockwood at the S.S.R.C. Conference on Economic Growth in Selected Areas (April 1952).

3. Unpublished study of Professor Takashi Nakano, Tokyo University of Education.

4. *A Sample Survey of Social Stratification and Mobility in the Six Large Cities of Japan* (Tokyo: Japan Sociological Society, 1953).

LANDES: FRENCH BUSINESS AND THE BUSINESSMAN: A SOCIAL AND CULTURAL ANALYSIS

1. The argument and materials presented in this paper are derived primarily from personal observation and conversation during nineteen months of study in Paris and the provinces. While this research was concerned with the role of the French businessman in the nineteenth century, it provides an unusual opportunity to meet some of the twentieth-century variety on a rather intimate and candid basis. I should like to take this occasion to express my thanks to the Sheldon Fund of Harvard University and to the Committee on Research in Economic History of the Social Science Research Council for the financial assistance that made this work possible.

2. For the purpose of a brief comparison, the United States has seemed preferable to countries like Germany or England whose backgrounds are far more like that of France, precisely because the marked contrast is ideally suited to bring out the pattern of French business activity. Here, however, a word of caution is in order. If the over-all contrast is marked—although far from antithetical—the differences between France and the United States, so far as the component elements of the pattern are concerned, are essentially a matter of degree. Two entirely unlike cakes may both contain milk; the point is, how much, and in combination with what other ingredients.

3. For the assumptions underlying this humanistic interpretation of an economic problem, see T. Parsons, *The Structure of Social Action* (New York and London, 1936).

4. During the nineteenth century, many French writers felt it necessary to point up the lack of initiative and enterprise of their own businessmen as against those of other countries. At first the paragon of entrepreneurial virtue was England, but the defeat of 1870 coupled with the remarkable industrialization of imperial Germany led to a whole literature of unfavorable comparisons of France with the Reich.

5. Thus W. Sombart, *The Quintessence of Capitalism* (New York, 1915), pp. 136–140; cf. W. Bowden, M. Karpovich, and A. P. Usher, *An Economic History of Europe Since 1750* (New York, 1937), pp. 457ff.

6. The briefness of this paper necessarily precludes an account of the regional and individual variations within the system to be described. The existence of such variations on a theme, as it were, by no means vitiates the theme. I cannot subscribe to any pluralistic interpretation of social behavior that implies that individual action is random, whether derived from some more or less whimsical soul within, or from a rationalistic reaction to personal problems taken *in vacuo.* Were individual behavior random in either sense, we might just as well throw the social sciences out the window.

7. Perhaps the most convenient picture is given by P. George, "Étude statistique des dimensions des établissements industriels," in G. Dessus, P. George, and J. Weulersse, *Matériaux pour une géographie volontaire de l'industrie française* (Paris, 1949), pp. 129–143. One can only regret that

more recent figures are not yet available to supplement the prewar censuses on which the article is based. For comparable statistics on American industry, see U.S. Dept. of Commerce, *Census of Manufactures,* "Wage Earners and Wages in Establishments Classified According to Number of Wage Earners: 1937" (offset, dated July 7, 1939), pp. 2–3.

8. See on this point Max Weber, *General Economic History* (London, n.d.), pp. 226ff., who implies that this unity, characteristic of European enterprise in the late medieval and early modern period—he cites the Medici as an example—disappears with further economic development and sophistication.

9. Note in this connection the French attitude toward bankruptcy, which was long considered almost a hereditary stain on a family's reputation. The classical picture is given by Balzac in *Grandeur et décadence de César Birotteau.* In contrast, the American attitude has generally been one of tolerance, to the point where at certain times and in certain places, one or two failures have been looked on as an almost indispensable preliminary to a successful business career. On the contrast in this respect between the United States and Europe, especially England, see Gilbert Burck, "The American Genius for Bankruptcy," *Fortune,* 37:130ff. (April 1948).

10. This system of family effort and family rewards is only one aspect of a generalized group basis for status distinctions within French society as a whole. In other words, compared with the United States, for example, the position of the individual is less dependent on such things as personal activity or achievement than on the position of the kinship group. As a member of the *Académie Française* remarked of one of his colleagues, famous in a field even more honorific than business: "I sometimes wonder if the Prince de Broglie is more proud to be one of the world's great mathematicians and the winner of a Nobel prize, or simply a Broglie."

11. The *commandite par actions* is a form of sleeping partnership whose distinguishing characteristic is the representation of ownership, as opposed to management, by stock negotiable in the market. The active partners, as might be expected, are in sole charge of operations and are liable to the full extent of their fortunes for any debts incurred by the company. This type of firm has also been popular in Germany, where it is known as a *Kommanditgesellschaft auf Aktien.* It is interesting to note that although the same form of business organization is provided for by statute in various states of the United States, it has to all intents and purposes never been used.

12. According to the Ministère du Commerce et de l'Industrie, there were in France at the end of 1939, 151,044 partnerships of various types as against 43,078 corporations. (*Annuaire statistique,* 1946, résumé rétrospectif, p. 70); cf. also for the trend, "Sociétés commerciales," *Larousse commercial,* p. 1196. As a point of comparison, there were in the United States in 1936, 530,779 corporations and 237,367 partnerships, with the former gaining every year. (U.S. Temporary National Economic Committee, *Verbatim Record of the Proceedings* [Washington: Bureau of National Affairs, 1939], 1, Reference Data Section, p. 59). Such figures, of course, can only give a two-dimensional picture, as it were. For the strategic importance of the corporation in France and its role in given sectors of the economy, see the *Annuaire Chaix* of the leading joint-stock companies. Note above all the

limited number of such firms in manufacturing, especially in industries producing consumers' goods.

13. The semi-invisibility of this all-important form of capital formation has led analysts of the French investment picture either to neglect it entirely or to accord it short shrift in studies devoted almost exclusively to corporation finance and government investment. Cf. the treatment of C. Bettelheim, *Bilan de l'économie française, 1919–1946* (Paris, 1947), pp. 113–17. And yet even in the case of corporations, self-financing has always played a more important role than the more obvious and measurable techniques of stock and bond issues.

14. It has long been a favorite sport of historians to whip the French banks for the inadequacy and parsimony of medium- and long-term credits to industry. To a certain extent such criticism is justified, but there is good reason to believe that the real culprit is industry itself, in that, at least until quite recently, no successful firm, hence no good risk, wanted any part of bank credit. This, of course, does not include the discount of short-term commercial paper.

15. Émile Zola, *Le Ventre de Paris*. Cf. also François Coppée's delightful poem, "Petit-Bourgeois." This subsistence production, as it might be called, is apparently equally alien to the thinking of most economists and economic historians, who continue to base their analyses of the classical assumption that the end of business enterprise is to maximize profit. And yet enough examples exist to the contrary in both advanced and primitive economies to indicate that the supposed rule is the exception, and that the famous diminishing returns embrace social and cultural considerations that often diminish far more rapidly than pecuniary ones.

16. See the above-cited article by George, "Étude statistique des dimensions des établissements industriels," pp. 113, 115, 116–118, 133, 135, and *passim*. George is especially struck by this coexistence of big and small in the metalworking industries, where one-third of the working force in 1936 was employed in plants of over 500 men (average 1,600), and one-third in a *"poussière de petits établissements"* of 10 to 25 men each. In seeking to explain this phenomenon, however, George offers another example of the economist apparently unable to free himself from the traditional assumptions, in this case that of more or less perfect competition.

17. In the 150 years from 1800 to the present, the population of France has increased about 45 per cent, from 28,250,000 to about 41,000,000. That of the United States has jumped over 2,700 per cent, from 5,300,000 to almost 150,000,000. As for the French overseas territories, their role as an important outlet for French manufactured products still lies in the future. See the chapter by Dudley Kirk on population factors in Earle, *Modern France.*

18. This is supplemented by certain social security benefits, plus family allotments which in the last analysis barely keep a growing family from being swamped. On workers' wages and budgets, see the *Bulletin de la statistique générale de la France,* supplements of January–March and July–September, 1949. On p. 37 of the earlier number, there is a useful bibliography of similar surveys of family budgets. For more detailed pictures of individual cases, which make up in human interest and insight what they lose in statistical objectivity, see Sherry Mangan, "French Worker," *Fortune,*

38:102ff (December 1948), and "Condition du salarié français," *Réalités*, 36ff (January 1950). The outstanding feature of all these budgets is the high percentage of income devoted simply to nourishment and the correspondingly insignificant expenditures for manufactured articles.

19. In 1931, of 2,421,933 exploitations in agriculture and forestry, 1,341,112 had no hired help. (*Annuaire statistique*, 1938, p. 103). Few of these could have yielded much surplus revenue applicable to manufactured goods.

20. In this regard, Italy furnished a good example of such a situation carried to an exponential power, where there is not one market, but two, one handling extremely well made but costly articles for the "haves," the other purveying necessities like food and shoddy manufactured goods to the "have-not's."

21. As we shall see below, conspicuous consumption exists in France, but it is oriented in a distinctly different direction from the American variety.

22. Thus, for income-tax purposes, certain *"revenus forfaitaires"* have been established on the basis of real property, domestic personnel, automobiles, etc.

23. In the sense that a certain degree of fluidity is indispensable in any Western society, given the economic and social pressures of the present day. Because of this and other considerations—the shopkeepers in France have proved an exceptionally well organized and effective political force—the small merchant has generally been carefully protected by law against the incursions of such monopolistic phenomena as department, five-and-dime, and chain stores.

24. Of course, the introduction of the fixed price sometime in the nineteenth century has imposed certain limitations on this silent warfare, although fixed prices are not nearly so universal as one might think, even in Paris. But the fixed price simply impersonalizes the relationship; the underlying conflict, the pattern of buyer vs. seller, remains the same.

25. The following personal experience may be taken for what it is worth. I once had occasion to ask the director of one of the largest Parisian stores, which does little if any advertising, why this was the case. The answer was that advertising would be simply a waste of money. And to my question why this was so, he replied that he did not know, that he did not care to know, that he operated purely pragmatically, and that he was not interested in *why* things do or do not work, but simply *whether* they do or do not.

26. This dogged refusal of the French merchant to sell at a loss was most intelligently exploited by the government in its recent campaign to drive down the price of gold. By simply refusing credit to tide retailers and wholesalers over a period of stagnation, the Ministère des Finances compelled them to liquidate stocks of gold and dollars hoarded during the war years and after. As a result, gold lost about 40 per cent of its value in the few months from January to May 1949.

27. The interplay of these two factors, sales pattern and consumption pattern, is an excellent illustration of the inextricable concatenation of elements in a socioeconomic problem of this type.

28. This discussion of the qualitative consumption pattern will necessarily emphasize the bourgeois classes of society. These are the people whose pecuniary means give them a semimonopoly of the market for non-necessities,

and whose social prestige endows their taste and standards with a charisma which influences to a greater or lesser degree the standards of other sections of the population. As regards these other groups, the effect of their qualitative consumption patterns is obviously limited by their pocketbooks, or, in the case of certain well-to-do farmers, by a concentration of effort and wealth toward a goal of landownership that drastically curtails purchases of manufactured consumers' goods.

29. On the economic effects of our consumption pattern on the structure of the American garment industry, see "Adam Smith on Fifth Avenue," *Fortune*, 39:73ff (January 1949).

30. There is, of course, a demand for American cars, although government restrictions make it impossible to say how strong or effective it is. It is generally accepted, however, that from the standpoint of originality and style, our big luxury models leave something to be desired.

31. This analogy was suggested to the writer by Mr. Jesse R. Pitts.

32. In point of fact, it is hard to say how much the preference for personal service owes to the relative cheapness of labor—the average *maîtresse de maison* considers $20 or $25 a month for a maid exorbitant—and how much to the prestige value of domestic personnel. The French attitude toward machinery in general is an excellent illustration of the conservative force of existing behavior patterns, of the natural congeniality of familiar ways. There are progressive housewives who have purchased such devices as pressure cookers or washing machines, only to find that they had to prepare the vegetables or do the wash themselves—the maid would have no part of such new-fangled gadgets. Similarly, many a businessman is convinced that no machine can possibly do a given industrial operation as well as the traditional hand methods. This attitude has played and still plays an important role in retarding mechanization in French industry.

33. A recent survey of the market for textiles and clothing showed not only a remarkably low per-capita consumption of such goods, but—even more significant for our purposes—a general agreement on the part of those questioned that this low consumption was not the result of excessive prices. The only exception was sheets, where almost half felt that the cost was too high. "Une Enquête par sondage sur le marché de textiles," *Bulletin de la statistique générale de la France*, 36:250–262 (Supplement of July–September 1948). It is worth noting in this respect that linen has always been considered in France a form of wealth, to be saved and passed on from one generation to another like silver and dinnerware, and hence possesses exceptional prestige value.

34. This diversification of output in an effort to reduce risk should be carefully distinguished from the desire to guarantee independence by what is often excessive integration.

35. This, of course, is true of American firms as well, though once again to a far smaller degree. The case comes to mind of a leading French steel producer who in 1929, if not later, was using, together with the most modern types of hydraulic press, water-driven tail hammers of the sort used in the fourteenth century. *Les Établissements Jacob Holtzer* (privately printed, n.d. [1929]).

36. The colonies form a desirable field of action, not only because the rate of profit is likely to be higher in what is still an underexploited area, but also because the colonial franc, which is worth twice as much as the

metropolitan franc, is considered a more solid currency. The ideal spot, of course, is Morocco, where the special commercial régime growing out of the nineteenth-century treaties of the Western powers with the local rulers has created a minor twentieth-century business paradise.

37. Laws of March 2–17 and June 14, 1791.

38. *Le Monde,* December 25–26, 1949, p. 6.

39. It goes without saying that the above paragraph is not meant to imply that failure and bankruptcy are unknown in French business life. There is such a thing as being too marginal. Once again, it is a question of degree, the tolerance here being far greater than in more competitive economies.

40. A. Mayer, *"La Crise de structure de la société française," The French Review,* 16:5–15 (October 1942), 16:122–133 (December 1942).

41. Compare Landes, "French Entrepreneurship and Industrial Growth in the Nineteenth Century," *Journal of Economic History,* 9:52 and n13 (1949).

42. As already indicated, the primary purpose of this paper is to present the dominant pattern of entrepreneurial behavior in France, without undue attention to the "but's" and "however's." It would be worse than unfair, however, to give the picture of a stagnant economy totally unleavened by the ferment of innovation. The point is that French business is far from unchanging, as the above paragraph hints only too briefly, but that it proceeds according to certain rules more conservative than those of other societies in Western Europe. Every society, indeed every social or professional group, has such rules and regulations, and all have more or less effective ways and means to penalize nonconformists.

43. Superficially, in that this situation is and always has been much more common than Americans, with their orientation of free enterprise and their big business economy, tend to think. Other European economies than the French could yield even more marked examples.

44. Émile Zola, *La Curée.*

45. In this connection, the worker is apt to prove a far more serious obstacle than the employer. It should be remembered that the introduction of time and motion programs, while superficially easy, involves the creation of a discipline utterly alien at present to the mentality of most French labor.

46. In a recent analysis of the projected French antitrust law, soon to be proposed largely at American behest, M. Robert Buron, Secrétaire d'État aux Affaires économiques and head of the government office charged with preparing the measure, differentiated between good and bad agreements (*ententes*) on the following basis: "the good being those which lighten the task of the owners of small and medium enterprises." *Le Monde,* February 1, 1950, p. 4.

47. On the ideological background of this corporate movement and its development since the First World War, see G. Pirou, *Essais sur le corporatisme* (Paris, 1938); O. de Magondeaux, *Les Ententes industrielles obligatoires et le corporatisme en France* (Paris, 1937); and especially, A. Piettre, *L'Évolution des ententes industrielles en France depuis la crise* (Paris, 1936). For a good statement of the businessman's point of view, see H. L. Dubly, *Vers un ordre économique et social: Eugène Mathon, 1860–1935* (Paris, privately printed, 1946). Mathon was an outstanding textile manufacturer in a city of outstanding textile manufacturers, Roubaix.

48. Cf. John E. Sawyer, "Strains in the Social Structure of Modern France," in Earle, *Modern France*. This suggestive chapter provides an institutional frame of reference for further research in French economic and social history.

PART IV

AITKEN: THE ENTREPRENEUR AS AN INDIVIDUAL

1. For a more extended treatment, see Harold C. Passer, *The Electric Manufacturers, 1875–1900: A Study in Competition, Entrepreneurship, Technical Change, and Economic Growth* (Cambridge, Mass., 1953).
2. See also Michael W. Flinn, *Men of Iron: The Crowleys in the Early Iron Industry* (Edinburgh University Publications: History, Philosophy, Economics, No. 14. Chicago, Aldine Publishing Company, 1962). The interested reader may also consult M. W. Flinn (ed.), *The Law Book of the Crowley Ironworks* (Publications of the Surtees Society, Vol. 167, Durham, 1957) and, for a general survey, Sidney Pollard, "Factory Discipline in the Industrial Revolution," *The Economic History Review*, 16:254–271 (December 1963).

PASSER: THE ELECTRIC LIGHT AND THE GAS LIGHT: INNOVATION AND CONTINUITY IN ECONOMIC HISTORY

1. Martin, T. C., *Forty Years of Edison Service*, New York, 1922, p. 9.
2. *Ibid.*, p. 11.
3. "Progress of the Electric Light in England," a report submitted to the House of Commons, Ottawa, Canada, March 10, 1882. Quoted in the Edison Electric Light Company *Bulletin* no. 9, May 15, 1882, p. 16.
4. Martin, *Forty Years of Edison*, p. 38.
5. This meter can be seen in the restored Menlo Park Laboratory, Edison Institute, Dearborn, Michigan.
6. The Edison Electric Light Company *Bulletin* no. 16, February 2, 1883, p. 31.
7. The Edison Electric Light Company *Bulletin* no. 16, February 2, 1883, pp. 33, 34.
8. The Cincinnati Water Works installed an electric light plant in 1884 and for a period of several months used almost no gas. But its gas bill each month was the same as before. *Cincinnati Enquirer*, February 16, 1885. Quoted in the Edison Company for Isolated Lighting *Bulletin for Agents* no. 6, September 15, 1885, p. 3.
9. *American Gas Light Journal*, July 3, 1882, p. 5.
10. *Ibid.*
11. It might be argued that by coincidence the cost of electric light may have been equal to the price of gas light and that no inference can be drawn from the fact of identical prices of gas and electric light. My cost data and calculations are not yet complete but they indicate that the cost of electric light was substantially below the price set.
12. *American Gas Light Journal*, July 3, 1882, p. 5.
13. *Edison Electric Light Company booklet*, 1884. In the historical file of the General Electric Company, Schenectady, New York.

14. Quoted in Edison Electric Light Company *Bulletin* no 17, April 6, 1883, pp. 21–22.

15. The Edison Electric Light Company *Bulletin* no. 9, May 15, 1882, pp. 6–7.

CHAPMAN: WILLIAM BROWN OF DUNDEE, 1791–1864: MANAGEMENT IN A SCOTTISH FLAX MILL

1. *Dundee, Perth and Coupar Advertiser.*

2. Alexander J. Warden, *The Linen Trade, Ancient and Modern* (2nd ed., London, 1867).

3. W. Norrie, *Dundee Celebrities of the Nineteenth Century* (Dundee, 1873).

4. See Dennis Chapman, "The Combination of Hecklers in the East of Scotland," *Scottish Historical Review*, 27:156–164 (Oct. 1948).

5. One spyndle was equal to 14,400 yards.

FLINN: SIR AMBROSE CROWLEY, IRONMONGER, 1658–1713

1. British Museum, Add. Ms. 34,555.

2. *Victoria County History of Durham* 2:281–287 (London, 1906); W. A. Young, "Works Organisation in the Seventeenth Century," *Transactions of the Newcomen Society*, 4:73–93 (1923–1924); William Bourn, *History of the Parish of Ryton* (Carlisle, 1896); *Whickham Parish: Its History, Antiquities, and Industries* (Carlisle, 1893); *and Annals of the Parish of Whickham* (Consett, 1902). Particularly valuable is the genealogical work of Mr. A. L. Reade in his *The Reades of Blackwood Hill in the Parish of Horton Staffordshire* (London, 1906); and his *Johnsonian Gleanings* (1909–1939).

3. *Monthly Chronicle of North Country Lore and Legend*, 1:98 (Newcastle-on-Tyne, 1887).

4. E. Lipson, *Economic History of England*, vol. II, 4th ed. (London 1947), p. 178.

5. Referred to hereafter as "Lloyd Mss."

6. Referred to hereafter as "Marlow Mss." I am indebted to Mr. Lloyd firstly for the loan of these letters, and secondly for permission to reproduce extracts from some of these letters.

7. Referred to hereafter as "Ashburnham Mss."

8. Referred to hereafter as "Council Instructions." I wish to express my thanks to Mr. Frank Kojay of Winlaton for first drawing my attention to these letters.

9. I am grateful to Mr. Percival Boyd, Master of the Drapers' Company 1926–1927, for this and other information taken from the manuscript records of the Drapers' Company in London. See also Percival Boyd, *Roll of the Drapers Company of London* (London, 1934).

10. Ambrose Crowley to his half-brother, John Crowley, 13 Oct. 1707 (Marlow Mss.).

11. *Universal Magazine*, 83:57 (August 1788).

12. Drapers' Company records. By the time of Crowley's death in 1713 no fewer than 43 apprentices had served their time with him. It is interest-

ing to notice that many of these apprentices came from Crowley's native county of Worcester, while others came from the neighborhood of his works in County Durham. Several of them remained in his service after completion of their terms of apprenticeship. One, Daniel Walter, bound in 1706, only left the firm of Crowley in 1739.

13. Ambrose Crowley to his father, 10 February 1684/5 (Lloyd Mss.).

14. The brother was probably Samuel (born 1669), his eldest half-brother, was apprenticed to him in the same year 1685.

15. In 1688 Crowley petitioned the King to order that his Catholic workmen might continue to work in Sunderland unmolested (*State Papers Domestic,* Entry Book 44, no. 236, pp. 24–25). James II, as might be expected, was sympathetic to his petition, and, "being graciously disposed to give the Petitioner all fitting Encouragement," referred the matter to his Attorney General, as a result of which the Privy Council instructed the Bishop of Durham to take "speedy and effectuall care that the Petitioners workemen be protected." (*Privy Council Register* [P. C. 2] no. 72, p. 702).

16. The place of the foreign workers at Winlaton was possibly taken later by women: in 1702 Crowley launched a scheme for the employment of women as nailers. "Whereas I have found that the want of having employment for girls and women hath not only born hard upon their parents, but hath lead them into a slothful and lazy life, and the little worke they have done hath been where great numbers have been employed, whereby they have learned much vice and ludeness, and have debached their principles and become odious in the eyes of all good people; for remedy I have known of severall women nayling in Staffordshire and the adjacent countries; and hearing of severall lately learning the same, do therefore think fitt to give the following encouragement to all that shall learne to nayle . . . " (Council Instruction no. 46, 27 January 1701/2, verse 173).

17. Inventory of the Estate of John Crowley, 16th Schedule (Ashburnham Mss.) After the death of Sir Ambrose's son, John, in 1728, his executors had an inventory of the estate made for probate purposes. This inventory, reputed to contain 3000 sheets, and to have taken one year to produce, is immensely informative. John Crowley's estate was valued at nearly £250,000. Not only was every nail and every bracket in the many warehouses accounted for, but the details of leases held by John Crowley at his death help to reconstruct the history of the business.

18. J. Brand, *History and Antiquities of the Town . . . of Newcastle-upon-Tyne* (Newcastle, 2 vols. 1789), II 501.

19. Between 1684 and 1686 Crowley's address was given in the records of the Drapers' Company as "Carey Street," in London. It seems likely that the Thames Street premises were occupied from 1686 onward.

20. Even as late as 1702, out of 197 men and boys employed in the manufacture of ironware at Winlaton, 81 were nailers. (Council Instructions no. 48, February 1701–1702, verse 185).

21. "As to carradg of the nails to the most usuall markets which are between Sunderland and Exon [Exeter], any of which places there is frequent commerce by shipping, London beeing about the middle port . . . " (Ambrose Crowley to his father, 10 February 1684/5, Lloyd Mss.).

22. Ambrose Crowley to Sampson Lloyd, 14 April 1704 (Marlow Mss.). It is characteristic of Crowley that after this announcement to his brother-in-

law, he plunged immediately into details of the building of the warehouse—the engaging of bricklayers, the finding of lime and sand, and the purchase of hinges.

23. *Notes and Queries*, 2nd ser., 3:48 (January 1857); 6th ser., 12:48 (16 July 1885); 6th ser., 12:191 (5 September 1885).

24. Inventory of the Estate of John Crowley, 1st Schedule (Ashburnham Mss.).

25. Council Instructions no. 1, 10 October 1700; no. 31, 14 August 1701; no. 32, 19 August 1701; no. 33, 23 August 1701.

26. Indenture dated 17 November 1740 concerning the estate of John Crowley (Ashburnham Mss.).

27. W. Bourn, *History of the Parish of Ryton*, p. 122 (Winlaton and Winlaton Mill lay in the parish of Ryton). Bourn clearly had access to records of the Crowley business now no longer traceable. For this reason his local histories are extremely valuable.

28. Inventory of the estate of John Crowley, 16th Schedule, (Ashburnham Mss.) In 1707, the leases at Swalwell were assigned by Edward Harrison and his partners to Gregory Page, a friend and neighbor of Crowley at Greenwich, and, like Crowley, a wealthy London merchant. As there must have been a reason for the mention of this assignment to Page in the Inventory, it seems probable that Page was acting as an intermediary on Crowley's behalf.

29. Indenture dated 17 November 1740 concerning the estate of John Crowley (Ashburnham Mss.).

30. *Law Book of the Crowley Ironworks*, Laws 29 and 30.

31. If not impassable, at least passable only at carriage rates which Crowley was reluctant to pay. (See Council Instruction no. 4, 26 November 1700, verse 17, "Leading": "The price fixed for bringing up iron from Bladon to Winlaton is from May day to March 9d. per Tun but by reason of extraordinary wet the price was raised before Martlemas. This is therefore to put yow in mind to make restitucion when good weather shall happen before May Day.").

32. Though not as slow as is often imagined. Crowley kept a very careful check on the time taken for a letter from London to reach Newcastle (300 miles). This was normally four days. (See Council Instructions no. 8, 17 December 1700; and no. 9, 21 December 1700).

33. In 1711 Crowley took a lease for 18 years of Axwell Hall, near Winlaton, from Sir John Clavering, but no evidence has yet come to light to show that he or his successors ever resided there for long periods. (Inventory of the estate of John Crowley, Ashburnham Mss.).

34. Ambrose Crowley to Sampson Lloyd, 4 November 1704 (Marlow Mss.).

35. For some account of the iron business of Richard Knight and his partners, see B. L. C. Johnson, "The Foley Partnerships: the Iron Industry at the end of the Charcoal Era," *Economic History Review*, 2nd. ser. 4:322–340 (1952); R. L. Downes, "The Stour Partnership 1726–36", *ibid.* 2nd ser., 3:90–96 (1950).

36. Ambrose Crowley to Sampson Lloyd, 10 July 1711 (Lloyd Mss.).

37. Ambrose Crowley to Sampson Lloyd, 5 July 1711 (Lloyd Mss.).

38. *Ibid.* 26 January 1711–1722 (Lloyd Mss.).

39. There was a pathetic discrepancy between the bequests in the father's will, which totaled £3,357 (P. C. C. 125 Buckingham), and the value of his estate after his death, estimated to amount to £1,811 (even this sum included £600 of "debts, part whereof are desparate") (Inventory of Goods of Ambrose Crowley, Lloyd Mss.).

40. Ambrose Crowley to his father, 14 October 1710 (Marlow Mss.).

41. Ambrose Crowley to James Crowley, 20 July 1710 (Lloyd Mss.).

42. Ambrose Crowley to John Crowley, copy attached to letter to Sampson Lloyd, 13 October 1707 (Marlow Mss.).

43. Council Instruction no. 46, 27 January 1701/2, verse 175.

44. Council Instruction no. 49, 14 March 1701/2, verse 187.

45. Jonathan Story first joined the Crowley business in November 1697 when he was bound apprentice to Crowley. He became free of the Drapers' Company in 1705, but remained in Crowley's service. (Drapers' Company Ms. records).

46. Will of Sir Ambrose Crowley (P. C. C. 222 Leeds).

47. *Commons' Journal*, 22:851–852.

48. Compare Council Instruction no. 9, 21 December 1700, verse 40: "I have for many years made it my observacion, that when those that have done the broad busynes have grown negligent they have sometimes stifled my letters, at other times deferr'd the communicating them to the Councell, thinking thereby to cloud their evill actions. For remedy, I shall make an order, and for the present doe order (1) that noe letters be opened by any person otherwayes than one of the Councell. Such letters shall not be opened but in the presence of as many of the Councell as are in the way and to be then read. (2) That in case any Councellor shall open any letter and not communicate it to the rest of the Councell as soon as he shall see them shall pay 12d. to the Councell Box; if he keeping the same secret after he hath seen any of the Councell twelve houres, 2s; If 24 houres 5s, and after the rate of 5s p. day for everyday anyone shall stifle or conceal any letter from the rest of the Councell."

49. Notably by W. A. Young, in *Transactions of the Newcomen Society*, 4:73–101 (1923–1924); and by E. Lipson, *Economic History of England*, 2:178–183. (London, 1931).

50. Inventory of the Estate of John Crowley, 2nd Schedule (Ashburnham Mss.) Of this sum, £1,672.15. 5d. was owed by Deptford. By Lady Day 1732, there were £15,000 of Navy bills outstanding. (A Calculation of how the Estate stood . . . at Lady Day 1732, Ashburnham Mss.).

51. Account of the Crowley Estate . . . 25 March 1739/40 (Ashburnham Mss.).

52. Crowley claimed to have lost £15,000 in discounting Navy Tallies (*Calendar of Treasury Papers 1708–1714*, vol. 143, no. 33).

53. Compare *The Sergison Papers*, ed. R. D. Merriman (Navy Records Society, London, 1950) pp. 58–61.

54. Alfred B. Beaven, *The Aldermen of the City of London* (London, 1908, 2 vols.) I, pp. 142, 258; II, p. 122.

55. After the election, Pitt petitioned the House of Commons, claiming that "Sir Ambrose Crowley and Agents was guilty of Bribery; and, by that means procured himself to be returned." (*Commons' Journal*, 17:489.

56. A. Raistrick, *Quakers in Science and Industry* (London, 1950) p. 168.

57. Rhys Jenkins, "The Hollow Blade Sword Company and Sword Making at Shotley Bridge," *Transactions of the Newcomen Society,* 15:185–194 (1934–1935); J. D. Aylward, "The Hollow Blade Sword Company," *Notes and Queries,* 4 and 11 September 1948.

58. J. U. Nef, *The Rise of the British Coal Industry* (London 1932) II, p. 51; T. S. Ashton & J. Sykes, *The Coal Industry of the Eighteenth Century* (Manchester, 1929) p. 4.

59. E. Hughes, *North Country Life in the Eighteenth Century,* (London, 1952) *passim.*

60. Sir John Clapham, *The Bank of England* (London, 1944) I, p. 30.

61. *Autobiography of William Stout of Lancaster,* ed. J. Harland (1851).

62. It is inaccurate to call Crowley, as he is so often called, an *ironmaster.* He was mainly concerned with the finishing processes of ironmaking.

63. This assertion underlies the widely held belief that Addison's essay in the *Spectator* no. 299, 12 February 1711–1712 is a caricature of Crowley. Even a cursory comparison of Crowley's career with that of Addison's Sir John Enville shows that there can be no foundation for this identification.

64. John Halford to James Crowley, 27 November 1712.

65. Council Instruction no. 3, 5 November 1700, verse 12, "Furnaces."

66. *Ibid.,* no. 38, 25 September 1701, verse 141, "Brasses."

67. "Plating" was a process used in the edge-tool industry. The body of a tool was made of iron and a tip of steel which took the edge was welded to the iron. This was necessary on account of the high price of good steel. The welding of the steel to the iron body was called "plating."

68. An early example of prefabrication?

69. Council Instruction no. 32, 19 August 1701, verse 127, "Forge Plateing."

70. Rhys Jenkins, "Notes on the early History of Steel making in England," *Transactions of the Newcomen Society,* 3:16–40 (1922–1923). The process concerned was that of the making of "shear" or "German" steel. Before the introduction of this process from Germany, "blister" steel had been made by the cementation process. Shear steel was superior in quality to blister steel.

71. Jonathan Swift, *The Intelligencer,* no. XIX, 2 December 1728.

72. Compare Boyne (ed. G. C. Williamson), *Trade Tokens of the 17th Century; "Tradesmen's Tokens of the 17th Century in the Cabinet of the Society"* (Newcastle Society of Antiquaries, 1854).

73. Law No. 13, "Coals Deliver'd."

74. The word "Reckoning" here has a particular and not a general meaning. It will already be apparent that Crowley evolved a highly specialized terminology.

75. References to the Current Bills are copious. The principal sources for the above brief account are: Law No. 5, "Bills Currant"; Council Instructions No. 6, 5 December 1700, Verse 29, "Want of Money"; and No. 8, 17 December 1700, Verse 33, "Money Wanting."

76. Council Instruction no. 51, 30 April 1702, verse 193, "Dunning."

77. Ambrose Crowley to James Crowley, 8 December 1711 (Lloyd Mss.). Crowley chose poor ground on which to criticize young James: his own handwriting was far from impeccable!

78. Ambrose Crowley to his father, 14 October 1710 (Marlow Mss.).

79. Council Instruction no. 52, 13 June 1702, verse 199.

80. *Historical Manuscripts Commission,* Portland Mss. V, p. 222.
81. *The Northern Tribune* (Newcastle), 1:26 (1854).
82. William Bourn, *History of the Parish of Ryton,* p. 118.
83. Council Instruction no. 49, 14 March 1701/2, verse 187.

McLAUGHLIN: THE STANLEY STEAMER: A STUDY IN UNSUCCESSFUL INNOVATION

1. Floyd Clymer, *Treasury of Early American Automobiles* (New York, 1950), p. 179.
2. *Ibid.,* pp. 38–40. See also E. L. Throm and J. S. Crenshaw, *Popular Mechanics Auto Album,* (New York, 1952), pp. 61–64.
3. R. Matthes, J. Geschelin, and others, "Automotive Industry," *Collier's Encyclopedia* (New York, 1950), II, 558.
4. The power output of the gasoline engine is comparatively low at 900 to 2,500 rpm, and at its highest at about 3,600 rpm. See C. F. Kettering, N. Shidle, J. Gilbert, "Motorcar," *Encyclopaedia Britannica* (1952) XV, 889.
5. E. Hamilton, "Motor Vehicles," *Collier's Encyclopedia,* II, 889.
6. For a list of steam automobile manufacturers in the U.S., see Clymer, *Treasury,* p. 23.
7. Arthur Pound, *The Turning Wheel: The Story of General Motors through Twenty-five Years* (New York, 1934), p. 48.
8. When propelling a car at 60 mph, the Stanley engine would be running at 994 rpm. See George Woodbury, *The Story of a Stanley Steamer* (New York, 1950) p. 253.
9. The White Motor Company, *The Albatross, A Quarter Century of White Transportation,* 1900–1925 (Cleveland, 1925), p. 8.
10. Woodbury, *The Story of a Stanley Steamer,* p. 211.
11. Wallace W. Abbey, "Steam Cools Your Train," *Trains,* 2:17 (August 1951).
12. Woodbury, *The Story of a Stanley Steamer,* pp. 170–178.
13. Interview with Frederick E. Haenel, violin appraiser, June 1953.
14. Interview with Carleton F. Stanley, a cousin of the Stanley brothers and a violin maker, April 1952.
15. Woodbury, *The Story of a Stanley Steamer,* pp. 170–178.
16. Carleton F. Stanley, "Early History of the Stanley Company" as quoted in Floyd Clymer, *Historical Motor Scrapbook, Steam Car Edition* (Los Angeles, 1945) vol. I, p. 23.
17. F. O. Stanley, as quoted in Thomas S. Derr, *The Modern Steam Car and its Background,* with a supplement by F. Clymer (Los Angeles, 1945) p. 45.
18. Interview with Fred Marriott, driver of the Stanley racer, 10 April 1952: Woodbury, *Story of a Stanley Steamer,* pp. 177, 239.
19. F. O. Stanley, as quoted in Derr, *Modern Steam Car,* pp. 45–49.
20. Interview with C. F. Stanley; Ralph C. Epstein, *The Automobile Industry, its Economic and Commercial Development* (New York, 1926) p. 124.
21. Edward D. Kennedy, *The Automobile Industry, the Story of Capitalism's Favorite Child* (New York, 1941) pp. 38–39.
22. Interview with Fred Marriott.
23. Interview with C. F. Stanley.

24. Kennedy, *Automobile Industry*, pp. 36–37; Clymer, *Treasury*, p. 188.
25. Interview with C. F. Stanley.
26. Epstein, *Automobile Industry*, p. 187; Kennedy, *Automobile Industry*, pp. 114, 129.
27. R. W. Stanley, as quoted in F. Clymer, *Historical Motor Scrapbook, Steam Car Edition* (Los Angeles, 1945) I, 19.
28. Kennedy, *Automobile Industry*, p. 151.
29. *Ibid.*, p. 52.
30. Pound, *The Turning Wheel*, p. 48.
31. *The Albatross*, p. 10.
32. Arthur Pound, *Detroit, Dynamic City* (New York, 1940) p. 282.
33. *The Story of a Stanley Steamer*, p. 113.
34. Kennedy, *Automobile Industry*, p. 82.
35. Martin Tuttle, *Automotive Statistics* (Motor List Co., Des Moines, 1927) p. 79.
36. Derr, *Modern Steam Car*, p. 87.
37. C. F. Stanley in Clymer, *Scrapbook, Steam Car Edition*, I, 24–25; Federal Trade Commission, *Report on the Price of Gasoline in 1915* (Washington, D.C., 1915).
38. Test by Doble Company, 1918 [?], in Clymer, *Scrapbook, Steam Car Edition*, I, 145.
39. S. O. White, as quoted in Derr, *Modern Steam Car*, p. 145.

PART V

AITKEN: HISTORICAL VARIETIES

1. For a fuller discussion, see Bernard Bailyn, *The New England Merchants in the Seventeenth Century* (Cambridge, Mass., 1955).
2. For a more extended treatment, see Peter Mathias, *The Brewing Industry in England 1700–1830* (Cambridge, England, 1959).
3. Bert F. Hoselitz, "Entrepreneurship and Traditional Elites," *Explorations in Entrepreneurial History*, 2d ser., 1:36–49 (Fall, 1963).
4. Lawrence Stone, in an article dealing with a somewhat earlier period in England, takes a more positive view of the contributions of aristocratic entrepreneurs; see his "The Nobility in Business, 1540–1640," *Explorations in Entrepreneurial History*, 10:54–61 (December 1957).

MINCHINTON: THE MERCHANTS IN ENGLAND IN THE EIGHTEENTH CENTURY

1. Some aspects of this subject have been explored in R. Westerfield, "Middlemen in English Business between 1660 and 1760," *Transactions of the Connecticut Academy of Arts and Sciences*, XIX (1915), particularly pp. 394–412 and in T. S. Ashton, *An Economic History of England: The 18th Century* (London, 1955), pp. 130–140. For a discussion of the merchant class in the early eighteenth century, see J. H. Plumb, *Sir Robert Walpole* (London, 1956), pp. 22–29.
2. M. Ginsberg, "Class Consciousness," *Encyclopedia of the Social Sciences* (New York, 1935), III, 536.
3. I gratefully acknowledge the help given by Mrs. Carter, M. M. Schofield, W. G. Hoskins, M. Newman, and Mrs. M. Stacey in the preparation of this paper.

4. For 1696, see Gregory King, *Natural and Political Observations on the State and Condition of England in 1696* (London, 1696): for 1750, M. Postlethwayt, *The Universal Dictionary of Trade and Commerce*, 4th ed. (London, 1774), under "People": and for 1812, P. Colquhoun, *A Treatise on the Wealth, Power and Resources of the British Empire* (London, 1815).

5. Bristol Apprentice Books, Council House, Bristol.

6. *England in the Age of the American Revolution* (London, 1930), p. 9.

7. *The Newcastle Merchant Adventurers*, Surtees Society, CI (1899), xxiv and Bristol Apprentice Books.

8. Bristol Apprentice Books. See also I. V. Hall, "The Whitson Court Sugar House, Bristol, 1665–1824," *Trans. Bristol and Gloucestershire Archaeological Society*, 65:76–80 (1944).

9. E. Hughes, *North Country Life in the Eighteenth Century* (London, 1952), pp. 104–109.

10. *Ibid.*, pp. 106–107 and Bristol Apprentice Books.

11. Hughes, *North Country Life*, p. 105.

12. Richard Pares, "A London West-India merchant house, 1740–69" in *Essays Presented to Sir Lewis Namier*, ed. Richard Pares and A. J. P. Taylor (London, 1956), p. 81.

13. I am indebted to Gordon Jackson for this information.

14. For Bacon, see L. B. Namier, "Anthony Bacon, M.P., an Eighteenth-Century Merchant," *Journal of Economic and Business History*, 2:20–70 (1929): for Standidge, see J. Symons, *High Street, Hull* (Hull, 1862), p. 10: for Wraxall, see my *Trade of Bristol in the Eighteenth Century*, Bristol Record Society, 20:107 (1957); and for Blundell, see H. Fox Bourne, *English Merchants*, 2nd. ed. (London, 1886), pp. 316–318.

15. H. Fox Bourne, *English Merchants*, I, 16–17; E. Williams, *Capitalism and Slavery* (Chapel Hill, N.C., 1945), p. 74.

16. W. R. Savadge, "The west country and the American mainland colonies, 1763–83" (unpublished thesis), pp. 108–109.

17. Hughes, *North Country Life*, p. 105.

18. G. E. Weare, *Edmund Burke's Connection with Bristol* (Bristol, 1894), pp. 7–8.

19. See H. J. Wade, *My Grandfather's Pocket Book* (1931); and C. Wilson, *Anglo-Dutch Commerce and Finance in the Eighteenth Century* (Cambridge, Eng., 1941).

20. *Life of the Norths*, ed. A. Jessop (1890), I, 156.

21. Hughes, *North Country Life*, pp. 164–166.

22. C. Northcote Parkinson, *The Rise of the Port of Liverpool* (Liverpool, 1952), p. 75.

23. Information kindly contributed by J. E. Williams and O. Wood.

24. See, for example, C. and J. Ackers, *London Directory* (1749).

25. Namier, "Anthony Bacon, M.P.," p. 22.

26. For Lyde see my *Trade of Bristol*, p. 101; for Coghlan, see my "The voyage of the Snow *Africa*," *Mariner's Mirror*, 37:188 (1951).

27. *The Story and Origin of Hunt, Roope & Co. London and Oporto* (1951).

28. W. G. Hoskins, *Industry, Trade and People of Exeter* (Manchester, 1935), p. 48.

29. Information from W. G. Hoskins.

30. Henry Hobhouse, *Memoirs of the Hobhouse Family* (Taunton, 1927).

31. John Hughes, *Liverpool Banks and Bankers,* 1760–1837 (Liverpool, 1906), p. 141.

32. Liverpool corporation petition of 1699 cited in F. A. Bailey, *The Story of Liverpool* (Liverpool, 1951), p. 29.

33. H. L. Bradfer-Lawrence, "The Merchants of Lynn," in *Supplement to Blomefield's Norfolk,* ed. C. Ingleby (London, 1930), p. 187.

34. R. Brooke, *Liverpool As it was During the Last Quarter of the Eighteenth Century* (Liverpool, 1853).

35. See Bristol Burgess Books (Council House, Bristol) and Directories.

36. As an analysis of Bristol Directories for the eighteenth century shows.

37. Savadge, "The west country," p. 103.

38. *Proceedings of the Huguenot Society.*

39. Wilson, *Anglo-Dutch Commerce,* p. 115.

40. E. R. Samuel, "Anglo-Jewish Notaries and Scrivenors," *Transactions of the Jewish Historical Society of England,* 17:113–160 (1951–1952).

41. *Matthews's Bristol Directory* (1794).

42. Hoskins, *Industry, Trade and People,* p. 42.

43. W. Minet, *The Huguenot Family of Minet* (London, 1892).

44. Susan Gay, *Old Falmouth* (London, 1903), p. 101 .

45. See *Gore's Liverpool Directory for . . . 1767* (Liverpool, 1767) and later years.

46. T. Baines, *History of the Commerce and Town of Liverpool* (Liverpool, 1852), p. 427.

47. Chatterton's phrase.

48. R. James, "Bristol Society in the Eighteenth Century" in *Bristol and the Adjoining Counties,* ed. C. M. MacInnes and W. F. Whittard (Bristol, 1955), p. 232.

49. N. Hans, *New Trends in Education in the Eighteenth Century* (London, 1951), pp. 26–27. In Scotland, where there was a different educational tradition, more merchants went to the University. See, for example, *James Finlay & Co. Ltd.* (Glasgow, 1951).

50. C. P. Hill, *History of Bristol Grammar School* (Bristol, 1951).

51. For William Braund's library, see L. S. Sutherland, *A London Merchant* (London, 1933), pp. 1–2.

52. E. C. Mossner, *Life of David Hume* (Edinburgh, 1954), p. 90.

53. *The Character of an Honest Merchant* (London, 1686). Many other similar programmes were published in the course of the eighteenth century.

54. Hans, *New Trends in Education,* pp. 38–41.

55. H. McLachlan, *Warrington Academy, its History and Influence* (Chetham Society, 1943).

56. H. Owen, *Two Centuries of Ceramic Art* (Gloucester, 1873), p. 40.

57. Thomas Mortimer, *Elements of Commerce* (London, 1772).

58. Hughes, *North Country Life,* p. 104.

59. Savadge, "The west country," p. 89.

60. See Gay, *Old Falmouth;* W. Stout, *Autobiography* (London, 1851); A. Raistrick, *Quakers in Science and Industry* (London, 1950).

61. See *Proceedings of the Huguenot Society of London.*

62. For Liverpool, see J. Enfield, *History of Liverpool* (Liverpool, 1809); for Whitehaven, C. Caine, *A History of the Churches of the Rural Deanery of Whitehaven* (Whitehaven, 1916); for Hull, Symons, *High Street, Hull* (Kingston-upon-Hull, 1862).

63. "Onslow MSS." Historical Manuscripts Commission, *14th Report*, appendix, IX, pp. 469–470.
64. Bristol Society of Friends, Minutes of Men's Monthly Meeting, CCIX, 148 (10 April 1775); 275 (7 Oct. 1775); CCX, 350 (11 Aug. 1777); 257 (28 June 1779); CCXI, 81 (12 June 1780).
65. See S. G. Checkland, "Economic Attitudes in Liverpool, 1793–1807," *Econ. Hist. Rev. 2nd ser.* 5:63 (1952).
66. L. B. Namier, *The Structure of Politics at the Accession of George III* (London, 1929), I, 59–60.
67. G. P. Judd, *Members of Parliament, 1734–1832* (New Haven, Conn. 1955), p. 57.
68. Namier, *The Structure of Politics*, pp. 16–19.
69. L. B. Namier, "Brice Fisher M.P., a Mid-Eighteenth Century Merchant and his Connections," *English Historical Review*, 42:514–532 (1927).
70. Namier, "Anthony Bacon, M.P.," pp. 20–70.
71. Pares, "A London West-India merchant house," in Pares and Taylor, *Essays Presented.*
72. Judd, *Members of Parliament*, pp. 26, 57.
73. The converse—downward mobility—by its very nature is much more difficult to document. The successful are remembered, the unsuccessful forgotten.
74. Hughes, *North Country Life*, p. xix.
75. *Matthew's Bristol Directory for the Year 1793–4* (Bristol, 1794).
76. Walter Ison, *Georgian Buildings of Bristol* (London, 1952), pp. 23–24, 32, 40, 43, 45, 106, 181–189.
77. Lucy Sutherland, "The City of London in Eighteenth-Century Politics" in Pares and Taylor, *Essays Presented*, p. 61.
78. Information from M. W. Flinn.
79. Genealogies are given in C. H. Cave, *A History of Banking in Bristol* (Bristol, 1899).
80. W. Bagehot, *The English Constitution*, World's Classics ed. (London, 1928), p. 145.
81. *A General Description of All Trades* (1747), p. 140.
82. *Ibid.*
83. See, L. S. Pressnell, *Country Banking in the Industrial Revolution* (Oxford, 1956), pp. 45–56.
84. Bourne, *English Merchants*, 2nd ed. p. 304.
85. Transcript of will, Exeter Record Office.
86. Bourne, *English Merchants*, p. 323.
87. R. Hidy, *The House of Baring in American Trade and Finance* (Cambridge, Mass. 1949), p. 8.
88. Sutherland, "The City of London," in Pares and Taylor, *Essays Presented*, pp. 9–13.
89. Wilson, *Anglo-Dutch Commerce*, pp. 28–30.
90. Pares, "A London West-India Merchant House" in Pares and Taylor, *Essays Presented*, p. 80.
91. Minchinton, *Trade of Bristol*, pp. 88–89.
92. F. B. Tolles, *Meeting House and Counting House* (Chapel Hill, N.C., 1948), pp. 90–91.
93. Wilson, *Anglo-Dutch Commerce*, p. 117.
94. Richard Pares, *A West-India Fortune* (London, 1950), p. 212.

95. *Boswell's Life of Johnson,* ed. G. B. Hill (Oxford, 1934), IV, 4.

96. See, for comparison, T. S. Willan, *The Muscovy Merchants of 1555* (Manchester, 1953), chap. iv.

97. Pares, "A London West-India Merchant House," in Pares and Taylor, *Essays Presented,* p. 106.

98. R. Welford, *Men of Mark Twixt Tyne and Tweed* (London, 1895), I, 297–316.

99. England in *The European Nobility in the Eighteenth Century,* ed. A. Goodwin (London, 1953), p. 16.

100. *The Story of Hunt, Roope* (London, no date).

101. See J. F. Gibson, *Brocklebanks 1770–1950* (Liverpool, 1953).

102. J. C. G. Hill, *Shipshape and Bristol Fashion* (Liverpool, 1952).

103. Donovan Dawe, *Skilbecks: Drysalters 1650–1950* (1950).

BAILYN: KINSHIP AND TRADE IN SEVENTEENTH CENTURY NEW ENGLAND

1. *Winthrop Papers* (Boston, 1929–1947), II, 112.

2. Letter from John White, Dorchester, England, to John Winthrop, Nov. 16, 1636, *ibid.,* III, 322.

3. *The Diaries of John Hull . . . (Transactions and Collections of the American Antiquarian Society,* III, 1857), 168.

4. Nathaniel B. Shurtleff, ed., *Records of the Governor and Company of the Massachusetts Bay in New England* (Boston, 1853–1854), I, 142.

5. *Note-Book Kept by Thomas Lechford, Esq. . . . from June 27, 1638, to July 29, 1641 (Transactions and Collections of the American Antiquarian Society,* VII, 1885), 74n., 75.

6. James Savage, *A Genealogical Dictionary of . . . New England . . .* (Boston, 1860–1862), II, 420; *A Volume Relating to the Early History of Boston Containing the Aspinwall Notarial Records from 1644 to 1651 (Thirty-second Report of the Record Commissioners of the City of Boston,* Boston, 1903), 197.

7. *Boston Town Records (Second Report of the Record Commissioners of the City of Boston,* Boston, 1877), 40; William H. Sumner, *A History of East Boston* (Boston, 1858), 187–191; *Asp. Records,* 181, 410, 397, 398, 402, 404, 406.

8. Viola F. Barnes, "Richard Wharton, a Seventeenth Century New England Colonial," *Publications of the Colonial Society of Massachusetts,* XXVI (Transactions, 1924–1926), 249.

9. *The Clarendon Papers (Collections of the New York Historical Society for the Year 1869,* New York, 1870), 84.

10. *Diary of Samuel Sewall (Collections of the Massachusetts Historical Society,* fifth series, V), 132, 217.

11. *Ibid.,* 102, 158.

MATHIAS: THE ENTREPRENEUR IN BREWING, 1700–1830

1. One of the best general discussions remains that of P. Mantoux, *The Industrial Revolution in the Eighteenth Century.* (London, 1948 ed.), pp. 374–408. See also C. Wilson, "The Entrepreneur in the Industrial Revolution," *Explorations in Entrepreneurial History,* 7:129–145 (February 1955).

2. T. S. Ashton, *An Eighteenth Century Industrialist* (Manchester, 1939), pp. 71–86. See also P. Mathias, "Industrial Revolution in Brewing: Developments in the Brewing Industry in England: 1700–1830," *Explorations . . .*, 5:208–224 (May 1953). Statistics from *Excise Statistics, 1662–1805* (ms. at Customs and Excise, London), pp. 17, 20–21, 144, 147; *Excise* mss. 1749, 3069, 3070. London figures are in mss. at Barclays, being copied from Excise mss.

3. I would like to acknowledge with gratitude a grant to help with my research from the Houblon Norman Fund and the owners of all mss. cited who made it possible. They allowed me to study many records still remaining in the breweries whose past they document and many in private hands.

4. Brewing Victuallers in London are ignored, being always under 50 in number with an insignificant percentage of production in their hands. The number of brewers declines in London and increases in the country during this period, from the trend toward larger production in individual units of production. In the country this was squeezing out brewing victuallers, in London the smaller Common Brewers.

5. See the Table printed in Mathias, "Industrial Revolution in Brewing," p. 217. A figure of 100,000 barrels implies almost 15 million retail transactions (at one quart each), a scale of operations from a single unit of production which was not to be met with in many sectors of the economy in the 1780s, when this range was first reached.

6. John Smiths (Oundle), *Sales Book,* 1798–1800; Gardners (Cheltenham), *Ledger, 1800–7;* Palmers (Bath), D.N.B., *Gents Mag.* 1818 (II), 276.

7. Information from the Company. I owe this reference to Mr. B. Spiller.

8. Public Record Office, *Administration,* 110.

9. Samuel Whitbread II had interests in lime-burning in Essex, and John Martineau in sugar refining (*Partnership Deeds* (*1812*) *at Whitbreads*).

10. A. Barnard, *Noted Breweries of Great Britain and Ireland* (1889), I, 117, *et seq.* P. Mathias, *House Journal,* Ind Coope and Allsopp, X Nos. 5–6 (1956).

11. *Allsopp Records: Personal Ledger 1779–95, Letter Books.* The shortness of the brewing season also gave these persons time and opportunity to profit by other things.

12. Palmers (Bath),: Lacons (Yarmouth), *Cash Book 1759–69; Valuations,* 1742, 1752, 1758; Cobbold (Ipswich), *Cliffe Brewery, Ipswich,* 1723–1923. There is a very widespread connection, too, with the wine and spirit trade, which was a natural extension to supplying publicans with beer. In addition many coastal brewers were "agents for London Porter."

13. Mathias, "Industrial Revolution in Brewing."

14. M. Combrune, *Theory and Practice of Brewing* (London, 1758); John Richardson, *Statical* [sic] *Estimates of the Materials of Brewing; or, a Treatise on the application and use of the saccharometer* (London, 1784); J. Baverstock, Jr., *Treatises on Brewing* (London, 1824), Preface and Appendix; P.R.O. Adm. 110/37 fol. 359 *et seq.* Baverstock and Richardson in particular were not so circumstanced in the London porter market to have the problems of efficiency and large-scale production thrust upon them. It seems to be more professional pride that urged Combrune on, although all of them acknowledged the economic utility of their innovations in print.

15. *London and Country Brewer* (1742), pp. 179, 182; P.R.O. Adm. 110/26 fol. 101.

16. P. Mathias, "Steam Power comes to Chiswell Street," *House of Whitbread* XIV (1954). For Whitbreads' innovation of underground cisterns for storage see *Do.* XII (1952), based on *Southill MSS. Property Book.*

17. *Gents Mag.* 1798 (I), pp. 536–537. The brewery was sold by his son for £70,000.

18. Mathias, "Industrial Revolution in Brewing."

19. *Whitbreads Brewery* (1951).

20. *Thraliana* (ed. K. Balderston, 1951), I, 501; Rylands Lib. *Eng.* MS. 600 (7), 600 (II).

21. *Whitbreads Records: Private Ledgers; Gratuity Book,* 1798–1850; *Southill MSS. Brewery 4638.* In 1781 Mrs. Thrale considered keeping Perkins on a salary, which with bonuses might have reached £1,200 p.a. (*Letters of Samuel Johnson* (ed. R. W. Chapman), II, No. 725).

22. *Whitbreads Records: Gratuity Book,* W. P. Serocold, *Story of Watneys* (1949); *Gents Mag.* 1818 (II), p. 83; *Faringdon Diary* (ed. J. Greig) IV, 55; II, 187–188.

23. Partnership Deeds at the breweries. *Faringdon Diary,* V, 130, 279; VI, 98; *Gents Mag.* 1830 (II), 563.

24. Herts. C.R.O. *MSS. Nos.* 61134, 61137, Series 61144; *Southill MSS.* 4652–4676, 4727.

25. *Excise MSS. Trials,* 556, 582, 584; Guildhall Library, Pam. 3802.

26. Needless to say this feature varied completely over the country in response to the urban markets. For example, there were few public brewers of any kind near Birmingham.

27. *General Description of all Trades* (1747), p. 34.

28. Boswell, *Life of Johnson* (Oxford, 1946 edn.), II, 69.

29. T. F. Buxton's mother was a daughter of Osgood Hanbury. He married Hannah Gurney, daughter of John Gurney of Earlham Hall, Norfolk.

30. The younger Samuel Whitbread gave most of his time, energy, and money to matters other than business. He dispersed his own shares of the brewery in partnerships, fell heavily into debt personally, and committed suicide in 1815. Robert Hucks "spent his money on the turf and sold the brewery . . ." (*Notes and Queries,* 12 Ser. II, 93).

31. *Thraliana,* I, 333.

32. *Southill MSS. Property Book.*

33. This was true until the increase in taxation in the Napoleonic Wars raised the stake which excise had in the price from 20 to 22 per cent to 45 to 47 per cent.

34. Rylands Lib *Eng.* MS. 616, Box I, *Note Book,* entry 8 July 1773.

35. In addition to these mss. at the breweries see T. C. Barker and J. R. Harris, *St. Helens 1750–1900* (Liverpool, 1954), pp. 90–107 where the point is admirably brought out.

36. *Alsopp Records, Letter Books,* B. Wilson to Jackson, 30 September 1791.

37. *Parl. Papers,* 1819, V, *Report . . . on Public Breweries,* Evidence of T. Clough, J. Taylor.

38. Whitbread commissioned malting from his entry into trade (*Whitbread Records: Trade Ledger,* 1746–1752). Martineau (joined with Whitbreads after 1812) had malt houses in Norfolk at least by 1787 (*Rest Books,*

1812–1830), Goodwyns by 1784 at latest (*Charrington Records: Goodwyn Ledger,* 1784–1786), Barclays by 1787 (*Barclay Records: Cash Books,* 1787), Calverts by 1818 (*Parl. Papers,* 1818, V, Evidence of Calvert, pp. 18, 25).

39. *Truman Records: Letter Books,* S. Hanbury to Wright and Casburne, 18 November 1802; to J. Kemp, 11 November 1802.

40. T. Pennant, *History of London* (London, 1790), pp. 278–279; *Whitbreads Brewery.*

41. D.N.B. (Parsons); E. P. Hughson, *History of London* (London, 1805–1809), II, 195.

42. See note 7 above.

43. 24 Geo. II c. 4; 31 Geo. II c. 29.

44. W. Bagehot, *Lombard Street* (London, 1873 edn.), pp. 268–9.

HABAKKUK: ECONOMIC FUNCTIONS OF ENGLISH LANDOWNERS IN THE SEVENTEENTH AND EIGHTEENTH CENTURIES

1. Many collections of estate papers have been deposited in the record offices of the various counties. A number of studies of specific estates and families are now in progress. Mr. J. P. Cooper, Trinity College, Oxford, is working on the records of a number of landowners in the sixteenth and seventeenth centuries. Miss Mary Finch is writing a thesis on certain Northamptonshire families, 1540–1640; and Mr. E. Kerridge has investigated the archives of the Herbert family, Earls of Pembroke. Mrs. Long is working on one of the smaller gentry families, the Blounts of Mapledurham, and Mrs. V. Varley on a number of Cornish families in the later seventeenth and eighteenth centuries. Mr. R. A. C. Parker has in progress a study of certain of the larger landowners of the eighteenth century. A valuable study of the Essex estates of the Petre family, 1540–1640, by Mr. W. R. Emerson, is to appear in the Oxford Historical Series.

2. For the traditional view of the improving landlords see P. Mantoux, *The Industrial Revolution in the Eighteenth Century* (London, 1928), 163–165. For some examples see Naomi Riches, *The Agricultural Revolution in Norfolk,* (Chapel Hill, N.C.) 32–34; A. H. Dodd, *The Industrial Revolution in North Wales* (Cardiff, 1933), chap. 11. There is a good account of an improving landlord, the 3rd Earl of Egremont, in Hugh Wyndham, *A Family History, 1688–1837,* 245–260. Mr. R. A. C. Parker is making a detailed study of the estates of the Coke family in the eighteenth century, which will make possible a more accurate assessment of the significance of Thomas Coke.

3. Adam Smith, *Wealth of Nations,* ii, 479. (All references are the World Classics Edition, published by the Oxford University Press.) Smith incidentally though the practice "generally a foolish one," "generally the effect of the landlord's conceit of his own superior knowledge (a conceit in most cases very ill-founded)."

4. Nathaniel Kent, for example, with his partners Claridge and Pearce, appears to have managed a number of estates.

5. Smith, *Wealth of Nations,* pp. i, 430.

6. W. E. Tate, "The Cost of Parliamentary Enclosure in England," *Economic History Review,* 2nd ser. vol. V, p. 265.

7. There is no good study of the financial aspects of the draining of the fens, one of the most important examples of economic activity by landowners, but there is a good deal of information in H. C. Darby, *The Draining of the Fen* (Cambridge, Eng.).

8. G. E. Mingay, "The Duke of Kingston and his Estates," unpub. diss. University of Nottingham.

9. G. Scott Thomson, *The Russells in Bloomsbury, 1669–1771,* 301.

10. Smith, *Wealth of Nations,* pp. i, 454.

11. There is valuable information about the activities of landowners in the iron and coal industries in J. U. Nef, *The Rise of the British Coal Industry,* I, 265–343 (London); T. S. Ashton, *Iron and Steel in the Industrial Revolution* (Manchester, 1951 ed.), 4–5, and T. S. Ashton and Joseph Sykes, *The Coal Industry of the Eighteenth Century* (Manchester), p. 2, and chap. xi.

12. This is suggested by the industrialization of South Wales; see A. H. John, *The Industrial Development of South Wales* (Cardiff) 8–10. See also Dodd, *The Industrial Revolution,* pp. 305–308.

13. See W. H. B. Court, *The Rise of the Midland Industries* (London 1938), pp. 73, 86.

14. T. S. Willan, *River Navigation in England* (London, 1938), 138, chap. III and IV, contains information about the activities of landowners in river improvements.

15. For the Duke of Bridgewater, see W. H. Chaloner, "Francis Egerton, Third Duke of Bridgewater", *Explorations in Entrepreneurial History,* V, 181–185. For the activities of other landowners, see John Phillips, *A General History of Inland Navigation* (London, 1793).

16. Nef, *Rise of the British Coal Industry,* pp. 1, 342.

17. John Summerson, *Georgian London* (London, 1945), especially chaps. III, VII, XII, and XIV.

18. Percy Ford, "Tobacco and Coal: a Note on the Economic History of Whitehaven," *Economica,* 9:192–196 (1929).

19. Thomson, *The Russells in Bloomsbury,* p. 312.

20. I am indebted here to some stimulating observations by Professor Viner, *International Trade and Economic Development,* (Glencoe, Ill., 1952), pp. 106–107.

ROSOVSKY: THE SERF ENTREPRENEUR IN RUSSIA

I wish to thank the Research Center in Entrepreneurial History for the grant which made this study possible. I am particularly indebted to Dr. Fritz Redlich for suggesting the topic and for unsparing guidance during the writing. My special thanks are due to Mr. Serge Cheremeteff for information supplied about his family and particularly for giving me a feeling of the period which cannot be obtained from books. I have translated into English all quotations from the Russian, as well as most of the longer French and German excerpts.

1. N. Turgenev, *La Russie et les Russes* (Paris, 1847) vol. II, p. 128. Through the period covered in this essay, 1700–1850, bank notes (assignats) and silver rubles circulated in Russia. Silver rubles were always worth more, but their value *vis-à-vis* bank notes fluctuated considerably. Unless specifically mentioned, all ruble figures are quoted in assignats.

2. *Ibid.*, p. 127.

3. Alexander Gerschenkron, "Social Attitudes, Entrepreneurship, and Economic Development," *Explorations in Entrepreneurial History*, 6:6–7 (October, 1953). This quotation comes from an earlier version of Professor Gerschenkron's paper. It is slightly more appropriate for my purposes than the revised version.

4. A few words must be said about the technical difficulties of doing research in this field. Periodicals and books about Russia of pre-1860 vintage are largely unavailable in this country. Archives, which would be the logical source material, are available only in the Soviet Union. Secondary sources largely ignore the serf entrepreneur, or mention him only in passing. This is true for a variety of reasons, but mainly because Marxist historians like to play down the individual and the entrepreneur in particular. For example, see speech by F. Konstantinov, in *Pravda,* July 1, 1953.

5. P. I. Lyashchenko, *History of the National Economy of Russia* (New York,1949) p. 389. (A translation of *Istoriya Narodnogo Khozyastva SSSR,* Moscow, 1947; all citations refer to the English edition.)

6. *Ibid.*

7. *Ibid.*, p. 309.

8. *Ibid.*, p. 310.

	Barshchina	*Obrok*
Black Soil Region	71.2%	28.8%
Volga Area	73.3%	26.7%
Eastern Steppe Lands	83.0%	17.0%

9. *Ibid.*

10. Compare G. von Schulze-Gaevernitz, *Volkswirtschaftliche Studien aus Russland* (Leipzig, 1899) pp. 21ff.

11. M. Tugan-Baranowskii, *Russkaya Fabrika v Proshlom i Nastoyashchem* (Moscow, 1898) pp. 88–117.

12. A. Freiherrn von Haxthausen, *Studien über die innere Zustande, des Volksleben und insbesondere die ländlichen Einrichtungen Russlands* (Hannover, 1847), cited by Schulze-Gaevernitz, *Volkswirtschaftliche Studien aus Russland,* who adds: " . . . ein Satz der gewiss nicht bloss auf die Russen passt." p. 24.

13. S. G. Strumilin, *Promyshlenni Perevorot v Rossii* (Moscow, 1944) pp. 13–47.

14. It was possible, in some instances, to have part of one's family perform *barshchina* obligations, and then let the other members of the family carry on independent economic activity; but this was certainly not typical.

15. On the general question of commutation and its effects on the peasantry, see the two classics by G. F. Knapp, *Grundherrschaft und Rittergut* (Leipzig, 1897), and *Die Bauernbefreiung*, etc. (Leipzig, 1927).

16. On the vast and complicated question of serf law, see *Krepostnaya Rossiya: Sbornik Statei* (Leningrad, 1930) pp. 247–266, and J. Engelmann, *Die Leibeigenschaft in Russland* (Leipzig, 1884).

17. A. Yatsevich, *Krepostnoi Peterburg Pushkinskogo Vremeni* (Leningrad, 1937) p. 67.

18. This is an indirect, but important, example of the influence of nobility on economic development. For a more detailed treatment of this problem

see *Explorations in Entrepreneurial History*, 6:77–130 (December, 1953), particularly Dr. Redlich's introductory remarks.

19. Yatsevich, *Krepostnoi Peterburg Pushkinskogo Vremini*, pp. 65–76.

20. *Ibid.*

21. Lyashchenko, *History of the National Economy of Russia*, p. 315. These figures include only the monetary obligations of the peasantry. Some nonmonetary duties often remained; e.g., Count Sheremetev required all his serfs resident in St. Petersburg to participate in fire-fighting. See Yatsevich, *Krepostnoi Peterburg Pushkinskogo Vremini*, p. 52.

22. P. A. Khromov, *Ekonomicheskoe Razvitie Rossii v XIX-XX Vekakh* (Moscow, 1950) pp. 9–12.

23. J. A. Schumpeter, *The Theory of Economic Development* (Cambridge, Mass., 1934) pp. 84, 89.

24. Compare Fritz Redlich, *History of American Business Leaders* (Ann Arbor, 1940) vol. I, chap. 1.

25. Schumpeter, *The Theory of Economic Development*, p. 84.

26. For this section I have borrowed freely from V. O. Kliuchevski's *History of Russia* (New York, 1911).

27. I. V. Meshalin, *Tekstil'naya Promyshlennost' Krest'yan* (Moscow, 1950) pp. 40–41. Breaking the social barrier by economic means was done in Russia as far back as the 14th century. That country's most prominent salt mine owners were the Stroganovs, originally peasants from villages in the Solvychegodsk area who had achieved titles of nobility by the 18th century. But this career, spectacular though it was, is of no particular interest to us since the Stroganovs made their move upward long before serfdom was imposed on the Russian people. It is noteworthy that while one branch of this family became enormously wealthy and even respected members of society, another branch remained peasants, in due course became serfs in Solvychegodsk, and never distinguished themselves in any sense. On the Stroganovs, see Lyashchenko, *History of the National Economy of Russia*, p. 211, n. 7., and Otto Brunner, "Europäisches and Russisches Bürgertum," *Vierteljahrschrift für Social und Wirtschafts Geschichte*, vol. 40, no. 1, p. 10.

28. Meshalin, *Tekstil'naya Promyshlennost' Krest'yan*, p. 48.

29. Writing about Russia frequently creates what I have called the "War and Peace Problem," that overabundance of Russian names, diminutives, patronymics, largely incomprehensible and confusing to the English-speaking reader. To avoid this difficulty I have reduced the use of proper names to the absolute minimum in this section. A comprehensive list of Russian serf entrepreneurs is available at the Research Center in Entrepreneurial History, for all those with specific interests in the field.

30. It is noteworthy that Ivanovo and Pavlovo, both textile centers, were strongholds of the religious "Old Believers," an economically active and successful minority.

31. Haxthausen, *Studien über die innere Zustande*, vol. III, p. 76. This would seem to be among the largest number of serfs or slaves ever owned by a nonsovereign. (Mr. S. Cheremeteff estimates that his family owned over 350,000 male serfs.)

32. Yatsevich, *Krepostnoi Peterburg Pushkinskogo Vremini*, p. 70.

33. *Ibid.*, p. 71.

34. Tugan-Baranowskii, *Russkaya Fabrika v Proshlom i Nastoyashchem*, p. 82.

35. *Ibid.*, pp. 84–85.

36. Ya. Garelin, *Gorod Ivanovo-Voznesensk*, pp. 204–205; cited by Tugan-Baranowskii, *Russkaya Fabrika y Proshlom i Nashtoyashchem*, p. 83.

37. Meshalin, *Tekstil'naya Promyshlennost' Krest'yan*, p. 103.

38. V. Borisov, *Vladimirskie Gubernskie Vedemosti*, no. 4, 1842; cited by Tugan-Baranowskii, *Russkaya Fabrika v Proshlom i Nastoyashchem*, p. 180.

39. See Meshalin, *Tekstil'naya Promyshlennost' Krest'yan*, p. 106, and Tugan-Baranowskii, *Russkaya Fabrika v Proshlom i Nastoyashchem*, pp. 72–87, for extensive discussions of the early careers of Grachev and Garelin.

40. Peasant putting-out systems in the production of calico and linen were not started by the larger peasant entrepreneurs. Particularly in calico they were promulgated by the smaller enterprises, those still nearer to *Kustar* status, and it was only in the early 19th century that the bigger businessmen followed suit. It is estimated that in 1850 150,000 peasants were weaving calico in Vladimir Province under the putting-out system; see Meshalin, *Tekstil'naya Promyshlennost' Krest'yan*, p. 113.

41. *Ibid.*, p. 122. Relations between the merchant "front men," in some sense traitors to their class, and the serf bourgeoisie were not always without conflict. Yamonovski, another Ivanovo serf entrepreneur, was ruined by some of his merchant "acquaintances" in 1822 and forced to abandon production.

42. One *arshin* equals 28 inches.

43. Meshalin, *Tekstil'naya Promyshlennost' Krest'yan*, p. 178.

44. " . . . et qui servisse patrem suum parum, immo nimium, meminisset"; Pliny the Younger, *Letters*, Bk. III/14. I am indebted to Professor Gerschenkron for calling this quotation to my attention.

45. A similar case involves the Mossolov enterprises, state peasants of the Klomenski districts who became large-scale linen tablecloth manufacturers. In 1847 peasants of these districts made a complaint to the Ministry of Interior particularly directed against Mossolov. They claimed that money wages were never paid out, and that in their stead they were forced to accept various foodstuffs all of the worst quality and sometimes actually spoiled. Peasants accused the Mossolovs of using two scales: one for the market which weighed heavy, and one for the workers which weighed light. The peasants also alleged that manufacturers of the districts maintained a blacklist of "malcontents," which made complaints exceedingly dangerous. An official investigation revealed the truth of the peasant accusations. The truck system seems to have been widely practiced, but local officialdom remained, in the best Russian tradition, well bribed, so that little was ever done to relieve the situation. See Tugan-Baranowskii, *Russkaya Fabrika v Proshlom i Nastoyashchem*, p. 270.

46. *Materiali po Istorii Krest'yanskoi Promyshlennosti*, vol. II (Moscow, 1950) pp. 89–107. I do not wish to add anything, pro or con, to the famous and arid Tugan-Baranowskii-Populist controversy concerning the conflict between the *Kustars* and the early Russian factories. Even if Tugan-Baranowskii's thesis is wrong, and it seems to me that it is, there is little doubt that as a group *Kustars* represented more competition for the merchants than the large-scale serf entrepreneurs. *Kustars* also represent a form of entrepreneurial activity, but a much tamer sort than we are discussing at the moment.

47. Biographical material on the Morosovs taken from Meshalin, *Tekstil'naya Promyshlennost' Krest'yan*, pp. 229ff, Lyashchenko, *History of the National Economy of Russia*, pp. 296ff., and Schulze-Gaevernitz, *Volkswirtschaftliche Studien aus Russland*, pp. 24ff.

48. Ch. M. Ioksimovich, *Manufacturnaya Promyshlennost' v Proshlom i Nastoyashchem*, 1915, vol. I, pp. 1–4.

49. One of the men running the Morosov putting-out system was a serf named Egorov. He supervised the production of 66 peasant looms, handed out the materials to the weavers, collected the finished goods, paid them, etc. It is quite certain that Egorov represented some form of entrepreneurial talent, but it cannot be compared to Morosov. Yet all this does bring into focus the important point (made originally by Schumpeter) that entrepreneurial activity takes place on two general levels. First we have the vigorous innovating entrepreneur discussed most frequently in economic theory, and then we have the smaller-scale general entrepreneurial activities which are less noticeable but not necessarily less important. The agrarian Russian value system being what it was, I would suggest that almost any serf in business or industry (unless he was an ordinary wage worker) could be considered an entrepreneur. If innovation is a valid criterion, all of them left the well-trodden path of their class and especially of their class values, and tried something new. Compare Meshalin, *Tekstil'naya Promyshlennost' Krest'yan*, p. 236.

50. Morosov was instrumental in starting the career of the fabulous Knoop who secured English textile machinery for him despite the exportation ban. This astounding feat started Knoop's career in Russia. Compare Schulze-Gaevernitz, *Volkswirtschaftliche Studien aus Russland*, p. 92.

51. Maurice Verstraete, *La Russie Industrielle* (Paris, 1897) p. 163.

52. The name is frequently spelled Kondrashev. For the factual material in this section I have used mainly Meshalin, *Tekstil'naya Promyshlennost' Krest'yan*, pp. 207ff.

53. He also went by the name of M. Kyrilov.

54. *Zhurn. Manuf. i Torg.*, 1828, no. 1, p. 100, cited *ibid.*, p. 217.

55. P. M. Luk'yanov, *Istoriya Khimicheskikh Promyslov i Khimicheskoi Promyshlennosti Rossii* (Moscow, 1949) vol. III, pp. 94–120.

56. The size of this plant may, of course, have been a function of general Russian backwardness; the export figures make this even more probable, in view of the well-known thesis of the Swedish economic historians. Compare A. Gerschenkron, "An Economic History of Russia" (a review of Lyashchenko) *Journal of Economic History*, Spring, 1952, p. 155, and by the same author, "Economic Backwardness in Historical Perspective," in B. F. Hoselitz (ed.), *The Progress of Underdeveloped Areas* (Chicago, 1952) pp. 8ff.

57. Luk'yanov, *Istoriya Khimicheskikh Promyslov i Khimicheskoi Promyshlennosti Rossii*, vol. II, p. 143; my italics.

58. Meshalin, *Tekstil'naya Promyshlennost' Krest'yan*, p. 202. The decrease was greater in silk than in cotton.

59. A typical failure is the case of Ivan Spiridonov. Compare *ibid.*, p. 129.

60. Yatsevich, *Krepostnoi Peterburg Pushkinskogo Vremini*, pp. 19–52, and A. de Holstein and D. B. Montefiore, *Serf Life in Russia* (London, 1906) p. 55.

61. Schulze-Gaevernitz, *Volkswirtschaftliche Studien aus Russland*, p. 62.

62. Meshalin, *Tekstil'naya Promyshlennost' Krest'yan*, p. 113.

63. F. Bodenstedt, *Russische Fragmente* (Leipzig, 1892) vol. II, pp. 307–316. Article written by Ivan Aksakov.

64. *Ibid.*, p. 308. This quotation would bear out my contention that the "normal" serf entrepreneur was to be found in many Russian villages.

65. One of the best examples is the Stakheef Company, managed by Botolin, a man stemming from the peasantry. See *Ford Archives*, Accession 140, Box 13A, for his dealings with the Ford Motor Co. in 1919.

Index

Bei Fragen zur Produktsicherheit wenden Sie sich bitte an:
If you have any questions regarding product safety,
please contact:

Walter de Gruyter GmbH
Genthiner Straße 13
10785 Berlin
productsafety@degruyterbrill.com